American Educational Research Journal

Volume 46, Number 1—March 2009

American Educational Research Journal
Volume 46, Number 1—March 2009

Section on Social and
Institutional Analysis

*The SIA articles in this issue were accepted under the editorship of Margaret A. Gallego and Sandra Holllingsworth.

Section on Teaching, Learning,
and Human Development

American Educational Research Association

American Educational Research Journal (ISSN 0002-8312) (J589) is published quarterly—in March, June, September, and December—on behalf of the American Educational Research Association by SAGE Publications, Thousand Oaks, CA 91320. Copyright © 2009 by American Educational Research Association. All rights reserved. No portion of the contents may be reproduced in any form without written permission from the publisher. Periodicals postage paid at Thousand Oaks, California, and at additional mailing offices. **Change of Address:** Six weeks' advance notice must be given when notifying of change of address. Please send the old address label along with the new address to ensure proper identification. Please specify name of journal. POSTMASTER: Send address changes to AERA Membership Department, 1430 K Street NW, Washington, DC 20005.

Manuscript Submission: Authors should submit manuscripts electronically to the corresponding editorial team via Manuscript Central (Section on Social and Institutional Analysis: http://mc .manuscriptcentral.com/aerj-sia; Section on Teaching, Learning, and Human Development: http://mc.manuscriptcentral.com/aerj-tlhd). For more information regarding submission guidelines, please see the Manuscript Submission section of the American Educational Research Journal's Web site: http://aerj.aera.net.

Member Information: American Educational Research Association (AERA) member inquiries, member renewal requests, changes of address, and membership subscription inquiries should be addressed to the AERA Membership Department, 1430 K Street NW, Washington, DC 20005; fax (202) 238-3250; phone (202) 238-3200; e-mail: members@aera.net; Web site: www.aera.net. AERA annual membership dues are $120 (Regular and Affiliate Members), $100 (International Affiliates), and $35 (Graduate and Undergraduate Student Affiliates). **Claims:** Claims for undelivered copies must be made no later than six months following month of publication. Beyond six months and at the request of the American Educational Research Association, the publisher will supply replacement issues when losses have been sustained in transit and when the reserve stock permits.

Subscription Information: All nonmember subscription inquiries, orders, back-issue requests, claims, and renewals should be addressed to SAGE Publications, 2455 Teller Road, Thousand Oaks, CA 91320; telephone (800) 818-SAGE (7243) and (805) 499-0721; fax (805) 375-1700; e-mail journals@sagepub.com; http://www.sagepublications.com. **Subscription Price:** Institutions $309; Individuals $52. For all customers outside the Americas, please visit http://www.sagepub.co.uk/ customerCare.nav for information. **Claims (nonmembers):** Claims for undelivered copies must be made no later than six months following month of publication. The publisher will supply replacement issues when losses have been sustained in transit and when the reserve stock will permit.

Abstracting and Indexing: This journal is abstracted or indexed in Current Abstracts-EBSCO, Current Contents: Social & Behavioral Sciences, ERIC (Education Resources Information Center), Higher Education Abstracts, ProQuest Education Journals, PsycINFO, Scopus, Social Sciences Citation Index (Web of Science) Premier-EBSCO, and Wilson Education Index/Abstracts.

Copyright Permission: Permission requests to photocopy or otherwise reproduce copyrighted material published in this journal should be submitted by accessing the article online on the journal's Web site, http://aerj.aera.net, and selecting the "Request Permission" link. Permission may also be requested by contacting the Copyright Clearance Center via their Web site at http://www.copyright.com, or via e-mail at info@copyright.com.

Advertising and Reprints: Current advertising rates and specifications may be obtained by contacting the advertising coordinator in the Thousand Oaks office at (805) 410-7763 or by sending an e-mail to advertising@sagepub.com. To order reprints, please e-mail reprint@sagepub.com. Acceptance of advertising in this journal in no way implies endorsement of the advertised product or service by SAGE or the journal's affiliated society(ies). No endorsement is intended or implied. SAGE reserves the right to reject any advertising it deems as inappropriate for this journal.

Printed on acid-free paper

Social and Institutional
Analysis

American Educational Research Journal
March 2009, Vol. 46, No. 1, pp. 6–8
DOI: 10.3102/0002831208328979
© *AERA 2009. http://aerj.aera.net*

Editorial Statement

*A*ERJ-SIA is a peer-reviewed research journal that consistently pub-
lishes high-quality scholarship. Our emphasis is on "significant political, cultural, social, economic, and organization issues in education" (in the
words of our AERA mandate), and our editorial team will continue to pursue this broad-based research agenda. While both acknowledging the appropriateness of *AERJ*-SIA's traditional direction and continuing to publish the
best scholarship and analysis on key contemporary issues, we seek to
broaden and enrich the journal by taking into account changing global circumstances and educational trends.

Education faces dramatic change in the 21st century, and it is important
for *AERJ*-SIA to embrace new realities and directions. Globalization—in the
world economy, in patterns of migration, and increasingly, in education—
affects all of us. One need only look at the 2008 global economic meltdown
to get a sense of our interdependence. Education contributes to the success
of the knowledge economy—and is affected by it. The increasingly globalized and knowledge-based economy renders the linkages between education and social and economic outcomes empirically "up for grabs" while
simultaneously more important than ever. *AERJ*-SIA must explore the educational consequences of this economy both internationally and here at
home.

A Global Perspective

Our editorial team seeks to signal the importance of new patterns of
migration and immigration as well as the international context more generally. The influx of immigrants to economically powerful nations has deep
implications for education and social structure. Whether possessing "flexible
citizenship" by virtue of high-status knowledge or occupying a more marginal status in economically powerful nations like the United States, immigrants bring new demands to our educational systems. While continuing to
focus on the education of historically marginalized groups in the population,
we seek increased attention to these new groups, including disadvantaged
immigrant, migrant, and refugee students, most notably, those with limited
English proficiency and those from non-Western cultures, as educating these
groups now constitutes one of our biggest challenges.

It is similarly important that research in a variety of nations becomes part
of mainstream discourse. While *AERJ*-SIA will continue to publish high-quality research related to a range of key political, cultural, social, economic, and
organizational issues in U.S. education, including, among others, research on

tracking, segregation, and high-stakes testing, it is important to recognize the increasing complexity of the global situation as well as its impact on American educational policy, practice, and institutional outcomes. By way of example, American school reforms in the 1960s were partly driven by the international brain race fueled by Sputnik. Later, the rise of Japan, and more recently China and India, has fueled questioning about the direction of American education. This further underscores the need to acknowledge the larger context within which we live, and we seek to publish more articles that reflect global realities and can inform American thinking and practice.

Higher Education and Pre-K: The Educational Spectrum

The global knowledge economy further demands that we focus more carefully on higher education, with specific focus on the systemic linkages between high school, college/university access, and "success," as measured by college completion and linked social and economic outcomes. While there has been much focus on "access" to college, researchers must continue to press the "access to what" question and the ways in which the seemingly well-established linkages between high schools and particular kinds of colleges are now being renegotiated in light of changing global circumstances. We must, in other words, push the boundaries of *AERJ*-SIA's largely K-12 research focus, while publishing more articles related to higher education. Much excellent research has focused on the mechanisms of exclusion at the secondary school level, and *AERJ*-SIA has, impressively, been at the forefront of research in this broad area. Given increased access to higher education— in terms of sheer numbers who attend tertiary-level institutions as well as the large proportion of the age group attending college and university—and the centrality of higher education in the global knowledge economy, we seek increased attention to the pre-K through 16 plus pipeline. While a number of top-tier journals are devoted to higher education, attention to the "extended pipeline" is uncommon. Research on the extended pipeline must be folded into mainstream discussion about schools, schooling, and educational and economic outcomes. In a similar vein, as new research on the efficacy of universal pre-K policy emerges, the importance of early childhood education and access to quality preschools for disadvantaged children deserve more attention. We seek, then, to signal the importance of these broader issues by including more research on both early childhood education and higher education—in other words, pre-K through 16 plus—as we press to situate our research inside changing global realities.

Policy Debates

Without question, the stakes with regard to education are more intense than ever, and we must make concerted effort to inform and guide current and future national educational policy through publication of more policy-enlightening research. There has been a shift in the focus on national educational policy from equity to excellence during the past two decades while there have been simultaneous setbacks in the desired national progress toward closing the achievement gap. While the No Child Left Behind Act helped raise awareness of the achievement gap, it simultaneously generated debates about "what works" in education and what kind of research evidence matters for educational-policy decision making. This debate, however, often narrowed the focus of educational research and practice. Rather than seeking the "one best" method or practice, we wish to open up research possibilities by promoting more diverse methods and innovative approaches. This, combined with our earlier point as to the importance of publishing high-quality research on the pre-K through 16 plus pipeline for varying groups of students, will enable us to participate in critical policy debates of the future.

AERJ-SIA is one of the premier peer-reviewed research journals on education in the world, and we are very proud of its standing. It is, however, time to take into account more seriously the broader and more challenging national and global context within which educational policies, practices, and outcomes play. We will continue to publish important and high-quality research pieces across a wide variety of areas, while opening up possibilities with regard to changing world circumstance. We welcome multiple perspectives that draw upon the interdisciplinary nature of educational research as well as our strong tradition of multiple methods that enable us to answer critically important research questions. It is an honor to be entrusted with *AERJ*-SIA.

—Lois Weis, Editor
Philip Altbach and Jaekyung Lee, Associate Editors

American Educational Research Journal
March 2009, Vol. 46, No. 1, pp. 9–44
DOI: 10.3102/0002831208320573
© 2009 AERA. http://aerj.aera.net

Threat Rigidity, School Reform, and How Teachers View Their Work Inside Current Education Policy Contexts

Brad Olsen
Dena Sexton
University of California, Santa Cruz

This article reports on a study of teachers at one reforming high school. Though it is not their task to debate No Child Left Behind (NCLB), the authors locate their investigation inside the current policy context to which NCLB is attached. Specifically, they present their analysis through the organizational behavior lens of threat rigidity to discuss the ways that current federal and state policy contexts influence schools and how those affected schools in turn adopt corresponding reforms that influence teachers' work. The analysis demonstrates that on both levels, such influence occurs in similar ways: by centralizing and restricting the flow of information, by constricting control, by emphasizing routinized and simplified instructional/assessment practices, and by applying strong pressure for school personnel to conform.

KEYWORDS: educational policy, educational reform, qualitative research, teaching context

> Teaching is a job with a lot of contradictions in it, and I think it requires a lot of perseverance and idealism. Without the idealism, you know, why would you be there?
>
> —One of the teachers interviewed

The current education policy climate in the United States is controversial and complex. After decades of allegiance to decentralized state and local control of schools, the recent movement toward school accountability, standardization, and federal control began in the 1980s as response to *A Nation at Risk* (National Commission on Excellence in Education, 1983); it gained momentum during Bill Clinton's 1990s administration, and it burst open with George W. Bush's appointment of Rod Paige as education secretary and with the subsequent enactment of the No Child Left Behind Act of 2001 (NCLB;

McGuinn, 2006; Rowan, 1990; Sleeter, 2007). NCLB has become a lightning rod for concentrated attacks, defenses, punditry, and sweeping education reforms in our country's public schools. Although it is not the task of this article to debate NCLB, we locate our analysis inside the influential policy context of which NCLB is considered the pointed and public face.[1] Over the last several years, the policy culture in education writ large has engendered significant changes in how schools operate. For example, how to define and measure "highly qualified" teachers has affected teacher preparation and licensure; at the same time, it has also increased the scrutiny of and support for various "backdoor" alternative paths and internships into the profession (Ingersoll, 2002; Peyser & Costrell, 2004). Most public schools now focus on and often-times fear annual school scores based on aggregated results of state-developed indicators (Elmore, Abelmann, & Furhman, 1996; McDermott, 2007). Many teachers and administrators contend with not only increased public scrutiny of their practice but also concerns about job security and state receivership of their schools. Numerous states and city school districts require strict adherence to purchased curricula, prescriptive teaching methods, and mandated text-books. Finally, heated rhetoric has gathered around the topic of whether pub-lic education is flawed beyond repair or able to improve if left to its own devices (Berliner & Biddle, 1995; Will, 2006). For better or worse—and perhaps it is both—the policy landscape of education in the United States has been turned inside out.

This article reports on a qualitative study of six teachers at one reform-ing California high school. The research question that we set out to answer was twofold: First, how does a school's reform climate (influenced by local, state, and federal education policy cultures) affect teachers and their careers? Second, how do these teachers in turn affect the school's reform cli-mate? The study was designed to examine reciprocal relationships among teachers' perspectives on their work as situated within the school and larger education policy reform climates. Because all parts of the equation—teachers' views, work, and careers; school contexts; larger policy climates and pressures—are not discrete but inextricably connected, we adopted an ecological research design.[2] Utilizing an inductive analytical method, we first

---

BRAD OLSEN is assistant professor of education at the University of California, Santa Cruz, 1156 High Street, Santa Cruz, CA 95064; e-mail: *bolsen@ucsc.edu*. His research and teaching focus on teachers, teaching, teacher education, and school reform. Recent publications include *Teaching What They Learn, Learning What They Live: How Teachers' Personal Histories Shape Their Professional Development* (2008) and "How Reasons for Entry Into the Profession Illuminate Teacher Identity Development," in *Teacher Education Quarterly* (2008).

DENA SEXTON, is a doctoral student in the Education Department at the University of California, Santa Cruz, 1156 High Street, Santa Cruz, CA 95064; e-mail: *dmsexton@ucsc.edu*. Her research centers on teachers, teacher education, and teach-ers' work. She recently published "Student Teachers Negotiating Identity, Role, and Agency," in *Teacher Education Quarterly* (2008).

---

studied the collected data through two related research frames: school reform implementation (Berman & McLaughlin, 1978; Fullan & Pomfret, 1977) and school restructuring (Elmore, Peterson, & McCarthy, 1996; Rosenholtz, 1991). We then conducted a fuller, fine-grained analysis of the data through the lens of threat rigidity effects in organizational behavior (Staw, Sandelands, & Dutton, 1981). We discuss these research lenses and introduce threat rigidity as our theoretical frame after first presenting our study design.

Study Design

To examine the interrelationships among teachers, current reform approaches, top-down policy pressures, and the school context, we selected six teachers from one academic department (English) at one large underperforming high school in Southern California.[3] The school was selected partly because its demographic and student performance details make it the kind of school current educational reforms target and partly because its recent site history is steeped in multiple active attempts at school reform. Teacher selection was guided by our desire to represent a range of professional experiences, including teacher preparation, multiple roles within teaching, and years in the profession. The resulting stratified random sample included English teachers who attended various teacher preparation programs (undergraduate, graduate, and intern) at public and private universities. Furthermore, all participants had taken on different leadership roles as teachers, and the sample varied in number of years teaching, from 3 to 25, which we grouped into early-career teachers ($n = 2$), midcareer teachers ($n = 2$), and later-career teachers ($n = 2$).[4] Additional teacher information is included in Table 1.

We met with each teacher in the fall, winter, and spring of 2005–2006 to conduct audiotaped, hour-long semistructured interviews. Interview protocols focused on uncovering teachers' personal and professional histories; past and current education practice; perspectives on teaching, their school, and various education/policy reforms; and career plans. The school principal declined our two interview requests. We also collected documents and artifacts about the federal, state, district, and school contexts: published reports, Web site data, news articles, and teacher materials.

Choosing Our Analytical Frame: School Reform Research

Contours and consequences of modern school reform have been well documented in research on school reform implementation in the 1970s and on school restructuring in the 1980s and 1990s. Our own data analysis began with those research frames. School reform implementation as a research domain resulted from an investigation into why the first modern federally mandated school reform programs failed: the so-called *Sputnik* reforms of 1958 (i.e., the National Defense Education Act) and the Elementary and Secondary Education Act of 1965 (Sarason, 1982; Twight, 1994). Berman and McLaughlin (1978), Fullan and Pomfret (1977), and Sarason (1982) found the implementation

Table 1
Demographic Information on the Teachers in the Sample

Name	Years Teaching	Age	Race/Ethnicity (Self-Reported)	Gender
Melissa	3	34	White/Anglo	Female
Sophia	3	30	White/Middle Eastern	Female
Layla	6	36	White/Anglo	Female
Susan	10	37	White/Anglo	Female
Richard	13	52	White/Anglo	Male
Bill	25	56	White/Anglo	Male

Note. All names are pseudonyms.

of school reforms to be its own active force. Implementation is not an inert, simple process of putting into practice some chosen educational change. Instead, it carries its own influences and effects that become intertwined with and work to alter both school and reform. This research lens allowed us to examine ways in which the reform implementation process mediated the reforms being implemented and the teachers' perspectives on their work.

In the 1980s and 1990s, the school restructuring movement and its accompanying research picked up on active roles of reform implementation; yet, it also foregrounded the ways in which the school context is an active variable in reform (Little, 1982; Osborn & Broadfoot, 1992; Rosenholtz, 1991; Sisken, 1994; Woods, Jeffrey, & Bayle, 1997). Considering that a school's history, its administrative culture, its teaching staff (i.e., the characteristics of), and its contextual details mediate how or if reforms take effect, school restructuring advocates called for implementing school reforms carefully and holistically. The school restructuring movement held that reform implementation is a fragile, complex, site-specific phenomenon and that any reforming school or district should match its program of reform implementation to the specific contours of its context. This research frame enabled us to investigate how the school's history, culture, and staff characteristics affected its reform process.

Both analytical phases illuminated how teachers were affected by school change attempts and how the change attempts were affected by the teachers; yet, we believed that there was a deeper, more novel phenomenon inside our data. Preliminary analysis had identified a pattern whereby the federal and state education policy climate appeared to be pressuring the local school administration and school board in ways that produced an identifiable kind of threat mentality. We found that from the school administration and teaching staff came rigid defensiveness, coupled with a psychological myopia, that sabotaged the reform attempts and created a hostile work environment for the teachers whom we studied. To better understand this phenomenon, we turned to sociological research regarding how organizations cope with adversity. Specifically, we took up the concept of threat rigidity.

Organizational Behavior and Threat Rigidity

Threat rigidity as an analytical frame emerges from the sociological field of organizational behavior, and it can be located inside the natural systems perspective on organizations and the new institutionalism theory. The natural systems perspective focuses on the relationship between an organization and its goals, to highlight how organizations are guided by not only their stated goals but also their inherent desire for continued existence (Bolman & Deal, 1991; Scott, 2003). This perspective holds that it is an organization's survival that becomes the primary task for those involved and that the organization's stated goals become eclipsed by its desire to sustain itself (Scott, 2003). For example, a preschool created to serve children from the community over time becomes a place focused on keeping itself afloat, with the staff's working in part to ensure its continued employment. Natural systems theory treats individuals within an organization not as mere group members solely committed to the goals of the organization but as "more expansive, social, and motivationally complex [actors]" (p. 87) with sometimes-competing loyalties.

Complementing the natural systems perspective, the new institutionalism theory explains the safeguarding of organizations through institutional legitimacy (DiMaggio & Powell, 1983; Rowan, 1982). The underlying premise is that organizational forms and behaviors reflect prevailing societal beliefs that, over time, become taken-for-granted norms. Meyer and Rowan (1977) refer to this as *myth and ceremony*, where an organization's external structures and internal activities are loosely coupled so that the organization can appear legitimate despite possible inconsistencies: "To maintain ceremonial conformity, organizations that reflect institutional rules tend to [be able to] buffer their formal structures from the uncertainties of technical activities by becoming loosely coupled, building gaps between their formal structures and actual work activities" (p. 341). For example, as a public organization supported through tax revenue, a school earns external legitimacy when its visible structures resemble what society expects a successful school to look like: a recognizable architecture, a U.S. flag out front, knowledge demarcated by class periods with familiar names, teachers with official credentials. This societal validation seals off and protects the school's core work (i.e., learning and teaching) from outside intrusion or suspicion. Within this perspective, then, recent wholesale attacks on the legitimacy of schools as effective learning organizations (e.g., the current press for accountability, teacher quality concerns) compel different levels of the organization to respond in particular ways because the "forces maintaining the structure are themselves activated by forces threatening the equilibrium" (Scott, 2003, p. 61).

We combined these two perspectives to understand how actors, as complex individuals within a school, responded to multilevel attacks on their legitimacy and their school's legitimacy. As such, we turned to Staw and colleagues' work (1981) on threat rigidity.[5] We applied threat rigidity, as created by Staw et al. and as derived from business management studies, to examine how the current federal education policy context influences schools and how those affected schools in turn adopt corresponding reforms that influence teachers' work. We found that on both levels, threat rigidity occurs in a number of similar ways: by centralizing and restricting the flow of information, by constricting control, by emphasizing routinized and simplified instructional/assessment practices, and by applying strong pressure for school personnel to conform. These adaptations, or threat rigidity effects, created in the teachers the very responses that Staw et al. identified in business organization members: psychological stress, intergroup and intragroup difficulties, defensiveness/resentment, a desire to hide one's practice, and a move to replace the first-tier leadership. We describe threat rigidity in detail later, but first we introduce the school context.

The Context: Hawthorne High School

The school, which we call Hawthorne High School, is located in Southern California. Hawthorne is a large, comprehensive high school located in a rural, agricultural community. The community has a long history of drawing in members of various minority groups (Chinese, Japanese, Filipino, Mexican) for agricultural labor. The school has roughly 3,500 students, of which more than one third are classified as English learners (predominantly, Spanish speakers). About two thirds of the students qualify for free or reduced-price lunches. The majority of the students are Latino (93%), with the balance comprising White/other (5%) and Asian American (2%). The mostly White teaching staff is experienced, with an average of 14 years of teaching. Situated at the nexus of contested ideas about achievement, Hawthorne is considered *underperforming* by the teachers in this study and the community, even though according to the state and federal achievement markers (academic performance index and adequate yearly progress), Hawthorne met its performance goals for the 2005–2006 school year.[6]

During the year of data collection, Hawthorne was engaged in several schoolwide reforms: establishing small learning communities (SLCs), creating and implementing departmental curricular maps, adopting a new block schedule, and inserting into the beginning of the school day an "advisory" period for all students. Adoption of these reforms was met by mixed, mostly negative response by teachers. One reform in particular (the move to SLCs) was reportedly adopted—or "steamrolled though," as one teacher put it—by the administration through means that some teachers considered underhanded. Additionally, in spring the school was having its accreditation reviewed by the Western Association for Schools and Colleges (WASC) for the third time in 9 years; this was treated as a very high-stakes event. According to the teachers, this eventual WASC review did not go well. Not only was Hawthorne granted only a 3-year accreditation period (essentially, a probationary stamp of disapproval), but during the weeklong review, Hawthorne teachers shared school rumors, complaints, and other "dirty laundry" with the review team and resented the artificial nature of the "dog and pony show" that they were being asked to perform.

Largely because of these school reform efforts and WASC pressures, during this year Hawthorne experienced considerable friction between administration and faculty and among faculty subgroups and individual teachers. Dominating our interviews was teacher-initiated talk about school tensions and frustrations that affected teaching practice and teacher perspectives. A group of 20 teachers (not in our research sample) who opposed the changes implemented by the principal led a campaign of resistance against him, resulting in his departure at the end of the year. As the school year came to a close, tensions had polarized groups of teachers and increased hostilities between teachers and administration. Three of the four assistant principals at Hawthorne were offered early retirement or were transferred. Several teachers at Hawthorne left, including one of the six in our sample. Two more in our sample said that they were preparing to leave after the following year; one said that she was considering leaving; and another said that he was ready for retirement. We found that the content of the school reforms, the manner of their implementation, the generally hostile personnel climate, and the attitudes and career perspectives of the six teachers were all related. Understanding this emic reality—what we call "the Hawthorne situation"— became our analytical task and so constitutes the remainder of this article.

Threat Rigidity and Survival
Responses to the Hawthorne Reforms

In the relatively besieged work environment at Hawthorne, dysfunctional patterns of communication, leadership, and staff behavior arose that, rather than move reform successfully along, hindered and even sabotaged initial reform efforts. We believe that this maladaptive response phenomenon fits precisely with what Staw et al. (1981) termed *threat rigidity effects in organizational behavior*. Threat rigidity is the theory that an organization, when perceiving itself under siege (i.e., threatened or in crisis), responds in identifiable ways: Structures tighten; centralized control increases; conformity is stressed; accountability and efficiency measures are emphasized; and alternative or innovative thinking is discouraged.

These organizational adaptations, or threat rigidity effects, result in a set of threat rigidity responses by the individuals and subgroups of the organization. Psychological stress emerges and so limits the cognitive ability of organization members to discriminate unfamiliar stimuli and think flexibly or innovatively. Groups within the organization quarrel over power, resources, and support for their solutions to the threat. The group that typically prevails (often temporarily) increases its intragroup relations; overall, however, intergroup ties lessen, and the losing group suffers a marked decrease in intragroup cohesiveness. Conformity, efficiency, and standardization measures decrease individuals' perceptions of their value to the organization. Finally, the first-tier leadership of the organization is replaced, whereas the second-tier leadership gains power. These are the maladaptive phenomena that Staw et al. (1981) found to occur when organizations find themselves in a kind of survival mode. This model fits our data perfectly.

15

We found threat rigidity at play in two ways: one federal/macro and the other one local/micro. Because our study focused on local effects of threat rigidity, we center our analysis on those micro-dimensions of threat rigidity dimensions. However, to situate our localized analysis inside the larger context, a brief introduction to threat rigidity at the federal level is helpful. The macro-minded manifestation of threat rigidity is that the current educational policy zeitgeist in the United States can be seen as a threat rigidity effect of recent social and political views of education—namely, that public education is failing. These views are often referred to as "the crisis of education." They were ushered in by *A Nation at Risk* (National Commission on Excellence in Education, 1983), and they were intensified in recent calls for increased accountability, high-stakes standardized testing, and "teacher-proof" instruction (Berliner & Biddle, 1995; McGuinn, 2006). The thumbnail analysis goes like this: Since the early 1980s, factions in society have concluded that U.S. public education is failing and/or has become a threat—to national security, to individual social mobility, to economic dominance abroad, to performance on various international indicators (such as literacy rates and the Trends in International Mathematics and Science Study), and so on. Concluding that education is in crisis, those factions enacted a set of reforms as response: high-stakes accountability, an emphasis on standardized testing, new frames of teacher professionalization, the NCLB, and an embrace of scripted curricula and prescriptive pedagogies in many K–12 districts.[7] This response corresponds to precisely the kinds of responses that Staw et al. (1981) discuss: restriction of information, constriction of control and centralization of authority, inability to discriminate unfamiliar stimuli, a reversion to simplistic routinized behaviors, eroded group cohesion, increased attention to fiscal efficiency, and increased emphasis on conformity and uniformity.

Almost any look at the current policy culture in education would reveal it to be a textbook threat rigidity effect. Such a view is consistent with studies that have found that most policy aspirations do not match achievement results (McDermott, 2007). Threat rigidity characteristics also fit analyses faulting the oversimplified rigidity of NCLB's accountability mechanisms—what Popham (2005) calls *instructionally insensitive achievement tests*—for being ill-suited to the complex contours of teaching and learning. Popham points out that under NCLB many states, including California, have felt pressured to use diagnostic student tests for school evaluation purposes: an example of the kind of self-defeating misalignment that follows from pressures to overprivilege conformity, standardization, and efficiency.

There is, however, a second, more localized way in which Staw and colleagues' organizational theory (1981) illuminates the situation that our study investigated: This is our micro-minded view of threat rigidity effects and, thus, the primary concern of our study. We found that the situation at Hawthorne High School during 2005–2006 was itself a next-level effect of the national policy culture. In other words, if national education and political perceptions were the first-level threat that led to the first-level effect (i.e., NCLB and its connected policy cultures), then we can view the local pressures on and

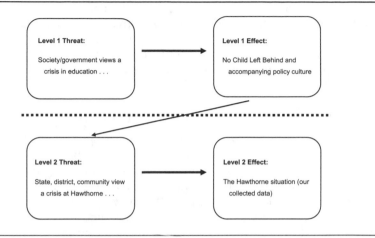

Figure 1. **Two levels of threat rigidity effects explain the Hawthorne situation.**

perceptions of Hawthorne as an underperforming school as a Level 1 effect (on the national and state stage) and a Level 2 threat in the local Hawthorne community. The visual representation depicted in Figure 1 displays this two-tiered effect.

Specifically, various Hawthorne stakeholders and administrators felt pressure to respond to the external threat of its school as a failing one—for example, its being maligned by local media in relation to policy benchmarks, its posting merely satisfactory academic performance index and adequate yearly progress scores, its being considered deficient by parents and students, its scoring badly on past WASC reviews. As such, the school board and administration initiated changes and effects that caused threat rigidity at Hawthorne; that is, Level 2 threat → Level 2 effect. Viewed by community members and education boards through current accountability lenses, Hawthorne was considered a school in crisis. For example, the·local newspaper carried multiple stories that were critical of controversial decisions by the school principal and that reported friction among teachers, administration, and the community.[8] The visible structures of the school as an effective organization had crumbled, which eroded societal support for the legitimacy of the school. As we demonstrate, the school principal's response to the threat was to initiate school changes that—sometimes inadvertently and sometimes intentionally—centralized and restricted the flow of information, constricted control, emphasized routinized and simplified instructional/ assessment practices, and applied strong pressure for school personnel to conform. These adaptations exacerbated or created, in many of the Hawthorne teachers, the very responses that Staw et al. (1981) had identified: psychological stress, intergroup and intragroup difficulties, defensiveness/ resentment, a desire to hide one's practice, and a move to replace the first-tier leadership. As individual actors in the school organization, the teachers reacted by privileging their individual perspectives over their organizational commitments. Below, we discuss these maladaptive responses inside three categories, which we developed to capture the effects of threat rigidity: intergroup and intragroup tensions; cognitive and structural inflexibility; and professional autonomy, isolation, and visibility.

Intergroup and Intragroup Tensions

The various school changes and surrounding professional climate at Hawthorne included many kinds of tension among teachers and school leaders. We found evidence of tensions between teachers and administration, between some late-career teachers and newer teachers, and among teachers inside and across academic departments. Not only were these group tensions a product of threat rigidity, but they also exacerbated it. As such, our data revealed the following: The principal favored the newer teachers; many teachers possessed negative attitudes toward the Hawthorne administration; personnel tensions affected student learning; the teachers interpreted Hawthorne's reform climate as deprofessionalizing; escalation of tensions caused the leadership change. We take them up individually.

The Principal's Favoring the New Teachers

Four teachers spoke in ways that suggest that the principal favored newer teachers as a whole (i.e., who came to the school when this principal was hired). The three most recently hired teachers in the English department (Melissa, Layla, Sophia) articulated cooperative, constructivist philosophies of education in their conversations with us that seemed to align with the contours of the adopted school reforms. All three—who were recently prepared in university programs—talked about privileging group learning, student-centered pedagogy, and teaching for understanding in their classrooms. For example, they viewed the move to block schedules as a useful constructivist challenge, whereas the later-career teachers in our sample were far more skeptical. We suspect that the administration considered the early-career teachers' constructivist pedagogies as being compatible with Hawthorne reforms. As well, we suspect that the principal perceived the newer teachers as being more malleable.[9] Regardless of the cause, the evidence suggests that they were favored over the later-career teachers. Layla reported that the principal told her, "You're one of the ones I want to keep." And at another point, Layla said, "[The administrators] pretty much know that I'm doing my job, they like what I do, so they concentrate on those teachers who are—well, the trouble people, basically." Likewise, Melissa said,

> When I learned that the English department is losing five [teacher] spots, and here I am [without seniority], I thought to myself, "Oh god, I'm going to be in trouble; my job's in jeopardy." But I learned that [the principal] actually had carved out a little niche for me as being a

model classroom next year, one that showcases SLCs, which is a little overwhelming but great, because it means I have a job.[10]

Two early-career teachers suggested that there was a common perception that many of the later-career teachers inside and outside the English department were reluctant to change because it would require too much effort and that they resisted collaboration. One teacher said that many Hawthorne teachers had not changed their practice over the years as the community and student population had changed from a predominance of White students to one of students of color—thereby suggesting that the later-career teachers' pedagogies did not match the student realities of these non-dominant-culture students (Ladson-Billings, 1994; Moll, Amanti, Neff, & Gonzalez, 1992). The following teacher said that many later-career teachers became alarmed at the move to block scheduling and then significantly more concerned about SLCs:

> So [adopting a block schedule] was huge; some people were upset. And then the small learning communities [decision was made], and everyone got scared. It was like, "Oh god, we're going to be moving into small learning communities—that means I'm going to be stuck with a group of teachers all the time, forced to collaborate." A lot of teachers don't like to collaborate. You know, they don't like to go to meetings. They view it as extra work—having to change their entire curriculum so everything aligns, which [to me] makes so much more sense. [But] it's like, you've got a teacher who's been doing the same thing for 35 years, and they've been doing a pretty good job. They don't want to change. They're looking at retirement.

Notice how she moves from the specific—these later-career teachers—to what seems to be a more general indictment of "a lot of" and "so many" 35-year teachers. This shift suggests that there may be a subtle process at work by which this teacher is relying on a common stereotype about later-career teachers (parts of which may be true, parts of which are probably false) that affects her interpretation of the Hawthorne situation as it related to teachers' career-cycle influences (Huberman, 1993a; Olsen & Kirtman, 2002). Another teacher talked about "the old school vets," telling us that they "don't like change—they don't like having to change, having to turn their curriculum upside down, having to create new curriculum." This same teacher spoke in a later interview about how the administration was "going after them" but that she herself was not worried: "I've got an 'in' with the principal—he likes how I teach and leaves me alone."

We found that the more experienced teachers in our sample shared a cynicism toward Hawthorne's school reforms, although none was in the group of 20 teachers directly involved in the public feud between teachers and administration. The later-career teachers in our sample revealed a kind of "been there, done that" response to school reform. They shared both a weariness and a wariness toward school change efforts. Richard said, "This is the thing that we do in education: The pendulum swings, we try new programs, we get rid of new programs. Sometimes they work, most of the time they're just new programs." This perspective confirms research around later-career teachers' becoming cynical and embittered, given their multiple generations of school reform experience (Hargreaves, 2005; Huberman, 1993a; Little, 1996).

Whatever the causes, we found tensions between newer teachers (who, intentionally or not, put some of the later-career teachers on the defensive) and later-stage teachers (who may have felt misunderstood, slighted, or fatigued by cycling reform attempts). We think that these already-existent tensions flared up largely because of the frustration, loss of professional autonomy, and other threat rigidity effects that the administrative climate and school reform culture engendered. Teachers quarreled over resources and interpretations of what was happening to Hawthorne. We heard complaints against former and current teacher leaders, conversations about faculty meetings rife with "yelling," "screaming" and "BMW—a lot of bitching, moaning, and whining."

Teachers' Negative Attitudes Toward Administration

All six teachers in our sample believed that the school was suffering from a "leadership crisis." About this there was consensus. The teachers reported that the administration was "weak," "in over its head," and had become "Stalin—doing to teachers things you would never do to your students." This complaint was sometimes couched in partial sympathy for the administration: The school and district administrators were between a rock and a hard place in terms of external policy pressures on the one side and the interests of students and teachers on the other. This explanation suggests that the administration was forced to make these school changes and thus act callously toward teachers. With a softening of tone, some of the English teachers told us that the administrators were good people at heart but underexperienced and overwhelmed. This perspective connects to the two-tier model of threat rigidity introduced earlier: From the perspective of these sympathetic teachers, Hawthorne leaders were caught in the place where the macro-level effect of threat rigidity (NCLB policy culture as response to education in crisis) becomes the micro-level threat (local pressure to respond to the larger sociopolicy response).

In other versions of this complaint, however, there was less sympathy and more hostility—less of a sense of administration as victim and more that it constituted malevolent leadership:

> [When the new principal came in], nobody expected a dictator. . . .
> And when you have that—when you have this "shoot one of the sol-
> diers to keep the others in line" kind of philosophy . . . it's not right.
> The stage we're at right now is the hatred, the development of hatred
> [by teachers toward administration]. People are hiding their heads.
> People are just "whoosh!" You know? Do your eight [hours of work]
> and hit the [school] gate. Don't get involved in anything.

Within this perspective, the fault lies less in the federal policy climate and more in inept school leadership. Here, there were three primary complaints against the administration: One is that the chosen and implemented school reforms were not good ones; the later-career teachers were more likely than newer teachers to level this complaint. The second concerned the manner in which those reforms were decided and implemented—that is, how the administration mandated restrictive changes while preaching democratic reform, teacher buy-in, and consensus building. Most teachers in our sample shared this perspective. And the third complaint was that the school administration generally had "clamped down" on teachers and students in such draconian ways as to lower morale and anger teachers; all six teachers voiced this position.

Deriving from these complaints were the psychological stress, narrowed thinking, and group power struggles consistent with that of previous threat rigidity research. We found significant unease, intergroup and intragroup fighting, and defensiveness toward the administration, which combined with other threat rigidity maladaptations to produce the Hawthorne situation. For example, the ways in which the English department chair pressured teachers to follow the administration's emphasis on standardized teaching exacerbated teachers' ill feelings toward the administration and thus created interdepartmental tensions. Melissa believed that these pressures were antithetical to engaging students in the passion and power of literature:

> The worst thing about it is that so many teachers are forced to focus on teaching to the test. We're not teaching literature, not having fun with it. We're not teaching kids to love poetry and books. I feel the hair on my back of my neck raise when I'm doing *To Kill A Mockingbird* with my accelerated class and the department chair asks me, "Well, what standard are you teaching to with that?" I'm like, "Oh my god, what standard am I *not* covering?!" *To Kill a Mockingbird* is one of the greatest pieces of literature. They're learning about dialect, and they're learning about theme and character as well as the world.

Sophia spoke of a similar pressure: "Our department chair passes the administration's information to us. And so, because of her and the administration's opinion about how our teaching should look, there's more pressure than I have felt in years."

Interpersonal Tensions as Negatively Affecting Student Learning Opportunities

Not only were the complaints and group tensions both an effect and a cause of the Hawthorne situation, but they were also reported to affect student learning. We found evidence that these tensions among educators spilled onto students in various ways. For example, teachers talked about how the constricted flow of communication meant that multiple kinds of school information never got to students correctly, on time, or sometimes at all: Administrative messages were not relayed to teachers; class and roster schedules changed without notice or explanation; frequent intercom messages to teachers and students interrupted class time. The teachers told us that student learning suffered as a result—specifically, in the form of breaks in student concentration; significant class time being squandered on sharing, clarifying, or correcting school information; and student and teacher stress over having insufficient information.

Three teachers talked about how they could not help but bring their schoolwide frustrations into interactions with students. Near the beginning of the school year, Melissa prophetically told us,

> [At the beginning of the school year, administration] looked at the master schedule, got rid of all of our long-term subs, reassigned a few teachers, some of us had to move rooms, some of us had to actually change teaching assignments. Everything kind of shut down, and it was a really ugly process, and people were very, very angry, and that was kind of the start of this whole snowballing—just rage, really, among a group of teachers that is really, I think, probably going to play out ultimately in some kind of ugly way. But I'm just kind of trying to stay out of it. . . . Most of the time, I can come in and just focus on my class and be fine. On the days I have to attend a meeting before school, [my frustration at the meeting] affects me as a teacher. And I really became aware of it one day when I came in after meetings, and I just yelled at a student. There was shock on the little faces around me. I said, you know, "I'm really sorry. I was just in a meeting that made me really mad, and I think I'm still just kind of in a bad mood." And then I just realized, "Wow, this is really getting to me and I don't want it to."

Three themes in this passage are worth noting. First, Melissa suggests that most of her time with colleagues was unpleasant—and we heard this sentiment from four of the six teachers in our sample. This finding further confirmed one effect of the Hawthorne rigidity—namely, that collegial relations among teachers were seriously strained. A second theme is that the unpleasantness occasionally affected interactions with students, although that seemed to be rare and something quickly addressed by Melissa. A third theme is that, in this passage, Melissa represents the classroom as a kind of safe place—a refuge from the school complications and a place where she can do what she entered teaching to do: work with students. As Sophia commented on "hiding in my classroom" and Susan described her classroom as a "fake world, [where] you just create whatever world you want," Melissa invoked the theme of teacher isolation and invisibility as a buffer against the Hawthorne hostilities; we discuss this theme later in the article.

Teachers' Interpretation of Hawthorne's Reform Climate as Deprofessionalizing

We found that threat rigidity made teachers believe that neither the larger education policy climate nor the Hawthorne administration respected their professional practice. Specifically, all six teachers in our study were disheartened by the deprofessionalization and decreased trust: It made them resentful; it led them to isolate themselves in their classroom ("put my head down, focus on the students, and just teach)"; and it sometimes pushed them into leaving, or considering leaving, Hawthorne. The teachers spoke about how the macro-policy climate of standardization, conformity, and high-stakes testing—all threat rigidity effects—ignored the teachers' training, talent, artistry, and skill as educators. They acknowledged that the school administration was responding to federal and state pressures in these areas, but they believed that it was not doing it well. So there were two targets of their displeasure: their school and the larger policy climate.

When asked about the new textbook series that Hawthorne administrators adopted and expected teachers to follow, Sophia talked about how the book in particular and the administrative action in general neglected her competence: "I don't need [the book publishing company] to tell me how to engage students." And she went on to talk about how prescriptive textbooks ignore her professional training, her teaching experience, and her knowledge of the students in her classroom. Melissa lamented that pushes for standardization and high-stakes standardized tests conceive of learning as rote facts rather than deep understandings and learning strategies. Bill said that the tests are racist for privileging White middle-class cultural literacies. Sophia said that the Hawthorne reforms made her feel like a worker bee. All the teachers mentioned how demoralizing it is to have to follow education mandates created by nonteaching educators, people who have not taught in decades, and/or politicians outside the education field. When asked if the education mandates around testing and prescriptive curricula bothered her, Melissa offered this reply:

> Yes it bothers me. . . . I think it's fine to have some core pieces of literature and some core themes, but I also love to supplement that with short stories and teach other things, poems I want them to read. And if someone starts telling me I can't do that any more, I'm not going to like that. It takes the pride out of your work—if you've developed a unit or something, I think being told, "No, you have to do this instead," is very demoralizing. It makes me feel like, then, you don't really need trained teachers; you just need trained monkeys. It's disrespectful to teachers.

In the teachers' words and nonverbal cues, we frequently noticed a strong affective dimension to the threat rigidity effects around deprofessionalism; the teachers were filled with more despair than hope. These were teachers who believed that they were doing well amid difficult circumstances, working as hard as they could, and they took it personally that they were continually critiqued by their own administrators, who knew them, and infantilized by the policy culture, which did not know them. Bill offered an analogy:

> [It's like] someone going in to the community hospital and getting all the doctors and nurses together and saying, "You people! What's wrong with you? We have too many sick people coming into this hospital and they're not getting any better." . . . You know, would we punish the doctors or the nurses? No. Because we understand that it's a dynamic institution, that you address what comes through that door

in the state that they come to you. There are a lot of variables. You may have 34 or 35 kids in your classroom, and you can't just lecture to them. You have to figure what's going on with them and reach them in ways they'll understand, and, boy, it's real tiring sometimes. I don't think the powers-that-be understand this.

Escalation of Tensions and the Subsequent Leadership Change

Group tensions at Hawthorne had escalated and boiled over by the end of the year. By late spring, the public feud between a group "of about 20 disgruntled veteran teachers" and the school principal had surfaced. This feud appeared to have two related components: one, a personal opposition between the group of later-career teachers and the principal (i.e., there appeared to be mutual antipathy); two, a kind of philosophical split (part ideological and part career location) between attitudes toward school change. Administration was mandating a set of specific changes: The 20 disgruntled later-career teachers actively opposed the school reforms, and the other teachers opposed the reforms to various degrees in private or were frustrated but supported the reforms nonetheless. In late winter, Layla told us,

> I'm starting to feel the lines are being drawn again. Some of the veteran teachers will start screaming at you in front of people. I feel a lot of tension, like when we're in meetings; I feel that tenseness. There's a sort of veteran alliance—veterans teaming together—that whole veteran thing happening.

Sophia bemoaned some of these teachers who were so actively resisting current reforms: "They get really upset by things, by the changes that are happening. There's just a lot of griping." However, Richard—one of the later-career teachers in our sample—saw it differently. His perspective was that the group of later-career teachers was fighting admirably for something that it believed in:

> The way [that the principal] is handling the situation and the way he's treating the staff—I knew that morale was low and a lot of people were unhappy. [Until recently] I did not realize that it was these [20 later-career] teachers specifically [who were leading the protest]—they're all excellent teachers, teachers whose integrity or care for students can't be questioned. I can't stomach [all the negativity] any more, but I understand them. They're putting their jobs on the line and saying [to the principal], "You've got to do something different."

Near the end of the academic year, the principal left the school for a job in another district, and several assistant principals chose to leave or were pushed out. Of the 20 disgruntled veterans, most remained (perhaps all; it is not clear which). This outcome matches Staw and colleagues' finding (1981) that in threat rigidity cases, the second-tier leadership (in this case, the 20 later-career teachers) often takes out the first-tier leadership (here, the recently installed Hawthorne administration). Overall, threat rigidity illuminates the brittle dynamics that had emerged among adults at Hawthorne: demarcated battle lines, deteriorating communication, heightened emotions, and increased defensiveness.

Cognitive and Structural Inflexibility

One way to view threat rigidity is as an organizational circling of the wagons—a way that groups tighten up and fixate in response to danger. As an effect of the macro-threat rigidity, NCLB and policy culture can be characterized here as a tightening of educational procedures, outcomes, and teaching models in schools and districts and as a clamping down on alternative thinking or decentralized attitudes toward reform. As an effect of the micro-threat rigidity, the policy culture can be seen as having instigated or heightened various localized school-level inflexibilities at Hawthorne. Teacher interviews revealed the following: First, school structures and personnel policies tightened up, resulting in an increased pressure to standardize one's practice; second, communication was constricted and made more hierarchical; third, there was increased pressure to conform to the administration's reform vision, thereby leaving no or little attention to flexible or alternative thinking.

Tightened Structures and Policies and the Pressure to Standardize

School structures and personnel policies tightened up, and the teachers' felt increased pressure to standardize their practice. Of the multiple reforms taking place at Hawthorne during the 2005–2006 school year, the implementation of curricular mandates took center stage, such as the development and use of curricular maps and the adoption of a new textbook series. We found both tangible and symbolic effects from these mandates. Here, we examine the adoption of curricular maps.

The development of, and unevenly forced adherence to, these maps dominated the teachers' work during the year. As well, opportunities for professional growth were co-opted under the auspice of this reform: Just about all Hawthorne professional development days were reportedly devoted to curricular maps and the WASC visit, which disappointed teachers who expected more substantive development opportunities from their in-service professional days. Sophia said,

> We had to do a lot of—they weren't really professional development days but happened during those times. They were days when we spent a lot of hours together—days where we had to build the whole curriculum map thing.

Not only did the teachers believe that the curricular maps constrained their teaching work, but they also believed that their professional autonomy suffered and their expertise was slighted. Weighing in on this point, Melissa told us,

25

> I feel like you need to give kids a broad range of skills, and there are a lot of classroom experiences that they will benefit tremendously from in life, things learned in high school that are not necessarily in the standards or the map. And so I'm certainly not going to limit myself to those [curriculum mandates]. I'll do them, and I'm completely willing to be accountable for the things I'm supposed to teach, but I am in no way going to limit myself to them—even though that's what I think this school wants. I shouldn't have to justify why I'm having students give a speech or an oral presentation. If someone can't see the value in that, then I can't explain it to them. It's frustrating.

None of the six teachers in our study opposed the concept of curricular maps; they all discussed positive aspects of having the maps as a shared resource, and four teachers talked about the value of vertically and horizontally integrating course contents. However, the administration's reported hypocrisy and contradictory insistence on strict adherence rankled teachers. The perceived hypocrisy was that the administration mandated these maps as a useful way for departments to open up their practice and create useful guides to follow, but the reality—according to the teachers in our sample—was that the maps were used by administration as a way to control and standardize teaching. Sophia said, "If we don't have the map at hand, we're made to feel that somehow we're not doing our job.

In practice, most teachers did not meaningfully collaborate on the development of these maps; instead, most departments, we were told, treated them as busy work: perfunctorily filling them in to have something to submit by the deadlines. There was an unevenness across departments, with some taking it seriously, with some farming it out to willing volunteers, and with some ignoring the mandate altogether. We were told that the maps were not used as a guide but as a script for standardizing teaching. Melissa said,

> We were told at various times over the course of the year: "This is your bible, and I [as assistant principal] want to be able to walk into any class English 1 class on a given Wednesday and see all of you on the same page and the same chapter."

The second complaint from teachers relates to the administration's contradictory insistence on strict adherence. Most of the teachers in our sample resented being told that they must follow the curricular maps; yet, at the same time, they knew that Hawthorne administrators were not going to conduct surveillance in teacher classrooms. None of the teachers with whom we spoke enacted the maps with any fidelity. They described the school's use of maps as a temporary reform: Teachers would use them when they had to, while waiting for the pendulum to swing back. They considered the maps ill-fitting to the needs of their students. Teachers had no reason to believe that the mandate would be enforced and so did not take the development very seriously. In the end, most teachers viewed the maps as merely a façade for the accreditation review. It was, they reasoned, all about the externally visible structures of schooling, not the core work of classroom teaching and learning. Melissa put it this way:

> This is all about WASC. When WASC comes, the administration has pretty much said, "You better be where you're supposed to be on your curricular map." And the thing that I hate is you have to pretend to be doing this and generate two days' worth of lesson plans, and I think that just beats the whole purpose of WASC, [which] is supposed to be so that we can reflect and see what's working and what isn't working. We're all faking for WASC. How are they going to be able to give us any valuable input? How are we going to grow? So I just think it's a sad state of affairs.

The teachers frequently talked about the curricular maps as a failed reform and an unpleasant and simultaneously unfair, unwarranted, and unsuccessful attempt at standardizing their practice. Most spoke in similar ways about the textbook adoption, the advisory period, and the move to SLCs.

Communication Constricted and Made More Hierarchical

Another dimension of the cognitive and structural inflexibility at Hawthorne was that communication was constricted between administration and teachers and among teachers. This created a stressful work environment and so limited opportunities for professional growth. Four teachers complained about not having a clear sense of what was happening in the school. Sophia said,

> Just constant lack of communication, and a lot of it just has to do with people being overwhelmed. There's too many people. We've got a failing technology system going on, and people aren't fully informed. There's no way to keep up on all of it.

Whereas all six teachers felt uninformed, four of the teachers described frustration over not having their voices heard within the administration; the perception was that administration was listening to only a small subset of Hawthorne's teachers to inform decision making. Richard told us, "It seems that the principal is listening to a very small cheerleading section and ignoring everyone else. And that's the part, I think, that's making everybody more upset." Other teachers, outside our sample, reported this sentiment to the local newspaper, including one who was quoted as saying that she felt intimidated by the principal and another administrator and had thus hired a lawyer to help her avoid reassignment. Susan likened the administration's leadership approach to that of a cruel classroom teacher:

> [Our administrators are] treating their teachers in a way you'd never treat your students. If you had a large group of students, and you had five who wouldn't do their work, who talked and misbehaved all the time, would you take your smartest kid or your best kid and punish the hell out of them? Hell no, you wouldn't do that. You'd go get some

> perspective. You'd go watch those guys. You'd make sure they do what they are supposed to do. You'd ride the trouble-causing ones a bit and compliment the good ones. You would not punish everybody!

Taken together, the restricted communication and the sense that the administration was unreceptive to most teacher input elevated frustrations about administrative decisions. Overall, the teachers complained that the decision-making process had became less transparent. With increasing frequency, teachers did not know the rationale behind the reforms being adopted. Teachers felt powerless to offer dissent or suggest alternatives. We also heard from the newer teachers that they believed that their jobs could be in jeopardy and that their working environment would be made more hostile if they voiced opposition to administrative decisions. For example, Layla said,

> I'm scared; I'm not going to go toe-to-toe with [the department chair or the principal] about anything, because the next thing I know, I'm going to get my [next year's class] schedule, and I'll be just like all those other teachers that are currently being screwed over—teachers who have a miserable schedule: five different preps in five different rooms.

A reported example of the lack of transparency and the disregard of teacher input involved the decision to restructure the school around SLCs. These were described as a school change that had been considered in previous years but repeatedly voted down. As such, there was anger toward the administration when the proposal to shift to SLCs was adopted the previous year. Richard told us,

> We were told the faculty was going to make the decision [about the SLCs]; we were told teachers were going to vote on it. We were told what the percentage would have to be: 75% of the voters would have to approve it. But a week before the vote, or 2 days before the vote, we were told that instead of 75%, it had suddenly dropped to 50% plus one. And then, at the last minute, somebody supposedly called targeted groups of parents, and all of a sudden a group of parents now had a vote. Nobody knows for sure—nobody's talking about what group of parents it was or who decided to make the phone calls to bring them into the equation and what they were told, but it wasn't every parent in the district or school. . . . So, of the teacher votes, out of about 130 people, it was something like 8 or 9 votes more in favor than against. It wouldn't have passed under the initial rules. The parent votes came out in favor. And teachers who were gone on school business that day were not allowed to vote. So it passed. The whole thing left a sour taste in most teachers' mouths.

Communication troubles also existed among teachers. As mentioned, we found a general apprehension toward collaboration: Four of the six teachers talked about not wanting to collaborate with others, and the other two spoke generally about how teachers at Hawthorne typically resist working together. The presence of the 20 disgruntled veterans, whose identities were largely unknown, revealed additional evidence of how communication was restricted among teachers. None of the teachers in our study—but for one later-career teacher, who knew of a few of these veterans—could (or would) identify this subgroup, which had amassed so much local power and which had forced the principal out of the school. This finding suggests not only that these 20 teachers felt the need to do their work in the shadows for fear of reprisal but also that lines of communication were so frayed at Hawthorne that no one knew what was happening outside his or her narrow field of vision, and so everyone's interpretation became its own subjective truth—a kind of *Rashomon* effect.

Restricted communication was also revealed in how teachers talked about the larger policy contexts in which the Hawthorne situation was situated. We found that five of the six teachers knew very little about NCLB—what it was, how it came about, how it might be influencing Hawthorne. Four of the teachers talked about NCLB in vague, broad, mostly negative terms:

Sophia: I can't keep the acronyms straight. All I know is that there's pressure for me to do certain things and it's told to me through my admin, to my department chair, and then down to me. I'm never let in on the larger picture.

Susan: I think [NCLB] is about doing stupid stuff with the money we're offered. I see crazy things. . . . You have this money that's all tied to [particular school changes]—foundations and grants—and those folks are all influenced by the legislature. And so then they say things like "Well, we're going to pay for, you know, SLCs or something like that. What we want to do is fund that!" And then your school goes running off and does it . . . because that's where the money says you have to go.

When pressed on particulars or asked to say more about NCLB, these teachers typically drew a blank or offered vague or inaccurate information. One readily acknowledged knowing nothing about it. The teacher in our sample who the newest to the profession was relatively knowledgeable about it: She had looked it up online and had read about it in professional journals, she said. Most teachers in the sample used it as a scapegoat on which to blame just about everything that they considered wrong in education. They had been exposed to sufficient anti-NCLB rhetoric in the press and in conversations with others so much so that it acted as a kind of proxy for some Orwellian future in schools: an education bogeyman just around the corner, waiting to pounce on everything that is good in schooling today. Generally, what we found is that the teachers were far more focused on the educational conditions right in front of them. The immediate school events and teaching policies that affected their daily work at school eclipsed any distant, higher-tier policy pressures that may or may not be trickling down.

This scenario makes sense. It is not surprising that people focus most closely on those conditions directly in front of them. But we suspect that it also suggests that Hawthorne's restricted communication and singular focus on WASC, which dominated school meetings and professional development days, precluded opportunities for administrators to explain, and for teachers to learn about, federal and state policies that factor into the reforms, policies, and climate of Hawthorne. Another school, one not experiencing the effects of a threat rigid environment, may have been freed up to dedicate professional time to learning the policies that shape daily operations and school changes. This open communication might have produced more awareness of the bind that the school was in (and, hence, more sympathy for those affected by it), some camaraderie among Hawthorne staff, and better conditions for shared problem solving. And these effects might have in turn looped back to improve personnel conditions and perhaps even encouraged innovative thinking; we return to this point in the conclusion.

Pressure to Conform to the Administration's Reform Vision

There was increased pressure to conform to the administration's reform vision, thereby leaving no or little attention to flexible thinking. That is, the threat rigidity response of cognitive and structural inflexibility is possibly best represented by the increased pressure on the teachers to conform, which left little or no room for attention to divergent thinking. Absent from the collected data was any attention on the part of the administration to encourage teachers to think differently about teaching and learning or about school improvement. Instead, the whole of the reforms, the school climate, and the various actions by the administration appeared to encourage a lockstep emphasis on conformity, which silenced opportunities for creative thinking. School conditions did not encourage innovative ideas; instead, they emphasized managing resources efficiently, controlling teaching, and bracing for attack. Sophia said that she had appreciated, in previous years, teacher meetings and professional development days as meaningful opportunities to think about her work—but no longer: "I am just getting really frustrated by things I hear in all these meetings throughout the year. It's all about WASC or how we have to follow the maps or adhere to the textbook. Or some administrator's complaints about us."

Job security was subtly present in the teachers' worries. Threats to job security were perhaps more symbolic than direct, but nonetheless, several of the teachers whom we studied believed that people in the administration were intentionally creating a perception that teachers who disobeyed in word or deed might be "pink-slipped" (i.e., released or transferred to another school in the district). Rumors emerged about falling student enrollments, which would lead to a loss of several English teacher positions. Teachers in our sample (especially, the newer ones) took this threat seriously; yet, at the same time, they were angry in their belief that this was a strong-arm tactic. The six teachers reacted in various ways: A few went undercover with their dislike of the situation while publicly maintaining appearances; a few tried to create their own personal niche within the department or with the principal, to secure their place at the school; most developed contingency plans to teach in another district or in another school within the district, if necessary; and Richard transferred to another school.

Going undercover—or, in Bill's words, embodying some variation of being "a good soldier"—was evident across the English teachers in our sample. Their general reaction was to publicly conform to the wishes and mandates of the administration but privately and carefully say and do what they wanted—both in their comments to us and in their practice (i.e., their closed-door classroom). There was also a sense that the more recently hired teachers needed to publicly support the principal so that their lack of seniority would not be used against them. Layla told us that she said to him, "'You're the principal, you're the boss. Tell me what to do and I'll do it.' I'd rather not lose my job." As such, Sophia began looking for other jobs within and outside of education; Richard interviewed at other schools in the district; and Susan changed departments within Hawthorne and put out feelers for jobs in other districts. Layla did consider teaching elsewhere. Richard described for us the personal toll that this year took on him and why the Hawthorne situation motivated him to migrate to another school:

> I was going home in a bad mood. My blood pressure was going up.
> I'd wake up in the morning and didn't want to go to work, didn't want
> to be there. And I've always loved my job. So when they came out in
> the spring and said that enrollment is decreasing and said we're going
> to have to eliminate six English teachers—either through retirement,
> transfers, or forced transfers. . . . I don't enjoy coming here in the
> morning, and they're going to force somebody to move, so I may as
> well volunteer rather than have somebody who wants to stay here be
> asked to move somewhere new. So I did.

Finally, the WASC review not only interacted with existing changes but also acted as a direct influence on teachers, pushing them to conformity and restricting their flexible thinking. As we have mentioned, Hawthorne's recent WASC review history had not been favorable, and the current year's accreditation visit was important. The WASC as an external threat that operated in direct and indirect ways. In a direct way, WASC promised reviewer walk-throughs in which teachers had to ensure that their practice was in perfect conformity with school reforms and one another's classrooms. In an indirect way, WASC (as it was framed by the school administration) had created a schoolwide ethos of pressure to conform. Again, the WASC visit was a disappointment to many. Layla lamented the outcome:

> We teachers worked our butts off for this—tried really hard to get
> good scores, did what we were told to do. So many teachers were
> into it, involved in the work, and then we get this horrible report—
> nothing about anything we were doing right. Nobody wanted to talk
> about it or hear anything about it. It was all very strange.

Melissa characterized how the WASC experience had exacerbated existing tensions all year long and had blown the disenfranchisement wide open by late spring:

> We had WASC this year and had to go to all of these meetings that were so tedious and horrible, and people were really just starting to hate any kind of meeting time to the extent that I think nobody really feels like what they say matters or what they want matters in the eyes of the administration. People feel really disenfranchised and angry. It's really ugly right now, and it was never this ugly before, even though there were still problems.

Although the resentment and negativity were taking a significant toll on the attitudes of most teachers, they told us that what happened in their classrooms did not change much. The threat response emphases on conformity and standardization had created an unpleasant and stifling professional climate, but they do not appear to have changed the teachers' classroom practice. Teachers reported maintaining the appearance of adhering to maps, using the new textbooks, and following the administration's seemingly rigid rules (including a new mandatory teacher sign-in policy). And it is possible that the WASC review team identified the point that we make here: that there appeared to be a disconnect between how Hawthorne represented its practice and what actually occurred in classrooms. This finding raises themes of visibility and invisibility.

Professional Autonomy, Isolation, and Visibility

A significant phenomenon that links to the two previous sections involves the teachers' sense of autonomy, their control over their work, and their ideas about professional visibility. At Hawthorne, this phenomenon derived from an interaction between two factors: the threat rigidity effects present at the school and a history of "loose coupling" between classrooms and school policies, common in large public schools (Meyer & Rowan, 1977; Weick, 1976). We found that all six teachers expected a kind of autonomy in or control over their classrooms. Our analysis revealed that teachers' reliance on loose coupling emerged as a defense mechanism against threat rigidity. It acted as a kind of escape valve that allowed them to locate some degree of autonomy and professional freedom in an otherwise constraining organizational environment.

Why Teachers Gravitated Toward Autonomy

The teachers gravitated toward professional autonomy and the freedom to teach as they desired for several reasons. The way that the teachers conceived of, valued, and defended their professional autonomy varied according to their professional preparation experience, their locations on the career cycle, and their individual differences. Some teachers said that they had been professionally prepared to diagnose kids and learning situations, design curriculum and plan lessons accordingly, and react to each class's unfolding dynamic as they perceived it. Richard raised the conflict between his professional training and the current climate of standardization:

> The emphasis [in my preparation program] was on planning lessons, which now I do somewhat, but [these days] a lot of things are dictated—more than I thought they would be. I can't use what I learned. . . . There was great emphasis placed in my program on knowing the students—they were the focus. Now it's all about what's in the textbook and what the state standards tell you.

There was also a career cycle factor: The newer teachers were more receptive to peer support and administrative assistance, whereas midcareer and later-career teachers believed that they had earned commensurate levels of control and freedom inside their classrooms. We found that all six teachers equated autonomy in their classrooms with the notion of a high-quality teacher: Autonomy was considered a mark of professionalism. We also noticed that status entered into the equation: There was a sense, on the part of the teachers, that autonomy correlates with professional respect; that is, any teacher who is left alone must be a good teacher indeed.

These teachers' embedded presumptions correspond in part to a long history of the isolated nature of teaching (Cuban, 1993; Lortie, 1975) and the teacher as independent artisan (Huberman, 1993b). The teachers in this study all, to some degree or another, presumed that such control of their classrooms was part of the job and that each had earned it. In fact, several teachers referenced autonomy in the classroom as they explained why they became teachers and talked about their work. For example, Melissa bemoaned the current policy climate for removing the artistry from teaching:

> I think that some standardizing of [the curriculum] is fine, [but] I think trying to have the lockstep—you teach chapter 2 on Day 5—is ridiculous. That takes all the artistry out of teaching, and I think when you're supposed to have a student-driven classroom, some kids just don't understand things [the same way]. . . . It's completely inappropriate to expect teachers to just march through and expect the kids to get anything out of it.

All six teachers believed that having autonomy in their classroom, with their students, was part of the job, part of being a professional, and that it should only be eliminated if there are clear signs of a teacher's incompetence or if students are not being well served. Teachers blamed the policy culture in general and the Hawthorne climate in particular for threatening their professional autonomy.

We detected a powerful sentiment: that although these teachers supported the notion of standardizing curriculum to a limited extent and agreed with the general idea of accountability in principle, they found the Hawthorne reforms to be overly prescriptive, misaligned with student-centered instruction, and professionally demeaning. But the teachers told us that no one ever came in to check on them (except during the WASC preparation and visit); as such, no one was sure how to interpret the mixed messages. "So basically you feel like, who's running this zoo?" Melissa said. Several of the teachers mentioned that if efforts to script their teaching intensified or if unsupportive observers regularly came into their classrooms, they would move to another school. Melissa was one of them, telling us, "If the climate gets so ugly that I'm just miserable, I won't stay. I just won't keep doing it. Why be miserable? Life's too short."

However, for the most part, the teachers had the autonomy that they wanted, which derived from multiple factors. We describe these factors as existing inside three categories: One is the federal policy climate. Although both its letter and spirit advocate strong standardization and accountability, NCLB as policy focuses more so on the primary grades; that is, its indirect climate effects are weaker in most U.S. high schools. Despite being an underperforming school, Hawthorne had been meeting its academic performance index and adequate yearly progress scores and so was not technically a high-priority target. As Bill described, "NCLB is coming down the pike but hasn't parked here yet."

The second category is the local context. As a large, traditional, comprehensive high school, Hawthorne has a long history of loose coupling and "egg-crate" (i.e., isolated) teaching structures (Cuban, 1993; Weick, 1976), which has meant that for many decades, teacher isolation (and its more attractive companion, autonomy) has been the norm. Richard, who had taught at Hawthorne for 7 years, said,

> When I first started here, each teacher within the department was left very independent, very independent to come up with your own lessons. We were given a general description of the things we needed to cover during the year, and that was it.

This school—like many traditional high schools—had enacted a professional culture in which teachers taught how they wanted, avoided "talking shop" at lunch and otherwise steered clear of having deep discussions of practice (especially, those concerning their own weaknesses and challenges), and maintained mostly isolated classroom communities that the teachers in our study variously called their "fiefdoms," kingdoms," and "perfect little worlds."

The third category of explanation is that the Hawthorne administration was simultaneously focused on so many things that observing teachers seemed a low priority. This meant that the teachers were rarely observed, evaluated, or pressed to actually change their practice to align with the intent of the reforms. Bill said,

> I think most people—what they've done before is they close the door and teach their kids the very best way they can. They try to adhere to the standards, try to adhere to what we're being asked to do, but we're not doing either slavishly.

Sophia said that for many teachers the response to administrative coercion was to hide: "Teachers would just get upset, and so they would isolate themselves."

Sophia said that even though the department was required to develop and follow curricular maps, "I was like, 'Well, thank you, [but] I'm just still going to do what I have to do and pick my own [reading] selections.'" When we asked her if there might be consequences to ignoring the curricular maps, she told us, "In my 3 years of teaching, I've had one 10-minute evaluation. . . . Nobody knows what the heck I'm doing!" In another conversation she said, "Nobody ever comes in to check up on me. . . . It's like, 'You guys never come to see me! If you really cared, you'd come and bark at me.'" This connects to the logic of confidence (Meyer & Rowan, 1977) coming from new institutionalism theories that explain loose coupling. As mentioned earlier, education stakeholders (e.g., district officials, the tax-paying public, state politicians) are convinced that schools do their job well if they outwardly resemble the public's image of good schooling. This perception governs the external structures of schooling, such as the buildings, the teacher qualifications, and the rhetoric of successful and/or improved teaching. As long as these visible logics are met, the public remains confident that good teaching and learning are occurring inside the classrooms. At Hawthorne, this explains the administrative focus on teacher certification, curricular maps, and high-profile reforms such as block scheduling and a move to academies within the school. Such a phenomenon allows a school to appear improved without changing its classroom instruction much. For these three reasons, then, the teachers still mostly had the autonomy for which they were prepared, of which they desired, and with which they had become familiar. Layla said,

> It's not like there is anybody breathing down my neck at school, and they aren't going to breathe down my neck as long as I—and this is true for the whole culture at [Hawthorne]—as long as there is a hint that you're doing your job, no one is going to bother you. I could be literally locking the door and showing movies 24 hours a day, and as long there's the hint that I'm doing my job, they're not going to bother me.

In many ways, the WASC review presented an unwanted intrusion into the teachers' core work. The curricular maps had been implemented a few years earlier, apparently in response to district pressures to standardize and make visible the learning that occurred in classrooms (and perhaps as a threat effect from the previous WASC visit). The curricular maps had been unpopular from the beginning, but teachers reported little previous pressure to actually follow them: As long as the curricular maps existed in folders on shelves, the administration was satisfied. But this past year, because of the impending WASC review, teachers were expected to follow the maps—or at least ratchet up the appearance of following them via written lesson plans, posters on classroom walls, and stacks of color-coded paperwork visible on their desks. This façade annoyed the teachers in our sample.

To different degrees and in different ways, five of the six teachers said that they would move schools if their autonomy in the classroom were eliminated or severely threatened. All teachers reported a positive correlation between classroom autonomy and their commitment to the school and the profession. And throughout our interviews, the teachers shared a perception that the current policy culture was slowly eroding their professional freedom and autonomy in the classroom. Because this was, for them, a nonnegotiable requirement of their work, they were prepared to move or leave if their autonomy disappeared.[11] Loose coupling was a structural feature that allowed the Hawthorne teachers to endure this component of threat rigidity, at least to an extent.

The Effects of Loose Coupling on Autonomy and Otherwise

The loose coupling that allowed teachers some autonomy in their classrooms produced other effects, however. One effect was that of a culture that discouraged collaboration and honest conversations about teaching, learning, and assessment. The classroom autonomy meant that few teachers at the school were collaborating in any substantive way. Layla lamented this sentiment:

> It's a bummer because I'm very social. I need to have people to hang out with, talk to, get ideas from—sort of bounce ideas off of. I have to have a social circle at work. Just like students need each other to be successful and motivated, I need to hang out with people who know what teaching is all about, who know what teaching means.

Melissa shared her dislike of faculty meetings: "The minute I have to go to a meeting after school, I'm just like, 'Arghh!' At the end of fifth period, I could have another 8 hours with students, but [meetings] really get me down." We suspect that this isolated teaching culture at Hawthorne sacrificed potentially valuable opportunities for team teaching, cross-classroom observations, professional development, and authentic conversations about teaching and learning. These teachers reported receiving none or very little feedback on their practice (i.e., feedback from adults), and what they did report receiving was often secondhand (e.g., a fellow staff member said that she had heard from students that a teacher was doing well). The negative pressure of threat rigidity to cope with visibility (Keltchermans, 2006) meant that teachers had to keep up appearances—to talk and act as if everything in the classroom was going well and that the school reforms were being faithfully implemented. We additionally suspect a reciprocal link to the intergroup and intragroup tensions discussed above: Would those interpersonal tensions lessen if teachers were less isolated? Would the teachers become less isolated if there were not these external mandates to conform?

There was a sense, stronger in the newer and midcareer teachers, that visibility was desirable (e.g., opening up one's classroom for others to see, building collegial ties, engaging in collaborative teaching); however, there was also a distrust that Hawthorne's present attempts to raise teacher visibility had the teachers' or students' interests anywhere close at heart. Several teachers in our sample talked about their good work going unrecognized by school and district administrators, and they lamented that teachers and students were inadequately praised for having raised schoolwide test scores. Susan said,

> A couple years ago, we were unhappy with some of the things about the state and the government; they put a gun to our head a bit. We were pressured and we got stressed, and what happened was people pulled together, we made our [academic performance index], we've made our [adequate yearly progress] every year. We pulled that up. We made the reading program work. It happened. People did pull together. And it wasn't enough. When you have somebody continuing to say, "We're not making it, we're not making our target," and we're like, "We made it! We did it!" What the hell? Then what are you going to do? Just f—k it! Forget it! You know what I mean? . . . We should be having marching bands running through the rooms!

Like the effects of threat rigidity presented thus far, the decrease in professional autonomy and the multiple anxieties around visibility and invisibility not only affected the maladaptive school climate but were also affected by it. Like the other threat responses, it angered the teachers, constrained their work, and intensified schoolwide tensions about the direction of reform at Hawthorne.

Concluding Ideas About Threat Rigidity in Reforming Schools

When we applied threat rigidity as a model onto our data, patterns, responses, themes, and findings came into stark relief. Threat rigidity pushed Hawthorne leaders to adopt school changes whose content emphasized administrative control and teacher conformity and whose design restricted teacher feedback and transparent decision making. In addition, Hawthorne's manner of implementation created teacher hostility and disenfranchisement. This double-pronged threat rigidity is about the content and the implementation of education reform—the what and the how—and, in this way, it echoes earlier research on reform implementation (Berman & McLaughlin, 1978; Fullan & Pomfret, 1977). Control, surveillance, constricted communication, no official spaces for dissent or alternative thinking created an us-versus-them dynamic that made teachers feel unsafe and so sharpened opposition between them and the administration. Ultimately, owing to threat rigidity effects, Hawthorne was not an organization whose shared purposes allowed members to work together but a place split into factions competing for control while individual teachers spent considerable energy on self-protection. Fight-or-flight had sabotaged meaningful reform.

Our use of threat rigidity as analysis encourages a view of the current policy culture in education as a kind of toy top exerting its weight on the sharpened tip of local schools. This is how the multilevel policy culture operated on the teachers at Hawthorne High. Federal policy pressures, state reform mandates, political rhetoric, and social perceptions around diminished opportunities to learn have put many public school districts on the defensive, thereby producing at the local level the threatened status that we found at Hawthorne. This organizational behavior corresponds to the discussion at the beginning of this article in that when the external legitimacy of an organization comes under attack, the various subgroups of the organization feel threatened in complex, often competing ways. This threat stance then translates into a series of maladaptive effects and responses that influence the school's reform approach and organizational climate in the ways that we have presented here.

We do not mean to suggest, however, that the pressures are entirely unidirectional. Teacher resistance (Gitlin & Margonis, 1995; Solórzano & Bernal, 2001), teachers' mediating reform in individualized ways (Olsen & Kirtman, 2002), and the reciprocal relationships among teachers, school leaders, and policy contexts (Hargreaves, 1995; Little, Dorph, & SB 1274 Research Team, 1998) mark most school situations, and Hawthorne was no exception. Consider that a group of 20 teachers apparently managed to overthrow the Hawthorne leadership! And the current educational policy culture remains hotly contested (Glickman, 2004; Meier & Wood, 2004). But for the purposes of our study, we chose an analytical frame that focuses on how top-down pressures to change create and intensify organizational dysfunction. None of the teachers in our sample, none of the Hawthorne community members, none of the published reports and stories about Hawthorne described things as going well. There was unanimous agreement that Hawthorne's organizational dynamics were dysfunctional. Threat rigidity offers an explanatory model for why, in part, this context occurred. It also presents an account of why the current top-down, one-size-fits-all policy culture in education (represented by but not limited to NCLB) may be unable to substantively increase teacher effectiveness and improve schooling. Finally, we believe that this model and our corresponding analysis offer the following suggestions for school reform and teacher preparation.

Rethink How to Restructure a School Culture

There are better ways to restructure a school culture. We recommend that policy makers consider and predict threat rigidity effects before initiating reform programs and that school leaders, too, pay special attention to these maladaptive patterns before commencing whole-school reform initiatives. For example, school restructuring researchers might take a look at our data and exclaim, "Did we not learn these lessons already?" Although school restructuring as a systematic reform approach has not fully disappeared, its influence has fallen victim to a different and politically powerful paradigm currently en vogue: large-scale accountability, a focus on quantitative outcomes, and the top-down emergence of a coded disdain for teachers (Cochran-Smith, 2006; King, 2004; McDermott, 2007; Meier & Wood, 2004). Yet, the restructuring movement still offers useful recommendations: Go slowly; that is, implement multiple reforms in integrated or sequenced ways.

Foreground school context as an active variable. Scaffold candid conversations among administration, teachers, parents, and other stakeholders about the reforms. Include teachers in all reform phases and treat them like professionals. Use professional development wisely, avoiding one-time, onsite mandatory events and instead offering a network of teacher-chosen, off-site flexible projects and activities that align with reform goals.

Actively Avoid Threat Rigidity

A school that feels threatened by, yet has to abide to, the current policy culture will benefit from consciously striving for exactly the opposite of all threat rigidity effects. We understand that threat rigidity is a natural organizational response to a perceived external threat; therefore, we place partial responsibility for what happened at Hawthorne on federal and state policy pressures. But we also believe that if a school leadership team acknowledges and considers threat rigidity effects beforehand, then it can better respond to a threatening situation and wisely plan its course of reform. This agenda would include school leaders' discussing case studies like Hawthorne and opening communication, encouraging innovative thinking, supporting teachers, and striving to put forward a climate of cooperation and trust. Essentially, we advocate identifying potential threat rigidity effects and responses and then consciously doing what would prevent them. This kind of threat rigidity attention would not eliminate the perceived threat but position a school to successfully address the perceived crisis and adapt in response to it. Specifically, we suspect that earning the trust of teachers, encouraging innovative thinking, formalizing open lines of communication, and promoting an inclusive reform ethos would eliminate or significantly lessen threat rigidity responses.

**Encourage Teacher Education Programs
to Acknowledge Current Reality**

Teacher education should not neglect current education realities and contradictions. The current policy climate may intentionally or not be creating a professional landscape in teaching in which the creative, daring, and iconoclastic candidates will not enter teaching (precisely those whom we believe education should covet); rather, those who do enter the profession may be predisposed and so primed for conformity, decreased decision making, and passive acceptance. If public school teaching becomes known as a profession of following orders, only those comfortable with this kind of obedience will enter or remain in the profession. We fear that this would lower the quality of and innovations in learning and democracy in the United States.

In addition, the clichéd gap between theories of teaching and learning (held by university teacher education) and practice realities (which teachers confront in K–12 schools) is apt here. Although we find this theory-versus-practice split exaggerated and erroneous, we have noticed a powerful, rarely acknowledged contradiction: Teacher educators often prepare teachers to freely design, enact, and assess student learning, but many K–12 schools require teachers to deliver standardized curricula, follow teaching scripts, and abide by off-the-shelf high-stakes tests. As we found at Hawthorne, it can be pedagogically limiting and professionally insulting for well-prepared student-centered teachers to have to fit into such restrictive didactic teaching roles. If, as it appears, the current policy culture is here for a while, more teacher educators should formally address it as part of the professional landscape. We recommend that teacher education programs consider introducing effects of the policy climate in explicit, honest ways that seek to prepare beginning teachers for what it means to work in "underperforming" or "high priority" schools like Hawthorne. By addressing ways that teachers can interpret and navigate these tensions in today's mandate-heavy school landscape, teacher education can offer collaborative preservice development around current policy effects. Entering teachers would therefore already have some knowledge of, strategies for, and allies within the policy-related work contexts that they will face in schools. Thusly equipped, they will be prepared to interpret their professional contexts, interact with policy reforms, effectively resist (if they choose), successfully hybridize their practice (if they choose), and actively participate in school improvement deliberations. What this study has examined as threat rigidity might then be reframed by artful teachers and school administrators as transformation opportunity instead.

Limitations of This Study

As in most educational research, there were facets of our case that we were not able to view, and there were places where our methodological choices shaped our findings. Although we were careful to delimit bias, hew to evidentiary warrant, and conduct reflexive research, there are limitations to mention. We consider three such kinds to this study. One is that we were never able to talk with the principal at Hawthorne. We twice requested an interview with him, but our calls were not returned. Without his perspectives on the reform context and the reasoning behind his actions, we were forced to rely solely on the teachers and the newspaper accounts of the year at Hawthorne. Although we tried to be balanced and we made claims only when data were clear and sufficient, we realize that there may be another side to this Hawthorne story.

A second limitation is that there is always the chance of alternative explanations for any phenomenon as complex as this one. We attempted to arrive at the explanation most consistent with the data, and we triangulated findings by way of multiple teachers and published reports about Hawthorne. Yet, we know that there are always mediating circumstances and details that any single study cannot capture. Perhaps the situation that transpired at Hawthorne would have happened even if the school were not inside the throes of a top-down federal push for school reform; perhaps, this is more simply a story of poor school leadership. A longitudinal study might have delineated in more detail the extent to which accountability pressures interacted with preexisting dysfunctions at the school. Our present analysis holds that what happened at Hawthorne derived from an alignment of factors:

the national education climate, the concrete pressures and policies affecting Hawthorne, the school's recent history, and the manner of response put forward by the school principal. However, we realize that nothing within education reform is as simple as it might seem.

The third and final limitation is that our view into the Hawthorne reform situation was primarily afforded by the perspectives of the six participating teachers. Another group of teachers may have viewed Hawthorne in a substantively different way. We tried to protect against this bias in three ways: by employing stratified random sampling to select English teachers that represented a range of professional experiences and views, by conducting most of the interviews off-site, and by taking care to isolate any teacher claims or complaints that resulted from teachers' personal idiosyncrasies. As well, we were pleased that our teacher sample included two teachers initially unsupportive of the principal, two who were initially supportive, and two who were ambivalent; this balance allowed us to triangulate and confirm/disconfirm various teacher claims. But perhaps another set of teachers would have experienced and reported on the Hawthorne situation differently—for example, some of those 20 teachers who called for the removal of the principal, teachers in another department, or teachers with different racial/cultural backgrounds. That is surely possible and should thus be taken into account.

Notes

[1]For detailed discussions of No Child Left Behind, see Meier and Wood (2004) and U.S. Department of Education (n.d.). Although our study focuses on ways that threat rigidity affects schools at the local level, there exists a growing body of research on those large-scale/macroscopic ways that No Child Left Behind and the current educational policy culture appear to constrain education practice. See Glickman (2004), McDermott (2007), McGuinn (2006), Meier and Wood (2004), Popham (2005), and Sleeter (2007).

[2]By *ecological*, we mean to draw on an emerging research paradigm that seeks to capture the broad, integrated webs of influence on any aspect of educational life—that is, the overarching ecology, or ecosystem, in which an educational phenomenon exists (Wideen, Mayer-Smith, & Moon, 1998). Here, we consider the broader ecology that influences, and is influenced by, teachers. As such, it includes multiple levels of educational context; past, present, personal, and professional influences; and emotional, intellectual, technical, and moral dimensions of teachers' selves and education work. All constitute the ecosystem in which teachers operate and on which we collected and analyzed data.

[3]*Underperforming* is both a technical term used by the state of California and a lay term employed by those who talk about schools. In both cases, its use is a little misleading in describing this school; we discuss this confusion in Note 6.

[4]These cutoff points—and, therefore, these career stage categories—are rather arbitrary. As such, we labeled teachers with 3 years of teaching experience as *early career*; those with between 4 and 10 years, *midcareer*; and those with 13 or more years as *later career*.

[5]Readers interested in fuller discussions of organizational behavior research and the larger contexts of threat rigidity studies should see Burch (2007), DiMaggio and Powell (1983), Rowan and Miskel (1999), Staw (2006), and Weick (1979).

[6]As mentioned in Note 3, *underperforming* is a technical term used by the state to designate schools whose academic performance index is below target levels. Because Hawthorne has been meeting its index and adequate yearly progress targets, it is not—technically speaking—underperforming. But the term is also a common lay term to denote a school that falls below expectations. In that vein, teachers, school district members, and local newspaper writers typically characterized Hawthorne as underperforming. Further muddying the waters is that California offers additional program improvement money for schools

that are not technically underperforming but are close and that choose to apply for a quasi-underperforming status. Hawthorne applied for and received some of these funds.

[7]Yet, we do not mean to suggest that this is so simple, linear, or coherent. Instead, there are myriad influences, resource struggles, and sociopolitical forces whose collective interactions account for the current policy climate. Examples include the fact that many textbook, curriculum, and testing companies have recently penetrated the public education market (Lemann, 1999; McLaren, 1998) and that there may be a political undertaking to set up public schools to visibly fail and thus increase support for the privatization of schooling (Berliner & Biddle, 1995; Fuller & Elmore, 1996; Meier & Wood, 2004). As well, the resulting set of views and approaches is in no way coherent or tightly aligned. There are always disconnects, contradictions, and competing views and approaches; the U.S. education system remains a very decentralized network. Finally, we do not mean to suggest this is all circumscribed within No Child Left Behind; indeed, the recent movement toward accountability, standardized teaching, and testing existed during the Clinton administration and before.

[8]Although we collected multiple published documents and news stories, for reasons of confidentiality we are unable to cite them by name in this article.

[9]We have edited interview passages for flow, deleting most pause fillers and false starts, unless they were integral to the meaning.

[10]Job security, however, becomes more complicated for later-career teachers, namely, because of their pensions and benefits. The early-career teachers—having logged fewer years, having younger kids of their own (or no kids), and being less concerned with retirement—did not talk about staying, moving, or leaving in terms of employee benefits. However, later-career teachers and the more senior midcareer teacher always discussed their leaving within the boundaries of their employee benefits.

[11]We wonder if this situation is similar to current struggles in medicine regarding the lack of spaces for doctors to talk honestly about mistakes that they make. Owing to increased malpractice suits and insurance scrutiny, doctors are facing decreased opportunities for confidential, open conversations about professional practice, called "morbidity and mortality" meetings (Groopman, 2007).

References

Berliner, B., & Biddle, B. (1995). *The manufactured crisis: Myths, fraud, and the attack on America's public schools.* New York: Perseus.

Berman, P., & McLaughlin, M. (1978). *Federal programs supporting educational change: Vol. 8. Implementing and sustaining innovations.* Santa Monica, CA: RAND.

Bolman, L. G., & Deal, T. E. (1991). *Reframing organizations: Artistry, choice, and leadership.* San Francisco: Jossey-Bass.

Burch, P. (2007). Educational policy and practice from the perspective of institutional theory: Crafting a wider lens. *Educational Researcher, 36,* 84–95.

Cochran-Smith, M. (2006). Teacher education and the need for public intellectuals. *The New Educator, 2,* 1–26.

Cuban, L. (1993). *How teachers taught: Constancy and change in American classrooms.* New York: Teachers College Press.

DiMaggio, P. J., & Powell, W. W. (1983). The iron cage revisited: Institutional somorphism and collective rationality in organizational fields. *American Sociological Review, 48,* 63–82.

Elmore, R., Abelmann, C., & Furhman, S. (1996). The new accountability in state education reform: From process to performance. In H. Ladd (Ed.), *Holding schools accountable: Performance based reform in education* (pp. 65–98). Washington, DC: Brookings.

Elmore, R., Peterson, P., & McCarthey, S. (1996). *Restructuring in the classroom: Teaching, learning, and school organization.* San Francisco: Jossey-Bass.

Fullan, M., & Pomfret, A. (1977). Research on curriculum and instruction implementation. *Review of Educational Research, 47*(1), 335–397.

Fuller, B., & Elmore, R. (Eds.). (1996). *Who chooses? Who loses?* New York: Teachers College Press.

Gitlin, A., & Margonis, F. (1995). The political aspect of reform: Teacher resistance as good sense. *American Journal of Education, 103*(4), 377–405.

Glickman, C. (Ed.). (2004). *Letters to the next president: What we can do about the real crisis in public education.* New York: Teachers College Press.

Groopman, J. (2007). *How doctors think.* New York: Houghton Mifflin.

Hargreaves, A. (1995). *Changing teachers, changing times: Teachers' work and culture in the postmodern age.* London: Cassell.

Hargreaves, A. (2005). Educational change takes age: Life, career and generational factor in teachers' emotional responses to educational change. *Teaching and Teacher Education, 21,* 967–983.

Huberman, M. (1993a). *The lives of teachers.* London: Cassell.

Huberman, M. (1993b). The model of the independent artisan in teachers' professional relations. In M. Little & M. McLaughlin (Eds.), *Teachers' work: Individuals, colleagues and contexts* (pp. 11–50). New York: Teachers College Press.

Ingersoll, R. (2002). *Out of field teaching, educational inequality, and the organization of schools: An exploratory analysis.* Seattle: University of Washington, Center for the Study of Teaching and Policy.

Kelchtermans, G. (2006). Teacher collaboration and collegiality as workplace conditions: A review. *Zeitschrift für Pädagogik, 52*(2), 220–237.

King, J. (2004). Paige calls NEA "terrorist organization." *CNN.* Retrieved February 23, 2004, from http://www.cnn.com/2004/EDUCATION/02/23/paige.terrorist.nea

Ladson-Billings, G. (1994). *The dreamkeepers: Successful teachers of African-American children.* San Francisco: Jossey-Bass.

Lemann, N. (1999). *The big test: The secret history of the American meritocracy.* New York: Farrar, Straus and Giroux.

Little, J. W. (1982). Norms of collegiality and experimentation: Workplace conditions of school success. *American Educational Research Journal, 19*(3), 325–340.

Little, J. W. (1996). The emotional contours and career trajectories of (disappointed) reform enthusiasts. *Cambridge Journal of Education, 26*(3), 345–359.

Little, J. W., Dorph, R., & SB 1274 Research Team. (1998). *Final report: Lessons about comprehensive reform.* Berkeley: University of California.

Lortie, D. (1975). *Schoolteacher: A sociological study.* Chicago: University of Chicago Press.

McDermott, K. (2007). "Expanding the moral community" or "blaming the victim"? The politics of state education accountability policy. *American Educational Research Journal, 44*(1), 77–111.

McGuinn, P. (2006). *No Child Left Behind and the transformation of federal education policy, 1965–2006.* Lawrence: University Press of Kansas.

McLaren, P. (1998). *Life in schools.* New York: Longman.

Meier, D., & Wood, G. (Eds.). (2004). *Many children left behind.* Boston: Beacon Press.

Meyer, J., & Rowan, B. (1977). Institutionalized organizations: Formal structure as myth and ceremony. *American Journal of Sociology, 83,* 340–363.

Moll, L., Amanti, C., Neff, D., & Gonzalez, N. (1992). Funds of knowledge for teaching using a qualitative approach to connect homes and classrooms. *Theory Into Practice, 31,* 32–41.

National Commission on Excellence in Education. (1983). *A nation at risk.* Washington, DC: U.S. Department of Education.

Olsen, B., & Kirtman, L. (2002). Teacher as mediator of school reform: An examination of teacher practice in 36 California restructuring schools. *Teachers College Record, 104*(2), 301–324.

Osborn, M., & Broadfoot, P. (1992). A lesson in progress? Primary classrooms observed in England and France. *Oxford Review of Education, 18*(1), 3–15

Peyser, J., & Costrell, R. (2004). *Exploring the cost of accountability.* Retrieved May 22, 2008, from http://media.hoover.org/documents/ednext20042_22.pdf

Popham, J. (2005). *America's "failing" schools: How parents and teachers can cope with No Child Left Behind.* New York: Routledge.

Rosenholtz, S. (1991). *Teachers' workplace: The organization of schools.* New York: Teachers College Press.

Rowan, B. (1982). Organizational structure and the institutional environment: The case of public schools. *Administrative Science Quarterly, 27,* 259–279.

Rowan, B. (1990). Control and commitment: Alternative strategies for the organizational design of schools. In C. Cazden (Ed.), *Review of research in education* (Vol. 16, pp. 353–389). Washington, DC: American Educational Research Association.

Rowan, B., & Miskel, C. (1999). Institutional theory and the study of educational organizations. In J. Murphy & K. Lewis (Eds.), *Handbook of research on educational administration* (pp. 359–384). San Francisco: Jossey-Bass.

Sarason, S. (1982). *Culture of the school and the problem of change.* Boston: Allyn & Bacon.

Scott, W. R. (2003). *Organizations: Rational, natural, and open systems.* New Jersey: Prentice Hall.

Sisken, L. (1994). *Realms of knowledge: Academic departments in secondary schools.* London: Falmer Press.

Sleeter, C. (2007). *Facing accountability in education.* New York: Teachers College Press.

Solórzano, D., & Bernal, D. D. (2001). Examining transformational resistance through a critical race and LatCrit theory framework: Chicana and Chicano students in an urban context. *Urban Education, 36*(3), 308–342.

Staw, B. (2006). *Research in organizational behavior: An annual series of analytical essays.* Greenwich, CT: JAI Press.

Staw, B., Sandelands, L., & Dutton, J. (1981). Threat rigidity effects in organizational behavior: A multilevel analysis. *Administrative Science Quarterly, 26,* 501–524.

Twight, C. (1994). Origins of federal control over education. *The Freeman: Ideas on Liberty, 44*(12), 701–705.

U.S. Department of Education. (n.d.). *No Child Left Behind information centers.* Retrieved May 22, 2008, from http://www.ed.gov/nclb

Weick, K. (1976). Educational organizations as loosely coupled systems. *Administrative Science Quarterly, 21,* 1–19.

Weick, K. (1979). *The social psychology of organizing* (2nd ed.). Reading, MA: Addison-Wesley.

Wideen, M., Mayer-Smith, J., & Moon, B. (1998). A critical analysis of the research on learning to teach: making the case for an ecological perspective on inquiry. *Review of Educational Research, 68*(2), 130–178.

Will, G. (2006, January 16). Ed schools versus education: Prospective teachers are expected to have the correct "disposition," proof of which is espousing "progressive" political beliefs. *Newsweek.*

Woods, P., Jeffrey, B., & Bayle, M. (1997). *Restructuring schools, reconstructing teachers: Responding to change in the primary school.* London: Open University Press.

Manuscript received July 19, 2007
Revision received September 28, 2007
Accepted February 23, 2008

American Educational Research Journal
March 2009, Vol. 46, No. 1, pp. 45–72
DOI: 10.3102/0002831208323277
© 2009 AERA. http://aerj.aera.net

Toward a Theory of Generative Change in Culturally and Linguistically Complex Classrooms

Arnetha F. Ball
Stanford University

This article situates the preparation of teachers to teach in culturally and linguistically complex classrooms in international contexts. It investigates long-term social and institutional effects of professional development and documents processes that facilitate teachers' continued learning. Data from a decade-long study of U.S. and South African teachers supported a model of generative change that explained how professional development could be internalized by teachers, subsequently serving as a heuristic to help them organize their individual programs of instruction. Drawing primarily on two case studies, this article documents teachers' development of generative knowledge and illustrates how they drew on that knowledge in thinking about students and teaching. The results were to facilitate generative thinking on the part of their students as well.

KEYWORDS: culturally and linguistically complex classrooms, generative change, professional development, writing as a pedagogical tool

National and international concern about changing demographics, inequities in the distribution of educational resources, and continuing underachievement for some students has stirred renewed interest in the quality and organization of instruction for students who are attending urban

ARNETHA F. BALL is a professor in curriculum studies, teacher education, and educational linguistics in the School of Education at Stanford University, 485 Lasuen Mall, Stanford, CA 94305-3096; e-mail: *arnetha@stanford.edu*. Her research has been funded by the Spencer Foundation, and it focuses on the language and literacy practices of culturally and linguistically diverse populations in the United States and South Africa and on the professional development of teachers to work with diverse students. As the author of five books and numerous chapters and articles, Dr. Ball uses sociocultural, sociolinguistic, and ethnographic approaches to investigate the ways in which semiotic systems in general—and oral and written language in particular— serve as mediating tools in teaching and learning in multicultural and multilingual settings and in the processes of teacher change.

schools. The UNESCO Institute for Statistics (2005) reported that although half the global population now lives in urban areas, that figure is expected to rise to two thirds—or about 6 billion people—by 2050. In keeping with international tends, the National Center for Educational Statistics (2006) reported that by 2020, more than 50% of the U.S. public school population will be classified as students of color—from Latino, African American, Pacific Islander, and American Indian backgrounds. Since the beginning of the 20th century, urban classrooms around the globe have been experiencing the largest influx of students from diverse backgrounds. In general, these individuals initially settle in segregated local communities and receive schooling there. By the time those students reach secondary grades, however, previously segregated groups come together in classrooms with teachers who feel underprepared to teach students from cultural and linguistically diverse backgrounds (Hollins & Torres-Guzman, 2005). I use the term *culturally and linguistically complex classrooms* (CLCCs) to describe the learning environments that are created when these previously segregated groups come together in the same classrooms—classrooms serving students from two or more cultural and linguistic groups. Low academic achievement, high dropout rates, and low college graduation rates among low-income culturally and linguistically diverse students are far too frequent in these classrooms (UNESCO Institute for Statistics, 2005; Willms, 2006). One contributing factor to these trends is the disconnect between the backgrounds of the students and the teachers who teach them.

Although changes in student demographics have been dramatic, changes in the demographics of the teaching force have been slow. Most teachers continue to be monolingual and middle class. Many of the teachers who are assigned to teach a diverse student body in an urban setting are concerned because they lack confidence in their ability to do so, they feel uncomfortable interacting with parents from diverse backgrounds, they feel inadequately prepared to teach diverse students, and they prefer not to be placed in situations where they feel uncomfortable and inadequate (see Duhon & Manson, 2000; Hollins & Torres-Guzman, 2005). I propose that to address the cycle of student underachievement, we must increase teachers' knowledge of theory and best practices and their knowledge of students' cultural practices and values. In addition, we must assist teachers in replacing their feelings of insecurity, discomfort, and inadequacy with feelings of agency, advocacy, and efficacy.

Although an extensive body of research focuses on an array of topics related to preparing teachers for diversity (for syntheses of the research, see Duhon & Manson, 2000; Grant & Secada, 1990; Hollins & Torres-Guzman, 2005; Ladson-Billings, 1999, 2000; Sleeter, 2001; Weiner, 2000), few longitudinal studies—and even fewer cross-national longitudinal studies—exist on this topic because diversity has been neither a priority for funding agencies nor a focus of well-supported programmatic research (Hollins & Torres-Guzman, 2005). This article reports on data collected from U.S. and South African teachers in a longitudinal study of a teacher education course designed to instill theoretical knowledge, pedagogical skills, metacognitive awareness, and positive attitudes in teachers—including a sense of agency, advocacy, and efficacy—concerning their work with diverse student populations.

Preparing Teachers for CLCCs

This study grows out of a larger program of research where the investigative site was the teaching and learning practices of U.S. and South African teachers in a professional development course and their subsequent work with students in CLCCs. The data were collected within the context of a cross-national longitudinal study conducted between 1994 and 2005 to better understand the influence of professional development on teacher change. In designing the research, I reasoned that the challenge of preparing an adequate supply of qualified teachers who were prepared to teach all students should not be narrowly conceptualized as a ghetto problem, an inner-city problem, or even as a national problem. It is, rather, an international challenge, and addressing it requires a better understanding of the processes of teacher change and professional development in cross-national contexts.

This investigation of teacher change took place in two parts. The first part of the research documented the process of teacher change that took place while U.S. and South African teachers were participating in a professional development course; the second part documented the teachers' continued learning after the course had ended (Ball, 2000, 2006). The analysis reported in this article was designed to advance knowledge concerning the social and institutional effects of professional development on teachers' generative change and to investigate the aspects of the professional development that affected the teachers' effectiveness in CLCCs. The central questions guiding this analysis were as follows: What is the role of generativity in the preparation of teachers to teach diverse student populations? How can teacher professional development be organized to facilitate the development of the generativity that is necessary for pedagogical problem solving? I propose that generativity is critical to the success of teachers in CLCCs.

I use the term *generativity* to refer to the teachers' ability to continually add to their understanding by connecting their personal and professional knowledge with the knowledge that they gain from their students to produce or originate knowledge that is useful to them in pedagogical problem solving and in meeting the educational needs of their students. According to Franke, Carpenter, Levi, and Fennema (2001),

> when individuals learn with understanding, they can apply their knowledge to learn new topics and solve new and unfamiliar problems. . . . Knowledge becomes generative when the learner sees the need to integrate new knowledge with existing knowledge and continually reconsiders existing knowledge in light of the new knowledge that they are learning. (pp. 655–656)

Building on this, I use the term *generative change* to refer to a process of self-perpetuating change wherein a teacher's pedagogical practices are inspired and influenced by the instructional approaches and theory that he or she is exposed to in a professional development program. That knowledge becomes generative when the teacher continues that learning by making connections with his or her students' knowledge and needs and begins planning the teaching based on what he or she is learning. Generative change occurred in this study as teachers integrated the knowledge they gained in my course with the knowledge they gained from their students in their pedagogical problem solving.

The analysis of the data revealed one distinguishing characteristic of effective teacher-student engagement in these diverse classrooms—namely, that as the teachers were developing their voices on issues of diversity and becoming generative in their thinking, they were building on the same instructional model that they experienced in my professional development course to inspire their students to become generative thinkers as well. I also found that as the teachers assumed the stance of learners, they began to talk to and listen to their students so that they could learn from them and use that knowledge in their student-teacher interactions and in their instructional problem solving to figure out how to meet the students' needs. This required the teachers to engage in generative change on an ongoing basis.

Professional Development and the Preparation of Teachers for Diversity

Borko (2004) noted that we are only beginning to learn what and how teachers learn from professional development and its impact on student outcomes. Adding to our knowledge base in these areas is Darling-Hammond and Bransford's focus (2005) on core knowledge needed for teaching; Franke and colleagues' work (2001) on school restructuring to encourage teacher reflection in generative ways; Desimone, Porter, Garet, Yoon, and Birman's work (2002) on the effects of professional development on teachers' instruction; and Sarason's work (1996) on creating school cultures that facilitate teachers' growth. However, this knowledge still needs to be applied to the preparation of teachers to work in CLCCs. I proposed that professional development programs that are designed to prepare these teachers must build on our knowledge of how people learn, be structured so that teachers reflect on their knowledge and daily practices in generative ways, focus on instructional practices that support their use of those practices in the classroom, and create cultures where serious discussions of educational equity take place regularly. I further proposed that teachers' strategic engagement with challenging theoretical perspectives, integration of action research in the professional development curriculum, ongoing work with diverse student populations, and use of writing as a pedagogical tool are additional features that should be integrated into the professional development program when preparing teachers for diverse classrooms.

Theoretical Framework for the Course

The professional development program that I designed centered on the use of narrative as a tool for developing teachers' metacognitive thinking. Many researchers have emphasized the importance of narrative in the human experience and consider narrative as the framework through which human beings comprehend life. It is the process by which we make sense of our experiences. Jerome Bruner (1994) asserted that culture "gives meaning to action by situating its underlying intentional states in an interpretive system" (p. 34; see also, Bruner, 1990) that includes narrative explication. He further posited that it is through narrative that people make sense of themselves and their world. A second and equally important function of narrative is that it can serve as an artifact through which to make actions, thoughts, and feelings intelligible to "others" (Said, 1978). The sharing of narratives with others can result in a facilitation of problem definition and resolution, and it can expand understandings of the practices of students and teachers in informed and sensitive ways. I conceptualized my classroom as a contact zone where the narratives of teachers' autobiographies and their students' literacy biographies could be used as tools for increasing metacognitive awareness of the centrality of critical literacies in teaching and learning. In addition, I used introspection to facilitate ideological becoming, and I used critique to facilitate internalization of new information. As teachers engaged in and used narrative to make meaning of new theory, they experienced an increased sense of agency, advocacy, and efficacy, as well as the emergence of their own voices. Later in the course, they used narrative to make meaning of their action research projects and to consider transforming action plans into practice.

Building on narrative as a tool for meaning making, the theoretical framework for the course was built around four concepts: metacognitive awareness, ideological becoming, internalization, and efficacy. According to Bransford, Brown, and Cocking (2000), the notion of metacognitive awareness refers to one's ability to think about his or her thinking, to predict one's performances on various tasks, and to monitor one's current levels of mastery and understanding. Teachers with high levels of metacognitive awareness can identify their barriers to learning, change the strategies they are using to attain their goals, and modify their teaching and learning strategies based on awareness of their effectiveness. Effective teachers are those who are metacognitively aware of their strengths and weaknesses and have a broad repertoire of tools and resources to assist them in attaining their goals. That repertoire includes a reconceptualization of their students as resources in the teaching–learning process.

Bakhtin's concept (1981) of ideological becoming suggests that the coming together of new perspectives, new ideas, and new voices is essential to a person's growth. According to Bakhtin, our engagement with the discourses of others can influence the way that we think, and it can contribute to forming what ultimately becomes internally persuasive discourses for us—thus influencing our ideologies, thoughts, beliefs, and ways of theorizing about a body of ideas, their origin, and how they operate. The process of ideological becoming is critically important to the development of a sense of agency because it is through this process that individuals can begin to generate their own ideologies about teaching in diverse classrooms.

Vygotsky's concept of internalization (1978) was also critical to the design of the course. Internalization is a concept that emerges from sociocultural theory, which holds that learning and development occur on two planes (Wertsch, 1985). First, learning and development appear on a social plane, occurring between people as an interpsychological category; then they appear on an internal psychological plane, occurring within an individual as an intrapsychological category. In this course, the social process of engaging teachers with theoretical concepts and having them conduct action research on diversity and literacy-related issues in their classrooms became an internalized activity when they took personal ownership of the knowledge learned and then applied that knowledge to solve problems within their classrooms. Through this process of internalization, teachers began to develop a sense of advocacy with the assistance of more knowledgeable others. Vygotsky's discussion of internalization can help us to better understand how teacher learning and development occur—how the information presented to teachers in a professional development program can move from an interpsychological plane, where there is a social exchange in which more informed others encourage learners to consider conceptual innovations, to an intrapsychological plane, where these socially conscious classroom activities are embraced by teachers to become an internal catalyst that facilitates a sense of advocacy.

Influenced by Bandura's self-efficacy theories (1977, 1997), *teacher efficacy* refers to a teacher's belief in his or her potential ability to effect positive change in the lives of students. A teacher's sense of efficacy is critical to his or her effectiveness in the classroom. By design, the teachers in my course engaged with new perspectives, new ideas, and new voices through the assigned readings, through discussions and reflective writing, and through their required interactions with diverse learners to facilitate metacognitive awareness, ideological becoming, and internalization. Specifically, the intended outcome was that teachers who had these experiences through professional development would have an increased sense of metacognitive awakening, agency, advocacy, and efficacy in their CLCCs.

The Course as a Site for Studying Teacher Change

The first part of the research documented the process of teacher change that took place while U.S. and South African teachers participated in a professional development course designed to facilitate teachers' development of the knowledge, skills, and dispositions necessary to effectively teach diverse students. When undertaking the development of a course that would prepare preservice and in-service teachers in the United States and South Africa, I wanted to design a course—based on the theory outlined above—that would help teachers consider the role of literacy in their lives and in the lives of their students, as well as understand literacy demands in various content areas. The course consisted of eight to twelve 3-hour sessions with approximately 30 students enrolled each time the course was taught. The course syllabus stated the following:

> This course will assist preservice and in-service teachers in developing a metacognitive awareness of the processes and strategies they use in their own reading and writing in order to help them think about what their students are experiencing each day. You will develop an awareness of the literacy abilities of one student through close observations and a video analysis of a *literacy event* in your class. You will also develop a *strategies notebook* containing literacy strategies you would like to use in your own teaching next year. In this course you will have opportunities to engage with theory that will help you consider the following questions: What does it mean for a person to be literate in our society and within various content area disciplines? What is critical literacy, and is it something I want for my students? How can multiple literacies be used in strategic ways in my classroom to teach content area materials effectively to all students? What important questions should I be asking about the literacy needs and capabilities of the students in my classes? What is my philosophy about how I can use literacies to support struggling students in my class, and where can I find resources to help them? and How does literacy relate to issues of equity and democracy? You will have an opportunity to find answers to some of these complex questions during our course, but you will also have an opportunity to begin a dialogue that will continue throughout your professional career.

Course requirements included in-class assignments, tutoring assignments in diverse classrooms, active participation in large and small group discussions, reflective journal writing, an action research project, literacy case study, and a strategies notebook. At the end of the course, students wrote their philosophies of how they thought that literacy should be integrated into their teaching.

The U.S. course was composed largely of preservice teachers, many of whom had prior teaching experiences in parochial schools, community-based organizations, and tutoring programs but were enrolled in the teacher education program to gain credentialing and professional development. In South Africa, the course was attended predominantly by practicing teachers who had been educated in underresourced schools. Thus, their educational experience mirrored those of the preservice teachers in the United States more closely than one would expect—not based on experience but based on exposure to theories of teaching. In both locations, the purpose of the course was to familiarize prospective and working teachers with theoretical perspectives and best practices for using reading, writing, and multiple literacies to teach effectively in multilingual and multicultural classrooms. The theoretical and practical topics in this course were strategically chosen to help classroom teachers (a) understand how sociocultural theory might be used to enhance their teaching in diverse classrooms and (b) consider how they might want to use multiple literacies to teach their subject matter effectively. In particular, I used writing as a pedagogical tool during the course to facilitate teachers' development of generative thinking skills, and I hoped that teachers would in turn use writing as a pedagogical tool with their students.

The writing required of these teachers went far beyond simple reflection on personal experiences, by requiring them to consider generative ways to use the knowledge they were gaining to support student learning. I accomplished this through the use of carefully designed writing prompts that called for teachers to respond with an introspective examination of their practices and beliefs about teaching and learning as dynamic, complex, and situated practice that occurred in the lives of students inside and outside the classroom. If teachers responded to the prompts with simple reflections on their personal experiences, they received written probes on their returned papers, asking them to consider relevant perspectives, theoretical readings, and class discussions and to resubmit the assignment after thoughtful revision.

After using extensive writing in these ways, teachers began to consider how they might use writing as a pedagogical tool in their efforts to build learning communities within their classrooms. During my follow-up visitations to their classes, I observed that teachers in my course were beginning to use writing as a pedagogical tool to facilitate the development of generative thinking on the part of the students in their classrooms. The next section provides examples of how this process occurred, explicating the influence of professional development on teachers' and students' generative development.

Data Collection and Analysis

During the first part of the study, the data collected from 50 U.S. teachers and 50 South African teachers included narrative essays of their literacy autobiographies, biographies that they wrote about their students' literacy experiences, transcripts of classroom and small group discussions, journal entries, and reflections written in response to carefully selected class readings assigned in the professional development course. Those readings required teachers to engage with the writings of Vygotsky (1978), Gee (1989), Bakhtin (1981), Delpit (1988), Giroux (1988), McElroy-Johnson (1993), and others and to write reflections about the work of these scholars. Throughout the analysis of the data, I returned to and drew heavily on the teachers' narrative reflections to locate evidence of their changing perspectives and cognitive change (Hollingsworth, 1989) as a result of their participation in the professional development course (Ball, 2006).

The second part of the study started in 1995 when I began visiting the classrooms of the teachers who had completed my professional development course and who were now teaching in CLCCs. I conducted these follow-up visits with about 10% of the U.S. and South African teachers from 1995 to 2005. During these follow-up visits with the focus teachers, I made audio- and videotaped recordings of their teaching and the dialogues that I had with them concerning their application of the theory, as learned in my course, to their classroom teaching. The follow-up interviews lasted about 2 hours and took place after my 2-hour classroom observations and videotaping. These tape-recorded interviews were transcribed and used to supplement the videotapes of the teachers' classroom teaching, field notes, and photographs taken at the time of our follow-up meetings.

Findings

The data shared in this article to illustrate the findings come from close case studies of two follow-up teachers in the study—one U.S. teacher and one South African teacher—selected because they constitute a representative sample of the many transitioning teachers whom I observed. The transitioning teachers were those who had not initially given issues of diversity much consideration but who eventually displayed evidence that a commitment to working with diverse students was developing (Ball, 2000, 2006).

Two Teacher Participants in the Course

Nomha and Niko were two transitioning teachers who had been somewhat timid and unsure of themselves at the beginning of the course. By the end of the course, however, both thought deeply about issues of teaching diverse students and about developing plans of action for their teaching practices, and in generative ways, they began to apply what they learned in the course to their classroom teaching. They also began to use what they were learning from their students—to tap into the rich cultural and linguistic resources that their students brought into the classroom—to encourage them to become generative thinkers.

Nomha was a South African female teacher who enrolled in the course while I was teaching at a major university located in the Western Cape Province of South Africa (Ball, 2006). Nomha came from a Black African language–speaking background and began her schooling at a lower primary school in one of the Black townships. When we met, Nomha was in her late 20s and had already been teaching in a township school for a few years, with class sizes of 60 to 65 students. At the beginning of the course, she was shy and soft-spoken, but I sensed that she was eager to learn about new perspectives and pedagogical strategies. She had received her teaching credential from an underresourced teachers college that had been established to train Black teachers to teach Black students. She had returned to the further diploma in education program offered at the university to receive additional training.

Niko was an Asian American female in her mid-20s who came from a middle-class community in the Midwestern United States (Ball, 2000). As she began the course, she shared thoughts on her early literacy experiences and voiced her growing awareness of the role that literacy played in her life. Niko grew up attending well-resourced schools. Her interest in the course was motivated by the realization that all students do not receive the type of education that she had; as such, she was developing a deep interest in working with some of our society's more needy populations.

Both Niko and Nomha began the course by sharing narrative reflections that served to increase their metacognitive awareness of their literacy experiences. In describing her early literacy experiences, Niko noted that she had always been taught in a positive atmosphere by empathetic and understanding teachers who sincerely desired to help make her learning environment an enjoyable and productive place. In contrast, Nomha reflected on the fact that her education began at a township school where teachers were rigid and strict and where repetition and recitation were the norm in teaching pedagogy. In learning to read, Nomha had been required to repeat after the teacher despite noncomprehension—"even if we were saying things that we did not understand." According to Nomha, "most of the time we were taught to memorize without meaning." Failure to successfully comply with the teachers' wishes resulted in the use of corporal punishment. These early literacy experiences of recitations, memorization, adherence to meaningless rules, and punishment laid a negative foundation for Nomha's perceptions about what it meant to be a teacher, whereas Niko's experiences were far more positive and far less authoritarian.

In parallel situations, the teachers were given the assignment to write a literacy biography of a student whom each was working with. As their metacognitive awareness increased, Nomha and Niko began to question some of the literacy experiences in their students' lives. The biographical activities served as readiness exercises that prepared teachers to consider different theoretical perspectives and new visions for generative literacy practices that they could try with the students in their classrooms.

Following the sharing of autobiographical literacy narratives and their students' biographies, the teachers were exposed to carefully selected readings written by sociocultural and critical theorists and to practical teaching strategies based on these theories. The readings were selected to broaden previously held views on literacy and classroom practice. Building on the assumption that teachers' developing ideologies can be affected by carefully selected course readings and well-designed course experiences, I exposed the teachers to readings that included *Teachers as Transformative Intellectuals*. Here, Giroux (1988) proposes that teacher education programs need to be developed where prospective teachers can be educated as transformative intellectuals able to affirm and practice the discourse of freedom and democracy. Other readings included but were not limited to Au's "An Expanded Definition of Literacy" (1993), Delpit's "The Silenced Dialogue" (1988), Gee's "What Is Literacy?" (1989), McElroy-Johnson's "Teaching and Practice: Giving Voice to the Voiceless" (1993), and short excerpts from Freire's *Pedagogy of the Oppressed* (1970), hooks's *Teaching to Transgress* (1994), Vygotsky (1978), and Bakhtin (1981).

Through much discussion of the ideas represented in these texts and the ideas of other authors, teachers began to consider which, if any, of these ideas would become a part of their discourses. Through this process, they began the initial stages of developing their voices on issues related to preparing teachers to work with students from culturally and linguistically diverse back-grounds. I coupled these readings with assigned observations and authentic teaching experiences and gave assignments that used writing as a pedagogical tool for inquiry to facilitate their ideological becoming. Later, the teachers completed action research projects. These activities served as the catalyst needed to motivate a sense of agency, advocacy, and efficacy on their part as they began making plans about how the course information would influence their work with students.

By the end of the term, I realized that Nomha, Niko, and other teachers in the course were beginning to use generative thinking in planning their class-room teaching. I also noted that they were drawing on the instructional approach used in the professional development course to plan and structure their classroom teaching. Their classroom discourses reflected an awakening to the important role that literacy plays in their lives and in the lives of their students. As this awakening occurred, I detected noticeable changes in their perspectives toward teaching diverse students and in their teaching practices. After demonstrating increased metacognition and a sense of awakening in their reflective writing, their introspective writing reflected a sense of agency, and a sense of advocacy was emerging in their critiques and future plans. Not only was Nomha becoming a generative thinker, but she was also becoming a more confident, more effective teacher as she applied the knowledge that she gained in our professional development course to learn new information about her students. As she asked her students to write about their interests and concerns, she was able to apply that knowledge in her interactions with them, and she integrated that knowledge into her content materials. In doing so, she was able to solve instructional and pedagogical problems in her classroom by making the materials more engaging for the students and more relevant to their inter-ests. Her ultimate goal was for students to generate plans of action to address some of the pressing social issues that existed in their community. Thus, the knowledge that she gained in the professional development course became generative knowledge as she saw the need to integrate this new knowledge with her existing knowledge, and she continually reconsidered that know-ledge in light of the needs of her students. When she was introduced to new readings in our course, Nomha applied that knowledge to her classroom teaching. In one of her reflective essays, she wrote,

> Au said that instead of telling the pupils to write a letter required by the syllabus, we should let them write letters to their pen-pals. . . . After reading these articles, I think that rather than giving pupils "top-ics" chosen by me, I will let them write about their own topics so as to enable them to write more freely. I will use these ideas in my teach-ing by changing my strategies for learning how my pupils learn, by allowing the pupils to use their mother-tongue as the base so as to make them proficient in reading and learning English, by letting pupils bring their experiences into the classroom so . . . every one should be able to learn from others, and by bringing into my classroom the students home learning environment.

Here, Nomha, a student who came from a strict teacher-centered educational background, talks about what she recalls from her reading of Au
(1993), and she determines that it would be a good idea to bring the students'
home learning environments into the classroom and to let students choose
their topics for writing. Although the strict mandates of school administrators
in the apartheid system and her early educational experiences had taught her
that multilingual students could not use their home languages in the classroom, she was beginning to realize that multilingualism can be used as a
resource in the English classroom. This realization was changing the way that
she thought about teaching and her teaching practices. Nomha went on to
say that her reading of Vygotsky (1978) had influenced her new choices of
pedagogical approaches that she was using in her classroom:

> And also after reading the article by Vygotsky that has changed my
> perception about literacy. I used to dictate the work [to my students]
> all the time. I told the students what assignments to go and do and
> how to do them. But after I read this article, I told the students to give me
> some topics to write about. I guide them so they can become inde-
> pendent to work without being guided. . . . As a result of these articles
> you gave us, I began to develop an interest in learning more about
> Action Research. My interest in teaching was crippled. . . . My self-
> esteem was taken away. My pride as a teacher was gone. . . . All in
> all, this course has brought back my confidence as a teacher. . . . This
> is causing me to consider changes in my teaching career.

According to Nomha, these experiences had also influenced her development of a new sense of confidence in her teaching and a sense of efficacy
as a teacher.

Similarly, during our follow-up interviews, Niko talked about using
critique and analytical writing to facilitate the process of making some of the
things that we covered in the course her own. Niko's action research consisted
of her participation in and writing about the class-assigned tutoring activities
that she engaged in while volunteering in her own ongoing tutoring and peer
counseling activities. As she struggled to integrate the new course theories
and best practices into her teaching activities, she wrote analytically and critically about her experiences and developing perspectives. Niko's writing for
the course provided evidence of her movement toward internalization of
some the concepts that we covered:

> Although we will have been educated as to "how to teach," we can
> never really learn without experiences, circumstances that provide for
> different variations of what works. We need to take heed to the pos-
> sibilities that the problems may reside in ourselves and not in the stu-
> dent. In any case, the responsibility to teach them (not only accept
> them) is the ideal that we need to instill in ourselves. . . . As I thought
> about how my readings inform my teaching, the idea that grabbed
> me most intensely was the idea that we need to "turn ourselves inside

out, giving up our own sense of who we are, and being willing to see ourselves in the unflattering light of another's angry gaze" [Delpit, 1995, p. 46]. More than applying this to teaching, this is something that should be applied to any and every situation. To understand our own power and not be afraid to expose our vulnerabilities and raise questions of discrimination is essential to almost every situation.

Here, Niko is questioning the pedagogy used in many teacher education courses that tell teachers how to teach or what to do on Monday morning. However, she notes that few programs prepare teachers to think in generative ways about the "different variations of what works" and what does not work in diverse contexts. As some of the course readings become internally persuasive for Niko, she invokes something that she has taken from Delpit and claims it as her own—the notion that we as teachers need to "turn ourselves inside out, giving up our own sense of who we are, and being willing to see ourselves in the unflattering light of another's angry gaze" as we gain the courage to raise questions about our vulnerabilities and issues of power in the classroom. Niko's statement that we as teachers "need to take heed to the possibilities that the problems may reside in ourselves and not in the student" and that we need to take "responsibility to teach" indicates movement toward advocacy. As Niko contemplated the application of what she has learned to her own teaching, she said,

Where do I begin to comment in my growth as a result of this class. Even now as I write these words, there are so many unresolved dilemmas, contradictions, questions—and I am trying to live with the worries I've confronted as a student who is soon to be a teacher. . . . I came into this course arrogant and self-assured. Critical thinking had always been my forte; it has been my natural disposition to try and search for deeper meaning and deeper truths. . . . I began with my personal essay about . . . what I wanted to do for the rest of my life. And in this way I began the course, with a love for literature, arrogance from acquired knowledge, and hope for a glorious future. . . . I began to ask lots of questions. . . . And from then on, my arrogance began to deflate. I began to realize my potential role within these students' lives. I was introduced to things I had never even considered. What if my students cannot read? How will they internalize this lack of skill? Who will they become as adults? How can I change this? How can I become the teacher I want to be? . . . I began trying to see through the student's eyes, trying to remember what it was like to be like them. The readings I have done for this class have elucidated cobwebs of half thoughts and have furnished solutions that had begun in my head. . . . In this way my thinking has evolved. . . . I am anxious about having been ignorant and insensitive to certain students. . . . I am afraid to make the wrong moves just as I am excited to make the right ones. But in the end, I take my future position . . . as a privilege to have the opportunity to help mold the wet clay that will one day become fine art. . . . It is their minds that I am exploring and trying to expand.

As Niko writes these words, she begins by recalling the "many unresolved dilemmas, contradictions, [and] questions" that she has been struggling with as she is "trying to live with the worries" that confront her "as a student who is soon to be a teacher." She notes that the course readings have helped her—they "have elucidated [the] cobwebs" in her mind and provided her with solutions to the questions that had begun in her head. As a result, her "thinking has evolved." She contemplates how she can extend similar experiences to the students in her CLCCs. She sees the need to try "to see the world through her students' eyes . . . to remember what it is like to be like them." Niko envisions her life as a teacher as a privilege and wants to provide her students with experiences that will expand their minds. As Niko talked and wrote analytically about theory and her teaching experiences in the presence of her peers and supportive instructors, she began to challenge her preconceived notions about teaching diverse student populations and to stretch herself to consider new possibilities for her future teaching. As she contemplated issues related to teaching for diversity, she noted that she is "anxious about having been ignorant and insensitive to certain students." Although she is afraid that she will make the wrong moves, she is "excited to make the right ones." As she struggled with theoretical notions in the context of her current tutoring projects and course activities, she voiced her changing perspectives in our classroom discussions and in her journal writing. And as I conducted follow-up visits in her classroom, it became evident that the course had generative effects beyond the professional development setting.

Generative Teaching of Diverse Learners

In the final stages of our professional development course, I encouraged teachers to express their own voices on issues of diversity and best practices in CLCCs. Their responses reflected an emerging sense of efficacy. Throughout this process, teachers talked and wrote not only about opportunities, challenges, and the perceived need for changes but also about the actions they planned to implement in their classrooms.

During my follow-up visits to the classrooms of the study's focus teachers, I was able to investigate the implementation of those plans of action in their classrooms. These teachers' journeys to becoming generative educators culminated in their acting on those plans as they became change agents in their schools. I observed generativity in these teachers' interactions with their students, in curricular innovations, and in the reorganization of their classroom structures that included reflective, introspective, analytical, and critical writing with their students. The transformation of the teachers' plans of action from the professional development course required generative thinking on the part of each teacher. For both Nomha and Niko, the ultimate goal of their teaching was for students to generate plans of action that addressed some of the pressing social issues that existed in the students' communities.

When I returned to observe and interview these teachers, I did not expect to see a specific set of strategies or lessons being implemented in their classrooms, because my course was not prescriptive in nature. Instead, after gaining an increased sense of metacognitive awareness, agency, advocacy, and voice during our course, I expected and saw increased supporting evidence of generativity. These teachers began to draw on the knowledge that they gained in my course, and they linked it to the knowledge they gained from their students; then they added to their understanding by applying that knowledge to solve instructional and pedagogical problems they encountered in their classrooms. I watched these teachers as they encouraged their students to explore a deeper understanding of what their textbooks were saying, to use critical thinking about how to respond to writing prompts that were assigned, and to pose questions that challenged the authoritative voices of the teacher, the textbooks, and their peers. I also observed the teachers as they presented alternative perspectives on the topics covered in their textbooks and as they invited alternative perspectives from their students. For example, the students in Niko's classroom wrote reflective and introspective narrative essays in response to their reading of literature, whereas in Nomha's classroom, the students were writing reflective and analytical essays and performing the powerful skits they had written on *Ten Years of Democracy in South Africa*. One student wrote the following:

> Ten years of democracy means celebrating and remembering those moments of struggle. It means appreciating what we have and hold on to it. . . . It has been a long journey, starting from 1994, the day that everybody was free and people voted for the party of their choice. It was the beginning of freedom for all and an end of apartheid. People couldn't believe it was actually true that they were voting. It was like a dream.
>
> In this ten years of democracy, I for one have gained something from it. . . . I think there is hope. . . . Women are starting to get noticed and rewarded for what they have done for our country, even in Parliament they have women in high places and their voices are heard. . . . We have women who are doing engineering, which means we are really improving every day. . . . I have decided that I will attend the tecknicon and take classes in engineering. . . . Maybe in another five or ten years there will be some other changes that will make life much easier.

This student is reflecting on the changes that she has seen in society around her in the past 10 years, and she is generating ideas about possibilities for change in her own life and plans for the future. Another student wrote,

> As we are . . . celebrating ten years of freedom, from 1994 forwards, now it is called the new South Africa. . . . Some people are saying that there are few changes because people are still starving and living in shacks. . . . My views are, Yes, there are changes, but there is

something that makes me feel unsatisfied with the government arrangements of this country. The people of South Africa are suffering (AIDS), unemployment, starvation, but the government has spent billion for arms deals for the sake of protecting the country for the next war. . . . I'm trying to say that I think the government should first solve the needs of the people like food, medicine, employment, and houses. . . . For us to become equal, everyone must have jobs, the government must give everyone equal settlements, and we must increase Black Economic Empowerment.

This student is using writing as a tool for introspection on how he feels "unsatisfied with the government arrangements of this country." He is also using writing to critique social and economic conditions in the country, and he is generative in his thinking about how the government should go about solving these problems. Another student wrote generatively on her thoughts about what she thinks should be happening in her community:

We must build houses, build the roads, provide good education, provide jobs, build health services, build our local towns, and provide police stations. . . . What I encourage is that black and white people in South Africa should learn one another's cultures and languages so that we can bridge the gap of communication and speak whatever language we choose. This can be achieved by the cooperation of each person who is a South African or claiming to be one.

This student is generative in her thinking as she recommends what should be happening between Black and White people and how it can be achieved. And finally, one student wrote,

I would like to say that I am proud of being South African because many things have happened but we have survived. . . . During the apartheid times, our parents and grandparents couldn't walk the streets without the passport and if the police found you without the pass . . . the police would put you in jail. They were really struggling from what was happening. . . . One person to thank for change is Mr. Mandela, who fought for our freedom. Now . . . many things are changing in the country such as the youth of South Africa and now it is necessary for the youth in our society to act as citizens of the country—to be highly politically educated so that they can earn more money to supply themselves with anything they want to have. And in this new democracy, if you study hard you will be given sponsorship to further your studies and your education will be free. But, we also have choices to make. . . . Peer pressure will always be there, but it is up to a person to overcome. . . . For every situation there is a solution!! We just need to be able to make the right choices for ourselves.

In his writing, this student has generated a plan of action that calls for youth to act as full citizens of the country—to be highly political and to take advantage of educational opportunities rather than give in to peer pressure. Although these students see positive changes in society and signs of hope, they are unsatisfied with current conditions, and they are generating plans for change. These essays illustrate the students' developing sense of voice— recommending that the government first solve the needs of the people by supplying food, medicine, employment, housing, and increased Black economic empowerment. They also illustrate students' developing sense of agency and generative thinking as they talk about plans to attend the tecknicon, recommend improving Black-White communication, and fight against peer pressure.

When I returned to Nomha's classes in 2005, she was busy coaching students who had been selected to represent their school in a formerly all-White regional oratory competition. In 2007, I received the following e-mail messages from one of Nomha's oratory students whom I had met during my 2004 and 2005 visitations. We had kept in contact, and he wrote about what he was doing to act on the generative knowledge that he had gained:

Subject: Grade 12 and the future

Dear Professor

I'm very happy to hear from you. . . .

As I have stated in my last email, grade 12 is becoming almost normal (i.e., when you exclude the pressure and piles of work.) I still LOVE languages . . . thus I have decided to go to a bible training school, their South African branch. There I will be doing translation work— translating publications from English to Afro languages.

So my dream of working with languages will be fulfilled after all (maybe even quicker), and I will get much more satisfaction from it.

Anyways, I will go now because we've just watched the SA budget speech and I need to download the Highlights and check them out.

Enjoy your day.

Peace

This student had developed a love of languages while in school with his teacher Nomha, and he was using generative thinking and problem-solving skills to seek ways to fulfill his lifelong passion of continuing to work with languages after completing high school even though his financial resources were limited. Several months later he wrote,

Subject: How's it Doc!

Dear Doc:

It's been a very long time since we last communicated, and trust me a lot has happened and changed since then. I am now involved in political leadership: I am branch executive committee member of an African National Congress Youth League branch; I'm Western Cape provincial chair person of the Congress of SA Students; and many other things. The list goes on. . . .

What I really wanted to share with you is that on the 8th of this month was the night of my school's matric ball (12th grade award ceremony and farewell) and . . . I was awarded top student in English!! . . . I am also into business now, co-managing an aspiring theatre productions company. . . .

That's it from me for now.

truly yours

This student expressed thanks for having teachers such as Ms. Nomha, who helped him to develop his visions for the future through the development of his oral and written skills. The student's writing tells of the many non-school contexts that he engages in where he has the opportunity to use generative thinking beyond the classroom boundaries. The voices of the students I have shared are typical of the many students whom I engaged with. Student after student told me of their plans to gain further schooling and the details of their entrepreneurial small business schemes, which they planned to implement. In addition, every one of the focus teachers in the study had organized extracurricular forums for their students to engage in, including drama clubs, art clubs, oratory and spoken-word clubs, after-school oral history clubs, and tutoring programs where they collected and shared information with the students on their community lives and discourse practices. Although the specific curriculum in these classrooms may have varied widely, the learning that was taking place within these different contexts on separate continents shared a common thread: the generative teaching and learning that was occurring between the teachers and students. Teachers were drawing on the knowledge they gained in the professional development course, combining it with knowledge they gained from their students, and they were using writing as a pedagogical tool to facilitate generative thinking.

When I visited Niko's school 3 months after the course ended, I observed her classroom of 22 African American and Latino students from low-income backgrounds. Niko presented her students a culturally enriched curriculum that reflected the multiple heritages represented in the school and surrounding community. She used literature, freewrites, exit slips, and assigned research projects designed to help her students learn more about themselves while helping her to learn more about her students' experiences and perspectives. Niko reported that she had reorganized her curriculum around her students and that she was using writing as a pedagogical tool to learn about them. The lesson that I observed during my visitation focused on the students' recent reading of several chapters of Sandra Cisneros's *The House on Mango Street* (1991). As Niko taught the literature lesson, she first had her students review the chapter in small groups; then she engaged the students in a lively class discussion punctuated by questions that helped them to link the story to their experiences and to similar settings in their community.

Students were asked to discuss several chapters that they had read and to consider the theme of community and their hopes and dreams. In small groups they were asked to remember Esperanza's recollections of her life while living on Mango Street and to discuss the various people whom she meets while there. The students recalled that although Esperanza's family had not always lived there, it was perhaps the most important place that she had lived and it represented her heritage and upbringing. They also recalled that Esperanza's central hope throughout the vignettes was to have a large comfortable house—one that she was not ashamed to own, one where she could have control of her destiny. After describing the house on Mango Street, the students discussed Esperanza's greatest dream: having her own house. One student noted,

> Esperanza realized that she was an important part of Mango Street and that it was an important part of her. Although she longed to travel and find a new home of her own, she realized that she would always return to Mango Street to help those who could not achieve their dreams.

After reviewing the vignettes that focused on hopes and dreams, students were supported in analyzing why the author chose to tell the stories as she did. Links were made between the students' lives and the characters' experiences with immigration and poverty. Students were then asked to compose a reflective journal entry to demonstrate an understanding of Esperanza's feelings and to create an artistic rendering of the house as it was depicted in the book. Students compared this story to others about immigration to understand how immigration affects the identity development of many people. Students used personal photos and pictures from magazines to create a collage, and they wrote an essay about the social importance of having hopes and dreams in the book and in their lives. The students discussed how they might make their hopes and dreams become a reality. Finally, they created a PowerPoint presentation and class Web site highlighting their stories and local community resources related to their hopes and dreams.

As her students recapped what they had learned during that day's lesson, I noted that Niko was using writing as a pedagogical tool to facilitate metacognitive awareness, critique, and generative thinking on the part of her students.

Ball

She gave her students class assignments that required extended writing as they struggled ideologically with issues related to the literature they were reading and to their personal experiences. The students' writing assignments went beyond simple reflection on personal experiences, requiring them to use writing as a pedagogical tool to analyze problems and to pose solutions that related to their lives outside the classroom.

Both Nomha's and Niko's classroom practices had been influenced by the course, theoretically and pedagogically. When I visited their classrooms, I observed that since the completion of the teacher education course, both teachers had added new writing assignments to their curriculum, which provided opportunities for their students to investigate and share information about their culturally influenced literacy practices. Students were also given opportunities to integrate their culture knowledge when completing academic assignments. In doing so, the teachers were reconceptualizing their curriculum around their students, and they were continuing to use writing as a pedagogical tool to learn about their students. In their efforts to create classrooms that possessed the qualities of a learning community, both teachers articulated a realization that they needed to learn more about their students on an ongoing basis. During my second follow-up visit to Nomha's classroom, she informed me of the thing that she remembered most from the course, namely, to guide her students to become independent—that is, generative—in their thinking. She recalled our conversations about Vygotsky (1978) on scaffolding and McElroy-Johnson (1993) on the development of one's own voice:

> What I did to build on the concept of voice was I let my students write books about their families, their different cultures, the way they do things, and their customs. Even though we are mostly Xhosa speakers in my classes, we practice our customs in different ways . . . independently. We do things according to our clans. So by writing those books we've learned things that we didn't know about each others' backgrounds and about things that are very important to them. . . . And then if something is bothering them, it comes out in their writing and using that I was able to help many of them.

Though Niko and Nomha were presented with diverse students in disparate contexts, their ability to be generative in their teaching resulted in students who were similarly engaged in generative thinking. For both teachers, their goal was to develop critical thinking skills and to teach their students to think generatively about plans of action to address some of the social issues in their community. Another teacher in my course explained the process best when she wrote the following:

> My exposure to reflective writing in your class caused me to want to use similar writing to reach and influence my students at my high school as a part of our service learning program. . . . Our focus area of study is homelessness in the area. . . . The program is designed to make students aware of the areas of need in their communities,

where and how they can be of service, and to question explanations for current conditions. To help facilitate the latter goal, I included an intense writing component in which students address one reflective writing topic each month. . . .The writing component was meant to be very similar to the one used in your course. In that class, I valued very much the way reflection was used both as a tool and a space for exploration, without too much regard to writing errors. As a result, I was free to challenge my own thinking and draw creative conclusions and connections between text and observation. . . . Reflective writing, then, as an experience became a very non-judgmental form of creative thinking, and I wanted to extend that relationship with writing to my students. . . . My experience with reflective writing . . . had one of the most lasting impacts on my development as an educator. It allowed me to manipulate the new concepts, challenge them, and reorganize them next to new ideas and emerging beliefs. . . . My students and I have had some very intriguing seminar discussions addressing such things as whether homelessness is a moral imperative (based on evidence drawn from Opposing Viewpoints articles), and whether community service makes a person more or less humane (based on their own observations).

A Model of Generative Change

Based on my analysis of the changing classroom practices of the transitioning teachers in my follow-up study, a model of generative change emerged. This model illustrates the professional development instructional approach that I used to support the teachers' growth toward generativity, which was subsequently taken up by the teachers and used in their instruction within their classrooms. My analysis showed that as teachers developed metacognitive awareness about the role of literacies and a sense of agency, advocacy, and efficacy, they developed personal voices and generative thinking skills to direct their continued development as teachers within their CLCCs. This process is depicted in Figure 1. My interviews and observations of the teachers' subsequent work with diverse students confirmed that the teachers were influenced by the instructional approach used in the professional development course and that they drew on this model of generative change when working with their students.

This model builds on Vygotsky's construct of mediation (1978) and is based on his emphasis on the powerful use of language as a cultural tool. Wertsch (1985) notes that mediation is best thought of as a process involving the potential of cultural tools to shape action. The model illustrates the notion of mediation as a process involving the strategic use of oral and especially written language as cultural tools to shape and influence teachers' considerations about how to use the knowledge that they gain about pedagogical problem solving to become generative agents of change in their classrooms. The process is generative in that the teachers were motivated to use the same cultural tools to shape their students' development as problem solvers and generative thinkers.

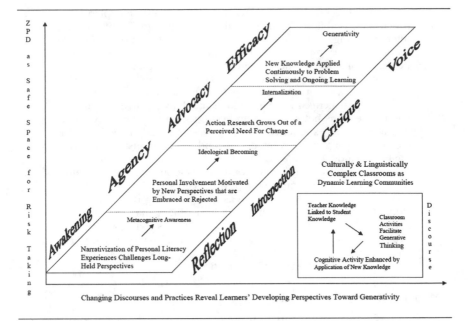

Figure 1. **Model of generative change: The processes through which teachers and students develop voice, generativity, and efficacy in their thinking and practice.**

To make this notion more understandable within the context of teachers' professional development and students' generative development, the model in Figure 1 depicts the strategic use of language—in particular, the use of writing as a pedagogical tool for reflection, introspection, and critique—within professional development and subsequently within CLCCs. The smaller legend inset in Figure 1 depicts the overarching goal of the course: to view professional development classrooms and, subsequently, CLCCs as dynamic learning communities in which oral and written discourses are strategically planned to create environments where cognitive activity is enhanced not only by the introduction of new information but by the application of that new knowledge such that (a) teacher knowledge is linked to student knowledge on an ongoing basis and (b) classroom activities are designed to facilitate generative thinking and problem solving on the part of teachers and students alike.

The model in Figure 1 depicts the processes of cognitive change—metacognitive awareness, ideological becoming, internalization, and generativity—that take place within an individual's zone of proximal development if he or she is allowed to grow within safe spaces where risk taking is encouraged. These processes of cognitive change are facilitated by the strategic use of multiple literacies in the course and particularly by the use of extended writing to engage learners as reflective, introspective, critical, and generative thinkers. As teachers (and, later, their students) move toward generativity, their internal changes are reflected in their changing discourses and practices over time. The model shows four stages in the process of generative change that take place when learning communities are organized such that Phase 1 emphasizes the use of reflection through the narrativization of personal experiences that motivate increased metacognitive awareness concerning the critical role of literacies in teachers' lives and in the lives of others. Engagement with this guided reflection results in an increased sense of personal awakening.

Phase 2 in the process of generative change emphasizes the use of guided introspection that requires teachers (and their students) to look within themselves to determine their role within the teaching/learning community. As teachers engaged in serious discussions and extended writing about important issues related to diversity and literacy, they were motivated by carefully selected readings to take a stand on issues, to locate their level of personal involvement, and to decide if these perspectives would be embraced (to become internally persuasive discourses) or rejected. These activities were designed to facilitate the process of ideological becoming, which resulted in an increased sense of agency.

During Phase 3, the classroom community focused on facilitating internalization through critiques of course readings and through the analysis of action research projects that teachers selected to work on to increase their sense of advocacy. The teachers developed action research projects focusing on the literacy practices of their students, which culminated in plans for implementation. Later, teachers asked their students to conduct ethnographies of community literacy practices and other research projects that linked classroom learning with their communities. Grounded in work that was important to them, the action research projects required teachers and students to formulate questions that were of real interest to them, to carefully describe the data they collected, and to engage in the processes of thoughtful discovery and problem solving as they were thinking and rethinking issues related to teaching, learning, literacy, and diversity. The action research projects served as a catalyst to facilitate the development of generative thinking skills.

The fourth and final phase of this recursive model represents the point at which learners combined theory, best practices, and actual work in communities with diverse populations in ways that facilitated their own theory posing and generative thinking. During this process, they wrote and talked not only about opportunities, challenges, and perceived need for changes but also about the actions they took as they implemented their plans. This process resulted in an increased sense of efficacy and the development of their voices on important issues of diversity.

During the follow-up interviews, teachers referred to the theory they were exposed to in the professional development and their own emerging ideological stance that guided them in their teaching. They spoke with confidence and a sense of efficacy about using writing as a pedagogical tool to learn about their students and then using that knowledge in their teaching. The use of writing as a pedagogical tool provided the teachers a medium for discovering their thoughts and needs; later, it provided a window through which to discover how best to support their students. As the teachers learned about their students through their writing, they integrated that new knowledge with their existing knowledge and used that combined knowledge to solve new and unfamiliar classroom problems. These teachers encouraged their students to explore a deeper understanding of what their textbooks were saying, to use critical thinking about how to respond to writing prompts that were assigned, to link content area topics to their life experiences, to pose queries that challenged their peers and the authoritative voices of the textbooks, and to engage in community building through participation in after-school clubs and community-based organizations. Teachers' modeling this kind of generative thinking with their students inspired the students to become generative thinkers as well.

Conclusions and Implications

The sites of some of the most challenging teaching taking place in the United States and abroad are classrooms that serve students from diverse cultural and linguistic backgrounds. A unique challenge facing teachers in CLCCs is the demand to make the appropriate pedagogical adjustments to meet the needs of their students without having the advantage of being able to draw heavily on their own personal cultural and linguistic experiences as a knowledge base for making those adjustments for many of their students. Because many of the teachers in diverse classrooms come from cultural, linguistic, and socioeconomic backgrounds that are very different from those of their students, it is imperative that they become generative in their pedagogical problem-solving skills. Although we as educational professionals are aware of these challenges, we often find that some of our least prepared teachers are found working in some of our most diverse and underresourced communities—armed with little knowledge about how to meet the teaching and learning needs of their students. It is in these complex classrooms that we need our best-prepared, most highly qualified teachers. Because we know that this is often not the case, a critical key to achieving our goal of preparing additional teachers for diverse classrooms lies in professional development that facilitates the development of teachers as generative practitioners.

This research was designed to increase understanding of how teachers can make use of the opportunities provided within professional development to think about how to apply what they are learning in the teacher education program to becoming effective teachers in their CLCCs. The purpose of this study was not simply to document whether teachers continued to implement particular principles after a program has ended; rather, it was an attempt to investigate teachers' continued learning and their development and use of generative knowledge.

According to Franke et al. (2001), knowledge becomes generative when the learner sees the need to integrate newly gained knowledge with existing knowledge to continue learning and when newly gained knowledge is applied to solve new and unfamiliar problems. Teachers in CLCCs must become what Giroux (1988) calls *teachers as transformative intellectuals*, who are capable of using acquired knowledge as a basis for reinventing their practices so that their teaching and learning are interdependent, rather than separate, functions. Achieving this vision requires changes in teacher education programs that include the development of teachers who are prepared to teach students from backgrounds different from their own. Achieving this vision also requires changes in teachers' conceptions of themselves as teachers and as learners. Teachers must be prepared to be generative in their thinking and generative in their teaching practices. Professional development programs must be reconceptualized as places where pedagogical approaches that are appropriate for working with diverse populations are modeled to scaffold teachers' development as generative practitioners. Moving forward, we must begin to view the preparation of teachers to teach diverse students as a global challenge, and we must look to the international community for ways to address the challenges we face.

In this article I present the model of generative change that emerged from my research to explain the instructional approach used in the professional development course, as well as the instructional approach later used by the teachers themselves in their growth toward becoming what they considered more effective teachers of diverse students. The model provides a foundation for future work on understanding teacher change and development. The model can also be used as a framework to guide the organization of instruction in professional development programs and as a heuristic to explain what needs to happen in programs aimed toward addressing the challenge of developing a highly skilled teaching force that has the skills, knowledge, and dispositions needed to ensure excellent education for all students. As a heuristic, the model illustrates an approach to teaching that facilitated teachers' metacognitive awareness, ideological becoming, internalization, and generativity and that encouraged teachers to discover solutions for themselves while drawing heavily on the use of writing as a pedagogical tool for deep thinking. Drawing on this model, teacher education programs can design instruction that helps teachers to recognize the need to modify their pedagogical practices and instructional organization in response to the information that they gain in their courses and, later, in response to the information that they gain from the students whom they teach. Teachers can subsequently use this model as a tool that helps them arrive at solutions to the day-to-day challenges they face in their classrooms.

This research can help leaders within the policy arena to acknowledge the importance of facilitating the development of teachers who are generative thinkers. According to Darling-Hammond and Bullmaster (1998), efforts to produce effective schools by teacher-proofing curriculum and by telling teachers what to do and how to do it have failed. These efforts have taught us that "regulations do not transform schools. Only [well trained] teachers can do that, in concert with parents, students, administrators, and the wider community" (p. 1072). Teachers remain the key factor in realizing the full educational potential of our students. Other initiatives are doomed to fail if the primary agents of instruction are incapable of acting as generative agents of change in our schools and classrooms. Becoming excellent teachers in CLCCs requires much more than the ability to implement a scripted curriculum. As Shulman (1983) pointed out over two decades ago, "no microcomputer will replace them, no television system will clone and distribute them, no scripted lessons will direct and control them, no voucher system will bypass them" (p. 504). Because teachers are the key factor to the successful teaching of all students, we are compelled to look closely at the complex challenge of preparing teachers for diversity and to think seriously about the preparation of teachers who can organize their classrooms to allow for variability in the delivery of instruction—teachers who can diversify their practice so that they can engage every student in learning. This requires generativity on the part of teachers and teacher education programs. Our teachers need support in developing these qualities, and we can provide that support if we reconceptualize current notions of professional development so that we place the preparation of teachers to teach in CLCCs at the center, rather than at the margins, of current reform efforts in teacher education. The model that I present supports us in placing at the center of our work a teachers' movement toward becoming reflective, thoughtful, critical, generative thinkers.

What is needed is the expansion of what we define as basic education for preservice and in-service teachers and an expanded conception of student knowledge as an important resource in the professional development of teachers. We can accomplish this as we open up the curriculum to a variety of perspectives and experiences and expose teachers to complex theoretical ideas that challenge them intellectually and require them to use critical thinking, reasoning, and problem solving to chart new directions for instruction that models how teachers can learn from their students and about their students so they can apply that knowledge to making necessary changes within their classrooms.

Note

This article is designed to provide the necessary empirical foundation to bring attention to the need for the development and support of teachers across national boundaries who are preparing to teach the world's poor, marginalized, and underachieving populations. Ideally, this work will serve to accelerate educational parity across racial and social boundaries, and the legacy of academic failure that plagues so many students will be overcome through an expanded understanding of the processes of generative change.

References

Au, K. (1993). An expanded definition of literacy. In *Literacy instruction in multicultural settings* (pp. 20–34). New York: Harcourt Brace.

Bakhtin, M. M. (1981). *The dialogic imagination.* Austin: University of Texas Press.

Ball, A. F. (2000). Preparing teachers for diversity: Lessons learned from the U.S. & South Africa. *Teaching and Teacher Education, 16,* 491–509.

Ball, A. F. (2006). *Multicultural strategies for education and social change: Carriers of the torch in the US and South Africa.* New York: Teachers College Press.

Bandura, A. (1977). Self-efficacy: Toward a unifying theory of behavioral change. *Psychological Review, 84,* 191–215.

Bandura, A. (1997). *Self-efficacy: The exercise of control.* New York: Freeman.

Borko, H. (2004). Professional development and teacher learning: Mapping the terrain. *Educational Researcher, 33*(8), 3–15.

Bransford, J. D., Brown, A. L., & Cocking, R. R. (Eds.). (2000). *How people learn: Brain, mind, experience, and school.* New York: National Academy Press.

Bruner, J. S. (1990). *Acts of meaning.* Cambridge, MA: Harvard University Press.

Bruner, J. S. (1994). Life as narrative. In A. H. Dyson & C. Genishi (Eds.), *The need for story: Cultural diversity in classroom and community* (pp. 28–37). Urbana, IL: National Council of Teachers of English.

Cisneros, S. (1991). *The house on Mango Street.* New York: Vintage.

Darling-Hammond, L., & Bransford, J. (Eds.). (2005). *Preparing teachers for a changing world: Report of the Committee on Teacher Education of the National Academy of Education.* San Francisco: Jossey-Bass.

Darling-Hammond, L., & Bullmaster, M. (1998). The changing social context of teaching in the United States. In B. J. Biddle, T. L., Godd, & I. F. Goodson (Eds.), *International handbook of teachers and teaching* (pp. 1053–1079). New York: Springer.

Delpit, L. (1988). The silenced dialogue: Power and pedagogy in educating other people's children. *Harvard Educational Review, 58*(3), 280–298.

Delpit, L. (1995). *Other people's children: Cultural conflict in the classroom.* New York: New Press.

Desimone, L., Porter, A., Garet, M., Yoon, K. S., & Birman, B. (2002). Effects of professional development on teachers' instruction: Results from a three-year longitudinal study. *Educational Evaluation and Policy Analysis, 24*(2), 81–112.

Duhon, G., & Manson, T. (Eds.). (2000). *Implications for teacher education: Cross-ethnic and cross-racial dynamics of instruction.* Lewiston, NY: Mellen.

Franke, M., Carpenter, T., Levi, L., & Fennema, E. (2001). Capturing teachers' generative change: A follow-up study of professional development in mathematics. *American Educational Research Journal, 38*(3), 653–689.

Freire, P. (1970). *Pedagogy of the oppressed.* New York: Continuum.

Gee, J. P. (1989). What is literacy? *Journal of Education, 171,* 18–25.

Giroux, H. A. (1988). *Teachers as intellectuals: Toward a critical pedagogy of learning.* Westport, CT: Greenwood.

Grant, C. A., & Secada, W. G. (1990). Preparing teachers for diversity. In W. R. Houston (Ed.), *Handbook of research on teacher education* (pp. 403–422). New York: Macmillan.

Hollingsworth, S. (1989). Prior beliefs and cognitive change in learning to teach. *American Educational Research Journal, 26*(2), 160–189.

Hollins, E., & Torres-Guzman, M. E. (2005). The preparation of candidates for teaching diverse student populations. In M. Cochra-Smith & K. Zeichner (Eds.), *Studying teacher education: The report of the AERA panel on research and teacher education* (pp. 201–225). Mahwah, NJ: Lawrence Erlbaum.

hooks, b. (1994). *Teaching to transgress: Education as the practice of freedom.* New York: Routledge.

Ladson-Billings, G. (1999). Preparing teachers for diverse student populations: A critical race theory perspective. In A. Iran-Nejad & D. Pearson (Eds.), *Review of research in education* (Vol. 24, pp. 211–248). Washington, DC: American Educational Research Association.

Ladson-Billings, G. (2000). Fighting for our lives: Preparing teachers to teach African American students. *Journal of Teacher Education, 51*(3), 206–214.

McElroy-Johnson, B. (1993). Teaching and practice: Giving voice to the voiceless. *Harvard Educational Review, 63*(1), 85–104.

National Center for Educational Statistics. (2006). *Characteristics of the 100 largest public elementary and secondary school districts in the United States: 2003–04 statistical analysis report.* Washington DC: U.S. Department of Education.

Said, E. (1978). *Orientalism.* New York: Vintage Books.

Sarason, S. (1996). *Revisiting "The culture of the school and the problem of change."* New York: Teachers College Press.

Shulman, L. S. (1983). Autonomy and obligation. In L. S. Shulman & G. Sykes (Eds.), *Handbook of teaching and policy* (pp. 484-504). New York: Longman.

Sleeter, C. E. (2001). Preparing teachers for culturally diverse schools: Research and the overwhelming presence of whiteness. *Journal of Teacher Education, 52*(2), 94–106.

UNESCO Institute for Statistics. (2005). *Global education digest 2005: Comparing education statistics across the world.* Montreal, CA: Author.

Vygotsky, L. S. (1978). *Mind in society: The development of higher psychological processes* (M. Cole, V. John-Steiner, S. Scribner, & E. Souberman, Eds.). Cambridge, MA: Cambridge University Press.

Weiner, L. (2000). Research in the 90s: Implications for urban teacher preparation. *Review of Educational Research, 70*(3), 369–406.

Wertsch, J. (Ed.). (1985). *Culture, communication, and cognition: Vygotskian perspectives.* Cambridge, MA: Cambridge University Press.

Willms, J. D. (2006). *Learning divides: Ten policy questions about the performance and equity of schools and schooling systems.* Montreal, CA: UNESCO Institute for Statistics.

Manuscript received December 3, 2007
Revision received June 8, 2008
Accepted June 16, 2008

American Educational Research Journal
March 2009, Vol. 46, No. 1, pp. 73–114
DOI: 10.3102/0002831208323279
© 2009 AERA. http://aerj.aera.net

What Does It Mean to Be African American? Constructions of Race and Academic Identity in an Urban Public High School

Na'ilah Suad Nasir
Milbrey W. McLaughlin
Amina Jones
Stanford University

In this article, the authors explore variation in the meanings of racial identity for African American students in a predominantly African American urban high school. They view racial identity as both related to membership in a racial group and as fluid and reconstructed in the local school setting. They draw on both survey data and observational data to examine the nature of racial identity meanings for African American students, their relation to academic engagement and achievement, and how they were fostered by the school context. Findings show that students embraced (and were offered differential access to) different meanings of African American racial identity and that these meanings were differentially related to achievement and engagement.

KEYWORDS: African American students, racial identity, urban schools

Research on the relation between the racial/ethnic identities[1] of African American students and school-related outcomes has produced conflicting findings (Harper & Tuckman, 2006; Lowe, 2006). Some studies have found

NA'ILAH SUAD NASIR is an associate professor of education and African American studies in the Graduate School of Education, University of California, Berkeley, Tolman Hall, Berkeley, CA 94720; e-mail: *nailahs@berkeley.edu*. She specializes in race, culture, and learning; identity processes and educational trajectories; and redressing inequities in educational access and outcomes.

MILBREY W. MCLAUGHLIN is David Jacks Professor of Education and Public Policy, Stanford University, School of Education, CERAS, 520 Galvez Mall, Stanford, CA 94305; e-mail: *Milbrey@stanford.edu*. She specializes in contexts for teaching and learning, policy implementation, and community youth development.

AMINA JONES is a graduate student at Stanford University, School of Education, CERAS, 520 Galvez Mall, Stanford, CA 94305; e-mail: *Amina.jones@stanford.edu*. She specializes in disenfranchised and disconnected youth, the social construction of educational pathways, and emerging adulthood.

that when students hold strong identities as African Americans, their academic achievement suffers and/or academic identification decreases, especially when they view being African American as antithetical to doing well in school (Fordham, 1988, 1996; Fordham & Ogbu, 1986; Noguera, 2003; Osborne, 1997). Others have found the opposite relationship and argue that racial/ethnic identity is a facilitative and protective factor for education for African Americans (Chavous et al., 2003; Oyserman, Harrison, & Bybee, 2001), even buffering the effect of racial discrimination (Sellers, Copeland-Linder, Martin, & Lewis, 2006; Wong, Eccles, & Sameroff, 2003). Other research has argued that there is not an overarching linear relationship between racial/ethnic identity and academic outcomes for African American students, but rather that it varies depending on the nature of the African American identity (Carter, 2005; Chavous et al., 2003; Harper & Tuckman, 2006; Sellers, Chavous, & Cooke, 1998; Spencer, Noll, Stolfus, & Harpalani, 2001).

What may explain these conflicting findings? It may be that findings on the relation between racial/ethnic identity and school outcomes conflict for at least two reasons. First, researchers have used a variety of definitions and measures of racial/ethnic identities; and a range of attitudes, behaviors, and beliefs have characterized African American racial/ethnic identity, depending on the study (Harper & Tuckman, 2006; Lowe, 2006). Such differences in definitions and measures may contribute to the lack of consensus in the literature, as various aspects of African American racial identity may be differentially related to academic outcomes.

Second, there may be differences due to the way in which racial/ethnic identities get constructed and play out in local settings that it may be difficult to capture with survey methods alone. Too often, research on racial and ethnic and academic identities and achievement for African American students has failed to explore the school, institutional, and neighborhood contexts that students are negotiating and the way in which such contexts may support particular kinds of identities or may mediate the relation between racial/ethnic identities and academic outcomes (Davidson, 1996, is an important exception). This may be particularly important as we know that racial/ethnic identity is related to perceptions of one's group within the larger social context—such perceptions may be fundamentally influenced by local experiences with race and ethnicity.

In this article, we present data on the racial identity meanings of African American high school students and the ways in which these meanings were related to school achievement and academic identity. We highlight youth's local conceptions of their African American racial identity and the importance of considering the local school context as well as broader levels of context in understanding students racial/ethnic and academic identities and the relations between them.

Variations in Racial/Ethnic Identity Content

Much of the literature on ethnic identity has viewed ethnic identity as a measure of how much one identifies with and participates in the practices of his or her ethnic group. Increasingly, scholars have also indicated that there are variations in types of racial/ethnic identity; much of this work has focused on African American identities (Cross, 1991; Cross & Fhagen-Smith, 2001; Oyserman et al., 2001; Sellers et al., 1998; Sellers, Rowley, Chavous, Shelton, & Smith, 1997). Researchers have argued that the kind of racial identities students hold may have implications for their sense of themselves as students and for their achievement.

For instance, Sellers et al. (1998) contend that there is no single set of attitudes or behaviors that define racial identification; rather, each individual decides if he or she identifies with the race and what that identification means to him or her. Sellers et al. propose three stable aspects of racial identity (centrality, regard, and ideology) that exist alongside its situational properties. Centrality describes how important one's race is to his or her self-concept. Regard describes how one feels about his or her racial group (private regard) and how one thinks others feel about his or her group (public regard). Ideology refers to one's beliefs about how his or her racial group should act and interact in society. These aspects of racial identity have been shown to be related to academic achievement for African American students. Among college students, high centrality was positively correlated with grade point average, as was public regard (Sellers et al., 1998; Shelton & Sellers, 2003). These findings point to the existence of multiple possibilities of how one thinks about oneself racially and the importance of understanding the nuance of these identity meanings.

Spencer et al. (2001) have also examined how variation in African American identity might relate to achievement. They draw on Cross's (1991) model of the development of racial identity for African Americans, in which he identifies several stages of Black identity development.[2] Spencer showed that African American students that held a Eurocentric orientation showed lower academic achievement and lower self-esteem than students who held a proactive Afrocentric orientation. This research showed that the relation between racial identity and academic success was mediated by content of the racial identity that students held. Similarly, Oyserman et al. (2001) reported that when African American students' racial identities included academic achievement, students had higher levels of academic efficacy. These studies illustrate three critical aspects of racial/ethnic identities: degree of affiliation with being African American, a connection to an African and/or African American tradition, and achievement as a part of one's racial/ethnic identity. Oyserman et al. also found that achievement ideology mattered more for female students, whereas connection to an African American tradition mattered more for male students.

Qualitative work has also supported the notion that there are multiple ways that African American students position themselves both with respect to race and school and that some patterns are conducive to high achievement whereas other patterns are less conducive to doing well in school (Carter, 2005; Davidson, 1996; Fordham & Ogbu, 1986; O'Connor, 1999). For example in Carter's study of African American and Latino students, she identified three categories that describe how students made sense of themselves both racially and academically: cultural mainstreamers, cultural straddlers, and noncompliant believers. In Carter's formulation, cultural mainstreamers are students that assimilate to a mainstream culture, cultural straddlers tap into the resources of American society while maintaining a strong sense of cultural identity, and noncompliant believers espouse an achievement ideology and yet behave in resistant and oppositional ways in school. In Carter's study, male minority students were more likely than female minority students to be noncompliant believers.

Similarly, Fordham and Ogbu (1986) highlight the ways that African American students can come to define their racial identity in opposition to school success and either perform poorly or "act White" in order to succeed. In a small qualitative study of schooling of African Americans in an urban school in Washington, DC, in the 1980s, Fordham and Ogbu found that some African American students felt that doing well in school was tantamount to rejecting their racial identity and that such students didn't trust educators or the education system. Subsequently, Fordham (1988) suggested that other youth adopt what she termed a "raceless persona" in which they distanced themselves from their race by avoiding ethnically similar peers who were disengaged from school and by taking on language and a style of behavior that met with the approval of teachers.

These studies have been critical in elucidating students' perspectives on their racial identities and its relation to school, and furthermore, these studies have pointed to interesting profiles of these beliefs and behaviors on the part of youth. However, some of this work implies that African American youth see their racial/ethnic identities in opposition to school success (at worst) and as a cultural identity that can be straddled with an alternative identity that includes success in school (at best). That notwithstanding, this line of research also points to the complexity and potentially local nature of the meaning that African American students ascribe to their racial/ethnic identity, with some students in some places seeing a lack of congruence between their racial/ethnic and academic achievement, and other students successfully integrating the two cultures.

The Multiple Contexts of African American Racial/Ethnic Identity

We view two levels of context as critical to bring to bear on youth's racial/ethnic and academic identities: (a) the school and local context and (b) the historical and national media context.

School context. Davidson (1996) has pointed out that racial/ethnic identities are negotiated in school and classroom contexts and that these contexts can support or fail to support the extent to which youth see school as a part of or in opposition to their racial/ethnic identities. Specifically, Davidson found that features of school contexts that contributed to manifestations of disengagement and opposition for students of color included academic tracking, negative expectations, racial discrimination, bureaucratized relationships and practices, and barriers to information. Conversely, Mehan, Villanueva, Hubbard, and Lintz (2004) have argued that in school settings where students are expected to succeed and are given information about college and other support, racial/ethnic identities of marginalized students need not be defined in opposition to school success.

Clearly, then, one important factor in understanding racial/ethnic identities and their relation to schooling outcomes is the nature of schooling practices that students are exposed to. The idea that school context has a significant effect on students' racial and academic identities is supported by theories that view the self as fluid across contexts (Markus & Kunda, 1986; Shelton & Sellers, 2000; Stryker & Serpe, 1994). Part of the reason that such school contexts are important is because they make different configurations of identities possible, through modeling, norms, and social interaction.

Historical and media context. Similarly, historical time shifts the possibilities for who one can become. Clearly, the possibilities for what it meant to be African American in the 1950s are likely quite different than the possibilities for what it means today. In the 1950s, as today, there was considerable range in the economic resources, values, and lifestyles of African Americans. However, due to more explicit racism in the United States at the time, there were severe limitations placed on African Americans' participation in mainstream society. Movies rarely portrayed African Americans, and in the new era of television, there was little to no African American presence. Despite the institutionalized and interpersonal racism, in general African Americans considered themselves to be Americans, did not express strong connections with Africa, and saw education as the key to social mobility. Women straightened their hair, and both men and women wore formal clothing in public places.

Today, a markedly different national and media context exists for youth. The media has a much stronger presence in the identity choices offered to African Americans. And although there is considerable variation, as in the 1950s, contemporary media images tend to portray African Americans, particularly young males, most often as thugs, athletes, or entertainers. The prevalence of this "gangsta" identity is related to a consumer economy where gangsta rap is a multimillion-dollar industry.

Indeed, heated debates over the term that should be used to refer to African Americans in this country has occurred every 20 years or so (from "Colored" to "Black" to "African American"), and underlying these debates are assumptions and values around what it means to be African American. "Colored" identified African Americans in relation to Whites and as citizens with fewer rights; "Black" indicated that African Americans had embraced the power of their skin and their uniqueness as a people; "African American" identified African Americans with a country, Africa, yet recognized their long legacy in this country.

A recent example of such an historical (yet local) shift in possible African American identity meanings occurred in 2006 in some high schools in northern California, when the identity of the African American skate boarder had been made available as a potential identity by the release of a rap song (Vans, by The Pack) by a local group. These African American students wear Vans (a brand of tennis shoes associated with surfers) and carry skateboards around their high school—an identity that was not available for African American students in Bay Area high schools prior to the song release.[3]

It is also important to understand contemporary African American youth's racial/ethnic identities given the shifting national climate around race (in a postaffirmative action era), where conversations about race are decreasingly explicit (Pollock, 2005). Furthermore, at the same time that issues of race have become less explicit, youth are exposed at unprecedented levels to an increasingly globalized media culture (Goodman & Dretzin, 2001), which blurs the lines between racial groups yet profits from "gangsta" stereotypes of African Americans (Jhally, 1997; Ro, 1996). Although the epitome of African American maleness is portrayed as "gangsta" or "hard," the African American female is often portrayed as the gangsta's hypersexualized counterpart—the "video vixen" (Steffans & Hunter, 2005), a scantily clad party girl present for the enjoyment of men.

Media portrayals of African Americans must be understood as a part of a long history of racism, discrimination, and exploitation in the United States (Frederickson, 2002). The media has consistently offered a relatively narrow set of identity choices for nondominant people and youth in particular (Page, 1997). For African American youth, media images reinforce stereotypes of these groups as potentially dangerous, anti-intellectual, and downtrodden. As Essed (2002, as cited in Spencer, 2006) argues, these racial images, by virtue of their repeated use, become "common-sense," thus making them both pervasive and insidious. Spencer (2006) has written about the developmental consequences of the prevalence of negative stereotypes in the media for African American students. She has argued that the presence of negative stereotypes makes difficult the developmental task of managing an ego-supporting identity while coping with generalized negative imagery. Under such conditions, African American students (particularly males) may be left to cope with normative developmental tasks with few supports and may "deploy coping methods that prove to be less than constructive" (p. 857). Other research has confirmed that adolescents (and even young children) understand stereotypes about their own and other groups (Baron & Banaji, 2006; Hudley & Graham, 2005; McKown & Weinstein, 2003). Thus, prevalent stereotypes about African American students and the ways those stereotypes are perceived by students may form an important part of the context that students negotiate (Steele, 1997).

Using both ethnographic and survey data, the study reported in this article examines both students' perceptions of the racial identity meanings available to them and how the endorsement of various meanings relate to academic identity and achievement. It also explores how multiple configurations of racial identity meanings were made available in the same high school context. We consider carefully both youth's local and stereotypical conceptions of what it means to be African American and the nature of the school context that informs their racial identities. The high school context was complex, in that the school had a strong African American cultural tradition, yet was underresourced and highly tracked in ways that offered very different sets of social and academic resources to different students.

In considering both students' perceptions of their racial and academic identities and the ways in which these are afforded by multiple layers of social context, this study moves beyond simple oppositional culture theories (Diamond, in press) as well as theories that place identity solely in the minds of youth and their communities. We consider both the local and the broader social space that African American youth are navigating as they construct a sense of themselves and as they process the multiple identity expectations conveyed to them by their social and cultural worlds. As such, this study contributes to the literature on relationship between racial identity and academic achievement and highlights the role of both local and distal contexts in this relationship.

Theoretical Frame

In order to understand the way in which students' racial and academic identities developed in the context of their experience at school and in society more broadly, we draw on sociocultural (Cole, 1996; Engestrom, 1999; Rogoff, 2003; Wenger, 1999) and ecological theories (Bronfenbrenner, 1979, 1993; Lerner, 1991; Spencer, 2006) in that we take cultural activities and practices to be central in the developmental trajectories of individuals. By cultural practices and activities, we mean reoccurring, goal-directed activities that involve two or more people. From sociocultural and ecological perspectives, developmental processes are deeply informed by the social context—through the organization of activities that people participate in, and through the values, norms, and expectations conveyed in those activities (Gonzalez, 1999; Gutierrez & Rogoff, 2003; Nasir, 2004). Cultural theories of development also highlight the layered nature of context, such that it involves both immediate (proximal) contexts, such as activities or cultural practices, but also more distal contexts, such as institutions and society (Bronfenbrenner, 1993). We find this frame important for considerations of identity, as identities are inherently social and identity meanings are part of culturally figured worlds (Holland, LaChicotte, Skinner, & Cain, 1999). This theoretical lens also highlights the situational, local, and historically bound nature of identities (Wenger, 1999).

We view racial/ethnic identities as being coherent within racial/ethnic groups (i.e., there is something that we recognize as an African American identity) yet also fluid over individuals, time, and space. Furthermore, racial/ethnic identities are tied to participation in institutions and are offered through the norms, conventions, and available roles within cultural practices in these institutional settings. Finally, racial/ethnic identities are also informed by broader societal conceptions about what racial group membership means, such as racial stereotypes. These broader societal conceptions constitute ideational artifacts (Cole, 1996; Nasir, 2004) that get taken up and acted upon in local settings.

79

Understanding racial identity in this way is also consonant with the sociological literature on identity, particularly with a social interactionist perspective. Social interactionism has its roots in the work of philosopher and sociologist George Herbert Meade, and it takes as its premise that who we are is fundamentally shaped by our participation in the social world and by our social interactions with those around us, through which particular values, norms, and expectations are conveyed. As we mirror these expectations that others have of us, our sense of self is constructed. Sociologists from the symbolic interactionist school highlight the ways in which identities are negotiated moment-to-moment in social interaction in daily life and take as central the idea that social reality is created and negotiated by people through the names and meanings (symbols) they attach to things when communicating with one another.

This frame on identity allows us to better understand how students develop conceptions of themselves academically and racially as they participate in the multiple settings of their lives, including school.

Method

The data for this article are drawn from a larger 2-year study on youth connection and disconnection in an urban public high school attended by primarily African American students. Our research combined focus groups, observations, and interviews of case study students, teacher interviews, and survey methods. We used multiple methods because we were centrally concerned with both students' experiences and their perceptions of those experiences. Furthermore, our focus on identity required both an understanding of how students were thinking about themselves and their place in the world and in their school and a concern for the ways in which their school context afforded or constrained particular identity choices. For the former, we captured with interviews and surveys; for the latter, we relied on systematic observations. For the purposes of this article, we draw on observational, interview, and survey data.

Negotiating Access

Our initial access to students in our focal high school, Jackson High, came through a preexisting formal partnership between the school and a university research center at our university. As a part of that partnership, the research center ran an after-school program at the school site. Initial conversations about the possibility of the study took place between the third author and the principal, who granted us permission to carry out the study at Jackson High. However, having the permission of the school administration did not mean that students would trust us or want to be a part of our study. Thus, as a first step into understanding the experiences of students, we conducted a series of hour-long focus groups. We recruited students to come to these focus groups by providing food and offering students the opportunity to have their opinions about the school heard. Students were also recommended to us by the school counselor. We asked the counselor to help us identify a range of students—both students who were connected to the school, teachers, and academics, and those who were less connected. Initially, we conducted one-time focus groups with the goal of getting insight into students' perspectives on aspects of their school experience that connected them to school and those that disconnected them. We found the focus group format to be productive and saw potential for developing relationships with students, so we decided to create a regular focus group to lead activities and discussions with students.

These groups met weekly for nine sessions with two groups of students selected with the assistance of teachers and the guidance counselor: students who were identified as relatively "connected" and students who were seen as relatively "disconnected." By connected, we meant students who seemed to have solid relationships with teachers and peers and who were viewed as participating in the ways one might expect that students would participate in school: They went to class and completed schoolwork with some degree of regularity. By disconnected, we meant students who teachers and counselors felt might be at risk for dropping out. One focus group consisted of connected students and the other of disconnected students. The connected group consisted of 11 African American students, 6 males and 5 females, all of whom attended regularly (no student missed more than two sessions). The disconnected group consisted of 9 participants, 8 African American and 1 Asian, with 4 males and 5 females. Overall, attendance was regular (the mean attendance was 5.8 sessions), though this group did have some attrition (it started out with 12 students and lost 3). Three students had less regular attendance and attended only four of the nine sessions (2 of these students dropped out of school during the course of our study). Each of the two focus groups met once a week at lunch time for 9 weeks, under the leadership of the first two authors. The structure of the focus groups was informal. Students worked in groups on various tasks designed to elicit students' perceptions of their school and community environments. For instance, one task involved students taking pictures of positive and negative spaces in their school, then creating a poster board and presenting the pictures on their board to the whole group. The sessions were audio-taped and transcribed. In these sessions, issues of race and the meaning of racial identity arose spontaneously. Once it did, we asked students specifically about what it meant to them to be African American. We also collected and analyzed academic performance and attendance records for focus group participants.

At the end of these 9-week sessions, we introduced the idea to students that we would like to "shadow" them to learn more about their lives in school and outside of school. Students were generally receptive to this possibility. We chose case study students to represent both male and female experiences and a range of achievement levels. Students were primarily 10th and 11th graders in the first year of our study.

Observations. All told, we accompanied 7 case study students (6 were African American) as they attended classes and interacted with teachers and peers during class time, lunch time, and in passing through the halls between classes. We shadowed each student for at least 8 full days, resulting in at least 56 hours of observations for each case study student.

We also recorded informal conversations and interviewed participants on several occasions. In these interviews, students were asked to reflect on their class attendance behaviors, the importance of school to their sense of self, relationships with teachers, and safety and instructional practices. These interviews were audio-taped and transcribed. Academic performance and attendance records were also collected and analyzed. These case studies provided us with a close-up vision of students' experiences as they negotiated a range of classes and other school activities.

Survey. In the second year of the study, we designed a survey to explore the nature of school connection for students and to examine the relationship between connection and students' academic and racial identities. Our survey questionnaire consisted of five main scales: interpersonal connection, institutional connection, academic identity, and two scales for students' racial identities. We also collected background information and self-report information on student achievement. Academic identity and connectedness findings are reported in another article (Nasir, Jones, & McLaughlin, 2007). In this article, we report information from the academic identity, ethnic identity, racial/ethnic identity meanings, and achievement measures.

Achievement was measured with three questions that had a yes/no response format (Have you been on the honor roll in the last year? How you been enrolled in an AP class in the last year? and Have you failed a class within the last year?). We used these questions instead of student grades because our pilot work and conversations with students revealed that students rarely knew their own GPA or grades, and our survey was anonymous, which made matching survey responses with student records unavailable.

The Academic Identity Scale included four items (adapted from Osborne, 1997). Examples of these items include, "How important is doing well in school to who you are?" "How much do your grades matter to you?" Inter-item reliability for this scale was $\alpha = .73$.

The Ethnic Identity Scale was adapted from the Multigroup Ethnic Identity Measure (Phinney, 1992). It included 11 items, such as "I have a clear sense of my racial group and what it means to me" and "I have a strong sense of belonging to my racial group." For all measures, the response scale was from 1 to 5, with 1 being *not at all true* and 5 being *very true*. Inter-item reliability for this scale was $\alpha = .80$. Specific items that made up each of the scales are presented in Appendix A. We included this scale as one way to measure racial/ethnic identities.

The *racial/ethnic identity meanings* measure was more complex. We wanted to capture (in an ecologically valid way) what it meant to African American students to be African American. Since the goal of this measure was to tap into youth's locally held definitions of *racial/ethnic identity*, we began by holding two focus groups with youth to ask them what it meant for them to be African American. The traits and behaviors generated by students during focus groups were compiled and put on a checklist for the survey. The survey instructed students to check all selections that captured what it meant for them to be a member of their racial/ethnic group.

In analysis, items on the checklist were grouped into categories of like items. There were five different categories of meanings of African American identity. These were as follows: (a) understanding the history of African Americans, (b) expressing behaviors/beliefs that support school success (positive school), (c) expressing behaviors/beliefs that do not support school success (negative school), (d) wearing a particular clothing style or using Ebonics (personal style), and (e) expressing behaviors/beliefs that support a "gangsta" persona (gangsta). The specific items that made up these subscales are listed in Appendix B. Students received a score of either 0 (*item not checked*) or 1 (*item checked*) for each item on this measure. A score was derived for each of the racial identity meaning categories by calculating the mean score of the items that made up each category. Thus, students received a score between 0 and 1 for each of the racial identity meaning categories, with a higher score indicating that the student believes membership in his or her race group is associated with that category.

We surveyed 121 students: 31% were 9th graders, 18% were 10th graders, 29% were 11th graders, and 22% were 12th graders. Gender was balanced: 49.5% were male and 50.5% were female. Racially, the sample included 68 African American students, 13 Asian students, 9 mixed, 8 Latino, and 17 students who declined to state ethnicity. This sample was fairly representative of the school population. In this article, we consider only the data from the African American students.

Analysis

Analysis of the survey data began in the summer of the second year of the study. Data were coded and entered into a data analysis program (SPSS). In this article, our analyses focus on the racial identity scale, the racial identity meaning items, and the three achievement questions. The racial identity score was created by computing a mean of the answers to the 11 items; thus, these scores could range from 1 to 5. The racial identity meanings measure was scored as follows. Each item was coded 0 or 1: 0 if the item was not checked, 1 if it was checked. Some items were subsequently reverse-coded. A mean was computed for each of the five dimensions we identified above (understanding history, positive school, negative school, personal style, and "gangsta").

The focus group, interview, and observational data were interpreted qualitatively. Members of the research team (one African American female faculty member, one White female faculty member, and one African American female graduate student) met weekly over the course of the project, along with undergraduate students involved with the project to debrief the week's activities and to explore emerging findings. Formal analysis on the qualitative data began in the spring of Year 2. Members of the research team read through all transcripts and field notes and began an iterative process of coding that began with open coding and went through increasingly specific rounds of coding as particular issues and processes became apparent. Our final codes centered on three core issues: connection and disconnection (both how these were expressed by students and how the school offered opportunities for both), racial and academic identity, and an aspect of the organization of the school that we came to call the "two schools" phenomenon. We also developed cases for each of our case study students. In this article, we focus on the data that bears on issues of racial and academic identity. The two cases reported in this article were chosen because they were representative of the processes, trends, and patterns found across the cases.

School Context: Jackson High

Jackson High School is located in East Baysville, a historic section of a large northern California city. Nearly 20,000 people live in East Baysville, according to the 2000 U.S. Census. The population is 64% African American, 16% Latino, and 9% Asian Pacific Islander. Income levels in the neighborhood are the lowest in the county. Over two thirds of households in East Baysville earned less than $30,000 in 1999, as compared to 28% in the county as a whole. Half of the households in the poorest census tract earned less than $11,000. Almost half (45%) of East Baysville residents ages 25 and over do not have a high school degree, compared to 18% in the county as a whole.

East Baysville vies with another Baysville neighborhood for the title "murder capital" of the city. From January 2000 through August 2003, there were 22 homicides in East Baysville. The majority of homicide victims and offenders were African American (approximately 90%). Of homicides committed with a gun, about 6 in 10 in East Baysville were walk-by shootings at point-blank range. East Baysville experienced 433 aggravated assaults from 1998 to August 2003, and 103 involved a firearm (Wilson & Riley, 2004). At the time of this writing, a fatal shooting occurred three blocks from Jackson High. The victim was a senior and honor student at Jackson High School. She was sitting on a car outside of her home when she was struck by a stray bullet. The crime and fears of the surrounding neighborhood carry over into the school.

Jackson High is one of the five traditional comprehensive high schools in the Baysville Unified School District. Although it was built in the 1930s to serve 2,400 students, it is the district's smallest high school, enrolling 670 students. Its small size permits the school to emphasize personalization and relationships among staff and students. For the 1999-2000 school years, the pupil teacher ratio was 16.2 to 1, with a reported average class size of 21.5 students. Jackson High School has struggled with chronic absenteeism and with difficulties in getting students to attend classes once they arrive at school. These two factors significantly affected the school climate and physical environment.

Although the building was constructed to serve 2,000 students, at the time of the study, the school had fewer than 700 students enrolled. Faculty and staff estimated that approximately 500 students were present on an average school day. Observations revealed that although the average class size was around 25, class attendance typically was around 10 students on any given day. The vast physical space of building posed a challenge to the two security guards who patrolled the hallways for students skipping classes. Students often congregated in unmonitored areas inside the stairwells, along upper floors, and outside the building.

The school has a long history of poor academic performance and struggles to improve academic achievement in the face of an alarmingly high drop-out rate and test scores that are among the lowest in the state. The 4-year drop-out rate was 46% in 2000. In June of 2005, Jackson High graduated 33% of those students who matriculated as 9th graders in 2001, an increase from the previous graduating class that represented only 15% of those students who matriculated as 9th graders in 2000. By the end of our study, nearly two thirds of the 350 students who entered 9th grade in 2001 had drifted away.

However, despite these challenges, there existed a sense of "family" in the school, and students, staff, and faculty knew one another and greeted one another in the hallways. Additionally, at the time of our study, Jackson High was also in the midst of reforms to improve both its social climate and academic climate. Jackson High administration created Advanced Placement (AP) classes as part of their efforts to foster a more academic culture. Although AP classes were offered in several subjects, because most of the students were unprepared for AP material, the courses enrolled a broad range of achievement levels, and students were placed in the AP classes based on their potential rather than their past achievement. Very few students (only a handful in several years) have passed the AP exam; the AP situation illustrates the challenges Jackson High educators face in trying to boost academic expectations and experiences.

In many ways, the school constituted a unique and highly African American–centered cultural space. There was a high proportion of African American students and faculty in the school, and the faculty often initiated conversations with students about race and being African American. The school was deeply rooted in its historically African American neighborhood, such that many students came from families that had lived in East Baysville for generations and had parents and even grandparents who had attended Jackson. The main hallway was covered with a large mural depicting African and African American historical figures, and most of the office staff was African American.

This context was a particularly fruitful place to study contemporary African American and academic identities for several reasons. First, it was a school set in the heart of an urban neighborhood, and thus students were required to navigate a wide array of both local and societal identity challenges. Second, although students wrestled with such challenges, the school itself was relatively small and students were not subjected to the same kinds of depersonalization that has been described at large comprehensive high schools. Third, this institution was profoundly African American, with a long history in the African American community; it was a place where students would be less likely to encounter racial prejudice from students or teachers. Fourth, although historically low performing, the school was undergoing multiple reforms that sought to offer new opportunities for engaging academics. These characteristics made it a rich site to study students' experiences of connection and disconnection as well as the range of identities that African American students embraced.

Results

In this article, we explore the variations of African American racial identity meanings for African American students at Jackson High and the implications of these for achievement. In addressing these issues, we present both qualitative and quantitative findings. In the first section, we consider several cases that illustrate variations in African American racial identity meanings, how these meanings played out in classroom and school life, and their relation to academic achievement. We also examine how the social and institutional context of the school (as experienced by students) supported these configurations of racial identity meanings. In the second section, we bring quantitative data to bear on the variations in students' African American identity meanings and their relation to one another and explore how these relate to engagement and achievement in school.

Two Configurations of Racial and Academic Identity

Qualitative findings draw on observations, interviews, and focus groups, and show how students understood and expressed of the nature of their African American racial identities. In this section, we describe two versions of African American identity.[4] The first consists of a "thug" or "gangsta" identity and includes wearing popular clothing styles, speaking Ebonics, and not seeing one's African American identity as being connected to school. We call it a "street savvy"[5] African American identity. The other we call a "school-oriented and socially conscious" African American identity, and it involves being connected to school, community, and a cultural and historical legacy, and seeing oneself as a change agent and positive force in the community. It also includes wearing popular clothing styles and speaking Ebonics. We note that although we present these as distinct identity types, in reality, these aspects of identity might be conceptualized as particular configurations of possibilities available to students; for instance, a student might endorse some aspects of each of these or might even hold contradicting conceptions simultaneously. Later in the section, we consider two such students.

Students in both of the identity types we describe in this section consider themselves to be African American, though they differ as to what that means to them. They also differ in the level of critical thought about their racial identities—one type uncritically performs a racialized persona and the other constructs an African American identity as a product of a more thought-ful consideration of one's place in the world. Our purpose in presenting the cases that follow is not to argue that all students can be categorized in these ways but rather to illustrate the variation in the types of African American identities that students hold, how they play out in the lives of young people, and how they were linked to the social and institutional context of Jackson High School.

Street-Savvy African American Identity

In this version of African American identity, being African American meant being "gangsta" or being connected to "the street" or "the block."[6] It also included both the speaking of Ebonics and a clothing style that included baggy jeans, oversized T-shirts, and caps. In addition, this street-savvy identity was considered by some students to be antithetical to doing well in school or being a "nerd." This way of defining African American racial identity is most commonly represented in popular movies (e.g., *ATL, Freedom Writers*), music videos, and hip-hop and rap music (e.g., 50 cent, Too Short), especially those geared toward urban African American youth. This identity includes viewing African Americans as being drug dealers, pimps, and gangsters; not being well educated; and not caring about the law, citizenship, or their futures.

Claude, a sophomore at Jackson High School, typified this version of African American identity. Like many of his classmates, school for him was a place for social interaction rather than for intellectual development. Claude could often be found hanging out on campus instead of going to class, some-times shooting dice or chatting in the third floor hallway or near the gym.

Claude was born and raised by his grandmother in East Baysville. At 5'6", Claude was shorter than many of his peers. He hid his small frame beneath multiple layers of oversized T-shirts, jeans, and a yellow and black heavy leather coat that he wore daily and left on while in the school building. He was serious, and his light-brown skin had hints of acne. He had a reserved nature, but his timely interjections revealed that he was a very active listener during group conversations and had keen sense of when to speak in order to be heard. Claude only came to our sessions when his friend Zeus (a regular attendee) brought him. While Zeus was quite talkative, Claude spoke less often. He often needed to be coaxed into staying after he finished eating the free pizza offered at the start of each session. In general, he was relatively quiet as we discussed issues of teachers, school, administrators, and academics.

Claude clearly identified with the street life and joined the conversation only when the topic turned from school to discussions of "the block," drugs, or illegal activity. For instance, in one session, researchers introduced the idea of research assistants shadowing the youth participating in the study. A dis-cussion of what they do after school ensued. Claude (who had said very lit-tle the entire session) said loudly to the group that after school, he goes home to call his "PO" (probation officer). Then moments later, he repeated himself, "I call my PO and tell him I'm in the house." On this day and on others,

Claude persisted in positioning himself as "gangsta" and connected to "the block." Later in the session, the students were teasing one another, jokingly accusing one another of smoking "weed" (marijuana). There was friendly banter with students pointing fingers at one another, saying "You smoke weed," "No, you smoke weed." Claude shifted the conversation from playful accusations of others, to one about himself as he addressed another student "We was smoking and drinking together, huh, Chris?" Chris replied, "Yeah." In this comment, Claude took the opportunity to again position himself as "gangsta" and as a participant in illegal activities.

The social landscape of identifying with a gangsta lifestyle was observed to have an additional dimension among female students. Connie typified a female who secured her status as street savvy through her outlook and patterns of interaction, as well as through association with her boyfriend. At 16 years of age, Connie was a freshman at Jackson High School. She repeated fifth grade and after eighth grade, she was referred to a special district program for students with significant disruptive behaviors. Faculty described this additional year of remediation classes prior to entering high school as a "chance to catch up for kids who act-out and are not the school type." Several staff members also disclosed that they knew of Connie's long-term relationship with a high-profile drug dealer in the neighborhood, JD. He did not attend Jackson High, but had several family members who were students.

Connie was tall with a slender build and a rather fashionable general appearance. Like most of the other girls, she wore jeans often with color-coordinated sneakers, accessories, and tops. She did not have a large social network at Jackson High, in part because she did not enter with one of the local middle school cohorts. When Connie was introduced to research staff by a guidance counselor, he mentioned that Connie was "most known to the faculty because of her discipline problems." Connie laughed in response and then dismissively said, "What do they know!" During the first 5 months of school, Connie was suspended twice for fighting. The majority of Connie's peers from her block knew about her relationship with JD, though she did not openly discuss it during focus group sessions. In subsequent interviews, she disclosed that both of her fights involved female students whom she suspected of being jealous because "They always tryin' to get at me. JD's with me, but I know what they want. He ain't like these fake niggas up in here [Jackson High]." When probed further about what these girls wanted, she explained, "He gets paid and they want to roll with him like I do; for him to buy them all kinds of, well, I don't know, whatever they want." Connie did not boast about these fights but was confident that she did what was necessary to defend her relationship.

Claude, on the other hand, made sure that others knew he was knowledgeable about street activities. For instance, during one session, he looked around the room and noting the clothing of another student, declared, "He got all that blue on, he's a Crip. He be a gang banger." This statement turned the conversation to fighting and gun play on the street, during which Claude told the group, "I fight. I had a fight on Friday." He went on to make the argument that people don't often fight with their fists anymore and that guns are the preferred method of combat.

These portrayals of himself as "gangsta" were not lost on the other students. By the end of the session, students were engaged in a heated debate about selling drugs, with Claude and Zeus arguing strongly for merits of drug selling and corner life as a viable lifestyle, and another student, Victor, arguing strongly against it. Claude expressed the sentiment that life is not long and that you never know when you will die; thus, the fact that drug dealing is a short-term career that could end in death did not concern him. He said, "Well, I only got one life to live and I'm gonna make it fun," and "I don't wanna get really old." By the end of the session, he explicitly discussed drug dealing as a potential career for himself. In a consideration of the options available to him, Claude stated, "If I don't go to college I ain't gonna be flippin' no burgers." Another student asked, "So what are you going to do?" He responded, "I'm gonna be pushin' 500 Ki's, pushin' Ki's" (meaning selling drugs—kilos of cocaine). This proposal was challenged by Victor, who argued that selling drugs is easy but managing a drug operation is more difficult. He posed mathematical questions to Claude and Zeus about selling drugs (e.g., How many grams come in a Ki?) that they couldn't answer. Claude retreated and declared, "I'm gonna be a pimp when I get older. That's quick money. Yeah, that's easier than selling drugs." Through such statements, Claude continually positioned himself as an insider to street life, and he seemed to take pride in this sense of himself as cool, reckless, and tough.

In another session, students watched *Paid in Full*, a movie about a young man who starts out as a good student and son and becomes a drug dealer. The movie ends badly and is intended as a cautionary tale about street life. Our goal in showing this film was to spark conversation about life choices and the role of school in one's life. To our surprise, though the film was relatively obscure, Claude and Zeus had already seen it and told us that it was their favorite movie and they watched it at home regularly. As the movie played, they recited the characters' lines by heart. Connie also embraced the film's mixed messages. She enthusiastically engaged in conversations about the three female characters: the girlfriend of the senior drug dealer, the mother of the main character, and his younger sister. In a discussion following one scene where the girlfriend of the dealer helps him with packaging the drugs, Connie was adamant that the character had made the wrong decision. She repeated several times, "I would have said no. I would not do it." Although Connie had admitted earlier to regularly smoking marijuana, she used this instance to make it clear that she was not willing to participate in its distribution. She became visibly annoyed at the male students (Claude and Zeus in particular) who supported the girlfriend's decision to assist. In the session 2 weeks prior to this focus group, Connie was the first participant to justify the younger sister's decision to date a drug dealer, stating, "She want money." The other female participants were more accusatory and described the sister as lazy. Connie withdrew from the conversation as the other females continued to criticize the sister and the mother for accepting money for groceries from the boyfriend's drug sales. Like the character in the film, Connie's mother was raising her as a single parent. An office coordinator at the school who knew Connie's mother well said that she was supportive of her daughter's relationship despite the 10-year age difference and JD's criminal involvements. He believed that Connie's boyfriend was helping to financially support their family.

An important aspect of the thug or gangsta identity has to do with community. Claude and Zeus saw drug dealing not just as a viable way to make money but also as occurring within a social network with which they were familiar. Drug dealing, getting arrested, and even being shot were described by Claude and Zeus as "putting in work" for the block and thus being accountable and giving to their community.

We should note that Claude and Connie (and other students who subscribed to a street-savvy definition of being African American) rarely mentioned race explicitly. Might this mean that this identity for them was not racialized? Possibly. But we would argue that Claude's identity as a gangsta and Connie's identity as a girlfriend of a gangsta were highly racialized and reflect the versions of African American racial identity that are available to them in the local African American community (his block), in the school, and in the mainstream media. Connie and Claude and his group of friends commonly used the word "nigga"[7] to refer to themselves and others. The common use of this word as a self-identifier supports the notion that the gangsta identity was racialized, even if the students who endorsed it didn't articulate it as such. Race is also implied in Claude and Connie's identification with "the block" (i.e., their neighborhood) in that in this city, neighborhoods are segregated by race, such that Claude and Connie's neighborhood is almost entirely African American. The lack of explicit discussion about race may also reflect that this street-savvy identity was often less the product of thought and reflection and more a process of embracing a persona.

Indeed, although students who endorsed a gangsta identity rarely identified it as African American explicitly, other students openly articulated their struggles with "gangsta" as one of multiple competing definitions of African American–ness in their local context. One such student was Victor (who argued with Claude about drug dealing above). After attending a focus group where we talked explicitly with students about what it meant for them to be African American, Victor pulled us aside to express the tension he felt in trying to be African American in a way that fit with his perception of what his peer group thought. Victor felt that his peers thought that being African American was about being "hard," being "on the block," wearing particular kinds of clothes, and speaking Ebonics. Later, he said that he didn't really believe that, but he found himself endorsing it to fit in. Victor, despite being a strong student, later dropped out of school, as did both Claude and Zeus. Connie was expelled. In a more nuanced analysis than Victor's, Connie also articulated an awareness of the variance among her definitions of being African American. In testifying to the authenticity of her boyfriend's gangsta status, she would often juxtapose him with the males at her school who she dismissively described as "stupid niggas," "fake niggas," and most frequently as "fake gangstas." Her status as "girlfriend of a gangsta" was dependent on a perception that the intelligence and realness of her boyfriend's racialized identity involved being on the block and participating in the illegal dealings that had earned him his reputation.

Thus far, we have focused on perceptions that Claude and Connie had of themselves in the context of community, but less so within the context of school. For Claude, the academic side of school was simply outside of the scope of his definition of himself. Indeed, Claude rarely attended his classes, never carried a pencil or backpack, and did not join any conversation in our focus groups that had to do with school or the classroom. Although Connie attended the majority of her classes—70% for the first semester, which was above the student average—she was noticeably disengaged on most occasions. Like several other students in her classes, she was frequently observed sitting with her head down. Both of Connie's major physical altercations with other girls happened in the classroom.

In part, Claude and Connie taking up this street-savvy identity may be related to the identities they were offered access to in their neighborhood and at school. That is, the presence of this gangsta identity and the absence of a positive school identity are both supported by the school and classroom contexts in which Claude and Connie participated. One way that this gangsta identity (and the lack of importance attributed to school) was made available in the school context was by what we came to call the "two schools" phenomenon. At Jackson High, students experienced two very different school contexts. One school context offered students higher than average academic standards, viewed students as capable and college bound, provided a prevalence of information about college, and incorporated students in the leadership of the school. Another school context (the one Claude and Connie attended) provided students with little academic content and little information about college or even their own academic standing and requirements to graduate. These two schools coexisted in the same building and were not formally different schools. Rather, they were two different pathways for students within the same school. Students varied in their understanding and knowledge of these two tracks within the school, and there were some students that moved between classes from one track and classes from another track. The AP track was relatively small, consisting of approximately 5% to 10% of the student population.

The second school that was a part of Claude and Connie's daily reality was a place where students were largely invisible, where academic work was not demanded, and where students were allowed to fail. Students like Claude and Connie did not have access to information about graduation or college. As we noted, Claude spent most of his time during the school day wandering the hallways, in the bathroom, and socializing with friends in unmonitored areas around campus. Although Connie skipped class less frequently than Claude, her openly hostile relationship with school staff left her just as disconnected.

When they did attend class, Claude, Connie, and their peers in this "second school" experienced poor or nonexistent teaching in many of the classes, for example, in the music class where students watched popular culture movies every day, or the Spanish class where there was a long-term substitute who rarely conducted lessons and who spoke Portuguese but not Spanish. As we noted, issues of attendance plagued this second school and teacher absenteeism was also quite high; students complained that teachers were not there to teach them. The gym and the hallways were the most popular gathering spots for students in this second school who were cutting class. Physical education was scheduled as a double period class that made monitoring student attendance difficult and rarely attempted. Although the physical education instructor typically had 50 to 60 students on the roster, there was often about 30 additional students among the group. The students not registered to attend the class would sit among the others in the bleachers and/or roam the area socializing. On one occasion, an administrator entered the gym with the intention of sending the "cutters" back to their assigned classrooms. Connie was among the students instructed to leave the gym, but she was actually assigned to the class for that period. Connie began a verbal argument with the administrator and was sent to the principal's office. She continued using a loud tone with the principal and was informed that she was being suspended. Staff who witnessed the exchange reported that Connie's aggression escalated, and as a male staff member tried to restrain her, the principal stepped in between them. In the altercation, Connie hit the principal. Following a series of disciplinary appeal hearings in which two faulty members and Connie's mother spoke in her defense, she was expelled from Jackson High just before the end of her freshman year. At the time of the incident, Connie was 4 months pregnant with her first child, JD's third.

The hallways constituted another place of constant movement and activity. In one hallway on the third floor, gambling and marijuana were common during school hours. Claude was a regular participant in these activities, and his peer group consisted of others who also participated in these activities on the school grounds as well as other illegal activities outside of the school. Thus, the school context supported Claude's identity as a "gangsta" and Connie's identity as a "girlfriend of a gangsta" who did not participate in intellectual or academic activities—perhaps in part because they were not offered opportunities to high-quality instruction or to engage in a community of learners in a classroom.

In some ways, our presentation of these two students is stereotypical and confirms much of the media portrayals of urban youth. However, this consistency between Claude and Connie's self-portrayal and the media images of African American urban youth is an interesting point. It may be that such stereotypical portrayals do reflect the experience of some portion of the population. However, it may also be that Claude and Connie are taking up an African American racial identity that is made available to them both locally (on the block), in the school, and in society more broadly.

School-Oriented and Socially Conscious African American Identity

Students who embraced this version of African American identity were also deeply connected to their communities, but their conception of what their community was and what that commitment meant was different. These students held an African American identity that included a strong connection to the local, national, and historical African American community and a sense of oneself as a potential change agent in that community. This identity also included a sense of oneself as a student.

Consider Alonzo. Alonzo was an 18-year-old senior in high school, born and raised in East Baysville. He was tall and slender, with dark skin, a short haircut, and a ready smile. He carried himself with a confidence that fit his position in the school; he was student body president, school board student representative, salutatorian with a 3.7 GPA, newspaper editor, and contributing member of the football and track teams. Alonzo dressed in the clothing styles typical in his high school and in the African American community—large T-shirts and baggy jeans—and listened to popular hip-hop and R&B music. On several occasions, Alonzo wore oversized T-shirts or sweatshirts bearing the logos of local universities. When talking to friends (and sometimes in class), he often used Ebonics.

For Alonzo, his community included his family, the East Baysville community, and the African American community, locally, nationally, and historically. This sense of community is reflected in the way he framed his family's connection to Jackson High. He said during an interview, "There's a rich family history here [at Jackson]. My grandmother went here and my grandfather, my aunties and uncles." His senior project (a research paper mandatory for graduation) documented the history of African Americans in the city of Baysville. On one of our first encounters with him, Alonzo gave our research staff a guided tour of his evolving portfolio, pointing out pictures of Jackie Robinson and other historical African American figures with a sense of expertise and pride. In an interview, he told us that he aspired to be the mayor of Baysville after completing his undergraduate and graduate education.

Similarly, Adrienne was ranked in the top five of her class and had taken 7 AP classes by her senior year. Her mature demeanor and booming voice, combined with her tall height and heavy-set frame, made her appear older than she was, though her candor, high energy, and curiosity was quite fitting for her 17 years. She often wore jeans and T-shirts bearing African-centered slogans or college logos.

Like Alonzo, Adrienne took initiative over her learning. In class, she was the first to raise her hand and asked clarification questions when she didn't understand. Her English teacher described her as, "the type of person who is willing to push herself to academic success." She aspired to be a child psychologist—an interest that was sparked by her experience in a peer educator program. She also planned to write inspirational books for youth, to encourage people, she said. "Just being in the East Baysville community. . . life is hard. It's hard at home, and it's hard at school. I just want to speak to people and help young people understand that I know it's hard but you have to have a positive outlook." Thus, Adrienne, like Alonzo, aspired to be a positive change agent in East Baysville and saw herself as a part of this community.

Although Adrienne said that she has always been self-motivated, Alonzo noted that he didn't always hold such lofty goals. He said that in ninth and tenth grade,

> I thought all I wanted to do was play basketball. Yet my mind sort of shifted because I [pause] . . . I used to want to go to the NBA and stuff, and I had my other dreams I wanted that were like in-the-closet dreams, though. I knew what I wanted to do. I knew I wanted to write. I knew I liked politics. I knew . . . I knew that I wanted to do those things, but I was kind of. . . I kind of got stuck in a dream of being an NBA player. Because you know, its hard, society pushes black kids . . . that's all you can do. That's all you can do.

In this reflection, Alonzo articulated both a change for him over time in his goals but also the way that society "pushes" African American youth into particular pathways, such as sports, perhaps referring to prevalent stereotypes about African American students. Alonzo decided instead to pursue writing and politics through his involvement in school organizations such as student government and the school newspaper.

Observations on multiple occasions indicated the congruence of Alonzo's racial and academic selves. For instance, one morning Alonzo attended an English class where the teacher was not present. He explained to researchers that the teacher was proctoring the AP English exam and that students were to work on their senior projects. Twelve students came to class and sat down to work independently. The students turned on the radio, put in a hip-hop CD, and talked to one another while they worked. The conversation took place almost entirely in Ebonics, and occasionally a student danced a little to the music. Alonzo and two friends (all African American males) sat at a table together. One of the students said, "I can't concentrate with it that loud," and turned down the music a bit. At one point, their conversation turned to the topic of filling out scholarship applications.

The three students (Alonzo and two friends) discussed how they considered filling out scholarships a good use of time. One student said, "If you'll give me $2,000 to write an essay, I'll have it to you the next day." They updated each other on the scholarships they were currently working on. A joke sprouted up when Alonzo accused another student of "side dealin'." "*Side dealin'*" is a term that Alonzo invented, and it meant applying for a scholarship but not bringing it to the attention of your friends. This would theoretically increase your individual chances of receiving the money without competition, but it was viewed as a negative influence on the overall welfare of the group. They also used this word in the context of a teacher who only gave scholarship opportunities to some students at the expense of others. This term illustrates the incorporation of Alonzo's racial/cultural identity and his academic identity in that he created a slang term to talk about an academic subject, applying for scholarships. Interestingly, the term sounds like the term "drug dealin'" used to describe street activity.

Alonzo viewed himself as a part of the historical legacy of his family and the African American community and wanted to make his community a more positive place (this is what motivated his aspirations toward becoming mayor). He knew that drug dealing existed as an option in his community but saw those who chose that path as followers. In an interview, he said, "I consider people who sell drugs to be followers. A lot of people who sell drugs just doing it because they come from East Baysville, they may have seen their brother or uncle or dad doing it, so then they want to do it." Adrienne expressed similar views about the impact of drugs in her community. In response to viewing the same movie where Zeus and Claude celebrated the drug-dealing activities of the central characters, Adrienne was quite critical. She and Alonzo challenged the drug dealers' motives in "frontin' money" to family members and neighbors. Adrienne suggested, "But if you think about it, he's not really even giving back to the community because his profit is coming from him, making the community go down. Selling all them drugs to all those people." She expressed a similar disdain when commenting on other students who were not making the most of the educational opportunities at Jackson High. In a session where Adrienne identified the positive and negative aspects of the school, she highlighted students in the hallway during class and linked the school's attendance problems to reductions in funding for various advanced and elective classes.

Thus, Adrienne and Alonzo (and his friends) embraced a definition of what it meant to be African American that incorporated both a commitment to community that drew on a rich cultural history and a commitment to their own education. This congruence was more than just a fluid moving back and forth between conflicting identities or seeing two identities as compatible; it was a bending of identities, such that one implied the other. Because they viewed being African American as being committed to the positive development of family and community, a strong academic identity became a part of their racial identity.

The academic success that Alonzo and his friends and Adrienne found at Jackson High did not come at the expense of being "cool" or belonging. Indeed, Alonzo was very much at the social center of the school community and had a wide range of friends and associates. Similarly, when Adrienne walked down the hall, the walk was peppered with hugs and hellos from friends as well as from teachers and administrators. Other students in this group also played sports or were cheerleaders or were otherwise quite active on the campus social scene. As we noted, both Alonzo and Adrienne spoke Ebonics and wore the typical popular styles of clothing, though sometimes with African-centered slogans or college logos on the T-shirts. These styles were common for students that fit this identity type. Although Alonzo and Adrienne were central to the Jackson High social scene, they were in different friendship groups than Connie and Claude. Although they were not considered "nerds," they may not have been considered "cool" by Claude and Connie's social group, due to a different set of norms and expectations for behavior.

Late in the spring of his senior year, Alonzo was accepted to a prestigious university in the local area for the following fall. This outcome was celebrated by the administration and others in the school community. Adrienne and two of her classmates were admitted to the same university the following year.

Alonzo and Adrienne's identity as both racially conscious and strong students was supported by the schooling and classroom environments that they participated in. Alonzo and Adrienne attended the "first school." This school created a very different set of experiences and opportunities for identity construction than the "second school" that Claude and Connie attended.

Alonzo was identified early in his high school career as a student who had potential and was placed in the more academic, informal AP track. Adrienne, too, was placed in the AP track by her counselor in the 9th grade. While she acknowledged that AP was open to a range of students, she clearly considered herself a strong student. She said, "This year, they put a lot more people in AP that weren't ready for it. I think they just did it because Jackson was getting so much bad publicity. They were saying stuff about how we don't have a lot of AP classes and that students weren't really succeeding." As juniors and again as seniors, both Alonzo and Adrienne had access (and a key) to the "college room,"[8] as well as information about college and scholarships. Students in the AP track had close relationships with teachers that centered on academic mentoring, and such relationships were purposely created (in the form of an informal mentoring program) by faculty to support students' academic achievement. In the spring of her junior year, Adrienne was approached by the teacher who also volunteered as the school's scholarship liaison. She arranged for Adrienne to meet with the admissions outreach representative from the local university. This information was not distributed by the guidance office, nor did the counselors offer coaching in how to prepare applications. Adrienne and a small group of her peers at the top of their class met regularly with this teacher to draft their college essays and share information about local scholarship opportunities. Those who formed these close relationships with staff early in their academic careers, most often through the summer program or through developing personal connections with staff, were placed in upper-level courses. As one student reflected:

> The AP classes here are different from any other school in the sense that a lot of African American students don't have the chance to say I want to be in AP classes . . . to just say I want to be in there so I'm going to be in there. In a lot of other places, students have to go through a lot of tests and everything just to get into an AP class. Whereas [at Jackson] if he wanted to be in AP English they would have been able to get in. So I told my friends about it.

Thus, the AP track was used as a way to create experiences that supported both academic development and identities for students. For those on the AP leadership track, the school was a place where they could feel good about being students.

The teachers who taught AP courses were largely African American, and the content of the AP history class often touched on issues of African American history. In this way, students were encouraged to tie their developing academic knowledge to a cultural history of African Americans. Thus, for Alonzo and Adrienne, there were resources in the school context available to support the identity of a racial identity linked to history and school success.

Other Variations on These Two African American Identity Types

Thus far, we have described two ideal-type African American identities. In this section, we consider students who do not fit clearly into either ideal-type but who display aspects of each. Victor, whom we saw earlier as he argued with Claude about the viability of drug dealing as a lifestyle, is one such student. Victor was tall, with a slim, muscular build. His hair was twisted into the beginnings of locs, and he usually wore jeans and a button-down shirt. He had a confident air about him, and he enjoyed conversation, debate, and ideas. He was quick to share an interesting theory about why many students at Jackson High weren't doing well or about why Black people needed to be more connected to their history. He had a ready smile and related well to his peers across many social groups and achievement levels. Although his father was in and out of jail, he spoke fondly of their relationship and seemed to spend a significant amount of time with him.

He had a long history of participation in community-based programs (at one point, he was chosen as the school's representative in a national leadership conference) and often expressed strong, socially conscious opinions. One example of this, as we noted, was his argument with Claude. He credited his critiques of the social context and of the school to conversations with his father. In discussions, Victor often criticized both schools and societal structures. He regularly challenged teachers in class and was highly critical of what he felt was substandard teaching. In an interview, he describes the teachers that he has encountered, "Instead of trying to make sure you're on your task, they'll kind of give up on you. They'll base you on a stereotype, already thinking like 'you're going to fail, so get out of my class' type of thing."

Victor talked explicitly about feeling pressured by his social context to embrace a street-savvy identity, yet found it to be incompatible with his social consciousness. In one interaction during class, Victor was talking to a girl whose family immigrated to the United States from Ethiopia. After revealing that she was from Africa, she quickly (and defensively) asked him not to make fun of her because she is African. Victor responded, "I'm black! Why would I make fun of Africa?!" Victor clearly saw being African American in conflicting ways. On one hand, he saw it as positive—something to be proud of. On the other hand, he articulated a race-based perspective of the odds he would face as a minority in the United States. He said,

> Coming to Jackson, I'm well aware of where I stand as a Black man. I'm well aware of the chances that I've been given and what I'm deprived from, who I have to compete against. I haven't had the best of academics.

Academically, Victor was also somewhat in between the two schools. Early in his high school career, Victor described himself as academically strong. He was placed in many AP and other high-level classes, including AP English, chemistry, advanced algebra, and trigonometry. His peer group was wide ranging, but he saw himself as a part of the more academically successful group of students. His GPA in 9th and 10 grades were 2.8 and 2.9, respectively. In our initial interactions with him when he was a junior, he identified himself as different from the lower-achieving students in his focus group, though one or two of them were his friends. His class attendance, while not impeccable, was very good by Jackson High standards (75% for the random week we sampled). His goal was to attend a local university and major in architecture, and he maintained strong ties with an academically oriented social network.

As a senior, he still maintained higher than average attendance, though he missed an average of 20 class sessions from each of his classes over the course of the year. His participation (both in school activities and in the classroom), however, became more marginal. For instance, in one observation, he went to all of his classes, but sat at a table away from his peers and either put his head down or made conversation with the researcher (asking her to teach him vocabulary words). Despite the drop in his engagement in his senior year, he was transferred from regular history to AP history. By November, he was critical of the institution for transferring him into AP without the support he felt he needed to be successful and became discouraged academically. He said, "I gave up, but I don't want to fail so I just float by . . . At the end of the day, I felt like I was still stupid. So why feel stupid when you can be stupid? So that's what I'm doing." His GPA dropped to 1.8, his critiques of the structural inefficiencies of the school intensified, and he began to express disenchantment with school as a means to a future. Furthermore, perhaps in part due to not being successful in AP history, he no longer felt that he belonged in the AP track social network. During this time, he described himself as markedly different and less smart than Adrienne.

Although Victor was caught between his past performance as a strong student and a future he was unsure about, Terry was similarly caught between a student identity and a street-savvy identity. Terry was a fair-skinned African American girl with a clear, strong voice. She often wore a terry-cloth sweatsuit with her straight hair pulled back into a ponytail or bun and fashionable glasses. One of her teachers described her as possessing a maturity beyond her age, which may have stemmed from her troubled childhood. Both of her parents were addicted to drugs, and she herself was heavily into drug use as a 9th and 10th grader. An administrator says of Terry, "Any bad thing you can think of that can happen to a female teenager in the inner-city, it has happened to Terry. She dabbled in prostitution. She's been raped."

When asked what her teachers would say about her academic performance, Terry stated that they would say "that I've improved." She reported having difficult freshman and sophomore years but was adamant about being a successful student as a junior and senior. As a senior, she said, "I'm on the honor roll for the second marking period. I'm in my second year of foreign language. I'm in American Government and Econ, Math, and English 4. I'm focused on keeping my grades up." Terry's commitment to academics was also evident in our observations of her. She repeatedly demonstrated her commitment to her schoolwork, working on problem sets or Spanish translations, even when other students were not paying attention, and demanding help from teachers when she didn't understand. When other students were late to class or were disruptive, Terry scolded them and reminded them of her desire to learn. She prided herself on the way that she took initiative over her own learning and reported that she not only kept up with her schoolwork but that she also knew how many units she had and what classes she needed to graduate. At times, she left classes that she viewed as being unproductive to complete work for other classes. Due to her poor academic history, Terry, like Victor, had a foot in both "schools." Her closest mentors at school were not teachers of academic subjects but were the attendance clerk and a study skills teacher. She was enrolled in a couple of AP courses but did not see the students or teachers there as central to her social circle.

Like Connie, Terry also became pregnant when she was a senior. Her boyfriend, too, was a local drug dealer and gangster, though he was not older than she. Terry saw herself as street savvy and was connected to the streets both by virtue of her own personal history and through her boyfriend and others in her social circle. Like Connie, Terry also encountered physical and verbal altercations from other girls whom she perceived to be jealous of her relationship.

While at school, Terry was single-mindedly focused on her academic work; outside of school, conversations with her friends drifted to events and people in the local neighborhood (most of whom she reported had dropped out of school). In one observation, Terry was discussing a local shooting that had occurred over the Thanksgiving break. When asked if she knew the gunman, Terry laughed and answered, "Yeah I know him, but when the police come around, I don't." In another conversation, Terry expressed resentment at being compared to another student who is pregnant but who hasn't faced the difficulties that she has. She said, "Me and Hope have two different situations. First of all, my momma don't buy me [designer jeans and sneakers] . . . I been on my own since I was 12. Don't nobody give me nothin'." While Terry clearly viewed herself as street savvy, she also saw the hard side of street life. Nonetheless, her drug dealer boyfriend was a source of status for Terry, both at school and in the neighborhood.

Like Victor, Terry held a critical perspective on her access to resources by virtue of the opportunities that she had been afforded in her neighborhood and at Jackson High. In a discussion that occurred when Terry and six other Jackson students were on a visit to a local university campus, Terry tearfully acknowledged that she likely would never have access to such a beautiful and well-resourced campus and that being there made her feel frustrated and angry at the paucity of resources in her school and community.

These profiles of Terry and Victor illustrate the fluidity and variation in the categories of African American racial identity that we have identified. Their stories also reinforce the point that these identities are related to students' experiences at school and the opportunities that are afforded to them there, in addition to the identity choices they take up and challenge both locally and from the broader society. Both Terry and Victor had some (but not full) access to opportunities for participation in academics. Both held critical social views, yet did not share the sense of hope and personal responsibility for social change as did Alonzo and Adrienne. For Victor, this took the form of critique and embracing a connection to the African American community but not proactive action. Terry understood how racial and social stratification imposed limitations for her, but she also remained deeply connected to her street-savvy "girlfriend of a gangster" identity.

Discussion

This discussion of these two identity types brings to the fore several important issues. First, these data highlight that similar to other recent studies of urban, African American students (i.e., Carter, 2005; Oyserman et al., 2001), Alonzo and Adrienne did not have to act White to succeed academically. Rather, they were able to maintain a strong sense of themselves as a part of an historical legacy of African Americans and draw on that to support their academic achievement. Furthermore, they did not have give up being cool to succeed academically. In fact, Alonzo and his small circle of high-achieving friends as well as Adrienne were highly involved in the local school community and participated in student government, the school newspaper, as well as sports and peer tutoring. They were friendly with other high-achieving students as well as with low-achieving students, and Adrienne and Alonzo saw themselves as people who were "cool with" everyone at the school. They had wide friendship networks and were well liked across achievement levels. These data suggest that not only were Alonzo and Adrienne able to blend both strong school identities and strong racial identities but also that their identification with school became a part of their definition of what it meant to be African American.

Second, findings show that African American speech and clothing styles were not related to orientation toward school. All of the students consistently used Ebonics; listened to rap, R&B, and hip-hop music; and wore the latest urban clothing styles. However, school-oriented/socially conscious students often wore slogans or logos that expressed an Afrocentric perspective or were linked to colleges.

Third, it is important to remember that the identities that all of the students expressed were supported and made available to them in the local community and school contexts. In part, Alonzo and Adrienne were able to maintain a definition of being African American that included high achievement and racial consciousness because they were in a local school context where the majority of the student body was African American and where they were not required to choose between being African American and being high achievers. At Jackson High, students didn't need to straddle two cultures because it was an inherently African American institution. Related to this is the fact that Alonzo was a part of a small group of peers that supported one another in their definition of African American racial identity as well as in the practical aspects of school, such as scholarship and college applications.

Fourth, the findings that street-savvy youth were less aware of themselves racially and what that means in a social, political, and historical context further underscores the relation between racial and academic selves in this study. Although Alonzo and Adrienne were aware of local and national history of African Americans and saw themselves as potential positive agents for change in their community, Claude and Connie did not display an interest in or knowledge of African American history, though they did use the racialized term "nigga" with great frequency. This may confirm findings in the literature that shows that Afrocentric identities are protective and supportive of school success (Spencer et al., 2001). However, Terry and Victor's stories indicate that a social critique of a racialized society alone did not necessarily support school success or sustained positive engagement. A critical component of a positive racial identity may be a personal sense of agency and responsibility for supporting community uplift.

Findings also illustrate that all students were connected to their communities; however, they defined those communities quite differently. Alonzo's and Adrienne's communities included their families, school community, and the local and national African American community. Claude's and Connie's communities were defined by their block or neighborhood, which coincided with a particular drug turf. And although all of these students were committed to their communities, that commitment meant something different too. For Alonzo and Adrienne, it meant finding ways to improve the quality of living for all in the community, For Claude and Connie, it meant "putting in work," putting oneself at risk for the profit of others on the block, and being loyal to others on the block.

Finally, these divergent identities were not constructed in a vacuum; rather, they reflected the types of learning experiences that students had access to and the opportunities they were afforded. Thus, these identity choices on the part of youth were grounded in their experiences in school environments. Alonzo and Adrienne were offered a school context that affirmed the importance of the cultural history of African Americans and gave them multiple messages about the possibility of their academic success and college attendance. Claude and Connie, on the other hand, were not offered such opportunities to develop a sense of their academic possibilities and did not experience high-quality teaching or high expectations. Victor and Terry experienced aspects of each of the two schools. Such findings confirm the already strong literature on the negative effects of tracking (Gamoran, 1987; Oakes, 2005).

Survey Findings

The two identity types we described in the first part of this article consisted of several dimensions that we examined separately in our survey. In this section, we draw on our survey findings to examine the extent to which students' answers to the survey confirm the findings on racial identity and academic achievement that our qualitative data revealed. We consider five dimensions of African American racial identity meanings (all of which were present in various ways in the profiles we presented): (a) history: understanding the history of African Americans; (b) positive school: expressing behaviors and beliefs that support school success; (c) negative school: expressing behaviors and beliefs that do not support school success; (d) personal style: wearing a particular clothing style, listening or rap or hip-hop music, and using a Ebonics; and (e) gangsta: expressing behaviors and beliefs that support a gangster persona.

We explore the range of racial identity meanings that students endorsed on the survey, how they related to one another, and how they related to school achievement and engagement. We illustrate that confirming the qualitative data, the quantitative findings illustrate that there were multiple ways students conceptualized what it meant for them to be African American and that some aspects of these definitions related in systematic ways to other aspects as well as to academic achievement and engagement.

Variations in Students African American Racial Identity Meanings

Our first analysis examines the degree to which African American students embraced the five African American racial identity meanings (see Figure 1).

Figure 1 shows the mean proportion of male and female students that endorsed each category of racial identity meaning (of the times that it was possible to do so). Students most often endorsed understanding history (male 75%, female 64%) and positive school (male 40%, female 40%). Students moderately endorsed personal style (male 31%, female 23%), and they less often endorsed negative school (male 14%, female 7%) and gangsta persona (male 23%, female 7%). A one-way gender (male, female) on African American racial identity meanings (five dependent variables: history, positive school, personal style, negative school, gangsta persona) ANOVA revealed that while male students chose each at a slightly higher rate than female students, gender differences were only significant for gangsta persona ($df = 1$, $F = 4.22$, $p = .04$).

Relation Between the Five African American Identity Meanings

Our next analysis focused on how these five aspects of African American identity related to one another. In other words, were students who endorsed some of these meanings more or less likely to endorse others? More specifically, in a sample larger than our case studies, would we find

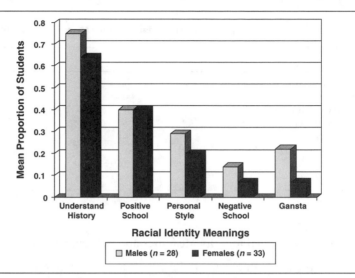

Figure 1. **Mean proportion of male and female students choosing the five racial identity meanings.**

that students who endorsed a definition of being African American as being "gangsta" also view being African American as having a negative conception of school? Conversely, would students who held a definition of being African American that included a connection to African American history also view being African American as being positively connected to school? We conducted bivariate correlations to explore how these five different identity meanings were correlated to one another (see Table 1). (Only significant correlations are shown in the table. Data are collapsed across gender here, as there were no significant differences between male and female students).

Findings indicate that students who felt that understanding their history was what it meant to be African American also thought that being African American meant expressing behaviors and beliefs that support school success (consistent with the profiles of Alonzo and Adrienne). Students who thought that being African American meant being "gangsta" also thought that it meant expressing behaviors and beliefs that did not support school success (similar to Connie and Claude). Most students thought that being African American meant to have a particular personal style and language practice—this identity meaning correlated significantly with positive school, negative school, and gangsta persona. This finding indicates that the degree to which students endorse popular urban clothing, music, and language styles did not distinguish between those who also endorsed positive school from those who endorsed negative school. It confirms the qualitative finding that students across identity types wore similar clothing and engaged in similar language practices.

Table 1
Correlations Among African American Identity Meanings (*N* = 61)

	I	II	III	IV	V
Type of African American Identity Meaning					
I. Understanding history	—				
II. Positive school	.35**	—			
III. Personal style	—	.29*	—		
IV. Negative school	—	—	.48**	—	
V. Gansta persona	—	—	.74**	.74**	—
M	.69	.40	.27	.11	.15
SD	.47	.41	.37	.29	.30

*$p < .05$. **$p < .01$.

Relation Between Racial Identity Meanings and Achievement Outcomes

Next, we explore the relation between these African American identity meanings and achievement. In general, we wanted to find out if endorsing the positive school or the negative school clusters had any relation to academic achievement or academic identity. We conducted linear regression analyses to examine the extent to which students' endorsements of the racial identity meanings predicted their achievement and academic identity. Again, as there were no significant differences between male and female students when these analyses were run separately, the data are reported collapsed across gender groups. Findings showed that students' endorsements of the racial identity meanings on the survey did not significantly predict academic identity nor significantly predict achievement. However, students' endorsement of the racial identity meaning "positive school" on achievement did approach significance, $b = .391$, $t(59) = 1.77$, $p = .08$, though this accounted for only a small proportion of the variance ($R^2 = .036$). These findings did not fully support our qualitative findings—in the qualitative data, students who embraced African American history and positive associations with school were also higher achieving.

However, analyses of individual items on the survey relating to school engagement did show significant relations with the African American identity meanings. Specifically, bivariate correlations showed that having an African American identity meaning of expressing behaviors and beliefs that support success in school (positive school) was mildly and negatively correlated with both coming late to class, $r(59) = -.270$, $p < .05$, and coming to class unprepared, $r(59) = -.277$, $p = .05$. Having an African American identity meaning of expressing behaviors and beliefs that do not support success in school (negative school) was negatively correlated with feeling comfortable talking to teachers about one's problems, $r(59) = -.255$, $p < .05$. This finding mildly supports the qualitative findings on the relationship between achievement and beliefs about school.

Furthermore, when regression analyses were conducted separately for students with high ethnic identity and students with low ethnic identity (using a mean split), findings showed that positive school predicted achievement for students with high ethnic identity, $b = .825$, $t(59) = 2.26$, $p = .03$, but not for students with low ethnic identity. This finding reinforces the qualitative findings that identifying with one's ethnic group may support academic achievement. Additionally, bivariate correlations showed that ethnic identity was significantly correlated with academic identity, $r(59) = .254$, $p < .05$.

Discussion

These data illustrate four critical points with respect to the racial identity meanings of the African American students in our sample. First, African American students endorsed a range of racial identity meanings—that is, they varied in what they felt it meant to be African American. Students were most likely to endorse African American racial identity meanings that included understanding the history of their group and doing well in school, not surprising as these are more socially desirable. Students were moderately likely to endorse meanings that incorporated personal style such as aspects of language and clothing. Students were least likely to endorse racial identity meanings that included doing poorly in school or being a gangster. Girls were less likely than boys to choose "gangsta" as an aspect of their racial identities.

Second, students' choices of these African American racial identity meanings tended to be grouped, such that when students chose "negative school," they were also likely to choose "gangsta." Similarly, students who chose "positive school" were more likely to choose "understanding history." Furthermore, personal style grouped with three other racial identity meanings: positive school, negative school, and gangsta. In other words, both students who endorsed positive school and those who endorsed negative school also felt that their language and clothing styles were an aspect of their African American racial identity. These findings supported the qualitative findings that aspects of students' African American identities clustered into identity types, such that students with a sense of connection to African American history also tended to view being African American as being positively connected to school and students who viewed being "gangsta" as a part of being African American also tended to view being African American as having a negative relation with school.

Findings showed less support for a relation between most of these racial identity meaning choices and achievement and did not fully confirm our qualitative findings. The "positive school" African American identity meaning did predict achievement, but only for students who were highly identified with their ethnic identity. This finding was interesting, given the qualitative data that showed a positive perspective of school as being clustered with a sense of one's connection to African American history and community, as well as the correlation between ethnic identity and academic identity. Surprisingly, there was no connection between students' racial identity meanings and their academic identity on the survey.

There was a relationship between the racial identity meaning of positive school and variables related to engagement, such that students who endorsed "positive school" as a part of their racial identity meaning were less likely to come to class late or unprepared, and those who endorsed "negative school" were less likely to feel comfortable talking to teachers about their problems.

The clustering of positive school with understanding history and negative school with gangsta (as well as the positive correlation with personal style for both) supported the qualitative finding about the ways in which aspects of African American students in our sample ascribed meaning to their African American identities. However, the absence of a relation between any of these (except positive school) and achievement is surprising. It may mean that while the racial identity meanings cluster, the important aspect for schooling outcomes is the extent to which students see achievement in school as a part of their racial and ethnic identity. It may also be that our achievement variable was just too rough to capture the nuance of the relation between achievement and our identity variables (recall that this variable consisted of three yes or no questions rather than students' grades).

More specifically, the lack of relationship between students' endorsement of "gangsta" as a racial identity meaning and achievement supports the notion that it may not be gangsta posturing in and of itself that is related to school outcomes. Indeed, students who identify with a street-savvy sense of what it means to be African American may be performing well or poorly in school (Dance, 2002), such as Victor and Terry, who both struggled with multiple and conflicting aspects of African American identity and whose school performance fluctuated. The quantitative data suggest that what seems to be more important is the extent to which students embrace a positive stance toward school as being a part of African American identity and, to some degree, the extent to which they embrace a negative stance toward school. However, for students in this study, those who felt that being African American meant to be "gangsta" also thought that being African American meant to have a negative stance toward school.

Another interesting finding had to do with the importance of the strength of one's ethnic identity, such that a stronger ethnic identity facilitated the relation between positive school and achievement. The strong ethnic identity might be linked to having a sense of oneself as a part of a historical legacy and may support a sense of oneself as positively oriented toward school in that such behavior carries on the tradition in the African American community. This may support the qualitative finding that students who held a socially conscious African American identity, such as Alonzo and Adrienne, were more likely to view being African American as encompassing a positive relation to school. Taken together, these qualitative and quantitative findings seem to indicate a complex picture of the multiple ways in which African American identity, academic identity, and achievement interact.

Conclusion

Findings from this study support the need for a nuanced conception of African American racial identity that considers both the strength of the identity and the local meaning of the identity—that is, what it means in the local setting and to the student to be African American.

The data illustrate that at Jackson High School, students could embrace a strong African American identity and be successful academically. Furthermore, findings illustrate that academic achievement was a part of the very definition of being African American for some students. This finding adds a level of nuance to our understanding of racial identities. Simply knowing the strength of one's sense of being African American does not determine the content or meaning of that identity, though it may be that the racial identity meanings that students hold may be more likely to exert an effect on achievement if they also identify strongly with being African American. This indicates the need to consider both the strength of one's identity and the local identity meanings that students are co-constructing and managing.

Qualitative findings show that both high-achieving and low-achieving students embraced African American identities, but what differs is what they view those identities as consisting of. Both high-achieving and low-achieving students viewed clothing styles and language patterns to be important for their African American identity. However, while some lower-achieving students defined being African American as related to street activity and having a negative relationship with school (consistent with both their local experiences of school and the broader media messages about African Americans), some higher-achieving students viewed their African American identity as incorporating doing well in school and created peer groups that shared and supported this sense of being African American for themselves and one another. Furthermore, these identities were supported in critical ways by the school context that offered different students access to different learning and identity resources.

Limitations

An important limitation of this study is the short-term nature of the research. Although we know that the experiences students have with respect to racial and academic identities in high school are critical, it is also true that the trajectories that we described began a long time before our study. An important difference between Alonzo and Adrienne and Claude and Connie may very well be the basic academic skills with which they entered high school. In that respect, it would be an overstatement to say that the trajectories of the students we present are fully the responsibility of the tracking system of the school. Rather, the system of tracking continued (and perhaps intensified) the unequal distribution of educational resources that began in elementary school.

Another limitation has to do with instrumentation for the quantitative portion of our study. While we drew items for our survey scales from other instruments, we did not validate or norm our instrument in its entirety for the population that we studied. Furthermore, we have no data on the psychometric properties of our racial/ethnic identity meanings measure. These limitations with respect to instrumentation should be considered when interpreting our quantitative findings.

An additional limitation lies in the focus group question used to elicit students' perceptions of being African American. In the focus groups, we asked students, "What does it mean to you to be African American?" We interpreted their answers (which we then based the survey question on) as authentic expressions of their ideas about what being African American meant to them. An alternative interpretation would be to view students' responses as expressions of their understanding of stereotypes about what it means to be African American, thus explaining the prevalence of stereotypes in their responses. This same critique might be made of students' responses to the survey. However, the responses from the focus group students mirror conversations that we heard among students. Furthermore, the survey responses show that while many students did choose stereotypical notions of being African American, more often, students chose "understanding African American history" and responses that indicated a positive connection to school.

A related concern is the assumption that students in the street-savvy group saw the gangsta version of African American identity as an authentic expression of their racial identity, despite the lack of explicit conversations about race in this group. It may be that had Claude or Connie pulled us aside for a private conversation about racial identity, they may have expressed concerns similar to that of Victor—that is, feeling as though the gangsta version of African American identity was one that they wore but that may not fully reflect who they are. Given the prevalence of this version of African American identity in the media, it would not be surprising if some students simply chose to wear this identity to be cool or to fit in, or simply because they didn't know there was a viable alternative. This possibility is consonant with our argument that students, in part, take up versions of African American identity that they see in the world around them, through their local interactions in cultural practices. However, not having the data to be able to make that distinction is a limitation of the current study.

Implications

Understanding the nuances of individuals constructing racial/ethnic identities in the contexts of schools (a process informed by broader media-informed images and stereotypes) can support both better teaching practices and program development in the context of schools. This work may also support researchers in attaining a deeper understanding of the complex relations between racial identity and academic achievement. Specifically, findings from this study have several important implications for research and practice.

One implication is that researchers who are concerned with issues of racial identity should consider the meanings (held locally) for racial identity made available to young people as well as the strength of these identities. This may mean that survey methods be augmented with focus groups, interviews, or other qualitative methods. This also raises issues with respect to how we think about and use existing measures on new populations. On one hand, existing measures have been vetted and validated and thus may be more reliable. On the other hand, if the definitions of racial identity are to some degree local, then using existing measures may obscure the local nature of racial identity meanings.

Another implication of this work is that teachers (and researchers) cannot assume that students' stylistic presentation (e.g., clothing and speech styles) is an indicator of students' orientations toward school. Nor should teachers or researchers assume that students feel that they must give up their cultural identities to achieve academically. Indeed, there is a long tradition in the African American community of high levels of achievement (Perry, Hilliard, & Steele, 2004) and service to the community, and it may be that connecting students to that history could positively support their achievement.

An open question is how we might create more opportunities for more students to thrive as Alonzo did and to come to define African American identity as including high academic achievement. Even at Jackson High, where such as identity was available, many students embraced the "street savvy" definition or struggled to construct a definition that included both academic success and peer acceptance. One possibility might be to develop programs that focus directly on students to make positive identity choices and to be purposeful about the definitions of African American identities that they take on.

Finally, this research points to the critical nature of offering students school contexts where they are provided with not only rich learning opportunities but also opportunities to develop a sense of a positive relation to school as being a part of being African American. Given this, these issues of identity are critical to foster social justice in schools.

In closing, we hope that the research presented in this article provides researchers and practitioners with conceptual tools that are useful to understand the complexities of African American youth's racial identities and their relation to school achievement.

Appendix A
Ethnic Identity and Academic Identity Scales

Scale	Items
Academic Identity	• How important is doing well in school to who you are? • How much do your grades matter to you? • How often do you take school seriously? • How often do you consider yourself to be a good student?
Ethnic Identity	• I have spent time trying to find out more about my own race group, such as history, traditions, and customs. • I have a clear sense of my race group and what it means to me. • I think a lot about how my life will be affected by my race group membership. • I am happy that I am a member of the race group I belong to. • I have a strong sense of belonging to my race group. • In order to learn more about my race background, I have often talked to other people about my ethnicity. • I have a lot of pride in my race group and its accomplishments. • I participate in cultural practices of my own race group, such as special food, music, or customs. • I feel a strong attachment toward my own race group. • I feel good about cultural or race background. • How important is race to you?

Appendix B
Items Combined to Form the Racial/
Ethnic Identity Meaning Categories

Category	Items
History	Understanding the history of African Americans
Positive school	Having a positive attitude toward school Being responsible Doing well in school Being smart in math
Negative school	Having a negative attitude toward school Not going to class
Personal style	Clothing style Using Ebonics Listening to hip-hop Listening to rap
Gangsta persona	Being a hustler Being a "gangsta" Cursing and swearing Wearing gold teeth Smoking weed

Notes

We are grateful to the Hewlett Foundation and Michael Wald for support of this research. Our research team represents a range of disciplinary backgrounds and perspectives. Na'ilah Nasir is a trained educational psychologist specializing in human development. Milbrey McLaughlin comes from a social policy perspective and is founding director of the John W. Gardner Center for Youth and Their Communities, and codirector of the Center for the Study of Research on Teaching research centers that undertake interdisciplinary research on policies affecting youth and their institutional contexts. Amina Jones is a trained educational anthropologist who focuses on the experiences of disenfranchised youth. This research was motivated by questions about the experiences of youth in high-poverty, urban high schools, and aims to inform changes in programs and resources that affect students of this population. It also aims to inform fundamental questions about the intersections between opportunities in the school context and educational pathways.

[1]Throughout this article, we use the term *racial/ethnic identity* to signal that we are referring both to ethnicity and race. Although racial identity and ethnic identity are closely related (Worrell & Gardner-Kitt, 2006), we do not assume that race and ethnicity are the same thing, nor do we assume that they have the same effects on achievement of psychological outcomes (Helms & Talleyrand, 1997).

[2]The most recent version of this framework (in Cross & Fhagen-Smith, 2001), like Sellers, acknowledges both a salience dimension and a content dimension.

[3]This example also illustrates the way that available identities are often created by and reflected in pop media culture, as the appearance of this identity on high school campuses was preceded by a hip-hop song about Vans tennis shoes that played on local radio stations.

[4]These identity types are ideal types (Dance, 2002; Weber, 1978) in that they are analytical categories that simplify reality for the sake of understanding. They do not capture the real-life dynamics and fluidity of these categories in daily life.

[5]We came to use this term independent of Dance (2002), but we share with her the use this of term as signaling the way in which these youth are "not sheltered from the criminal aspects of street culture (for example drug trafficking and gang violence)" (p. 3).

[6]"The block" refers to the immediate neighborhood, usually a several block radius.

[7]"Nigga" is a word with a historical legacy that is deeply tied to conceptions of race in the United States; we argue that it is this legacy that Claude's use of the term invokes. Although some youth have argued that their usage of the word "nigga" does not have racial connotations, such as when non–African American youth use it to refer to other non–African American youth, we disagree with this view, given that the prevalence of the word in the popular culture stems primarily from imitation of African American musicians, actors, and athletes.

[8]This was a small room in the school that housed college application materials and resources and served as an office for a part-time college counselor.

References

Baron, A., & Banaji, M. (2006). The development of implicit attitudes: Evidence of race evaluations from ages 6 and 10 and adulthood. *Psychological Science, 17*(1), 53–58.

Bronfenbrenner, U. (1979). *The ecology of human development: Experiments by nature and by design.* Cambridge, MA: Harvard University Press.

Bronfenbrenner, U. (1993). The ecology of cognitive development. In R. H. Wozniak & K. W. Fischer (Eds.), *Development in context: Acting and thinking in specific environments* (pp. 3–44). Hillsdale, NJ: Lawrence Erlbaum.

Carter, P. (2005). *Keeping it real.* New York: Oxford University Press.

Chavous, T., Bernat, D., Schmeelk-Cone, K., Caldwell, C., Kohn-Wood, L., & Zimmerman, M. (2003). Racial identity and academic attainment among African American adolescents. *Child Development, 74,* 1076–1090.

Cole, M. (1996) *Cultural psychology: A once and future discipline.* Cambridge, MA: Belknap.

Cross, W. (1991). *Shades of Black: Diversity in African American identity.* Philadelphia: Temple University Press.

Cross, W., & Fhagen-Smith, P. (2001). Patterns of African American identity development: A lifespan perspective. In C. Wijeyesinghe & B. Jackson (Eds.), *New perspectives on racial identity development: A theoretical and practical anthology* (pp. 243–270). New York: New York University Press.

Dance, J. L. (2002). *Tough fronts: The impact of street culture on schooling.* New York: Routledge.

Davidson, A. (1996). *Making and molding identities in schools: Student narratives on race, gender, and academic engagement.* Albany: State University of New York Press.

Diamond, J. (in press). Are we barking up the wrong tree? Rethinking oppositional culture explanations for the Black/white achievement gap in the U.S. *Journal of Curriculum Studies.*

Engestrom, Y. (1999). Activity theory and individual and social transformation. In Y. Engestrom, R. Miettinen, & R. Punamaki (Eds.), *Perspectives on activity theory* (pp. 19–38). New York: Cambridge University Press.

Essed, P. (2002). Everyday racism: A new approach to the study of racism. In P. Essed & D. Goldenberg (Eds.), *Race critical theories: Test and context.* (pp. 176–194). Cambridge, MA: Blackwell.

Fordham, S. (1988). Racelessness as a factor in Black students' school success. Pragmatic strategy or Pyrrhic victory? *Harvard Educational Review, 5*(8), 54–84.

Fordham, S. (1996). *Blacked out: Dilemmas of race, identity, and success at Capital High.* Chicago: University of Chicago Press.

Fordham, S., & Ogbu, J. (1986). Black students' school success: Coping with the burden of "acting white." *The Urban Review, 18,* 176–206.

Frederickson, G. (2002). *Racism: A short history.* Princeton, NJ: Princeton University Press.

Gamoran, A. (1987). The stratification of high school learning opportunities. *Sociology of Education, 60,* 135–155.

Gonzalez, N. (1999). What will we do when culture does not exist anymore? *Anthropology and Education Quarterly, 30*(4), 431–435.

Goodman, B., & Dretzin, R. (Producers). (2001, February 27). *Merchants of cool* [Television broadcast]. Washington, DC: Frontline PBS Special.

Gutierrez, K., & Rogoff, B. (2003). Cultural ways of learning: Individual traits or repertoires of practice. *Educational Researcher, 32*(5), 19–25.

Harper, B., & Tuckman, B. (2006). Racial identity beliefs and academic achievement: Does being black hold students back? *Social Psychology of Education, 9,* 381–403.

Helms, J., & Talleyrand, R. (1997). Race is not ethnicity. *American Psychologist, 51*(11), 1246–1247.

Holland, D., Lachicotte, W., Skinner, D., & Cain, C. (1998). *Identity and agency in cultural worlds.* New York: Cambridge University Press.

Hudley, C., & Graham, S. (2005). Stereotypes of achievement striving among early adolescents. *Social Psychology of Education, 5,* 201–224.

Jhally, S. (Producer). (1997). *bell hooks: Cultural criticism and transformation* [Motion picture]. Northampton, MA: Media Education Foundation.

Lerner, R., (1991). Changing organism-context relations as the basic process of development: A developmental contextual perspective. *Developmental Psychology, 27*(1), 27–32.

Lowe, A. (2006). *Contending with legacy: Stereotype threat, racial identity, and school culture.* Unpublished Doctoral dissertation, Stanford University, CA.

Markus, H., & Kunda, Z. (1986). Stability and malleability of the self-concept. *Journal of Personality and Social Psychology, 51,* 858–866.

McKown, C., & Weinstein, R. (2003). The development and consequences of stereotype consciousness in middle childhood. *Child Development, 74*(2), 498–515.

Mehan, H., Villanueva, I., Hubbard, L., & Lintz, A. (2004). *Constructing school success.* New York: Cambridge University Press.

Nasir, N. (2004). "Halal-ing" the child: Reframing identities of opposition in an urban Muslim school. *Harvard Educational Review, 74*(2), 153–174.

Nasir, N., Jones, A., & McLaughlin, M. (2007) *School connectedness for students in low-income urban high schools.* Unpublished document, Stanford University.

Noguera, P. (2003). The trouble with black boys: The role and influence of environmental and cultural factors on the academic performance of African American males. *Urban Education, 38,* 431–459.

Oakes, J. (2005). *Keeping track: How schools structure inequality.* New Haven, CT: Yale University Press.

O'Connor, C. (1999). Race, class, and gender in America: Narratives of opportunity among low-income African American youths. *Sociology of Education, 72*(3), 137–157.

Osborne, J. W. (1997). Race and academic disidentification. *Journal of Educational Psychology, 89*(4), 728–735.

Osyerman, D., Harrison, K., & Bybee, D. (2001). Can racial identity be promotive of academic efficacy? *International Journal of Behavioral Development, 25,* 379–385.

Page, H. (1997). "Black Male" imagery and media containment of African American men. *American Anthropologist, 99*(1), 99–111.

Perry, T., Hilliard, A., & Steele, C. (2004). *Young, gifted, and Black: Promoting high achievement among African American students.* Boston: Beacon.

Phinney, J. (1992). The Multigroup Ethnic Identity measure: A new scale for use with diverse groups. *Journal of Adolescent Research, 7*(2), 156–176.

Pollock, M. (2005). *Colormute: Race talk dilemmas in an American school.* Princeton, NJ: Princeton University Press.

Ro, R. (1996). *Gangsta: Merchandizing the rhymes of violence.* New York: St. Martin's.

Rogoff, B. (2003). *The cultural nature of human development.* New York: Oxford University Press.

Sellers, R., Chavous, T., & Cooke, D. (1998). Racial ideology and racial centrality as predictors of African American college students' academic performance. *Journal of Black Psychology, 24,* 8–27.

Sellers, R., Copeland-Linder, N., Martin, P., & Lewis, R. L. (2006). Racial identity matters: The relationship between racial discrimination and psychological functioning in African American adolescents. *Journal of Research on Adolescence, 16*(2), 187–216.

Sellers, R., Rowley, S., Chavous, T., Shelton, J., & Smith, M. (1997). Multidimensional inventory of Black identity: A preliminary investigation of reliability and construct validity. *Journal of Personality and Social Psychology, 73,* 805–815.

Shelton, J., & Sellers, R. (2000). Situational stability and variability in African American racial identity. *Journal of Black Psychology, 26,* 27–50.

Spencer, M. B. (2006). Phenomenology and ecological systems theory: Development of diverse groups. In W. Damon & R. Lerner (Eds.), *Handbook of child psychology: Theoretical models of human development* (6th ed., pp. 829–893). New York: John Wiley.

Spencer, M. B., Noll, E., Stolfus, J., & Harpalani, V. (2001). Identity and school adjustment: Revisiting the "acting white" assumption. *Educational Psychologist, 36*, 21–30.

Steele, C. (1997). A threat in the air: How stereotypes shape intellectual identity and performance. *American Psychologist, 52*(6), 613–629.

Steffans, K., & Hunter, K. (2005). *Confessions of a video vixen.* New York: HarperCollins.

Stryker, S., & Serpe, R. T. (1994). Identity salience and psychological centrality: Equivalent, overlapping, or complementary concepts? *Social Psychology Quarterly, 57*(1), 16–35.

Varenne, H., & McDermott, R. (1998). *Successful failure: The school American builds.* Boulder, CO: Westview.

Weber, M. (1978). *Economy and society.* Berkeley: University of California Press.

Wenger, E. (1999). *Communities of practice.* New York: Cambridge University Press.

Wilson, J., & Riley, K. J. (2004). *Violence in east and west Oakland: Description and intervention.* Santa Monica, CA: RAND.

Wong, C. A., Eccles, J. S., & Sameroff, A. (2003). The influence of ethnic discrimination and ethnic identification on African American adolescents' school and socioemotional adjustment. *Journal of Personality, 71*, 1197–1232.

Worrell, F., & Gardner-Kitt, D. (2006). The Cross Racial Identity Scale and the Multigroup Ethnic Identity measure. *Identity: An International Journal of Theory and Research, 6*(4), 293–315.

Manuscript received August 15, 2007
Revision received March 14, 2008
Accepted June 22, 2008

American Educational Research Journal
March 2009, Vol. 46, No. 1, pp. 115–144
DOI: 10.3102/0002831208322180
© 2009 AERA. http://aerj.aera.net

Discourses and Strategic Visions: The U.S. Research University as an Institutional Manifestation of Neoliberalism in a Global Era

Frank Gaffikin
Queen's University, Belfast
David C. Perry
University of Illinois at Chicago

It is argued widely that the academy today is in the process of significant change—in the institutional assumptions of what constitutes the university and the construction of knowledge and in its relations with the city and the world. This article addresses the evolution of the modern university in the context of the discourses of contemporary globalizing institutions. Further, it empirically assesses the organizational priorities of U.S. research universities in light of the application of these discourses to their objectives and practices, finding that they are playing a key role in the formal representation of the institutional direction, goals, and values of American higher education.

KEYWORDS: discourse processes, postsecondary education, educational policy, qualitative research

Perhaps the single most popular characterization of the present era is "globalization." While the concept is not totally new (Bender, 2000; Fainstein, 1990), contemporary global relations, at the human, technological, social, and economic levels, have been redefined in qualitatively different ways from previous times. One institution where much of this comes to ground is the university, and this article argues that the institutional priorities of the modern research university provide evidence of wider changing societal practices—priorities that are now influenced as much by the exogenous realities of "globalization" as they are by the historical institutional practices of the "academy." In essence, the purpose of this article is to explore how the American research university is institutionally reformulating itself in this global era, as indicated by universities' public representations of themselves in their strategic plans and statements.

Gaffikin, Perry

There are varied, often quite separate literatures on the elements of globalization and higher education, with nowhere near the synthetic and critical treatment of this literature that such a topic warrants. The first purpose of this article is to provide such a synthesis of interdisciplinary literature in order to better understand the larger purposes that globalization is playing in the development of universities and, conversely, the increased importance of universities in their global and urban surroundings. Also, to date, there has been little broad-based empirical study of the university as a "global institution." The literature is generally case based or experiential, with policy arguments often conflated to the national level. Therefore, the second goal here is to offer an exploratory review of the strategic plans of a select sample of the largest research universities in the United States to find out how deeply the discourses, or institutional languages, of globalization have penetrated into the vision, mission, goals, and practices of the modern research university. The intent here is to treat the university as a fully vested societal institution, at once more localized in its significance for economic development and more globalized in the virtual and collaborative spaces of research and learning. However, in examining how universities treat these discourses in their key strategic documents, the article does not claim that what they say about themselves is the same as what they actually deliver. Of course, the content of such strategies can contain the posturing of promotional rhetoric, unmerited claims, and post hoc rationalization. It is not the purpose of the article to decipher and expose these. Rather, its purpose is to identify the extent to which they at least feel obligated to prioritize and embrace globalization and its related agendas as important to their public institutional face.

To meet this objective, the article begins with an exposition of six preeminent discourses germane to overall global transformation, with subsequent consideration of how these issues have an impact on the institutional rearticulation of the academy. The term *discourse* here is not intended in a detailed poststructural sense of power analysis, linguistic interpretation, multiple meanings, and textual deconstruction (Foucault, 1972) but, rather, in its simpler definition as a disquisitional conversation about the key

---

FRANK GAFFIKIN is a professor of spatial planning in the School of Planning, Architecture and Civil Engineering and director of the Institute of Spatial and Environmental Planning at Queen's University, Belfast, Northern Ireland, BT9 5AG; e-mail: *f.gaffikin@qub.ac.uk.* He is director of the major research project Contested Cities and Urban Universities; government adviser on urban regeneration, regional planning, and employability; and senior fellow of the Great Cities Institute at the University of Illinois, Chicago. His key interests include planning in contested cities, integrated planning at the urban and regional levels, and the engaged urban university.

DAVID C. PERRY is director of the Great Cities Institute at the University of Illinois, 412 South Peoria Street, Suite 400, Chicago, IL 60607; e-mail: *dperry@uic.edu.* He is involved in leadership at the University of Illinois around engaged interdisciplinary, high-impact research and partnerships that address key urban issues at both the local and global levels. His key interests include the engaged urban university, planning in contested space, and the informal urban.

---

characteristics of contemporary society. Nevertheless, it is acknowledged that the dominant representations of these issues comprise partial knowledge, legitimated and challenged through power relations. Marked not only by coherence and systematicity but also by contradiction and contestation, such discourses are also embedded and performative in that they have penetrated pervasively into the social fabric and thereby contain substantial social force (Johnston, Gregory, Pratt, & Watts, 2000).

Following this framework, there is an analysis of the empirical data—the strategic plans of selected research universities—interrogating the nature and extent of the academy's engagement with, and internalization of, these discourses. The conclusion offers an appraisal of the wider implications of these trends in academy, as both recipient and agent of globalization.

Globalization and Its Discourses

To date, much of the appraisal of academy's reformulation within the context of globalization has been either anecdotal or case based (Breton & Lambert, 2004; Perry & Wiewel, 2005; Van der Wusten, 1998). But, even if globalization is an overarching theme of organizational mission and purpose, it is not a singularly understood concept. In fact, its ubiquity as a feature of modern sociopolitical and economic order is only matched by the level of disagreement over its definitional worth. For some, this new globalizing order is directed by a "neoliberal" ideology that frees, as it requires, the individual's execution of entrepreneurial powers and "skills in a political economy characterized by strong private property rights, free markets and free trade" (Harvey, 2005, p. 2).

If neoliberalism is the ideological discourse of globalization, the state best equipped to create and preserve globalization is one characterized as a *mixed economy welfare*, which in some places is defined as increasing privatization and in other places as the "Third Way": a state mixture of private opportunity, democratic rights, and a measure of social protection. The structures of both public and private institutions of the state are increasingly *corporate* in their practices of management, efficiency, and accountability. The order produced by such institutional features of state and market is balanced by new *civic engagement,* or community responsibility, along with societal inclusiveness, or *diversity.* In sum, the discourse of globalization is in fact many "globalizations," the product of several discourses in late modernity (Giddens, 1990) or *postmodernity.* Among them are the following six: the overarching concept of globalization itself; neoliberalism; the mixed economy of welfare, with its related issues of corporatism, managerialism, and efficiency; living with increasing diversity and difference; community/civic engagement; and postmodernist perspectives on knowledge itself. The following section examines each of these in turn and how they connect with campus concerns.

Changing Discourses on Campus

1. Globalization. As argued by Held and McGrew (2003), this is a deeply contested concept that defies simple summation. First, skeptics dispute its very validity, insisting on its weak specificity and explanatory worth; the existence of more globalized periods, such as the age of Imperialism; and the persistent autonomy of national sovereignty (Hirst & Thompson, 1999; Weiss, 1998). Indeed, some see in the concept an attempt to legitimate the global diffusion of capitalism as both inevitable and benign (Hoogvelt, 1997). Even among the globalists, distinction prevails. While most agree on its eminent features—the growing reach of transnational firms; round-the-clock, round-the-globe financial markets; the planetary interdependence suggested by global warming and environmental degradation; the spread of common popular culture; new communications such as the World Wide Web; and such like—the causal and impact analysis varies markedly. Some emphasize the mounting hegemony of market economics, with its assumed modernism, intensification of social inequity, and erosion of national sovereignty (Greider, 1997; Sassen, 1996). Some focus on the deterritorialization and "death of distance" achieved by transformations in global communication, such as wireless technology (Caircross, 1997). Others dismiss such explanations as either partial or reductionist, proposing instead a complex configuration of multiple factors in society, polity, and economy, not to mention theology (Castells, 1997).

Within this latter perspective, alongside due dismissal of the exaggerated demise of geography and history, there is recognition of a new era of increasing connectedness and spatial-temporal compression. But, this is seen to produce "many globalizations" (Berger & Huntington, 2002) that, far from generating uniformity, continue to accommodate diverse cultures and resistance (Jameson & Miyoshi, 1998). In this multilayered version, complication and ambivalence run counter to stark visions of a bipolar planet caught between private consumerism and religious fundamentalism or, as expressed by Barber (1995), between "McWorld and Jihad." Greater integration also generates varied differentiation and alternative modernities. For instance, particular phenomena, like the increasing evangelization of Pentecostal Protestantism, bear distinctive outcomes for cultural harmonization around individualism (Berger, 2002); parts of the national state can act as "protector of stakeholding communities [while other parts] are direct affiliates of global capital" (Appadurai, 2001, p. 2); close economic ties relate largely to the top countries in the Organization for Economic Cooperation and Development rather than to the whole of humanity; and the overall dynamic of a shrinking world contains its own contradictions that invite opposition and renew the relevance of both agency and the local.

Expression of this dynamic in the United States takes an acute form. Over the past four decades, its base economy has substantially shifted from industrial/manufacturing to postindustrial/service, a structural change that has had significant impact on the relations of production, the space and time of markets, and the products around which they are organized. With such restructuring, the institutional character of U.S. society has been transformed by not only a national but also a global shift in the primacy of the individual as the entrepreneurial center of a social order rooted in private property rights and free markets. The state, in turn, serves as site and guarantor of "an institutional framework appropriate to such practices" (Harvey, 2005, p. 2). As such, the state has been equally affected by changes characterized best by a shift from government to governance, suggesting that the relations of politics, the geographies of nation-state and city, and the very definition of the units of the state are in flux. But, increasingly, this political dimension is also being framed within the related discourse of the ideological ascendancy of neoliberalism and the attendant discourses of the mixed economy of welfare, corporatism and managerial efficiency, diversity, community engagement, and postmodernity.

2. Neoliberalism. This refers to the virtually ubiquitous political culture since the 1980s that has elided with globalization and that posits the benign impact of self-regulating markets and the corollary of minimalist government intervention designed to support economic demand management and social protection. This ideological turn, whose genesis is traceable to Hayek (1944), with subsequent intellectual development from Friedman (1962), emphasized retreat not only from command economy socialism but also from the egalitarian liberalism associated with Keynes and its underpinning of redistributative welfarism (Rawls, 2005). The visibility of this agenda was raised in the 1970s and took acute political expression in the 1980s in the transformative governments of Thatcher in the United Kingdom and Reagan in the United States: "These vanguard regimes took momentous steps to construct, in the name of economic liberalization, a capital-centric order in which the impediments to accelerated finance-oriented accumulation were minimized or removed" (Peck & Tickell, 2007, p. 28).

Advocates of neoliberalism extol a combination of a downsized state, free trade, flexible labor markets, enterprising individualism, and the compelling logic of competition. But, how deep these nostrums penetrate into contemporary polity remains contestable. Arguments persist about its uneven application; whether it represents a new "regime" of accumulation or a transitory disordered phase between the optimism of major government projects such as the Great Society in the 1960s and a new regulatory era yet to take clear form, or whether its high tide has ebbed in many places in favor of a more socially responsible capitalism, which though endorsing the preeminence of the market accommodates inventive forms of public-private partnership. Nevertheless, its dominance has narrowed the political space for collectivist manifestoes around public value and social equity, and with specific reference to academy, its influence has helped introduce a corporatist approach. Partly, this is reflected in the appropriation of business language and practice, with the associated elevation of efficiency and cost-effectiveness within institutional imperatives (Gumport, 2000). Partly, it can be represented in the reduction of collegial consultation and participation in favor of more managerialist leadership and decision making (Kerr, 1998), a related rise in central administrative staff, and the importation of an audit culture and ritualistic performance measurement (Bleiklie, 1998; Strathern, 2000). Overall, this shift in university governance is taken by many to be rooted in beliefs about the ascendancy of market principles and the efficacy of imitating business practice (Braun & Merrien, 1999).

Within neoliberalism, the claims for deregulated flexible labor markets rank high. Thus, within universities, a new class system is emerging, where not only is research privileged over teaching and service (Fairweather, 1996) but an increasing share of faculty are on restricted temporary contracts assigning them to a Fordist-style teaching of large numbers of undergraduates while tenured faculty are ever more dedicated to research and selective post-Fordist graduate teaching. Beyond such downsizing, this creation of a more entrepreneurial professoriate is supported by differential incentives that particularly reward the generation of research income and peer-reviewed journal publication (Anderson, 2002; Baldwin & Krotseng, 1995). In this new marketized environment, students become consumers, encouraged to view their college experience as the route to individual career and acquisitive ambition in an increasingly competitive economy (Leslie & Slaughter, 1995). Courses are more vocationally oriented, pursue a more instrumentalist pedagogy, pitch tuition fees on a more lucrative basis, and are valued in terms of their output of knowledge-intensive human capital. For some, the educational reform over recent times has followed a deliberate neoliberal agenda in not merely reacting to the market but rather in proactively lending the "hidden hand" a helping hand (Gordon & Whitty, 1997).

Such a shift holds contradictions for the academy. For instance, the development of a more hierarchical "line management" model is at odds with evidence that flatter, more collegial structures that accommodate more inclusive decision making, in turn, help promote more creative outcomes (Florida, 2005). Such inventiveness is a premium component of frontier intellectual inquiry, the central purpose of a research university. Moreover, insofar as the primary institutional focus is on its top-down administrative and fund-raising program, the intellectual energy that generates upward from its academic staff risks being undervalued or even stifled.

But, the impact of this agenda has not been peculiar to the United States. Rather, the global spread of these societal changes means that since the 1970s there has

> everywhere been an emphatic turn towards . . . [these] political economic practices and thinking. Deregulation, privatization and the withdrawal of the state from many areas of social provision have been all too common . . . . [And] have entailed much "creative destruction," not only of prior institutional frameworks and powers but also of divisions of labor, social relations, welfare provisions, and technological mixes ways of life and thought. (Harvey, 2005, p. 3)

In this view, the public good will be optimized through the extension of market relations into previously socialized realms, such as education.

However, it is important to acknowledge that this apparent hegemony has been uneven in operation and contains its own contradictions. As noted by Peck and Tickell (2007), its actual forms are hybrids of its "pure" version and leftovers of its antecedents:

> Only rhetorically does neoliberalism mean "less state": in reality, it entails a thorough-going reorganization of governmental systems and state-economy relations. . . . This program involves the roll-out of new state forms, new modes of regulation, new regimes of governance, with the aim of consolidating and managing both marketization and its consequences. (p. 33)

Thus, the application of the neoliberal project has been often more pragmatic than its more doctrinaire formulation might suggest. Similarly, the expression of neoliberalism in any particular institution such as the academy is likely to be uneven and to contain elements of former regimes as well as outcomes of resistance and prefigurative alternative formations.

Whether emphasized as neoliberalism and/or globalization, this institutional shift is evident not only at local and national levels but also in the widespread global networks of material and cultural relations. As the geography of political and economic change seems to be shifting outward, it also seems to contain a decidedly urban shift. Humans today live in an "urban world" made up of "global [i.e. increasingly diverse] cities" (D. Clark, 1999). Though this urban and global turn is far from new (Bender, 2000; Fainstein, 1990), what separates contemporary institutional transformations from the past are their scale, pace, and international character (Van Ginkel, 2003). Castells (1996) suggests that the time and space of these patterns are caught up in a whole new mode of societal production of information and communication technology—collapsing old notions of political economy through the erasure of borders and the simultaneous synchronicity of relations. Such compression of time and space renders the particular geography of the state, with its control of the territory within its borders and the space of production regulated by such geographic arrangements, secondary to new *networks* of relations—giving form to a "Network Society" (Castells, 1996). Part of this new networking involves the reconfiguration of private and public sectors and a new mixed economy of social provision.

3. Mixed economy of welfare. The mixed economy of welfare has involved processes of privatization and reductions in public funding, and this welfare pluralism has contributed to a falling share of university finances coming from the public purse. The impulses of the neoliberal state—at least rhetorically—to regressive taxation, fiscal rectitude, and welfare reform such as workfare, impose challenges to the concept of the public university supported by public funds. In turn, this has induced the sector to broaden its fiscal base by commercializing more of its operations (Newman, Couturier, & Scurry, 2004), including real estate development, partnerships with urban regeneration initiatives, high-technology transfers, incubator services, corporate sponsorships, equity and licensing arrangements, and a concentration on research that yields commercial dividends (Duryea, 2000; Powell & Owen-Smith, 1998). In short, the premium on leading-edge discovery and data in the "knowledge age" invites the academy to commodify its key product: knowledge.

But, such revenue streams have provoked controversy about the extent to which they compromise intellectual integrity, challenge academic freedom, produce conflicts of interest, and deform research agendas away from public concerns and toward private profit (Hollingsworth, 2000; Washburn, 2005). Indeed, writing about the Australian experience of this process, Marginson and Considine (2001) characterize it as the integration of the university into the capitalist mode of production, a claim echoed in what others refer to as "academic capitalism" (Slaughter & Leslie, 1998) and the "privatizing" of academy (Kelsey, 1998). This move to being a business like any other, according to Barnett and Griffin (1997), has led to an "end of knowledge" in higher education, nothing less than "a selling out" (Giroux, 2003). A central paradox identified by Meyer (2002) is how this new university can be at once "soulless" for staff and student alike and "contested" around all of the contentious features of the enterprise culture.

Counter to such reservations about this university-industrial complex, there are some who argue for a legitimate collaboration between the two (Giamatti, 1982). Recognizing knowledge-based enterprises as drivers of economic growth, they insist that public universities contribute to a public good when they help to promote economic development in their cities and hinterlands. In particular, they can link with local research-and-development centers, foster innovation, spin off start-ups and expansions with their intellectual property, and help to stimulate an entrepreneurial culture and creative milieu (Branscomb, Kodama, & Florida, 1999; Glazer & Grimes, 2004; Varga, 2000). For some time now, universities have been acknowledged for the multiplier impact they exert on local economies through their role as major employer, consumer, educator, land developer, researcher, culture provider, and such like. But, more recently, with respect to state and land-grant institutions, state governments are granting certain funds, in expectation that they focus even more closely on their unique contribution, through research, patents, disclosures, licensing, and workforce development, to their states' competitiveness and prosperity (Schmidt, 2000). But, in the view of Washburn (2005), this represents not so much a partnership as a corporate takeover:

> The problem is not university-industry relationship per se; it is the elimination of any clear boundary line separating academia from commerce. . . . The question of who owns academic research has grown increasingly contentious, as the openness and sharing that once characterized university life has given way to a new proprietary culture more akin to the business world. (pp. x–xi)

In this move to commercialize, Washburn (2005) sees the lure of another Silicon Valley inducing state legislators and college presidents to invest their hopes in university-led research in growth areas like pharmaceuticals and biotechnology. Yet, "in reality, a mere two dozen universities in the entire country make significant profits from technology licensing. Many others barely break even—or *lose* money" (p. xii). This circumspect view about the extent to which academia can contribute to state economic development is supported in other literature (Feller, 2004). Indeed, a wider critique of the intrusion of market ideology into the public realm identifies the difference between price and value and the potential mismatch between market mechanisms and the valid metrics for evaluating effectiveness in public service (Kuttner, 1997).

Universities once were privileged sites of knowledge and sites of national, often local, identity and accomplishment to which people physically traveled to learn and collaborate in knowledge production. Today, the transfer and production of knowledge are not limited to particular physical sites or, indeed, traditional institutions such as the academy. For some, this change is monumental, reflecting what one observer calls a "Copernican change" in the structure and practices of societal institutions, most distinctly evident in higher education (Van Ginkel, 2003, p. 76). For universities, these seismic shifts in institutional context, generated by neoliberalism and the globalizing relations of the "information society" (Castells, 1997), challenge and perhaps even redefine, to some extent, the essentially unique institutional purpose and practice of the academy (Van Ginkel, 2003).

Since they have forfeited any claim to monopoly in the creation of frontier knowledge, universities no longer command support as "sanctioned sites for the production of innovations in the arts, the sciences and the professions, and still less support for continuing as places of 'disinterested knowledge' in the quest for a better society" (Calas & Smircich, 2001, p. 148). Faced with new rivals, they are pressured to be more entrepreneurial and competitive (B. Clark, 1998). In reaching for wider recognition for their brand, they are tempted to translate complex critical appraisals into digestible media sound bites that catch headlines at the cost of deleting cautionary qualification. While critics like Bok (2003) acknowledge these dynamics, they remain convinced that the move into the marketplace has gone too far, to the deleterious consequence for core educational mission and other objectives such as addressing equity and diversity.

4. Diversity. This goal comprises many dimensions, including the racial/ethnic composition of student intake (Bowen & Bok, 1998); the efficacy of affirmative action and related policies of discriminatory admissions (Gurin et al., 2004); the implications for enhanced multicultural curriculum (Banks, 2002) and for standards and educational outcomes (Gurin, Dey, Hurtado, & Gurin, 2002); and the imperative for a less ethnocentric scholarship among faculty (Boyer, 1990). This visceral issue of diversity and inclusiveness has drawn both critic and advocate. While some associate it with a "political correctness" that augurs both a "dumbing down" and a disruptive intrusion of "culture wars" onto the campus, supporters insist that it properly reflects changing demographics and social heterogeneity, with potentially great educational dividend (Orfield & Kurlaender, 2001; Turner et al., 2002). Lasch (1996) complains that greater attention to diversity and pluralism offers little consolation to graduates, who are less literate than ever, and this theme is developed by Black (2004), who sees the

American university in freefall, debasing the minds and morals of its students: "The university today is an academic system that rewards novelty, extreme positions, and radical theories, and it favors any intellectual trope that panders to the prevailing anti-American bias of the academy" (p. xiv).

It should be acknowledged that such concerns are not new. For instance, the longer standing feminist agenda about gender access to, and power relations within, campus has disturbed, if not dislodged, the patriarchal comfort zone of an institution renowned for valuing tradition (Blackmore, 2003). However, an indication of the complexities of implementing a campus politics around equality and diversity is found in Cooper's (2004) work; he illustrates the plasticity and ambiguity attached to these concepts. Thus, for instance, the principle of pluralism cannot entail the endorsement of *all* difference, since power relations of discrimination and subordination determine certain forms of social difference and identity. While the campus has been trying to grapple with this thorny issue over recent decades, Cooper argues for a diversity anchored in a broader appreciation of human solidarity that facilitates choices and dissent—values that would seem to be very consonant with academy. But, in what way is this civic solidarity evident in university priorities?

5. Community engagement. Historically, the relationship between town and gown has operated along a spectrum between involvement and detachment (Bender, 1993). Certainly, recent decades have witnessed a reawakening of the civic responsibility of the academy, most evidently perhaps in the United States (Ehrlich, 2000), and of the reciprocities that can bestow mutual benefit (DeMulder & Eby, 1999). Advocates of university-community partnership have noted how the three conventional goals of universities—to teach, to research, and to serve—can operate in silos rather than in synergy and, indeed, how the service component can be relatively marginalized (Stukel, 1994). The Office of University Partnerships, established by the Department of Housing and Urban Development in 1994 and dismantled in 2004 by the federal government, was designed in large part to link the significant leverage of universities—physical, economic, political, technical, and intellectual—to the assets and capacities of the most vulnerable communities in a blend that works for both partners (Community Outreach Partnerships Centers, 2001). In this view, the academy is invariably seen as the senior partner, being a resource-rich institution of high social visibility and status, with the permanent presence to permit long-term strategic planning. By contrast, community is perceived as largely the recipient poor relation, with a more transitional social infrastructure.

But, a more radical engagement is conceivable beyond this standard outreach model (Feld, 1998; Maurrasse, 2001; Rubin, 1998). Rooted in a new scholarship that appreciates how "community" constitutes an important site of knowledge production (Boyer, 1996; Schon, 1995), it seeks a genuine cross-fertilization between formal and experiential learning as part of an effective social intervention for urban and regional development. But, this "engaged model" implies that the purpose and character of academy will be transformed in the dynamic of such a more equitable partnership (Silka, 1999; Walshok, 1995). For some, this change actually involves a "back to the future" rediscovery of the best traditions of the democratic cosmopolitan civic university (Benson & Harkavy, 2000), while for others, such a historic vision no longer suffices in the contemporary global context (Perry, 2005).

The university can contribute to the socioeconomic development of its urban hinterland in many ways: its *economic multipliers* in terms of targeted purchasing and employment strategies; use of *applied research* to tackle social problems and to optimize community assets; *knowledge, skills, and technology transfer* that equips local people to undertake their own research, evaluation, and development; *interdisciplinary perspectives* to illuminate cross-cutting and integrating approaches to local development; *comparative policy analysis* that permits the identification of model programs and best practice across the world and their customized transferability to local situations; *networking* local organizations into a wider regional and international milieu that enhances their social capital; use of *dialogic spaces,* by way of neutral secure locations for open engagement among diverse and contesting constituencies, with university facilitation where helpful; *outreach scholarship* that relates teaching to community needs and addresses the issue of educational underattainment and working-class access to postsecondary, professional education; *student community service* that also provides participants with "real life" learning opportunities and the relation of theory to practice; and *institutional leadership* in the whole realm of public policy.

However, this potential is debilitated by certain exigencies, including the *bureaucratic* traditions typical of large durable institutions; the *poor status* traditionally accorded to community engagement, as reflected in the university reward structure; the *culture of staff autonomy* that requires patient cajoling rather than instant coercion in order to spur staff cooperation with such an agenda; the tendency for departments to operate in *disciplinary silos,* with few incentives for staff to operate collegially or to create interdisciplinary research teams; the *financial pressure* on universities to maximize lucrative knowledge transfer in the new economy rather than to devote resources to less financially enriching activity; and the *stereotypical image of ivory tower institutions*, given over to detached esoteric study and theorization rather than to socially useful scientific investigation. In the United States, other negative factors can apply, such as the levy exemptions available to universities that in turn erode the tax base for local social consumption, and the way they can become major property developers, gentrifying rather than sustainably renewing their neighborhoods.

Finally, bringing together many of these themes, as the university is pressured to favor certain kinds of knowledge, to rethink ethnocentric perspectives, to appreciate different sites of knowledge production, and to commercialize knowledge transfer, the very issue of what constitutes valid knowledge is itself subject to contention amid the ferment generated by postmodernism.

6. *Postmodernist perspectives*. These disavow the certitude of unitary and universalist concepts such as truth and meaning, arguing that they do not exist independent of variant cultural interpretation and social contingency. Such a view cuts to the core of what universities have been about (Bloland, 1995). Indeed, it has been seen by some academics as a threat to the very currency of their profession, offering ambivalence and sophistry in place of "authentic" epistemology. As expressed by Willard (1994), "The heart of the university crisis is, in my view, the simple fact that the institutional structures and processes are no longer organized around knowledge" (p. 3). If all maxims, logic, and understanding are, if not delusional or absolutist, then certainly conditional and temporal (Willard, 1994), this relativist position is taken by such critics to render scientific insight as little more than discourse. Moreover, in extremis, the related loss of faith in rationality, alongside a greater respect for "multiple realities" and human emotive and intuitive capacities, is seen to degrade traditional categories like disciplines and standards. Finally, the adherence to relativism seems to warrant the volatility of endless textual analysis, a deconstruction in which denotative language, sublimation, and oblique reference are constantly subject to meticulous interrogation and dispute (Rorty, 1982).

In rejoinder, the adherents see such critiques as a vulgar misread of a subtle proposition. For instance, they insist that disavowal of totalistic metanarratives is not a contrivance for atheoreticism but rather a recognition that a complex contemporary world is not subject to discoverable social laws that contain prescriptive or predictive capacity. Pursuing knowledge in an age of uncertainty demands a more reflexive approach on the part of the academic, a rethink about the scope of science, and receptivity to the challenging pace and scale of change (Duderstadt, 2003). A "knowledge society" inevitably invites more dispute about the nature of knowledge itself, an unnerving process for higher education (Delanty, 2001), and in such context, part of the problem can be seen in terms of a more fundamental phenomenon—the current feast of information amid a famine of meaning (Baudrillard, 1988). Such intellectual parsing of the state of knowledge has found a very different way into the structure of the academy. The modern organization of the disciplines of the academy has become an object of increasing "revisioning" in the strategic nostrums of "interdisciplinarity," "multidisciplinarity," and "transdisciplinary" reach. While the *tenets* of science as characterized by the formal disciplines of the modern academy have not been fully engaged or critically rewritten, the academic units that contain them have become objects of strategic university restructuring, auguring a late modern if not postmodern institutional reconsideration of higher education.

Impact of Discourses on the U.S. Academy

In summary, the overarching discourse of globalization is the product of several discourses that, when taken collectively, offer an insight into universities in their global and city/regional contexts (Geiger, 2004; Rhodes, 2001; Slaughter & Rhoades, 2004). As such, universities are viewed as at once important to this new glocalizing order and yet required to undertake more of their economic and civic functions on their own. The synchronicity of this new order brings new opportunities for collaboration, but also new requisites of entrepreneurial independence and competition (Breton & Lambert, 2004; Shapiro, 2005). For example, the increasing importance of "knowledge-economy–driven" education to human capital development makes the university both more valued and more vulnerable in a new, open, often global quest for students, research funding, and private as well as public fiscal support (Gaffikin, 2008; Perry & Wiewel, 2008). At the same time, many in government and business view universities as "engines" for competitive economic development (CEOs for Cities, 2002; Initiatives for a Competitive Inner City, 2002)— a centerpiece of the "knowledge sector." This new sector depends, in turn, on innovation and collaboration between scholarship and entrepreneurship and strategic investment on the part of higher education in the local and global development economies of real estate, technology, and proprietary enterprise. For many universities, this constitutes new territory—where success will require new definitions of autonomy and collaboration and new institutional measures of achievement not found in traditional academic or even public policy metrics (Geiger, 2004; Rhodes, 2001; Slaughter & Rhoades, 2004).

While the pace, scale, and diffusion of this contemporary makeover can be unnerving for institutions habituated to autonomy and traditional status, universities cannot escape its repercussion (Goddard, 1999). In such a globalized environment, they face greater competition for students, staff, and research funding and, consequently, greater "consumer sovereignty" among students and corporate sponsors. Meanwhile, other providers contest their previous near monopoly in high-grade education and research services, and it even can be suggested that globalist information technologies, via interactive video and high-speed wireless platforms, can replace the centralist and elitist learning culture of the university with a more accessible and democratic online format. Already, universities in the United Kingdom are developing the concept of the e-university, and this is also being taken up by the European Union. More recently in the United States, the University of Illinois has floated a proposal to add a fully virtual campus to its system, called the Global Campus.

Amid such challenge and change, universities, especially public ones, find traditional state support substantially declining relative to their costs, even as their societal importance is being highlighted as never before, since recourse to the national state is constrained by its own reconfiguration and fiscal pressure within globalization (deWit, 2002). Moreover, in an age when intellectual capital is more mobile and transferable, universities have to opt whether to export their contribution via new distance-learning technologies or new campus plants overseas, or some collaborative franchising arrangement with other providers, or adopt some permutation of all three. Indeed, the whole concept of the university campus may be subject to a radical rethink, with some arguing that universities risk their competitiveness unless they reduce those production costs associated with expensive ancillary facilities such as sports fields, social centers, and libraries. Yet, others will insist that in a competitive environment, students

127

will select the campus that offers the best overall college experience in terms of amenities and ambience.

In short, thriving locally in this international age induces key institutions like universities to strive for a world-class pedigree (Kanter, 1995). But, this global entrepreneurialism need not necessarily imperil the local dimension (Deem, 2001), and it need not involve a shift from the principle of *knowledge as an end* to the expediency of *the end of knowledge* (Delanty, 1998). Rather, some see a combination of the global, national, and local focus—or what has been dubbed the "glonacal" (Marginson & Rhoades, 2002)—as offering a new synergy for academy. Apart from facilitating certain of its key canons, such as the free flow of ideas, it offers new networks and less ethnocentric perspectives. For instance, it allows for the *collaborative advantage* of international joint ventures among universities, rather than an exclusive concern about *competitive advantage,* in ways that do not prelude the local-national axis being both a source and beneficiary of leading-edge knowledge production. The inclusion of higher education in multilateral treaties testifies to this significant dimension, and for American universities, the increasing use of English as an international language offers further scope in this regard. Thus, instead of the predominant academic view of globalization as a fixed, uniformly negative, neoliberal project at odds with liberal education values, a more reflexive analysis suggests otherwise. In fact, improved global networking holds scope for university consortia to advance a transactional learning experience that enriches its participants, extends the boundaries of intellectual discovery, and opens the potential for a real transcultural engagement (Perorazio, 2004). On this argument, we need more rather than less globalization—but of a kind that enhances mutual learning and understanding and promotes democratic exchange.

Nevertheless, despite evidence of universities in the United States and elsewhere responding to this new world in ways that engender greater convergence in the global patterns in higher education (Scott, 1998) certain practical impediments are seen to persist. For instance, there is no global imprimatur for degree accreditation. Issues about patenting intellectual property, and indeed disseminating knowledge worldwide in the Internet age, remain vexed (Atkinson, 2001). Many ideas for a new global scholarship may be sound, but their implementation may not. For instance, while increasing recruitment of overseas students can offer a diversity that extends a still largely ethnocentric curriculum and better informs classroom dialogue, it may be used by university authorities as a means of mass teaching for job-related qualifications, alienating those home students that feel crowded out of college places by the new competition.

It is argued, therefore, that the institutional role of universities in this new era will be at once challenging and unsettling, since traditional models of either the ivory tower or old-style town-gown collaboration with civic agencies will no longer suffice if the contemporary university is to thrive (Rhodes, 2001). Forced to shake free of old dependencies, universities are being pressured to substantially alter both their makeup and agenda to optimize their stimulative role in this new political economy. This is said to require them "to strengthen and diversify their external relations with stakeholders, as well as their sources of financing. Consequently, universities must rethink their modes of governance, their financing, their internal structure and external relations, as well as their modes of operation" (Van Ginkel, 2003, p. 77). But, what causes concern for some is the extent to which these reconfigurations will alter the very nature of the academy and shift its fundamental, if not universalist, purposes of learning and knowledge creation into a corporatist institutional agent of the knowledge economy, seeking global reach and research for motives of market and entrepreneurial advantage.

In applying this synthesis of discourses of globalization to the American research university, we see something of the logic of the institutional changes they describe, of the transformations of organizational identity, and of the reinvigoration and redefinition of mission as they are found in studies of the modern research institution. However, it is not enough to simply offer a fresh synthesis of these composite discourses of globalization as they are played out in American higher education. The second goal is to see if they have any resonance in the formal purposive organizational discourses of university strategic planning.

Institutional Discourses of American Universities in the Era of Globalization

What follows is an exploratory review of the strategic documents of a select sample of the largest research universities in the United States in order to find evidence of how universities are responding to the institutional challenges of late modernity. Conceivably, the most important brand statement of the research university that embraces its full range of institutional/structural initiatives is what has come to be called the *strategic plan*. The "strategic" documents studied here are public reports that provide information on a research university's mission, vision, goals, actions, and outcomes. We have determined that the commonality of such plans offers comparable interinstitutional evidence with which to assess the presence of the key institutional discourses of globalization, discussed previously in this article. The subsequent content analysis of university plans seeks to determine how much these discourses of globalization have come to characterize the purposes and values of the contemporary research academy.

At the same time, we want to learn about how much the university is strategizing campus development within a vision of alternative institutional futures: beyond physical plants that are enclaves distant from the turmoil of urban and global life, to institutions that are at once "international" (Altbach & Umakoshi, 2004; Lambert & Butler, 2006) in their student profiles and knowledge clusters, socially "engaged" (Kellogg Commission, 1999) with their local hinterlands, and "entrepreneurial" (CEOs for Cities, 2002; Perry & Wiewel, 2008) in their research directions and their fiscal and developmental activities. Further, in an era when funding for the academy is shifting along with the role of state support for higher education, we also want to assess these planning documents for a strategic turn to proprietary, managerial, bottom-line, and "corporatist" forms of administration, which appear at odds the traditional precepts of academic autonomy and faculty governance.

Methodology

In terms of methodology, the study is focused on three different constellations of research universities: the top 127 research universities in the United States, as measured in terms of $20 million or more in research expenditures, and the top 50 American research universities, public and private, as measured along nine variables, including research expenditures, endowment, faculty awards, and student SAT/GRE ranking. To determine which American research universities to use for our study, we consulted a master list of American research universities compiled by the Lombardi Program on Measuring University Performance (2004). This program defined major research universities located in the United States and Canada as those whose total annual research expenditures were at least $20 million. Identifying schools that exceeded this threshold gave us 127 institutions in our initial analysis, and a sample of 23 of the top public and private universities was chosen randomly from the top 50 for more detailed analysis. It was split quite evenly between public (12) and private institutions (11).[1] Each university in the sample displayed some form of strategic plan or action document on its Web site, with a testament to its currency and its relevance to administrative decision making. For each sampled institution, a ranking system was employed to determine the extent and intensity of the discourses as a measure of the role they play in the university's institutional goals and strategic direction. In gathering the public records and electronic links to the available strategic documents of each of the 127 universities, note was taken as to whether each university had a strategic document as earlier defined. Thorough searching was done through the institution's home page and administrative sections to access the most comprehensive and *cross-departmental* overall strategic document. Separate plans and documents outlining strategies for specific schools, departments, or university offices were excluded. Strategic goals and initiatives related to more narrow subdivisions within the university, if included in the overall strategic document, were included in our analysis.

As Table 1 shows, roughly 73% of the major U.S. research universities made formal strategic plans publicly available. Public universities (85.33%) were more likely to have these than were private universities (55.77%). A much smaller number of universities publicly displayed other documents from which could be determined core elements of institutional strategic planning, even though these documents were not formal plans. When the two groups of documents were combined, almost all public universities and a smaller, but still impressive, number of private institutions evidenced recognizable public discussion of key elements of institutional strategic programming.[2]

Each public document of each university was then analyzed for the presence of one or all of the following key elements:

Vision—Overriding goal or possible landmark achievement that sets the framework for the university's planning future.
Mission—The things the university strives for, its ultimate ends and ambitions. The mission is what informs the university's activities to reach toward the stated vision.
Values—The principles, strengths, and ideals the institution will exercise as it conducts its activities.
Goals—Initiatives and benchmarks that will be met in the achievement of the vision.
Actions—Specific programs that will be created, specific research projects that will be undertaken, and specific action steps that will achieve the stated goals.

Of the 93 major American research universities, public and private, with some form of strategic planning document, a substantial percentage, sometimes higher than 90% and never lower than 40%, exhibited some, if not all, key elements of modern organizational planning (see Tables 2 and 3).

One obvious conclusion for this data is that most universities have generated a purposive public description of their institutional goals, practices, and aspirations. On this basis, we studied the public documents of university strategies outlining institutional vision, mission, values, goals, and action steps as an exploratory assessment, both quantitative and qualitative, of the role of global discourses in modern higher education.

Universities, Their Plans, and Globalizing Discourses

Every occurrence of a discourse within the text of the planning documents of each university in the sample was recorded, as were the times each discourse appeared. Because of a wide range in size for planning documents, a ratio of discourses per page was created. This ratio was developed by first converting all plan text into Word, deleting extended extraneous text (such as bibliographies, acknowledgements, copyrights, etc.), and re-creating each document using the metric of 250 words equaling a single page. The number

Table 1
Publicly Available Strategic Documents Among American Universities With Annual Research Expenditures of at Least $20 Million

	Total Schools	Publicly Available Documents	Percentage
Public universities	75	64	85.33
Private universities	52	29	55.77
All universities	127	93	73.23

Note. Expenditure data as of December 2004.

Table 2
**Presence of Plan Elements Among American Universities With
Annual Research Expenditures of at Least $20 Million**

	Public Universities	Private Universities	All Universities
Total	75	52	127
Vision	54	22	76
Mission	70	39	109
Values	52	19	71
Goals	71	28	99
Actions	65	21	86

Note. Expenditure data as of December 2004.

Table 3
Percentage of Schools Evidencing a Plan Element

	Public Universities	Private Universities	All Universities
Vision	72.00	42.31	59.84
Mission	93.33	75.00	85.83
Values	69.33	36.54	55.91
Goals	94.67	53.85	77.95
Actions	86.67	40.38	67.72

of discourse appearances was then divided by the number of pages, and the resulting ratio of appearances per page is used to give some quantitative rating of the presence of each discourse to overall strategic thinking. Grading the prevalence of a particular discourse in American higher education was then based on the percentage of the sample that scored a *weak, average, strong,* or *very strong* rate of appearances of each discourse per plan (see Table 4).

While not all discourses are evenly displayed in the purposive institutional discourses of higher education, it is clear that all six discourses are clearly in play in U.S. higher education today, with universities strategically positioning themselves as "engaged," "international/global," and increasingly "efficient" institutions, bent on maintaining and expanding "diversity" among their students and faculty.

But more than this, a quantitative measure of discourse appearances in the strategic plans was required to get a fuller indication of the perceived place of these issues in the future of research universities. Here we add a qualitative assessment of the sample institutions' strategic documents that measures the overall importance of each of the six discourses to a plan by rating its substantive centrality to the institution along a range of 0 to 3:

0 = the discourse is not mentioned at all;
1 = the discourse is mentioned among other ideas, but not emphasized;

Table 4

Quantitative Measure of the Global Discourses in the Public Plans of U.S. Research Universities

University	Type	Diversity	Postmodernism	Neoliberalism	Mixed Economy	Globalization	Community Engagement
Dartmouth University	Private	0.64	0.34	0.59	0.27	0.44	0.34
Duke University	Private	0.51	0.47	0.48	0.39	0.43	0.28
Emory University	Private	0.83	0.94	0.73	0.57	1.55	1.2
New York University	Private	0.19	0.04	0.95	0.34		0.38
Northwestern University	Private	0.09	1.28	1.7	0.38	0.17	0.09
Pennsylvania State University–University Park	Public	0.85	0.21	1.49	1.49	0.85	1.27
Princeton University	Private	0.17	0	0.5	0.2	0.06	0.01
Rice University	Private	0.2	0.49	0.88	0.25	0.56	0.58
Stanford University	Private	0.12	0.15	0.28	0.38	0.1	0.05
Texas A&M University	Public	0.28	0.3	0.74	0.83	0.64	0.46
University of Alabama–Birmingham	Public	2.34	0	3.51	2.93	1.76	2.93
University of Arizona	Public	1.08	0.26	0.73	0.96	0.64	0.73
University of California–Berkeley	Public	0.13	0.39	0.58	0.24	0.25	0.14
University of California–Davis	Public	0.98	0.73	1.46	2.32	1.46	1.58
University of Illinois–Urbana-Champaign	Public	0.29	0.23	0.41	0.7	1.34	0.58
University of Southern California	Private	0.17	0.6	0.77	0.38	1.83	0.72
University of Texas–Austin	Public	0.14	0.02	0.32	0.19	0.07	0.32
University of Washington–Seattle	Public	0.5	1	0.5	0	0.5	1.5
University of Wisconsin–Madison	Public	0.9	0.41	1.11	0.58	1.73	1.28
Johns Hopkins University	Private	0.26	0.28	1.18	0.33	0.51	0.28
Vanderbilt University	Private	0.14	0.24	0.33	0.08	0.03	0.08
Purdue University–West Lafayette	Public	0.51	0.61	0.7	0.7	1.4	1.26
University of Maryland–College Park	Public	1.05	0.13	0.57	0.75	0.29	1.7
Average all public		0.75416667	0.3575	1.01	0.974166667	0.910833333	1.145833333
Average all private		0.30181818	0.43909090 9	0.76272727	0.32545455	0.51636363 6	0.36454545
Average all schools		0.53782609	0.396521739	0.89173913	0.663478261	0.755	0.772173913

2 = the discourse is highly visible in the documents and elaborated in the documents; and

3 = the discourse is a central part of the university's plan and explicitly mentioned as part of all elements of the plan: mission, vision, and so forth (see Tables 5 and 6).

Findings[3]

With remarkable regularity, each of the discourses registered quite strongly in higher education. Some discourses were qualitatively more important than others, particularly the neoliberal, mixed economy, and community engagement discourses, but all six ranked as either *highly visible* or *central* elements of the institutional strategies (see Tables 5 and 6). Two discourses registered a bit less fully in this assessment. Postmodernity may have ranked lower because its position in the academy has shifted: What was before a challenging discourse that went to the heart of the sociology of knowledge has now become institutionalized as interdisciplinarity, represented by change in some of the more pervasive disciplinary silos of the institutions. The lower ranking of the globalization discourse itself may have a similar explanation in that it is now so intrinsic and pervasive in its institutional influence that it does not merit too much explicit particular mention. For instance, the New York University Presidential Transition Team (2002) report takes for granted that the global perspective is inescapable in the contemporary world. In similar vein, Duke University's (2001) strategic plan states simply: "Internationalization is an important intellectual trend in itself and has been a growing priority for Duke for several years" (p. 23). The University of Southern California, in its Plan for Excellence (2000), affirms that it

> will create a significant global presence that will increase international visibility, reach and impact of our research, scholarship, art, education and service. . . . To best serve the interests of Los Angeles and Southern California, our faculty need to understand the region in its global context. . . . The demand for education is increasingly worldwide, and the best students will view higher education as an international market, heightening competition and creating a truly global student body. (p. 2)

And the University of Pennsylvania's Building on Excellence plan (2002) perhaps puts this notion of the pervasiveness of globalization best:

> All twelve of Penn's schools and virtually every academic program incorporate a global perspective as part of their curricula, and faculty in a wide variety of disciplines view international issues and comparative approaches as integral to their own research agenda. Indeed, the global dimension of virtually every discipline is becoming increasingly important as technology reduces the natural barriers of time and space, and this trend is likely to continue. (p. 7)

For some universities, the particular imperative is to prepare their students for active involvement in a working and living environment that

Table 5

Qualitative Measures of the Globalizing Discourses of Higher Education

University	Public or Private	Diversity	Postmodernism	Neoliberalism	Mixed Economy	Globalization	Community Engagement
Dartmouth University	Private	3	2	3	2	3	2
Duke University	Private	3	2	3	3	3	3
Emory University	Private	2	3	3	1	2	3
New York University	Private	3	1	2	2	3	3
Northwestern University	Private	1	3	3	1	2	1
Pennsylvania State University–University Park	Public	2	2	3	3	2	3
Princeton University	Private	3	0	3	3	1	1
Rice University	Private	2	3	3	2	1	3
Stanford University	Private	2	3	3	3	2	1
Texas A&M University	Public	3	3	3	3	3	3
University of Alabama–Birmingham	Public	3	0	2	3	2	3
University of Arizona	Public	3	1	2	3	1	3
University of California-Berkeley	Public	2	3	3	3	2	2
University of California–Davis	Public	3	1	2	3	2	3
University of Illinois–Urbana-Champaign	Public	3	1	2	3	3	3
University of Southern California	Private	2	3	3	3	3	3
University of Texas–Austin	Public	2	1	3	2	1	2
University of Washington–Seattle	Public	1	2	2	0	2	2
University of Wisconsin–Madison	Public	2	2	3	3	3	3
Johns Hopkins University	Private	2	3	3	3	3	2
Vanderbilt University	Private	3	3	3	2	1	1
Purdue University–West Lafayette	Public	3	3	3	2	3	3
University of Maryland–College Park	Public	3	3	3	3	3	3
Number with Quality 3		12	11	17	13	10	15
Number with Quality 2		9	5	6	7	8	4
Number with Quality 1		2	5	0	2	5	4
Number with Quality 0		0	2	0	1	0	0

Table 6
**Percentage Distribution of Qualitative Measures of the
Globalizing Discourses of Higher Education**

Quality	Diversity	Postmodernism	Neoliberalism	Mixed Economy	Globalization	Community Engagement
3	52	48	74	56	43	65
2	39	22	26	30	34	17
1	9	22	0	9	22	17
0	0	9	0	4	0	0

reflects this increasingly "networked" reality. For instance, the University of Wisconsin–Madison (2005) strategic plan speaks of assisting "students in preparing for citizenship in a diverse and global world" (p. 5). In this shrinking arena, the influence of neoliberal emphasis on the need to compete and to subordinate educational goals to economic ones is apparent in the corporatist agenda emerging in many institutions. For instance, the strategic plan from the Princeton Board of Trustees (2000) affirms its determination to maintain a superior student-faculty ratio to that of competitor institutions, while the University of Wisconsin–Madison's strategic plan (2005a) states,

> We must find ways to better understand the needs of employers, and to identify new and emergent educational interests of potential students, allowing us to remain visible and relevant in all quarters as a source of graduate and professional education. (p. 9)

To achieve these objectives, many acknowledge the efficacy of a managerialist culture and efficiency measures for a lean, mean operation, in imitation of the corporate restructuring experienced in the private economy. As expressed by Rice University (1997) in its strategy, cost-cutting and downsizing measures similar to those practiced by many corporations are demanded. In similar vein, Penn State University (2003) affirms its restructuring to achieve cost-efficiency through further consolidation of administrative and academic units.

This focus on institutional restructuring and resource constraint has induced, or at least been paralleled by, the move of the academy to enter into new relationships with business, as evident in the spread of task forces to advance university-business relations. As expressed in Duke's (2005a) strategy, "We have begun to link our research efforts with those of the private sector and neighboring public universities in ways that should substantially enhance our quality in the next decade" (p. 24). Almost every university finding strategic direction in the mixed economy approach described research entrepreneurship as a key to their future. Penn State University (2003), for example, emphasized its determination to adapt its intellectual property into the commercial arena.

However, universities do not perceive this emphasis on "research entre-preneurialism" as incompatible with civic obligation to their local hinter-lands: Duke, for example, writes in its strategic plan that "our signature reflects a combination of place and scale and a relationship between campus and surrounding towns that is especially conducive to community" (p. 10). Similarly, the search for excellence, efficiency, and economic partners has not deflected Duke (2001a) from a concern about diversity, an issue it has included as a category for school and departmental reviews.

This goal of diversity has become a significant one in over 50% of the major research university plans in the sample. For instance, New York University and Princeton emphasize the significance of a diverse faculty and student body, a goal echoed in the strategic plan of Iowa State University (2005), which seeks in its 2010 plan to "expand the diversity of people, ideas, and cultures, and nurture an environment in which diversity can thrive" (p. 4). Virginia Tech University (2001) acknowledges how, within a leading university, diversity enriches the learning experience.

Though there is no direct reference to postmodernism to be found in these documents, new initiatives in interdisciplinarity, translational, and action-based research and study of identity have all contributed to the rethinking of the research process and the nature of knowledge. As indicated by Rice University, effective approaches to problem solving have made the boundaries of traditional disciplines more porous. Northwestern University (2004) takes an equally challenging look at the organization of knowledge in the academy in what it calls Northwestern: The Highest Order of Excellence: A Planning Framework, 2005-2010: "We appreciate the creative tension between strong disciplinary and interdisciplinary pursuits. . . . At the same time, we expect the boundaries of academic disciplines to change over time as they are influenced by what was once interdisciplinary" (p. 3). The University of Southern California, in its Plan for Excellence (2000), brings together many of the themes outlined here: "Some of the distinguishing features of our university, including our urban location, student diversity, breadth of disciplines and fields of study, strong reputation for interdisciplinary research and scholarship, close ties to the local community and the Pacific Rim" (p. 2).

Conclusion

Patently, the modern university is no longer an ivory tower or enclave (if it ever was in reality). What we find at the end of this two-part study of literature on modern higher education research units and of their strategic documents is that analysis of the primarily cased-based and experience-tinged literature of the global university is well displayed in the strategic documents of American research universities. However, as indicated in the analysis, there is no neat symmetry between the discourses and their translation into the institutional reformulation of academy. In particular, the somewhat rarified discussions about postmodernist epistemologies in the literature do not find clear resonance in the strategies and plans examined here.

Nevertheless, this article has argued that university strategic planning documents are key sites of institutional discourse, and the substantial presence in them of the global discourses identified here demonstrates that these themes are playing a key role in the institutional direction, goals, and values of contemporary American higher education. Whether this means that the "academy" has been truly transformed into a global institution is unclear. The "globalness" found in the studies and documents of the modern research university, reviewed here, is, at least, an expanded way to view the modern higher education research unit. But whether it portends a significant change in the direction of higher education of the magnitude of Clark Kerr's (1972) assessment of the "great transformation" of the postwar research university remains to be seen (p. 86 ff). As indicated at the start, this review of university strategic documents does not claim to assess the extent to which these themes are actually translated into actions. However, it does identify that, due to the diffusion of market ideas in the contemporary world, at least the universities feel the need to engage with these issues in how they publicly represent themselves via their core strategic statements.

At the same time, this article has emphasized the survival of rival imaginaries to the dominant neoliberal global order. As articulated by Leitner, Peck, and Sheppard (2007), these

> might promote collective rather than individual welfare; collaboration rather than competition; consensual rather than hierarchical decision making; recognition and respect for diversity rather than the promotion and commodification of individual identity; equity, justice, and social welfare rather than efficiency and competitiveness; and care for the environment rather than productivity, growth, and exploitation. (p. 319)

The content analysis of strategic documents undertaken here confirms that neoliberal globalization is a deeply contested concept within the academy as elsewhere. Will universities further appropriate the language and culture of business and marketing and seek to "brand" themselves globally as adaptive to dominant trends, particularly those that yield lucrative commercial return? Or, whatever the perceived political-economy hegemony, will they remain faithful to a core educational mission, involving challenge to orthodoxy and the independent pursuit of knowledge, while deploying all the positive potential of transnational and intersectoral networking in the global age? Thus far, the strategy statements and plans of leading U.S. universities demonstrate that there is no determinist logic influencing such choices. Whatever the *structural* pressures toward a convergent neoliberal and market-driven framework for institutional decision making, there remains political space for the *agency* of staff, students, community, and state to intervene with an alternative agenda.

Notes

This article derives from an international research project, known as Contested Cities and Urban Universities (CU2), involving the Institute of Spatial and Environmental

Planning at Queen's University, Belfast, and the Great Cities Institute at the University of Illinois, Chicago. We are grateful to researchers Jonah Katz, Gavan Rafferty, and Jessica Thompson for their work in data generation and organization.

[1]The top research universities among this master list of institutions were determined by their rank in the top 25 nationally in each of the following nine key criteria: (1) total research expenditures, (2) federal research expenditures, (3) endowment assets, (4) annual giving, (5) national academy members, (6) faculty awards, (7) doctorates awarded, (8) postdoctoral appointees, and (9) SAT/ACT range. Fifty-three total institutions appeared in the top 25 of university rankings based on their place in the ranking of the above nine criteria. Because the institutions were ranked based on their presence in a top 25 of just one of the nine criteria, many institutions tied with each other, creating a list of 53 universities that the report suggests represents the best in American research universities. Of these 53 schools, 26 are private research universities and 27 are public universities.

On this basis, the following schools were selected for the intensive discourse analysis:

Stanford University
Johns Hopkins University
Duke University
University of Southern California
University of California–Berkeley
University of Washington–Seattle
University of Wisconsin–Madison
Princeton University
Northwestern University
Emory University
University of Texas–Austin
Pennsylvania State University–University Park
University of Illinois–Urbana-Champaign
Texas A&M University
New York University
Dartmouth College
Rice University
Vanderbilt University
University of Arizona
University of California–Davis
Purdue University–West Lafayette
University of Maryland–College Park
University of Alabama–Birmingham

[2]Here a strategic plan is defined as a single document or series of Web pages formally describing future university plans. Other planning-type documents were not formally designated as strategic plans but still contained official university reports discussing the institution's future. (For example, some strategic elements were found in physical master plans and board of trustee reports.) These were also included in our analysis if other planning documents were unavailable. Noticeably, public and private universities did not fall evenly along the spectrum. To illustrate, four out of the top five schools with plans are private, while four out of the bottom with plans are public. The challenge was to find an even number of public and private plans that were (somewhat) evenly distributed throughout the ranking, enabling fair comparisons between both types. (For example, if all of the chosen private plans were in the top half of the list and all of the chosen public plans in the bottom half, correct comparison could not be drawn because any differences could be due to their place in the list.) Thus, the list of 53 universities was divided into thirds, each with similar ratio of public and private plans. These divisions were demarcated by the number of measures in the top 25: The first group had 1 to 2 measures in the top 25, the second group had 3 to 6, and the third group had 7 to 9. Four private and four public universities were randomly chosen from those with plans in Group 1, three private and four public universities from those with plans in Group 2, and four private and three public universities from those with plans in Group 3. This brought us to 23 plans—11 private and 12 public. This proportion of private universities to public universities was less than 5% different between the total proportion between private and public universities in the top 53.

³The quotations used in this section of the article are derived from electronic strategic documents, often unpaginated textually. They are cited as accurately as possible here and represent the Web-based enumeration of electronic pages. For more information, we direct the reader to the institutional home page Websites.

References

Altbach, P. G., & Umakoshi, T. (Eds.). (2004). *Asian universities: Historical perspectives and contemporary challenges*. Baltimore: Johns Hopkins University Press.

Anderson, E. (2002). *The new professoriate*. Washington, DC: American Council on Education.

Appadurai, A. (2001). Grassroots globalization and the research imagination. In A. Appadurai (Ed.), *Globalization*. Durham, NC: Duke University Press.

Atkinson, R. (2001, May 26). *The globalization of the university*. Inaugural address delivered at the Nagasaki University of Foreign Affairs, Japan. Retrieved from http://www.oap.ucsb.edu/diversity/docs/mitsuta.html

Baldwin, R., & Krotseng, M. (1995). *Incentives in the academy: Issues and options* (New Directions for Higher Education, No. 51). San Francisco: Jossey-Bass.

Banks, J. (2002). Multicultural education: Historical developments, dimensions and practice. In C. Turner, A. L. Antonio, M. Garcia, B. V. Laden, A. Nora, & C. L. Presley (Eds.), *Racial and ethnic diversity in higher education* (2nd ed., pp. 427–457). Boston: Pearson Custom.

Barber, B. (1995). *Jihad vs. McWorld*. New York: Ballantine.

Barnett, R., & Griffin, A. (Eds.). (1997). *The end of knowledge in higher education*. London: Cassell.

Baudrillard, J. (1988). *Selected writings* (M. Poster, Ed.). Stanford, CA: Stanford University Press.

Bender, T. (1993). *Intellect and public life: Essays on the social history of academic intellectuals in the United States*. Baltimore: John Hopkins University Press.

Bender, T. (2000, November). Lecture presented at the Chicago Humanities Festival.

Benson, L., & Harkavy, I. (2000). Integrating the American system of higher, secondary, and primary education to develop civic responsibility. In T. Ehrlich (Ed.), *Civic responsibility in higher education* (pp. 174–196). Phoenix, AZ: Oryx.

Berger, P. (2002). The cultural dynamics of globalization. In P. Berger & S. Huntington (Eds.), *Many globalizations: Cultural diversity in the contemporary world*. Oxford, UK: Oxford University Press.

Berger, P., & Huntington, S. (Eds.). (2002). *Many globalizations: Cultural diversity in the contemporary world*. Oxford, UK: Oxford University Press.

Black, J. N. (2004). *The freefall of the American university: How our colleges are corrupting the minds and morals of the next generation*. Nashville, TN: WND Books.

Blackmore, J. (2003). Tracking the nomadic life of the educational researcher: What future for feminist public intellectuals and the performative university? *Australian Educational Researcher, 30*(3), 1–24.

Bleiklie, I. (1998). Justifying the evaluative state: New public management ideals in higher education. *European Journal of Education, 33,* 299–316.

Bloland, H. (1995). Postmodernism and higher education. *Journal of Higher Education, 66,* 521–570.

Bok, D. (2003). *Universities in the marketplace: The commercialization of higher education*. Princeton, NJ: Princeton University Press.

Bowen, W. G., & Bok, D. (1998). *The shape of the river: Long-term consequences of considering race in college and university admissions*. Princeton, NJ: Princeton University Press.

Boyer, E. (1990). *Scholarship reconsidered: Priorities of the professoriate*. Princeton, NJ: Carnegie Foundation for the Advancement of Teaching.

Boyer, E. (1996). The scholarship of engagement. *Journal of Public Service and Outreach, 1,* 11–20.

Branscomb, M., Kodama, F., & Florida, R. (Eds.). (1999). *Industrializing knowledge: University-industry linkages in Japan and in the United States.* Cambridge, MA: MIT Press.

Braun, D., & Merrien, F.-X. (Eds.). (1999). *Towards a new model of governance for universities? A comparative view* (Higher Education Policy Series). London: Jessica Kingsley.

Breton, G., & Lambert, M. (Eds.). (2004). *Universities and globalization: Private linkages, public trust.* Paris: UNESCO.

Caircross, F. (1997). *The death of distance: How the communications revolution is changing our lives.* Boston: Harvard Business School Press.

Calas, M., & Smircich, L. (2001). Introduction: Does the house of knowledge have a future? *Organisation, 8,* 147–149.

Castells, M. (1996). *The rise of the network society.* Malden, MA: Blackwell.

Castells, M. (1997). *The information age: Economy, society and culture: Vol. 11. The power of identity* (2nd ed.). Malden, MA: Blackwell.

CEOs for Cities. (2002). *Leveraging colleges and universities for urban economic revitalization.* Boston: Author.

Clark, B. (1998). *Creating entrepreneurial universities: Organizational pathways of transformation.* Oxford, UK: Pergamon.

Clark, D. (1999). *Urban world/global city.* London: Routledge.

Cooper, C. (2004). *Challenging Diversity: Rethinking equality and the value of difference.* Cambridge, UK: Cambridge University Press.

Community Outreach Partnerships Centers. (2001). *COPC annual report 2000.* Washington, DC: U.S. Department of Housing and Urban Development.

Deem, R. (2001). Globalization, new managerialism, academic capitalism, and entrepreneurialism in universities: Is the local dimension still important? *Comparative Education, 37,* 7–20.

Delanty, G. (1998). The idea of a university in the global era: From knowledge as an end to the end of knowledge? *Social Epistemology, 12*(1), 3–25.

Delanty, G. (2001). *Challenging knowledge: The university in the knowledge society.* Buckingham, UK: Open University Press and Society for Research in Higher Education.

DeMulder, E., & Eby, K. (1999). Bridging troubled waters: Learning communities for the 21st century. *American Behavioral Scientist, 42,* 892–901.

deWit, H. (2002). *Internationalization of higher education in the United States of America and Europe: A historical, comparative, and conceptual analysis.* Westport, CT: Greenwood.

Duderstadt, J. J. (2003). *A university for the 21st century.* Ann Arbor: University of Michigan Press.

Duryea, E. (2000). *The academic corporation.* New York: Falmer.

Ehrlich, T. (Ed.). (2000). *Civic responsibility and higher education.* Phoenix: Oryx Press.

Fainstein, S. S. (1990). The changing world economy and urban restructuring. In D. Judd & M. Parkinson (Eds.), *Leadership and urban regeneration.* Newbury Park, CA: Sage.

Fairweather, J. (1996). *Faculty work and the public trust: Rethinking the value of teaching and public service in American academic life* (pp. 31–47). Boston: Allyn & Bacon.

Feld, M. (1998). Community outreach partnership centers: Forging new relationships between university and community, *Journal of Planning Education and Research, 17,* 285–290.

Feller, I. (2004, May). Virtuous and vicious cycles in the contribution of public research universities to state economic development objectives. *Economic Development Quarterly, 18,* 138–150.

Florida, R. (2005). *Cities and the creative class.* London: Routledge.

Foucault, M. (1972). *The archeology of knowledge* (A. M. Sheridan-Smith, Trans.). London: Tavistock.

Friedman, M. (1962). *Capitalism and freedom.* Chicago. University of Chicago Press.

Gaffikin, F. (2008). *Interface between academy and community in contested space: The difficult dialogue.* In W. Wiewel & D. Perry (Eds.), *Global universities and urban development: Case studies and analysis.* London. M. E. Sharpe.

Geiger, R. L. (2004). *Knowledge and money: Research universities and the paradox of the marketplace.* Stanford, CA.: Stanford University Press.

Giamatti, A. B. (1982). The university, industry, and cooperative research. *Science, 218,* 1278–1280.

Giddens, A. (1990). *The consequences of modernity.* Cambridge, UK: Polity.

Giroux, H. (2003). Selling out higher education. *Policy Futures in Education, 1*(1), 179–200.

Glazer, L., & Grimes, D. (2004). *A new path to prosperity? Manufacturing and knowledge-based industries as drivers of economic growth.* Michigan Future Inc. and the University of Michigan.

Goddard, J. (1999). How universities can thrive locally in a global economy. In H. Gray (Ed.), *Universities and the creation of wealth.* Buckingham, UK: Open University Press.

Gordon, L., & Whitty, G. (1997). Giving the "hidden hand" a "helping hand": The rhetoric and reality of neo-liberal education reform in England and New Zealand. *Comparative Education, 33,* 453–467.

Greider, W. (1997). *One world, ready or not: The manic logic of global capitalism.* New York: Simon & Schuster.

Gumport, P. (2000). Academic restructuring: Organizational change and institutional imperatives. *Higher Education, 39,* 67–91.

Gurin, P., Dey, E., Hurtado, S., & Gurin, G. (2002). Diversity and higher education: Theory and impact on educational outcomes. *Harvard Educational Review, 72,* 330–366.

Gurin, P., Lehman, J., Lewis, E., Dey, E., Gurin, G., & Hurtado, S. (2004). *Defending diversity: Affirmative action at the University of Michigan.* Ann Arbor: University of Michigan Press.

Harvey, D. (2005). *A brief history of neoliberalism.* Oxford, UK: Oxford University Press.

Hayek, F. (1944). *The road to serfdom.* London: Routledge.

Held, D., & McGrew, A. (Eds.). (2003). *The global transformation reader: An introduction to the globalization debate* (2nd ed.). Cambridge, UK: Polity.

Hirst, P., & Thompson, G. (1999). *Globalization in question* (2nd ed.). Cambridge, UK: Polity.

Hollingsworth, P. (Ed.). (2000). *Unfettered expression.* Ann Arbor: University of Michigan Press.

Hoogvelt, A. (1997). *Globalization and the postcolonial world: The new political economy of development.* London: Macmillan.

Initiatives for a Competitive Inner City. (2002). *Leveraging colleges and cities for urban economic development: An action agenda.* Boston: CEOs for Cities.

Jameson, F., & Miyoshi, M. (Eds.). (1998). *Cultures of globalization.* Durham, NC: Duke University Press.

Johnston, R. J., Gregory, D., Pratt, G., & Watts, M. (2000). *The dictionary of human geography.* Oxford, UK: Blackwell.

Kanter, R. (1995). *World class: Thriving locally in the global economy.* New York: Simon & Schuster.

Kellogg Commission. (1999). *Returning to our roots: The engaged institution.* Washington, DC: NASULGC.

Kelsey, J. (1998). Privatising the universities. *Journal of Law and Society, 25*(1), 51–70.

Kerr, C. (1972). *The uses of the university: With a postscript 1972.* Cambridge, MA: Harvard University Press.

Kerr, C. (1998). *Troubled times for American higher education.* Albany: State University of New York Press.

Kuttner, R. (1997). *Everything for sale: The virtues and limits of markets.* New York: Knopf.

Lambert, R., & Butler, N. (2006). *The future of European universities: Renaissance or decay?* London: Center for European Reform.

Lasch, C. (1996). *The revolt of the elites.* New York: Norton.

Leitner, H., Peck, J., & Sheppard, E. (2007). Squaring up to neoliberalism. In H. Leitner, J. Peck, & E. Sheppard (Eds.), *Contesting neoliberalism: Urban frontiers.* New York: Guilford.

Leslie, L., & Slaughter, S. (1995). The development and current status of market mechanisms in United States postsecondary education. *Higher Education Policy, 10,* 239–252.

Lombardi Program on Measuring University Performance. (2004). *The top American universities: A report.* Gainesville, FL: The Center.

Marginson, S., & Consindine, M. (2001). *The Enterprise University: Power, governance and reinvention in Australia.* Melbourne, Australia: Cambridge University Press.

Marginson, S., & Rhoades, G. (2002). Beyond national states, markets, and the systems of higher education: A glonacal agency heuristic. *Higher Education, 43,* 281–309.

Maurrasse, D. (2001). *Beyond the campus: How colleges and universities form partnerships with their communities.* New York: Routledge.

Meyer, H. (2002). Universal, entrepreneurial and soulless? The new university as a contested institution. *Comparative Education Review, 46,* 339–347.

Newman, F., Couturier, L., & Scurry, J. (2004). *The future of higher education: Rhetoric, reality and the risks of the market.* San Francisco: Jossey-Bass.

Orfield, G., & Kurlaender, M. (Eds.). (2001). *Diversity challenged: Evidence on the impact of affirmative action.* Cambridge, MA: Harvard Education Publishing Group.

Peck, J., & Tickell, A. (2007). Conceptualizing neoliberalism, thinking Thatcherism. In H. Leitner, J. Peck, & E. Sheppard (Eds.), *Contesting neoliberalism: Urban frontiers.* New York: Guilford.

Perorazio, T. (2004, November). *Moving forward: Refocusing the debate on globalization.* Paper presented at the Association for the Study of Higher Education, International Forum, Kansas City, KS.

Perry, D. (2005). *The engaged university.* Unpublished manuscript, The Great Cities Institute, University of Illinois, Chicago.

Perry, D. C., & Wiewel, W. (Eds.). (2005). *The university as urban developer: Case studies and analysis.* Armonk, NY: M. E. Sharpe.

Perry, D. C., & Wiewel, W. (2008). The university, the city and land: Context and introduction. In W. Wiewel & D. C. Perry (Eds.), *Global universities and urban development: Cases studies and analysis.* Armonk, NY: M.E. Sharpe.

Powell, W., & Owen-Smith, J. (1998). Universities and the market for intellectual property in the life sciences. *Journal of Policy Analysis and Management, 17,* 253–277.

Rawls, J. (2005). *Political liberalism.* New York: Columbia University Press.

Rhodes, F. (2001). *The creation of the future: The role of the American university.* Ithaca, NY: Cornell University Press.

Rorty, R. (1982). *Consequences of pragmatism*. Minneapolis: University of Minnesota Press.

Rubin, V. (1998). The role of universities in community-building initiatives. *Journal of Planning Education and Research, 17,* 302–311.

Sassen, S. (1996). *Losing control? Sovereignty in an age of globalization*. New York: Columbia University Press.

Schmidt, P. (2000, June 30). States set a course for higher education systems. *Chronicle of Higher Education, 46,* A27.

Schon, D. (1995). The new scholarship requires a new epistemology. *Change, 27,* 26–35.

Scott, P. (1997). The crisis of knowledge and the massification of higher education. In R. Barnett & A. Griffin (Eds.), *The end of knowledge in higher education*. London: Cassell.

Scott, P. (Ed.). (1998). *The globalization of higher education*. Buckingham, UK: Open University Press.

Shapiro, H. T. (2005). *A larger sense of purpose: Higher education and society*. Princeton, NJ: Princeton University Press.

Silka, L. (1999). Paradoxes of partnerships: Reflections on university-community collaborations. *Research in Politics and Society, 7,* 335–359.

Slaughter, S., & Leslie, J. (1998). *Academic capitalism: Politics, policy and the entrepreneurial university*. Baltimore: John Hopkins University Press.

Slaughter, S., & Rhoades, G. (2004). *Academic capitalism and the new economy: Markets, state, and higher education*. Baltimore: Johns Hopkins University Press.

Strathern, M. (Ed.). (2000). *Audit cultures: Anthropological studies in accountability, ethics and the academy*. London: Routledge.

Stukel, J., (1994). Urban and metropolitan universities: Leaders of the 21st century. *Metropolitan Universities, 5*(2), 87–92.

Turner, C., Antonio, M., Garcia, M., Laden, B. V., Nora, A., & Presley, C. L. (Eds.). (2002). *Racial and ethnic diversity in higher education* (2nd ed.). Boston: Pearson Custom Publishing.

Van der Wusten, H. (1998). *The urban university and its identity: Roots, locations, roles*. Boston: Kluwer Academic.

Van Ginkel, H. (2003). What does globalization mean for higher education? In G. Breton & M. Lambert (Eds.), *Universities and globalization: Private linkages, public trust*. Paris: UNESCO.

Varga, A. (2000). Local academic knowledge: Transfers and the concentration of economic activity. *Journal of Regional Science, 40,* 289–309.

Walshok, M. (1995). *Knowledge without boundaries: What America's universities can do for the economy, the workplace, and the community*. San Francisco: Jossey-Bass.

Washburn, J. (2005). *University Inc.: The corporate corruption of American higher education*. New York: Basic Books.

Weiss, L. (1998). *State capacity: Governing the economy in a global era*. Cambridge, UK: Polity.

Willard, D. (1994). The unhinging of the American mind: Derrida as pretext. In B. Smith (Ed.), *European philosophy and the American academy*. Chicago: Hegeler Institute, Monist Library of Philosophy, Las Salle, Illinois.

Manuscript received August 2, 2007
Revision received March 7, 2008
Accepted June 13, 2008

Teaching, Learning, and Human Development

American Educational Research Journal
March 2009, Vol. 46, No. 1, pp. 146–182
DOI: 10.3102/0002831208323280
© 2009 AERA. http://aerj.aera.net

Predicting Teacher Performance With Test Scores and Grade Point Average: A Meta-Analysis

Jerome V. D'Agostino
The Ohio State University
Sonya J. Powers
University of Iowa

A meta-analysis was conducted to examine the degree to which teachers' test scores and their performance in preparation programs as measured by their collegiate grade point average (GPA) predicted their teaching competence. Results from 123 studies that yielded 715 effect sizes were analyzed, and the mediating effects of test and GPA type, criterion type, teaching level, service level, and decade of data collection were considered. It was found that test scores were at best modestly related to teaching competence and that performance in preparation programs was a significantly better predictor of teaching skill. Results revealed that test scores likely do not provide additional information beyond preservice performance to safeguard the public from incompetent teaching.

KEYWORDS: teacher assessment, test theory/development, teacher knowledge, teacher education/development, testing, meta-analysis

Nearly since the beginning of the teacher certification process, teaching candidates have been tested to hold teacher preparation programs accountable to the public (Mehrens & Phillips, 1989; Porter, Young, & Odden, 2001). Requiring candidates to take a test was construed as a means

JEROME V. D'AGOSTINO is an associate professor at Ohio State University, Quantitative Research, Evaluation, & Measurement Section, College of Education & Human Ecology, 301 Ramseyer Hall, 29 West Woodruff Avenue, Columbus, OH 43210-1177; e-mail: *dagostino.22@osu.edu*. He specializes in applied measurement and program evaluation.

SONYA J. POWERS is a doctoral student at the University of Iowa, College of Education, 224 Lindquist Center, Iowa City, IA 52242-1529; e-mail: *sonya-powers@uiowa.edu*. She specializes in large-scale assessment issues, equating methods, and generalizability theory.

to ensure that preservice programs maintained high and uniform academic standards and provided candidates the opportunity to develop a wide range of skills necessary to teach effectively. Paper-pencil teacher tests, however, have been criticized severely for producing scores that lack both content and predictive validation evidence (Berliner, 2005; Darling-Hammond, Wise, & Klein, 1995; Glass, 2002).

When claiming that teacher test scores do not predict teaching performance, most critics site a study conducted by Quirk, Witten, and Weinberg (1973), which remains one of the few quantitative syntheses conducted on the topic. Their review, however, was limited to a small set of studies conducted between the 1940s and 1960s that focused on one teacher test. For this study, we used more contemporary meta-analytic techniques to review the criterion-related validity evidence on teacher tests and included primary studies on various types of teacher tests that date from 1903 to 2004. Because a primary reason for testing has been due to a mistrust of preparation programs, we also examined the predictive power of preservice teachers' grade point averages (GPAs) in college. Comparing the validity coefficients of tests and GPAs might elucidate the extent to which tests function to safeguard the public from faulty teacher preparation information about candidates.

Overview of Teacher Testing

The use of written tests to certify teachers dates back to the early 20th century (Cubberley, 1906), but oral certification exams date back to the late 1600s (Haney, Madaus, & Kreitzer, 1987). From 1940 to 1993, the National Teacher Exams (NTE) were used extensively by states. The Educational Testing Service (ETS), administrator of the NTE since 1951, developed the Praxis series in the early 1990s to replace the NTE. Presently, many states rely on the Praxis exams to certify teachers, while other states contract with the Evaluation Systems group of Pearson to develop tests based on their teacher standards (Gorth & Chernoff, 1986).

The number of states with certification tests has oscillated over time. In 1977, only 3 states had tests, but the number increased to 12 by 1980 and to 30 three years later (Sandefur, 1985). Today more than 40 states administer at least one type of teacher test. The exams vary considerably in terms of purpose and content, and states commonly use a variety of tests at different stages of teacher preparation. Several states and universities administer basic skill tests to students who are seeking admission to a preservice program. These tests, such as Praxis I, typically contain items that measure foundational skills in specific subject areas such as mathematics and language arts. As candidates approach the end of their preservice programs, they usually take a small battery of exams consisting of subject matter tests that typically contain items that reflect more challenging material than measured by the basic skills assessments. Candidates who plan to teach elementary school are administered content knowledge exams that indicate competency across the core subjects commonly taught to primary school students. Those who plan to teach secondary school usually must pass more advanced subject matter exams in the specific areas for which they are seeking certification.

Both elementary and secondary candidates also are expected to pass a professional knowledge or pedagogical skills exam. Most present content and professional knowledge tests were designed to measure various facets of state or national teaching standards, or theory-based models of teaching. For example, Shulman (1987) articulated seven teacher knowledge dimensions including content, general pedagogical, curricular, pedagogical content, learners and their characteristics, educational contexts, and educational ends, purposes, and values. Test developers craft items to reflect these various dimensions of teaching and typically ask educators to judge the relevance of the measured skills and alignment of items to dimensions (Reynolds, Tannenbaum, & Rosenfeld, 1992).

The ETS administers the Praxis II series that contains several content knowledge tests and the Praxis II: Principles of Teaching and Learning (PLT) exam, which measures professional knowledge. Pearson develops similar exams for the same purposes in the states for which it holds contracts. More recently, some states have issued provisional licenses to candidates who pass the paper-pencil exams and meet other requirements, and full licenses to those who pass a performance assessment, such as the ETS Praxis III, in their first year of teaching.

Paper-pencil tests consisting primarily of multiple-choice questions, however, remain the main form of teacher certification testing, likely because of the savings in testing time and cost and the ability to assess across a wide domain. The increased prevalence in teacher testing that occurred in the 1980s coincided with the release of *A Nation at Risk* (National Commission on Excellence in Education, 1983), which sparked resurgent criticism of initial teacher preparation programs (Borko, Liston, & Whitcomb, 2006). The authors of the report stressed that teacher preparation programs could be improved by (a) focusing less on teaching methods and more on academic disciplines, (b) maintaining higher educational standards for preservice teachers, and (c) being evaluated based on the degree to which they met those two goals.

Numerous other reports critical of teacher education programs followed *A Nation at Risk*. The Holmes Group (1986), for example, issued a report in the late 1980s calling for reform of conventional programs. Like *A Nation at Risk*, the report claimed that most programs lacked high standards and focused more on education than discipline courses. The Holmes Group recommended that preservice teachers first earn degrees in subject areas, followed by participation in a postbachelor's program consisting of education courses and an internship at a school. The National Commission on Teaching and America's Future (1996) argued that many education programs were not adequate to prepare teachers for the challenges facing contemporary schools. The organization called for improved quality through three interdependent reform areas, including adherence to the National Council for Accreditation of Teacher Education standards, initial licensure certification through the Interstate Teacher Assessment and Support Consortium (INTASC), and in-service certification through the National Board for Professional Teaching Standards process. To date, INTASC has developed, but not implemented, content, professional knowledge, and performance-based teacher assessments with funding and support from 15 states (Council of Chief State School Officers, 2006).

Driven by a prevailing belief that many preservice programs lacked rigor, overemphasized teaching courses, and taught a narrowly defined and often irrelevant set of teaching approaches, states relied on paper-pencil tests to ensure public protection from poor practice. Indeed, this role for teacher tests was embodied in the NTE Policy Council's *Guidelines for Proper Use of the NTE Tests,* which stipulated that such tests allowed schools and states to compare the skills of candidates from various preservice programs with different standards and grading expectations (Nelson, 1985). Mehrens and Phillips (1989) succinctly depicted the lack of confidence in preservice programs and the faith in teacher tests by stating,

> There is no question but that teacher training institutions have graduated individuals without the skills and knowledge necessary to protect the public. That is one of the reasons licensure tests have become so popular. Whether this has been a willful act of knowingly graduating those who are incompetent, based on poor judgment about what teachers need to know, or indeed based on ignorance of the students' ignorance, it is clear that at least at some institutions, good grades do not mean acquisition of the necessary knowledge. (p. 286)

Because tests are based on a uniform set of standards and content domain, one might assume that assessments yield more stable indicators of preparedness to teach than performance in teacher education programs.

Beginning in the late 1990s, the federal government reinforced the use of teacher tests to hold preservice programs accountable through two major laws, the 1998 reauthorization of the Higher Education Act (HEA) and the 2004 No Child Left Behind Act (NCLB). The HEA amendments of 1998 included accountability stipulations for states that received funds and for higher education institutions with teacher preparation programs that enrolled students receiving HEA aid. Under Title II, states were required to submit report cards that included, among other information, (a) a description of the state's teacher licensure assessments, (b) evidence of the alignment between state teacher standards and the assessments, (c) the percentage of teacher candidates that passed the assessments, (d) the percentage of passing candidates disaggregated by teacher preparation program, and (e) the criteria used by the state to assess teacher preparation program performance (Amendments to the Higher Education Act of 1965, 1998). States also were required to identify programs that did not meet the criteria standards and include the names of nonpassing programs in their annual report cards.

Unlike prior reauthorizations of the Elementary and Secondary Education Act of 1965, NCLB added teacher qualification requirements. Title II of the law mandated that states had to implement a plan to ensure that all core subject teachers were highly qualified by the end of the 2005–2006 school year. "Highly qualified" was defined as a person who (a) holds a full teaching license in the state or who has passed the state licensure tests, (b) holds the minimum of a bachelor's degree, and (c) has demonstrated subject matter competency in the areas taught by the person (No Child Left Behind Act of 2001, 2002). NCLB also stipulates that all new teachers must pass a subject matter and teaching skill test in reading, writing, mathematics, and other basic areas. The law, however, does not specify which tests are to be used but instead leaves it to states to make such decisions.

The teacher accountability provisions of HEA and NCLB, which rely heavily on certification exams, demonstrate an increased mistrust of teacher preservice programs to properly and comprehensively prepare candidates. Implicit in the logic model of both federal laws is the prevailing belief, which dates back at least to *A Nation at Risk*, that ostensible declines in student achievement in the United States are partly the result of shoddy teacher preparation, which can be improved by holding programs accountable to teacher test scores. Thus, tests were used at the federal level for the first time to ensure better quality control across preservice programs and as a mechanism to provide more valid information about teacher competency than candidates' higher education grades.

Teacher Test Scores and Criterion-Related Validation Evidence

Tests have been used for higher education accountability purposes and as a means to safeguard the public from poor teaching, but it remains debatable if teacher test scores must predict an examinee's future teaching competence to be considered sufficiently valid. According to the *Standards for Educational and Psychological Testing* (American Educational Research Association, American Psychological Association, & National Council on Measurement in Education, 1999), content-related evidence is the primary form of validity information for test scores used for credentialing purposes, and criterion-related evidence is less applicable due to the difficulty of conducting concurrent and predictive validity studies (also see Kane, 1994).

Numerous critics of teacher tests nonetheless have pointed to a lack of criterion-related validity evidence as a fundamental weakness of the exam scores (Darling-Hammond et al., 1995; Glass, 2002; Haney et al., 1987; Merwin, 1978; Mitchell, Robinson, Plake, & Knowles, 2001; Wilson & Youngs, 2005). Their position is predicated on the assumption that tests required of candidates should produce scores that accurately reflect the candidates' competencies to teach. A review conducted by Quirk et al. (1973), which mainly addressed the criterion-related validity of the NTE weighted common examinations total (WCET)[1] scores, often is cited as evidence that teacher test scores do not predict teaching performance.

The authors partitioned their findings into those based on (a) concurrent validation coefficients in which WCET scores were correlated with preservice measures of teaching performance, college GPA, and personal characteristics and (b) those based on predictive coefficients such as supervisor ratings, student ratings, student achievement, and classroom observation. They also reported findings from very small study sets (one to three studies) that focused on other relationships such as between performance ratings and certain NTE subtests, between college GPA and student teaching ratings conducted by field supervisors or principals, and between GPA and principal or supervisor ratings during the first year of teaching.

Among the 16 studies correlating test scores and college GPA, the median was .55 and the range was .23 to .74, but other median values were much less promising. The 6 studies included that provided correlations between college supervisor and principal ratings during student teaching and test scores yielded a median of .05 (range: −.03 to .18). The predictive validation coefficients were not much higher overall. WCET scores and principal or supervisor ratings during the first year of in-service, which were gleaned from 7 studies, produced a median of .11 (range: −.15 to .45).

Quirk et al. (1973) also reported other related findings from the studies they reviewed on the NTE. Three of the studies provided college GPA and principal or supervisor student teaching ratings correlations, which all were either .07 or .08. Another set of three studies reported GPA and ratings by principals or supervisors during the first teaching year, which varied from .08 to .31 with a median of .25. The authors did not accentuate the relative magnitude difference between the latter median value and the median concurrent and predictive validity coefficients of the WCET, likely due to the paucity of GPA coefficients reported by studies that focused on teacher tests.

Haney et al. (1987) argued that a validity coefficient of .11 not only has little utility in the candidate selection process but also is potentially damaging. After correcting for unreliability in teacher ratings, they computed acceptance accuracy hit rates while considering a 90% (which is rather typical of state certification tests) pass rate. A .11 coefficient would lead to a selection accuracy increase of 1 percentage point over random selection with no test scores considered (90% to 91%). From the states' or employers' perspectives, perhaps this slight increase might justify using the tests to certify teachers, but from the perspective of the candidates, the situation also would lead to an 80% false-rejection rate and a mere 20% false-positive rate, the authors contended. Besides many candidates being unjustly denied a teacher license, the educational system would suffer from the loss of qualified teachers from the available employee pool—an especially problematic issue in teacher shortage times.

Despite the reliance on the Quirk et al. (1973) review to draw conclusions about teacher test criterion–related validation evidence, there are a number of limitations with their study that detract from the generalizability of the findings. Besides the near sole focus on WCET scores, the reviewed studies were conducted between the 1940s and early 1970s on test forms that have long been defunct. That is, no newer test forms (such as the Praxis series or Pearson tests) based on more contemporary pedagogical approaches or more updated measures of teacher effectiveness were included. Further, because the WCET represented a weighted composite score, the authors did not include many studies that examined the validity evidence of subtest scores, such as basic skill, content knowledge, or professional knowledge exams. In one of the few studies they selected that was not based on WCET scores (McCamey, 1958), the three correlations between NTE Professional Information test scores and GPAs of preschool, elementary, and secondary teachers were .23, .28, and .30, respectively. These few data points were not enough for the authors to make reliable comparisons with the WCET-GPA correlations.

One final limitation with the Quirk et al. (1973) review relates to the available methods to conduct quantitative syntheses in the early 1970s. Due to the lack of advancement of the field at that time, the authors did not weight the studies based on individual study variance, which is influenced by sample size, nor did they consider random versus fixed effects models. Study sizes varied from less than 10 to more than 1,600 participants, which could have led to different average coefficients if the study effects were properly weighted.

Since the early 1970s, several other studies have examined the validation evidence of various teacher test scores and GPAs. Many of these studies provided sufficient statistics to be included in our quantitative synthesis, but some other studies were based on multiple regression designs in which test score and GPA effects could not be partitioned properly and, hence, could not be included. These latter studies tended to address several teacher characteristics simultaneously as predictors of student test score performance. Perhaps the seminal study of this kind was the Coleman report (Coleman et al., 1966), which revealed that a teacher's score on a small vocabulary test was one of the few significant predictors of student achievement.

Other production function studies followed. In the oft-cited analysis of district-level data in Texas, Ferguson (1991) found that about one fifth to a quarter of student test score variation after controlling for background characteristics could be accounted for by district average teacher scores on the Texas Examination of Current Administrators and Teachers (TECAT), which was a basic literacy test that Texas began to require of all its teachers in 1986. Average TECAT scores also predicted mean student change scores over time, especially for Grades 3 through 7, and primary-grade teachers' pass rates were better predictors of 11th-grade students' achievement levels than secondary teachers' pass rates in the same district. In a similarly designed study conducted by Strauss and Sawyer (1986) using North Carolina district-level data from 1977 to 1978, a 1% increase in average teacher NTE scores led to a 5% drop in the failure rate on a high school competency exam.

The purpose of the majority of production function studies, however, was to ascertain if school or teacher quality variables, such as teacher literacy skills, accounted for student test score variation. Consequently, the studies elucidated little about the criterion-related validity of specific teacher test scores. After Quirk and colleagues' (1973) review, however, a number of validation studies were conducted on the NTE and other tests, such as the Praxis exams. The results from many of those studies were included in our meta-analysis, as were findings from the Quirk et al. review and other studies not included in their analyses that predated the early 1970s.

Study Objectives and Research Questions

By selecting studies that addressed the relationship between any teacher test or college GPA and an indicator of teacher performance, we were able to locate studies that varied considerably on numerous variables. Studies were included that examined overall college GPA, education major GPA, and GPA in methods and student teaching. Both elementary and secondary teachers in the studies took basic skill, content knowledge, and professional knowledge tests, and measures of their teaching were obtained while they were enrolled in preservice programs or while they were in-service teachers. Besides measures of teaching produced by supervisors, their students, or outside observers, studies were included that defined teacher performance with student test scores. We located studies dating back to 1903 and as recent as this decade.

This assortment of data coupled with the availability of contemporary meta-analytic techniques allowed us to conduct a more expansive quantitative synthesis of the teacher test and GPA criterion–related validity evidence than performed by Quirk et al. (1973). Our analysis focused on addressing the following research questions:

1. To what degree do teacher test scores predict measures of teaching performance?
2. Given that tests have been used to hold preservice programs accountable, to what extent do teacher tests predict teaching performance better than candidates' performance in their preparation programs as measured by GPA?
3. How dependent are the criterion-related validity effects of teacher tests and GPA on certain study characteristics, including (a) the type of teaching performance measure, (b) whether examinees taught at the elementary or secondary level, (c) whether teaching performance was measured when examinees were in their preservice or in-service period, (d) how teaching performance was measured, and (e) the decade in which data were collected?

Because the subsamples of teacher tests and GPA were not of equal sizes across these contextual variables, it became apparent to us that any differences by test or GPA might be the result of data confounding. We conducted modified weighted regression analyses (Lipsey & Wilson, 2001) in which effect sizes served as outcomes and the conditions of each variable served as potential predictors to control for possible biases.

Method

Study Selection Procedure

The pool of potential manuscripts for our study came from past reviews, electronic abstract searches, and document reference lists. An annotated bibliography composed by Quirk, Witten, and Weinberg (1972) for their review (Quirk et al., 1973) served as the initial source of manuscripts. We then conducted several ERIC and Dissertation Abstracts searches using a variety of identifying words and phrases such as "teacher," "certification," "testing," "predictive," and "GPA." After locating manuscripts, we perused reference lists to flag other potential documents. Earlier annotated bibliographies (Barr, 1948; Domas & Tiedman, 1950; Morsh & Wilder, 1954) and a literature review (Hoyt, 1965) that provided additional manuscripts were discovered in that process. Searching continued until no other manuscripts could be found.

Over 500 manuscripts were located and reviewed for potential inclusion. Most manuscripts had to be removed because empirical findings were not provided (e.g., were opinion papers), the variables of interest to our study were not included, or the manuscript did not contain adequate statistical information to compute effect size indices. The great majority of selected manuscripts contained correlation coefficients between test scores or GPA and a measure of teaching proficiency, but in some cases t or F values were presented. In those cases, we converted the values to correlations using procedures described by Rosenthal (1994).

The selection process yielded 123 manuscripts that contained sufficient data to compute effect sizes. The appendix provides general descriptive information about the retained manuscripts. Most studies yielded data on multiple outcomes and predictors of interest: A total of 715 effect sizes were produced from the 123 manuscripts. As can be seen from the appendix table, many of the early studies examined the predictive strength of GPA, and several studies focused on one type of indicator and one criterion. There were, however, studies conducted on GPA and tests from all periods across an array of conditions.

Sixty-six of the studies were located in peer-reviewed journals, 28 were from dissertations, 27 were technical reports, and 2 were reported in books or book chapters. Hence, nearly half of the manuscripts were from unpublished sources. We could not locate primary manuscripts for some studies, but sufficient data from those studies were provided in secondary sources such as annotated bibliographies, technical reports, and literature reviews (the secondary sources for those studies are cited in the reference section).

Effect size estimates were classified by a number of characteristics, including indicator type, criterion type, service level, teaching level, and the decade of data collection. Indicator type reflected the general classification of teacher test or coursework upon which the collegiate GPA was based. Effects were coded as basic skill, content knowledge, WCET, or professional knowledge tests and overall, student teaching, or education major GPAs. The various measures of teaching performance were categorized by criterion type, which included principal or supervisor ratings, college instructor or mentor teacher ratings, student evaluations, observations conducted by researchers or other third-party individuals, student achievement, and self-ratings. In a small proportion of cases, it was not possible to determine the criterion type for effects. These cases were classified as unspecified. Some effects were from analyses conducted on examinees who were preservice teachers at the time that measures of their effectiveness were taken, while other effects were based on performance measures made while examinees were in-service teachers. Study descriptions were sufficient to classify each effect by either service level.

Most studies indicated if study participants were preparing to teach or were teaching at either the elementary or secondary levels. In some studies participants were not disaggregated by teaching level and thus were combined for the analyses. A minority of studies did not report the level of teaching for study participants, so we coded those effects as unspecified teaching level. As stated, studies were included that were conducted within a 100-year span. To increase cell counts for some periods, we classified studies as before the 1920s and by decade up to the 1990s. All studies conducted after 1990 were categorized into the last time period category.

Two raters worked independently to code each effect from the studies. Primarily because most of the variable classifications were low-inference judgments (it was rather obvious from the manuscript narratives how to classify the effects), the interrater agreement across all variables was 98%. The few discrepant classifications across the judges occurred when they attempted to distinguish early teacher tests as either basic skill or content knowledge. In those cases, the raters reread the test descriptions more carefully, conducted more research on the tests if necessary, and concurred on a final indicator type classification.

Table 1 presents the breakdown of effect sizes by condition of each variable. We categorized each teacher exam from the studies as either a basic skills test, professional knowledge exam, content knowledge exam, or NTE WCET. Effect sizes from the latter test were used to compare our results to the Quirk et al. (1973) review and as a baseline to examine if other teacher test types produced significantly different validity coefficients. The table indicates that almost half (44%) of the effects were derived from college GPAs. Among the 313 GPA effects, 171 were derived from students' overall undergraduate GPAs (55%), 63 were from student teaching course GPAs (20%), and 79 were education major GPAs (25%). The majority of

Table 1

Frequency Distributions of Key Variables

Variable							
Indicator	Content Knowledge	Basic Skills	Professional Knowledge	WCET	GPA		
	30 (4.2)	242 (33.8)	75 (10.5)	55 (7.7)	313 (43.8)		
Criterion	Principal/ Supervisor	Student Evaluation	Observation	Student Achievement	Self-Rating	College Instructor/ Mentor Teacher	Unspecified
	496 (69.4)	26 (3.6)	72 (10.1)	44 (6.2)	16 (2.2)	34 (4.8)	27 (3.8)
Service Level	Preservice	In-Service					
	201 (28.1)	514 (71.9)					
Decade Data Collected	Before 1920s	1920s	1930s	1940s	1950s		
	10 (1.4)	79 (11.0)	77 (10.8)	93 (13.0)	36 (5.0)		
	1960s	1970s	1980s	1990s and After			
	177 (24.8)	53 (7.4)	142 (19.9)	48 (6.7)			
Teaching Level	Elementary	Secondary	Combined	Unspecified			
	217 (30.3)	139 (19.4)	133 (18.6)	226 (31.6)			

Note. The first cell entry is the effect size count, and the row percentages are in parentheses. GPA = grade point average; WCET = weighted common examinations total.

effects for teacher tests were from basic skills exams that often are taken by candidates before entry into teacher education programs. Fewer effects were from content and professional knowledge tests, but there were sizable subsamples from those test types as well. Most studies relied on principal or supervisor evaluations when study participants held in-service positions (i.e., concurrent validity studies). Nearly 30% of the effect sizes, however, were based on preservice measures of performance, and about 30% of effects were based on a variety of other criteria, including third-party observation, self-appraisals, student evaluations, and student test scores. The 1960s and 1980s were "golden periods" of data collection, but studies were conducted throughout the last 100 years.

Computing Effect Sizes

We followed procedures for computing effect sizes from correlation estimates for random effects models as stipulated by Shaddish and Haddock (1994). To compute effect sizes, we first stabilized the correlation variance by transforming the values to Fisher z scores using the following formula:

$$z_i = .5\{\ln[(1 + r_i)/(1 - r_i)]\}, \tag{1}$$

where r_i represents the correlation coefficient from each unique effect. At smaller r values (e.g., below .40), r approximates z, but at larger values of r, the corresponding z values are greater. The z scores were treated as unweighted effect sizes, and because the underlying distributions were considered to be bivariate normal, the conditional variance of z_i was

$$v_i = \frac{1}{(n_i - 3)}. \tag{2}$$

A weight for each effect was computed by taking the inverse of the variance,

$$w_i = \frac{1}{v_i}, \tag{3}$$

and an average weighted effect size was computed with the formula

$$\bar{z}. = \frac{\sum\limits_{i=1}^{k} w_i z_i}{\sum\limits_{i=1}^{k} w_i}. \tag{4}$$

The average weighted effect was .18; however, this computational procedure assumes a common population effect (the fixed effect model), θ, which was doubtful given that effect sizes were derived from multiple factors such as

157

different indicators and performance criteria. A test of this assumption, computed with the formula

$$Q = \sum_{i=1}^{k} [(z_i - \bar{z}.)^2 / (v_i)],\tag{5}$$

was significant, $Q(714) = 3{,}633.52$, $p < .001$, indicating that a shared common effect size was unlikely and that population effect size parameters varied significantly (i.e., followed a random effects model). We assumed that underlying population parameters varied mostly due to the type of indicator, so we computed Q values separately for teacher tests and GPAs. Both tests were significant, $Q(401) = 944.58$, $p < .001$, and $Q(312) = 2{,}055.47$, $p < .001$, respectively, revealing that common parameters were unlikely for teacher tests and GPA when treated alone. Thus, we decided to employ the random effects model, and we assumed that a common population effect, θ, was not fixed but rather had its own distribution.

Under the random effects model, the variance component that is due to population parameter variance must be computed and combined with the variance of each observed effect, v_i. The computed variance component ($\hat{\sigma}_\theta^2 = .044$) was added to every v_i to estimate each effect's unconditional variance, v_i^*. These values were then used to compute the effects' weights and average weighted effects for the random model following the formulas outlined above.

We computed an overall weighted random model effect, $\bar{z}^*$, which was .17. Ninety-five percent confidence intervals were computed around the overall effect by first computing the overall random effects standard error based on the formula

$$v.^* = \sqrt{1 / \sum_{i=1}^{k} (1/v_i^*)}.\tag{6}$$

The standard error was multiplied by 1.96 and added and subtracted to the overall effect size to yield lower and upper bounds of .16 and .18. Because the interval did not contain 0, we rejected the hypothesis that the average population effect was 0. The average weighted effect for the random model, however, has limited interpretability because the model does not assume one underlying distribution of effects. We then computed random model weighted effects and 95% confidence intervals for each condition of indicator type, criterion type, service level, teaching level, and decade in which the data were collected to better reflect model assumptions.

Results

Before addressing our key research questions, we explored if published manuscripts yielded significantly greater effect sizes than unpublished

Table 2

Weighted Random Model Average Effect Sizes With 95% Confidence Intervals by Variable

Variable	Conditions						
Indicator	Content Knowledge	Basic Skills	Professional Knowledge	WCET	GPA	College Instructor/ Mentor Teacher	Unspecified
	.17 (.09–.24)	.09 (.06–.11)	.17 (.12–.21)	.12 (.07–.17)	.25 (.23–.27)	.23 (.17–.29)	.20 (.13–.27)
Criterion	Principal/ Supervisor	Student Evaluation	Observation	Student Performance	Self-Rating		
	.18 (.16–.19)	.09 (.00–.18)	.17 (.13–.22)	.08 (.01–.15)	.15 (.10–.20)		

Service Level	Preservice	In-Service
	.22 (.20–.25)	.15 (.13–.17)

Decade Data Collected	Before 1920s	1920s	1930s	1940s	1950s
	.37 (.26–.48)	.25 (.21–.29)	.29 (.24–.33)	.16 (.12–.21)	.12 (.05–.18)
	1960s	1970s	1980s	1990s and After	
	.14 (.11–.17)	.14 (.09–.19)	.13 (.11–.15)	.11 (.06–.17)	

Teaching Level	Elementary	Secondary	Combined	Unspecified
	.16 (.13–.18)	.18 (.15–.22)	.16 (.13–.19)	.19 (.16–.21)

Note. The first cell entry is the effect size, and values in parentheses are the 95% confidence intervals. GPA = grade point average; WCET = weighted common examinations total.

sources such as dissertations and technical reports. The average weighted effect sizes, assuming a random effects model for published and unpublished documents, both were the same value as the overall weighted effect size of .17, indicating no bias in favor of published sources. Table 2 presents the random model weighted effects and 95% confidence intervals for each condition of the variables presented in Table 1. Among indicator types, it is evident that GPAs yielded larger effects than any type of teacher test. The average weighted GPA effect of .25 was greater than the content and professional knowledge test effects (.17 for both) and the basic skill test effect (.09), and because none of the teacher effect estimates are greater than or equal to the 95% lower bound estimate of .23 for GPA, the difference was statistically significant, $p < .05$. The WCET effect (.12) was comparable to Quirk and colleagues' (1973) finding of .11 but smaller than the professional and content knowledge test effects. Because the WCET point estimate was within the lower bound estimates for those effects, however, it was not safe to conclude that teacher test scores other than those from the old WCET are better teacher performance predictors overall.

Effects also were computed by criterion type to examine if validity coefficients depended on how teacher performance was measured. As can be seen from Table 2, college instructor and mentor teachers' ratings tended to be most correlated with the indicators. Third-party observation and principal ratings yielded comparable effect sizes, and students' evaluations and their achievement test scores were correlated the least with the indicators.

We examined if effect sizes differed depending on whether teaching performance was measured when study participants were in the preservice or in-service stages of their careers. Effects derived from preservice measures were significantly larger, $p < .05$, than in-service effects. In terms of effects over time, Table 2 indicates that validity coefficients were relatively large until the 1930s and dropped significantly from the 1940s onward. Since the 1970s, there has been a slight but steady decline in effect size magnitude, and studies conducted over the last 15 years have yielded rather diminutive coefficients. Most of the more recent studies were based on contemporary tests or present university grading practices.

Table 2 reveals that validity coefficients for secondary teachers were slightly higher than for elementary teachers, but the difference was not statistically significant (i.e., the point estimate for each effect is within the confidence interval of the other effect). Some studies combined the two groups, which led to an average weighted effect that was between the values of the two groups separately. Other studies did not specify teaching level of participants, and those studies yielded comparably larger effects. There were no significant effect differences across the conditions, however.

Drawing conclusions based on the results presented in Table 2 alone, however, would have been premature given the potential study confounders. As is evident in the appendix table, the indicator types (tests and GPA), for example, were not equally balanced across time, with more GPA studies in the early years, so it was possible that effect sizes diminished not due to historical trends but due to an indicator-by-time confounder. Further, the larger effect for GPA relative to teacher tests could have resulted from a disproportionately large effect produced by some studies that collected grades in student teaching during preservice and an indicator of teaching effectiveness based on the course instructor or mentor teacher. Indeed, disaggregating GPA by type of course (education major, student teaching courses, and overall undergraduate) revealed that GPA in teaching produced a larger effect, .29 (95% CI: .24–.34), than overall undergraduate GPA, .24 (95% CI: 21–.27), and education major GPA, .22 (95% CI: .18–.26).

We attempted to control for potential codependence by conducting modified weighted regression analyses (see Lipsey & Wilson, 2001). The 715 Fisher z values served as outcomes, and sets of dummy codes indicated the various conditions of the variables explicated in Tables 1 and 2. The random model weights for the effects were used to weight the analyses, and standard errors of the regression coefficients were corrected by dividing the values by the square root of the regression mean square residual. Three regressions were run: one that included dummy variables that separated GPA and the various types of teacher tests (Model 1), one in which a dummy variable was included that distinguished GPA from all teacher tests combined (Model 2), and one that partitioned the unique effects of each GPA type (overall undergraduate, student teaching, and education major).

The regression results are presented in Table 3. It can be seen from the table that in all models, the decade in which data were collected was negatively and significantly related to weighted effects. The –.03 unstandardized regression coefficient for that variable indicates a .03 decrement in weighted average effect per decade. Because the coefficients for the dummy variables are unstandardized, the values represent the weighted average effect sizes after controlling for the other variables in the model. The –.10 coefficient for service level reveals a .10 smaller effect for test and GPA indicators when performance was measured during in-service relative to preservice. Hence, predictive validity studies produced significantly smaller effects than concurrent validity studies after controlling for other variable conditions in the regressions.

Results from all three models reveal that weighted effects did not vary significantly across most criterion indicators, except for student performance and self-rating. After considering other variables, there was a .16 decline in weighted effects for studies based on student achievement measures as the criterion of teaching performance, and self-rating studies produced a .25 decline in effects after controlling for other variables (Model 1). In terms of indicator effects, Model 1 results showed that no teacher test type led to significantly greater or lesser average weighted effects while considering all model variables. Model 2 revealed, however, that GPAs taken together yielded a .11 greater effect than all teacher tests combined, which was statistically significant, $p < .01$. Partitioning GPA by type (Model 3) indicated that all three GPA indicators led to larger average weighted effects relative

Table 3
Results From Weighted Regression Analyses (N = 715)

Variable	Model 1	Model 2	Model 3
Intercept	.42 (.059)*	.39 (.049)*	.40 (.049)*
Decade data collected	−.03 (.004)*	−.03 (.004)*	−.03 (.004)*
Service level	−.10 (.019)*	−.10 (.019)*	−.10 (.019)*
Indicator			
Content knowledge	.04 (.049)		
Basic skills	−.06 (.030)		
Professional knowledge	.01 (.037)		
GPA	.08 (.030)*	.11 (.016)*	
Undergraduate GPA			.10 (.019)*
Student teaching GPA			.16 (.026)*
Education major GPA			.07 (.025)*
Criterion			
Principal/supervisor	−.08 (.040)	−.09 (.040)	−.09 (.040)
Student evaluation	−.12 (.062)	−.10 (.060)	−.10 (.060)
Observation	−.02 (.044)	−.01 (.044)	−.01 (.044)
Student performance	−.16 (.053)*	−.16 (.053)*	−.17 (.053)*
Self-rating	−.25 (.068)*	−.24 (.066)*	−.28 (.080)*
College instructor/mentor teacher	−.10 (.050)	−.11 (.051)	−.17 (.082)
Teaching level			
Elementary	−.01 (.020)	−.01 (.020)	−.01 (.020)
Secondary	−.01 (.023)	.01 (.023)	.01 (.023)
Combined	.03 (.021)	.03 (.021)	.03 (.021)

Note. The indicator, criterion, and teaching level variables are dummy variables coded as 1 for the *condition* and 0 for *all other conditions*. The base condition (*all codes* = 0) for criterion and teaching level is unspecified. Model 1 includes indicator dummy variables that distinguish between each teacher test type and grade point average (GPA), with weighted common examinations total serving as the base condition. In Model 2, only one indicator dummy variable is included, with *all teacher tests* coded as 0 and *GPA* coded as 1. Model 3 includes three variables that distinguish between each *GPA type* (coded 1) and *all other indicators* (coded 0). Decade data collected was coded from 0 (*before 1920s*) to 8 (*1990s and after*). Service level was coded 0 for *preservice* and 1 for *in-service*. The first entry in each cell is the unstandardized regression coefficient, and the value in parentheses is the coefficient standard error. R^2 = .23 for Model 1, .22 for Model 2, and .23 for Model 3. Effect sizes were weighted by the random effects weights.
*$p < .01$.

to teacher tests, but that student teaching GPA yielded the largest effect after controlling for other variables, including service level and college instructor/ mentor teacher criterion measures.[2]

Discussion

The primary aims of this meta-analysis were to examine the degree to which teacher tests predict teaching performance and to compare the predictive capability of tests with preservice teachers' GPAs based on available evidence since the early 20th century. A quantitative review (Quirk et al., 1973), primarily of the NTE WCET, revealed a rather diminutive median validity coefficient (.11) for that test and for GPAs, but the study was limited in scope and size. Nonetheless, using more contemporary synthesis methods and including more studies produced an average effect for the NTE WCET, .12 (converting the .12 Fisher z value back to correlations yielded a .12 average r), that did not differ from the earlier review.

Though content and professional knowledge tests yielded slightly larger point estimate effects than the WCET, and basic skills tests had a slightly lower overall effect, we could not reject the null hypothesis that other teacher test types better predicted teaching than the WCET. This finding was corroborated by the regression results. After controlling for various study conditions, none of the regression coefficients for the test type indicator variables was statistically different from zero. Hence, though many teacher test reviews relied heavily on Quirk and colleagues' WCET findings to draw generalized inferences regarding the predictive capability of other teacher test types, we did not produce evidence that such claims were in error.

The reasons for this finding are elusive, but one possibility is that test scores used in the studies lacked variability, which would lead to attenuated test and criterion relationships. To explore this interpretation, we examined the correlations between test score standard deviations (when available from the manuscripts) and z values, but only a small relationship was detected. Another possible explanation is that examinee performance on teacher tests usually is reported as total test scores, yet more information might reside in examinee performance on certain item types, especially those pertaining to functional pedagogical knowledge (D'Agostino & Hester VanWinkle, 2007). It also is possible, however, that teacher test scores do not reflect actual teaching skills or teaching promise and thus do not correlate well with measures of performance. The scope and form of data collected in our study did not allow us to examine these plausible explanations in greater depth.

Considering the entire pool of studies, the criterion that defined teacher performance influenced the size of validity coefficients. College instructors' and mentor teachers' ratings tended to be most correlated with indicators, and student performance was the least related to indicators. The most ostensible explanation for the larger coefficients when college instructors or mentor teachers judged candidates is the close proximity of those measures to the time candidates take teacher tests and earn their GPAs. Also, instructors and mentor teachers probably had numerous opportunities to observe candidates while teaching across a variety of situations, perhaps leading to a more accurate and complete assessment of teaching skill. For GPA, it is possible that coefficients were inflated because instructors and mentor teachers likely were the same individuals who both judged candidates' teaching and administered their grades.

It is debatable if using student achievement as an indicator of performance directly reflects teaching skill. One position would hold that teaching performance is inconsequential if such skills do not influence students' learning. Indeed, improved student achievement is the ultimate purpose of federal laws that promote teacher testing, such as the No Child Left Behind and the Higher Education Acts. Based on the 44 effects derived from achievement measures, and especially after controlling for other conditions, the available evidence suggests that teachers with higher test scores or GPAs were no better at facilitating student learning than teachers with lower scores on those indicators. Regardless of one's perspective on the role that achievement should serve in evaluating testing and college performance, it should be noted that student achievement is one step removed from the indicator scores and thus is perhaps too distal to correlate with achievement. Further, though we identified a sizable number of achievement-based coefficients, most of the selected studies relied on simple pre-post student gains, which notoriously possess a great degree of measurement error.

We unexpectedly discovered that validity coefficients diminished from the beginning of the last century to the beginning of the present century. We first surmised that effects decreased due to increased grade inflation and decreased test difficulty over time, resulting in range restriction and shrunken effects. But after returning to the original manuscripts and culling indicator standard deviations when available, we found no evidence that indicator variability dropped over time. Another possible reason for this finding is that test scores and GPA levels changed meaning as teacher candidate pools changed across decades. Notice in Table 2 that effects dropped most precipitously during the 1940s. Before that decade, teaching was one of the few professional career options for women, which likely resulted in many talented individuals vying for the highest grades, test scores, and desirable teaching positions. Earning As in pre-service courses, consequently, required one to demonstrate a great degree of knowledge and teaching skill. As other professional fields opened for women after World War II, the talent pool likely decreased, possibly resulting in lower grading and testing expectations. Although not influencing the variability of indicator scores, changes in candidate expectations could have changed the meaning of the various score levels. Of course, this interpretation remains speculative on our part because the data are far too limited to test the assumption. Nonetheless, the diminished effect over time reveals that newer tests based on more contemporary models of teaching are not better predictors of performance than older tests and the NTE WCET.

Our primary finding was that preservice teachers' performance in college, especially during student teaching, predicted performance better than teacher tests. It is entirely possible, however, that GPA effects were inflated to some degree because most of the teacher performance measures were conducted by people and GPA involves more prosocial skills than teacher test scores. This might be especially the case for GPA effects based on performance ratings made by mentor teachers or college instructors who also likely administered students' course grades. The larger effects for GPA, however, remained after controlling for study conditions, as evinced by the significant and positive regression coefficients for GPA in general (Model 2) and

GPA partitioned by type (Model 3). We found from Model 3 that student teaching GPA led to a .16 overall larger effect compared to all other indicators combined. This relative effect difference is larger than most of the overall effects for teacher tests.

The GPA effect was unexpected given the findings from the Quirk et al. (1973) study, conventional wisdom, and the accountability role that tests serve. Although Quirk et al. included only a small number of GPA studies in their review, we assumed that GPA would be less a predictor of performance than tests due to the lack of uniformity in grading practices both within and between preparation institutions. It is important to note that the GPA studies we included provided data from either a single college or multiple colleges. Studies based on data from multiple sites yielded GPA effects comparable to studies from single sites, indicating that potential between-site grading differences did not attenuate GPA and performance correlations.

The conclusion that tests serve little purpose in the teacher licensure process, given that college performance is a better predictor of performance, should not be drawn from the study results. Though we found that tests reveal little about performance, assessments still can be an effective mechanism to encourage preservice programs to provide future teachers the opportunity to learn a broad set of skills and an expansive knowledge base. One might assume that teacher preparation instructors would be more inclined to maintain higher standards and to teach from multiple perspectives if tests that cover a large teaching knowledge and skill domain are required for licensure. It is not a requirement of an accountability mechanism that it directly relates to the ultimate outcome.

Furthermore, it is important to distinguish between the types and forms of tests included in our meta-analysis and more performance-based assessments or portfolios. We purposively excluded any studies on the latter types of tests, mainly because so few studies regarding the criterion-related validity of scores from those tests have been conducted to date. Even while considering the lower reliability of such assessments given that raters are involved in scoring, the scores might more authentically reflect actual teaching and thus might correlate better with measures of performance. In a sense, the GPA scores for student teaching that were part of our study could be classified as performance-based indicators, and those scores yielded the largest criterion-related effects.

The results of this study indicated an irony in state practices and federal laws pertaining to teacher testing. Conventional wisdom holds that preservice programs cannot be trusted to properly and comprehensively prepare teachers and thus must be held accountable with external tests. After reviewing a rather large body of validity evidence, we discovered that test scores have been less related to teaching performance than students' success levels in the preservice programs the tests were designed to hold accountable. Those involved in the teacher hiring and selection process probably should focus as much or more on students' grades than scores on the tests used for licensure purposes.

Appendix
Selected Studies With Descriptive Information

First Author (Unless Noted)	Publication Year	Sample Size	Number of Effect Sizes	Indicator(s)	Criterion/Criteria	Service Level(s)	Teaching Level(s)
Meriam	1905	1,185	6	GPA	Principal/supervisor	In-service	Elementary
Mead	1916	39–40	3	GPA	Principal/supervisor	Preservice	Unspecified
Ritter	1918	1,436	1	GPA	Unspecified	In-service	Combination
F. B. Knight	1922	6–97	9	Professional knowledge, GPA	Principal/supervisor, self-rating, college instructor/mentor teacher	In-service	Elementary, secondary, combination
Whitney	1922	780	1	GPA	Principal/supervisor	In-service	Unspecified
E. S. Jones	1923	44–45	3	GPA	Principal/supervisor	In-service	Secondary
Somers	1923	110–156	3	GPA	Principal/supervisor	Preservice, in-service	Unspecified
Whitney	1924	725	3	GPA	Principal/supervisor	In-service	Elementary
Crabbs	1925	151	2	Professional knowledge	Principal/supervisor, student performance	In-service	Combination
Hamrin	1927	108	2	GPA	Principal/supervisor	In-service	Unspecified
Boardman	1928	88	2	Professional knowledge	Principal/supervisor	In-service	Secondary
Pyle	1928	99	1	GPA	Principal/supervisor	In-service	Unspecified
Tiegs	1928	25	1	Professional knowledge	Principal/supervisor	In-service	Elementary
Broom	1929	148	1	GPA	Principal/supervisor	Preservice	Unspecified
Almy	1930	110	2	GPA	Unspecified	Preservice	Unspecified
McAfee	1930	98–112	2	GPA	Principal/supervisor, observation	In-service	Elementary
Ullman	1930	116	15	Professional knowledge, GPA	Principal/supervisor, self-rating	In-service, preservice	Secondary

(continued)

Appendix (continued)

First Author (Unless Noted)	Publication Year	Sample Size	Number of Effect Sizes	Indicator(s)	Criterion/Criteria	Service Level(s)	Teaching Level(s)
Wagenhorst	1930	191	1	GPA	Principal/supervisor	In-service	Unspecified
Whitney	1930	100	1	GPA	Unspecified	Preservice	Unspecified
Anderson	1931	590	1	GPA	Principal/supervisor	In-service	Unspecified
Bossing	1931	100	3	GPA	Principal/supervisor	In-service	Secondary
Breckenridge	1931	215	1	GPA	Principal/supervisor	In-service	Unspecified
Ullman	1931	116	12	Professional knowledge, GPA	College instructor/mentor teacher, self-rating	Preservice	Secondary
Broom	1932	232–240	6	GPA	Principal/supervisor	In-service, preservice	Unspecified
Broom & Ault	1932	46–81	8	GPA	Principal/supervisor	In-service, preservice	Unspecified
Betts	1933	61	2	Basic skills, professional knowledge	Student performance	In-service	Elementary
Coxe	1933	112–500	9	Basic skills, GPA	Principal/supervisor	In-service	Elementary
Dodd	1933	90	2	GPA, professional knowledge	Principal/supervisor	Preservice	Unspecified
Peterson	1934	63	1	GPA	Principal/supervisor	In-service	Unspecified
Barr	1935	66	6	Basic skills, professional knowledge	Principal/supervisor	In-service	Elementary
Hardesty	1935	127	3	GPA	Principal/supervisor	In-service	Unspecified
Kriner	1935	55	12	Basic skills, GPA	Principal/supervisor	In-service, preservice	Unspecified
Phillips	1935	173	2	GPA, professional knowledge	Principal/supervisor	In-service	Elementary
Odenweller	1936	560	8	GPA	Principal/supervisor	In-service	Elementary

(continued)

167

Appendix (continued)

First Author (Unless Noted)	Publication Year	Sample Size	Number of Effect Sizes	Indicator(s)	Criterion/Criteria	Service Level(s)	Teaching Level(s)
Bent	1937	597	7	Basic skills, GPA	Principal/supervisor, college instructor/mentor teacher	Preservice	Combination
Kriner	1937	42–94	14	Basic skills, GPA	Principal/supervisor	In-service	Unspecified
Sandiford	1937	336	6	GPA	Principal/supervisor	In-service	Unspecified
Stuit	1937	146	1	GPA	Principal/supervisor	In-service	Unspecified
Stewart	1940	193	3	GPA	Principal/supervisor	Preservice	Unspecified
Flanagan	1941	49	1	WCET	Principal/supervisor	In-service	Unspecified
Tudhope	1942	96	1	GPA	Principal/supervisor	In-service	Unspecified
Martin	1944	123	7	Basic skills, GPA	Principal/supervisor	In-service	Unspecified
Hult	1945	19	4	Basic skills, GPA	Principal/supervisor	In-service	Unspecified
Rolfe	1945	47	2	Basic skills	Student performance	In-service	Elementary
Rostker	1945	28	2	Basic skills	Student performance	In-service	Elementary
Seagoe	1945	31	5	Basic skills, GPA	Observation	Preservice	Elementary
R. D. Jones	1946	65	10	Basic skills, GPA	Principal/supervisor, student performance	In-service	Unspecified
Lins	1946	7–50	12	GPA, WCET	Principal/supervisor, student evaluation	In-service	Secondary
Seagoe	1946	25	18	Basic skills, professional knowledge	Principal/supervisor	In-service, preservice	Elementary
Gould	1947	113	2	Basic skills, GPA	Principal/supervisor	In-service	Unspecified
Stephens	1947	20–86	13	Basic skills, professional knowledge, GPA	Student performance	In-service	Elementary
Espenschade	1948	46	1	GPA	Principal/supervisor	In-service	Unspecified
Schwartz	1950	18	2	GPA	Principal/supervisor	In-service	Unspecified

(continued)

Appendix (continued)

First Author (Unless Noted)	Publication Year	Sample Size	Number of Effect Sizes	Indicator(s)	Criterion/Criteria	Service Level(s)	Teaching Level(s)
Ryans	1951	90–192	14	Professional knowledge, WCET	Principal/supervisor	In-service	Elementary
Bach	1952	69–73	12	GPA	Principal/supervisor	In-service	Unspecified
Delaney	1954	93	1	WCET	Principal/supervisor	In-service	Elementary
Shea	1955	110	2	WCET, GPA	Principal/supervisor	In-service	Unspecified
Stoelting	1955	88–189	14	Basic skills, GPA	Principal/supervisor, college instructor/mentor teacher	In-service, preservice	Unspecified
M. L. Jones	1956	46	2	GPA	Principal/supervisor	In-service	Secondary
Schick	1957	72	3	GPA	Principal/supervisor	In-service	Combination
Massey	1958	62	1	GPA	Principal/supervisor	In-service	Unspecified
Beecher	1961	78	4	Professional knowledge	Principal/supervisor, student evaluation, unspecified	In-service	Secondary
Cole	1961	140	3	Basic skills, GPA	Principal/supervisor	In-service	Combination
Ellis	1961	70	8	GPA	Principal/supervisor	In-service	Secondary
Freehill	1963	60	8	Basic skills	Principal/supervisor	In-service	Combination
Hankins	1964	117–121	2	GPA	Student evaluation, self-rating	In-service	Combination
Thacker	1964	126	24	Basic skills, professional knowledge, WCET, GPA	Principal/supervisor	In-service	Combination
Mathis	1965	107–145	10	GPA	Principal/supervisor	Preservice	Elementary, secondary
Popham	1965	49	2	Professional knowledge	Observation	Preservice	Secondary
Leimkuhler	1966	42	10	Basic skills, GPA	Principal/supervisor, student evaluation	In-service	Elementary
Eissey	1967	111	20	WCET, GPA	Principal/supervisor, college	In-service	Combination

(continued)

Appendix (continued)

First Author (Unless Noted)	Publication Year	Sample Size	Number of Effect Sizes	Indicator(s)	Criterion/Criteria	Service Level(s)	Teaching Level(s)
Walberg	1967	280	9	WCET, GPA	Principal/supervisor	Preservice	Elementary
Baker	1968	45–200	34	Basic skills, GPA	Principal/supervisor	In-service	Combination, elementary, secondary
Lewis	1968	45	1	Content knowledge	Principal/supervisor	Preservice	Unspecified
Carson	1969	241	4	Professional knowledge, WCET	Principal/supervisor	In-service	Combination
Cornett	1969	31–68	9	GPA	Principal/supervisor	In-service	Elementary, secondary, combination
Siegel	1969	393–617	7	GPA	Principal/supervisor	In-service	Elementary, secondary
Ducharme	1970	73–105	17	Basic skills, WCET, GPA	Principal/supervisor, student performance	In-service	Unspecified
Gerfen	1970	234–235	3	Basic skills	Principal/supervisor	In-service	Secondary
Erickson	1971	56	1	Content knowledge	Student evaluation	Preservice	Secondary
Short	1971	78	4	WCET, GPA	Principal/supervisor	In-service	Unspecified
Mercer	1972	75	4	WCET, GPA	Principal/supervisor	In-service	Secondary
Brown	1974	22–37	4	Content knowledge, WCET	Principal/supervisor	In-service	Elementary, secondary
Orebaugh	1974	108–220	2	GPA	Unspecified	In-service	Unspecified
Burns	1977	35	4	GPA	Principal/supervisor	In-service	Elementary
Eash	1977	227	1	GPA	Principal/supervisor	Preservice	Elementary
Gress	1977	63	2	Basic skills, GPA	Principal/supervisor	Preservice	Unspecified
Jenkins	1978	109	6	WCET, GPA	Principal/supervisor	In-service	Unspecified

(continued)

Appendix (continued)

First Author (Unless Noted)	Publication Year	Sample Size	Number of Effect Sizes	Indicator(s)	Criterion/Criteria	Service Level(s)	Teaching Level(s)
Ayers	1979	28–131	14	Content knowledge, WCET	Principal/supervisor, student evaluation, observation	In-service	Elementary, secondary, combination
Andrews	1980	269	1	Content knowledge	Principal/supervisor	Preservice	Unspecified
Piper	1981	32	1	Content knowledge	Principal/supervisor	Preservice	Elementary
Veal	1981	30	2	Basic skills, content knowledge	Principal/supervisor	Preservice	Unspecified
Southern Regional Education Board	1982	61–179	18	Content knowledge, professional knowledge, WCET	Observation	In-service	Unspecified
J. S. Knight	1983	93–123	13	Basic skills, content knowledge, WCET, GPA	Principal/supervisor	Preservice	Elementary
Olstad	1983	27–58	26	Basic skills, GPA	Principal/supervisor	Preservice	Elementary, secondary
Lovelace	1984	57–78	4	Basic skills, content knowledge, professional knowledge	Observation	Preservice	Combination
Webster	1984	31–288	12	Basic skills, WCET	Principal/supervisor	In-service	Combination, secondary
Dobry	1985	43	2	Professional knowledge, GPA	Observation	Preservice	Secondary
Onderdonk	1985	184	3	WCET, GPA	Principal/supervisor	In-service	Combination
Browne	1986	111	1	Content knowledge	Unspecified	Preservice	Elementary

(continued)

Appendix (continued)

First Author (Unless Noted)	Publication Year	Sample Size	Number of Effect Sizes	Indicator(s)	Criterion/Criteria	Service Level(s)	Teaching Level(s)
DeRee	1986	243	1	GPA	Principal/supervisor	In-service	Unspecified
Lawrence	1986	125	5	Basic skills, professional knowledge	Unspecified	In-service	Unspecified
Guyton	1987	232–269	3	Content knowledge, GPA	Observation	Preservice	Unspecified
Kodiyanplakkal	1987	60	1	Basic skills	Observation	In-service	Combination
Watkins	1987	26	8	Basic skills	Principal/supervisor, student performance, self-rating	In-service	Combination
Ayers	1988	17–46	16	Basic skills, content knowledge, professional knowledge	Principal/supervisor, student evaluation, observation	In-service	Elementary
Olstad	1988	24	1	GPA	Unspecified	Preservice	Secondary
Ayers	1989	29–34	9	Basic skills, professional knowledge	Observation	In-service	Unspecified
Chiu	1989	537	3	Basic skills, professional knowledge	Unspecified	In-service	Combination
Salzman	1989	279–305	6	Basic skills, professional knowledge	Observation	Preservice	Combination
Gatti-Carson	1990	17	6	Basic skills, content knowledge, professional knowledge, GPA	Unspecified	Preservice	Secondary
Riggs	1990	122	8	Basic skills, WCET, GPA	Principal/supervisor	Preservice	Elementary

(continued)

Appendix (continued)

First Author (Unless Noted)	Publication Year	Sample Size	Number of Effect Sizes	Indicator(s)	Criterion/Criteria	Service Level(s)	Teaching Level(s)
Moore	1991	663	4	Basic skills, professional knowledge, GPA	Unspecified	In-service	Unspecified
Moore et al.	1991	448–663	4	Basic skills, professional knowledge, GPA	Observation	In-service	Unspecified
Salzman	1991	607–610	4	Basic skills, GPA	Observation	Preservice	Combination
Hicken	1992	100	3	Basic skills, professional knowledge, GPA	Principal/supervisor	Preservice	Unspecified
Riggs	1992	146–392	10	Basic skills, WCET, GPA	Principal/supervisor, college instructor/mentor teacher	Preservice	Unspecified
Heller	1993	117–125	4	Basic skills, content knowledge, professional knowledge	Observation	In-service	Unspecified
Joshua	1996	90–135	8	Basic skills, WCET	Principal/supervisor	In-service	Elementary
Dybdahl	1997	375	3	Basic skills	Principal/supervisor	Preservice	Combination
Ukpolo	1998	58	3	Basic skills, professional knowledge	Principal/supervisor	In-service	Combination
Blue	2002	22–146	9	Basic skills, content knowledge, professional knowledge, GPA	Principal/supervisor	Preservice	Elementary
Chesley	2004	100	1	Basic skills	Observation	In-service	Combination

Note. GPA = grade point average; WCET = weighted common examinations total.

Notes

[1]The weighted common examinations total was a composite score of the National Teacher Exams Professional Education (i.e., professional knowledge) and General Education (i.e., content knowledge) exams.

[2]We also examined possible codependence effects by including certain variable interactions in the regression analyses. Although it was not possible to include all crossed interactions because some cells contained less than two effects, we included interactions for indicator type (tests vs. GPA) by time, indicator type by criterion, indicator type by service level, and indicator type by teaching level mainly to examine if the GPA-test gap effect generalized across conditions of these other variables. None of the interactions were significant, indicating that the magnitude of the GPA-test gap was not contingent on other study characteristics.

References

References included in the synthesis are marked with an asterisk (*).

*Almy, H. C., & Sorenson, H. (1930). A teacher-rating scale of determined reliability and validity. *Educational Administration and Supervision, 16*, 179–186.

Amendments to the Higher Education Act of 1965, Pub. L. No. 105-244, 112 Stat. 1581 (1998).

American Educational Research Association, American Psychological Association, & National Council on Measurement in Education. (1999). *Standards for educational and psychological testing.* Washington, DC: American Educational Research Association.

*Anderson, H. J. (1931). Correlation between academic achievement and teaching success. *Elementary School Journal, 32*, 22–29.

*Andrews, J. W., Blackmon, R., & Mackey, J. A. (1980). Preservice performance and the National Teacher Exams. *Phi Delta Kappan, 61*, 358.

*Ayers, J. B. (1988). Another look at the concurrent and predictive validity of the National Teacher Examinations. *Journal of Educational Research, 81*, 133–137.

*Ayers, J. B., Sibert, P. C., & Birdwell, L. A. (1989). *Follow-up evaluation of graduates of the teacher education programs of Tennessee Technological University.* Cookville: Center for Teacher Education Evaluation, Tennessee Technological University. (ERIC Document Reproduction Service No. ED312229)

*Ayers, J. B., & Qualls, G. S. (1979). Concurrent and predictive validity of the National Teacher Examinations. *Journal of Educational Research, 73*, 86–92.

*Bach, J. O. (1952). Practice teaching success in relation to other measures of teaching ability. *Journal of Experimental Education, 21*, 57–80.

*Baker, L. W. (1968). *An analysis of some assumed predictors of success in teaching.* Unpublished doctoral dissertation, United States International University, Nairobi, Kenya.

Barr, A. S. (1948). The measurement and prediction of teaching efficiency: A summary of investigations. *Journal of Experimental Education, 16*, 201–283.

*Barr, A. S., Torgerson, T. L., Johnson, C. E., Lyon, V. E., & Walvoord, A. C. (1935). The validity of certain instruments employed in the measurement of teaching ability. In H. M. Walker (Ed.), *The measurement of teaching efficiency* (pp. 73–141). New York: Macmillan.

*Beecher, C. (1961). Data-gathering devices employed in the Wisconsin studies. *Journal of Experimental Education, 30*, 30–47.

*Bent, R. K. (1937). Relationships between qualifying examinations, various other factors, and student teaching performance at the University of Minnesota. *Journal of Experimental Education, 5*, 251–255.

Berliner, D. C. (2005). The near impossibility of testing for teacher quality. *Journal of Teacher Education, 56*, 205–213.

*Betts, G. L. (1933). The education of teachers evaluated through measurement of teaching ability. National survey of the education of teachers. *U.S. Offices of Education Bulletin, 10*(5), 87–153.

*Blue, T. W., O'Grady, R. J., Toro, J. A., & Newell, E. A. (2002). *How do we find the best teachers? A study of the relationships among SAT, GPA, Praxis Series test scores, and teaching ratings.* Paper presented at the annual meeting of the Association of Teacher Educators, Denver, CO. (ERIC Document Reproduction Service No. ED467764)

*Boardman, C. W. (1928). *Professional tests as measures of teaching efficiency in high school* (Contributions to Education No. 327). New York: Bureau of Publications, Teachers College, Columbia University.

Borko, H., Liston, D., & Whitcomb, J. A. (2006). A conversation of many voices: Critiques and visions of teacher education. *Journal of Teacher Education, 57,* 199–204.

*Bossing, N. L. (1931). Teacher-aptitude tests and teacher selection. *U.S. Office of Education Bulletin, 12,* 117–133.

*Breckinridge, E. (1931). A study of the relation of preparatory school records and intelligence test scores to teaching success. *Educational Administration and Supervision, 17,* 649–660.

*Broom, M. E. (1929). The predictive value of three specified factors for success in practice-teaching. *Educational Administration and Supervision, 15,* 25–29.

*Broom, M. E. (1932). A note on predicting teaching success. *Educational Administration and Supervision, 18,* 64–67.

*Broom, M. E., & Ault, J. W. (1932). How may we measure teaching success? *Educational Administration and Supervision, 18,* 250–256.

*Brown, S. W. (1974). *The National Teacher Examination as an instrument of prediction of teacher success.* Paper presented at the annual meeting of the American Educational Research Association, Chicago. (ERIC Document Reproduction Service No. ED088947)

*Browne, B. A., & Rankin, R. J. (1986). Predicting employment in education: The relative efficiency of National Teacher Examinations scores and student teacher ratings. *Educational and Psychological Measurement, 46,* 191–197.

*Burns, M. L. (1977). Prediction of success in teacher training. *McGill Journal of Education, 12,* 279–286.

*Carson, E. M. (1969). *An analysis of National Teacher Examinations scores as predictors of teacher success in assignment.* Unpublished doctoral dissertation, University of Houston, Texas.

*Chesley, D. (2004). *The validity of teacher employment success predictors.* Unpublished doctoral dissertation, George Washington University, Washington, DC.

*Chiu, Y. C. (1989). *An investigation of the relationship between the National Teacher Examinations and a performance-based assessment of professional knowledge.* Unpublished doctoral dissertation, University of Virginia, Charlottesville.

*Cole, D. L. (1961). The prediction of teaching performance. *Journal of Educational Research, 54,* 345–348.

Coleman, J. S., Campbell, E., Hobson, C., McPartland, J., Mood, A., Weinfield, F., et al. (1966). *Equality of educational opportunity.* Washington, DC: Government Printing Office.

*Cornett, J. D. (1969). Effectiveness of three selective admissions criteria in predicting performance of first-year teachers. *Journal of Educational Research, 62,* 247–250.

Council of Chief State School Officers. (2006). *Test of teaching knowledge.* Retrieved November 8, 2006, from http://www.ccsso.org/projects/Interstate_New_Teacher_Assessment_and_Support_Consortium/Projects/Test_of_Teaching_Knowledge

*Coxe, W. W., & Cornell, E. L. (1933). *The prognosis of teaching ability of students in New York state normal schools* (University State of New York Bulletin No. 1033). Albany: New York State Education Department.

*Crabbs, L. M. (1925). *Measuring efficiency in supervision and teaching* (Contributions to Education No. 175). New York: Bureau of Publications, Teachers College, Columbia University.

Cubberley, E. P. (1906). The certification of teachers. In M. J. Holmes (Ed.), *The fifth yearbook of the National Society for the Scientific Study of Education* (pp. 5–88). Chicago: University of Chicago Press.

D'Agostino, J. V., & Hester VanWinkle, W. (2007). Identifying prepared and competent teachers with professional knowledge tests. *Journal of Personnel Evaluation in Education, 20*, 65–84.

Darling-Hammond, L., Wise, A. E., & Klein, S. P. (1995). *A license to teach: Building a profession for 21st-century schools*. Boulder, CO: Westview.

*Delaney, E. C. (1954). *Teacher selection and evaluation with special attention to the validity of the personal interview and the National Teacher Examinations as used in one selected community* (Elizabeth, New Jersey). Unpublished doctoral dissertation, Columbia University, New York.

*DeRee, H. G., Reynolds, B. J., & Martin-Reynolds, J. (1986). Grade point average and high school background as correlates of teacher effectiveness in rural settings. *Journal of Rural and Small Schools, 1*(1), 15–16.

*Dobry, A. M., Murphy, P. D., & Schmidt, D. M. (1985). Predicting teacher competence. *Action in Teacher Education, 7*, 69–74.

*Dodd, M. R. (1933). A study of teaching aptitude. *Journal of Educational Research, 26*, 517–521.

Domas, S. J., & Tiedman, D. V. (1950). Teacher competence: An annotated bibliography. *Journal of Experimental Education, 19*, 101–213.

*Ducharme, R. J. (1970). *Selected preservice factors related to success of the beginning teacher*. Unpublished doctoral dissertation, Louisiana State University.

*Dybdahl, C. S., Shaw, D. G., & Edwards, D. (1997). Teacher testing: Reason or rhetoric. *Journal of Research and Development in Education, 30*, 248–254.

*Eash, M. J., & Rasher, S. P. (1977). *An evaluation of changed inputs on outcomes in teacher education curriculum*. Paper presented at the annual meeting of the American Educational Research Association, New York. (ERIC Document Reproduction Service No. ED150203)

*Eissey, E. M. (1967). *Selected variables in teacher preparation and subsequent evaluation of teaching performance*. Unpublished doctoral dissertation, Florida State University, Tallahassee.

Elementary and Secondary Education Act of 1965, Pub. L. No. 89-10, 79 Stat. 27 (1965).

*Ellis, J. R. (1961). Relationships between aspects of preparation and measures of performance of secondary teachers of the social studies. *Journal of Educational Research, 55*, 24–28.

*Erickson, J. E. (1971). Three measures of a teachers' potential. *English Education, 2*(2), 95–99.

*Espenschade, A. (1948). Selection of women major students in physical education. *Research Quarterly, 19*, 70–76.

Ferguson, R. F. (1991). Paying for public education: New evidence on how and why money matters. *Harvard Journal on Legislation, 28*, 465–498.

*Flanagan, J. C. (1941). A preliminary study of the validity of the 1940 edition of the National Teacher Examinations. *School and Society, 54*, 59–64.

*Freehill, M. F. (1963). The prediction of teaching competence. *Journal of Experimental Education, 31*, 307–311.

*Gatti-Carson, S. R. (1990). *Predictors of future teacher effectiveness for nontraditional teacher certification candidates.* Unpublished doctoral dissertation, Colorado State University.

*Gerfen, R. L. (1970). *Analysis of selected variables in the preparation and performance of teachers.* Unpublished doctoral dissertation, University of Southern California, Los Angeles.

Glass, G. V. (2002). Teacher characteristics. In A. Molnar (Ed.), *School reform proposals: The research evidence* (pp. 155–174). Greenwich, CT: Information Age Publishing.

Gorth, W. P., & Chernoff, M. L. (1986). Introduction. In W. P. Gorth & M. L. Chernoff (Eds.), *Testing for teacher certification* (pp. 1–13). Hillsdale, NJ: Lawrence Erlbaum.

*Gould, G. (1947). The predictive value of certain selective measures. *Educational Administration and Supervision, 33,* 208–212.

*Gress, J. R. (1977). *A study of the reliability, validity, and usefulness of identified pre-teaching predictors.* Columbus: Ohio State Department of Education. (ERIC Document Reproduction Service No. ED151306)

*Guyton, E., & Farokhi, E. (1987). Relationships among academic performance, basic skills, subject matter knowledge, and teaching skills of teacher education graduates. *Journal of Teacher Education, 38*(5), 37–42.

*Hamrin, S. A. (1927). A comparative study of ratings of teachers-in-training and teachers-in-service. *Elementary School Journal, 28,* 39–44.

Haney, W., Madaus, G., & Kreitzer, A. (1987). Charms talismanic: Testing teachers for the improvement of American education. In E. Z. Rothkopf (Ed.), *Review of research in education* (Vol. 14, pp. 169–238). Washington, DC: AERA.

*Hankins, N. E. (1964). *A study of the relationship of selected factors to teaching effectiveness.* Unpublished doctoral dissertation, University of Tennessee.

*Hardesty, C. D. (1935). Can teaching success be rated? *The Nation's Schools, 15*(1), 27–28.

*Heller, W. H., & Clay, R. J. (1993). Predictors of teaching effectiveness: The efficacy of various standards to predict the success of graduates from a teacher education program. *ERS Spectrum, 11*(1), 7–11.

*Hicken, S. (1992). The Pre-Professional Skills Test: How it affects teacher aspirants and predicts performance in teacher preparation programs. *Urban Review, 24,* 253–261.

Holmes Group. (1986). *Tomorrow's teachers: A report of the Holmes Group.* East Lansing, MI: Author.

Hoyt, D. P. (1965). *The relationship between college grades and adult achievement* (ACT Research Reports Vol. 7). Iowa City: American College Testing Program.

*Hult, E. (1945). Study of achievement in educational psychology. *Journal of Experimental Education, 13,* 174–190.

*Jenkins, H. E. (1978). *The relationship of beginning teachers' scores on the National Teacher Examination and other selected variables to their competency in teaching.* Unpublished doctoral dissertation, Mississippi State University.

*Jones, E. S. (1923). The prediction of teaching success for the college student. *School and Society, 18,* 685–690.

*Jones, M. L. (1956). Analysis of certain aspects of teaching ability. *Journal of Experimental Education, 25,* 153–180.

*Jones, R. D. (1946). The prediction of teaching efficiency from objective measures. *Journal of Experimental Education, 15,* 85–100.

*Joshua, M. B. (1996). *The CBEST/NTE: Relationship between passing tests scores and first-year teacher performance.* Unpublished doctoral dissertation, Claremont Graduate School, Claremont, CA.

D'Agostino, Powers

Kane, M. T. (1994). Validating interpretive arguments for licensure and certification examinations. *Evaluation and the Health Professions, 17*, 133–159.

*Knight, F. B. (1922). *Qualities related to success in teaching* (Contributions to Education No. 120). New York: Bureau of Publications, Teachers College, Columbia University.

*Knight, J. S. (1983). *An analysis of the correlates of success in elementary teacher education.* Unpublished doctoral dissertation, University of Iowa.

*Kodiyanplakkal, L. J. (1987). *Evaluation of a competency test for teachers: The case of Guam.* Unpublished doctoral dissertation, University of Oregon.

*Kriner, H. L. (1935). Second report on a five-year study of teachers college admissions. *Educational Administration and Supervision, 21*, 56–60.

*Kriner, H. L. (1937). Five-year study of teacher college admissions. *Educational Administration and Supervision, 23*, 192–199.

*Lawrence, L. H. (1986). *The relationship between teacher competency assessment and teacher performance evaluation.* Unpublished doctoral dissertation, Arizona State University.

*Leimkuhler, B. D. (1966). *A follow-up study and evaluation of teacher competencies of a selected group of graduates of a teacher preparation institution.* Unpublished doctoral dissertation, Pennsylvania State University.

*Lewis, J. (1968). Tests of teachers. *Texas Outlook, 52*, 20–21.

*Lins, L. (1946). The prediction of teaching efficiency. *Journal of Experimental Education, 15*, 2–60.

Lipsey, M. W., & Wilson, D. B. (2001). *Practical meta-analysis.* Thousand Oaks, CA: Sage.

*Lovelace, T., & Martin, C. E. (1984). *The revised National Teacher Examinations as a predictor of teachers' performance in public school classrooms.* Lafayette: Board of Regents' Research and Development Program, University of Southwestern Louisiana. (ERIC Document Reproduction Service No. ED251416)

*Martin, L. O. (1944). *The prediction of success for students in teacher education.* New York: Teachers College, Columbia University.

*Massey, H. W., & Vineyard, E. E. (1958). Relationship between scholarship and first-year teaching success. *Journal of Teacher Education, 9*, 297–301.

*Mathis, C., & Park, Y. H. (1965). Some factors related to success in student teaching. *Journal of Educational Research, 58*, 420–422.

*McAfee, L. O. (1930). The reliability of the evidences of teaching efficiency secured in extension visitation. *Elementary School Journal, 30*, 746–754.

McCamey, J., Jr. (1958). *The correlation between certain academic factors and scores on the 1957 National Teacher Examinations of the 1957 graduates of the University of Hawaii Teachers' College.* Unpublished master's thesis, University of Hawaii.

*Mead, A. R., & Holley, C. E. (1916). Forecasting success in practice teaching. *Journal of Educational Psychology, 7*, 495–497.

Mehrens, W. A., & Phillips, S. E. (1989). Using college GPA and test scores in teacher licensure decisions: Conjunctive versus compensatory models. *Applied Measurement in Education, 2*, 277–288.

*Mercer, P. B. (1972). *A study of the relationship between scores on the National Teacher Examinations, teaching performance, and other variables in a selected group of secondary student teachers.* Unpublished doctoral dissertation, East Texas State University.

*Meriam, J. L. (1905). *Normal school education and efficiency in teaching* (Contributions to Education No. 1). New York: Bureau of Publications, Teachers College, Columbia University.

Merwin, J. C. (1978). Review of the National Teacher Examination. In O. K. Buros (Ed.), *The eighth mental measurements yearbook* (Vol. 1, pp. 514–516). Highland Park, NJ: Gryphon Press.

Mitchell, K. J., Robinson, D. Z., Plake, B. S., & Knowles, K. T. (Eds.), for the Committee on Assessment and Teacher Quality, Center for Education, Board on Testing and Assessment, National Research Council. (2001). *Testing teacher candidates: The role of licensure tests in improving teacher quality.* Washington, DC: National Academies Press.

*Moore, D., Schurr, K. T., & Henriksen, L. W. (1991). Correlations of National Teacher Examination core battery scores and college grade point average with teaching effectiveness of first-year teachers. *Educational and Psychological Measurement, 51*, 1023–1028.

*Moore, D. E. (1991). *The relationship among selected appraisals in predicting effective beginning teaching.* Unpublished doctoral dissertation, Ball State University, Muncie, IN.

Morsh, J. E., & Wilder, E. W. (1954). *Identifying the effective instructor: A review of the quantitative studies 1900–1952* (Research Bulletin TR-54-44). San Antonio, TX: Lackland Air Force Base, Air Force Personnel and Training Research Center.

National Commission on Excellence in Education. (1983). *A nation at risk: The imperative for educational reform.* Washington, DC: Author.

National Commission on Teaching and America's Future. (1996). *What matters most: Teaching for America's future. Report of the National Commission on Teaching and America's Future.* New York: Author.

Nelson, E. A. (1985). Review of NTE programs. In J. V. Mitchell, Jr. (Ed.), *The ninth mental measurements yearbook* (Vol. 2, pp. 1187–1188). Lincoln: University of Nebraska Press.

No Child Left Behind Act of 2001, Pub. L. No. 107-110, 115 Stat. 1425 (2002).

*Odenweller, A. L. (1936). *Predicting the quality of teaching* (Contributions to Education No. 676). New York: Bureau of Publications, Teachers College, Columbia University.

*Olstad, R. G. (1988). *The relationship of NTE exams to teacher education admission, performance, and employment.* Paper presented at the annual meeting of the American Association of Colleges for Teacher Education, New Orleans, LA. (ERIC Document Reproduction Service No. ED291698)

*Olstad, R. G., Beal, J. L., Schlick-Noe, K. L., & Schaefer, C. C. (1983). *Preservice teaching performance: A search for predictor variables.* Seattle: Teacher Education Research Center, College of Education, University of Washington. (ERIC Document Reproduction Service No. ED231810)

*Onderdonk, L. E. (1985). *Relationships between specified variables and success of beginning teachers in the mobile county public school system.* Unpublished doctoral dissertation, Auburn University.

*Orebaugh, F. E. (1974). *The analysis of selected employment criteria and their relationship to the performance ratings of teachers.* Unpublished doctoral dissertation, University of Cincinnati.

*Peterson, H. A., Obourn, G., Wallace, H., & Smith, O. W. (1934). Relation of scholarship during college career to success in teaching judged by salary. *Educational Administration and Supervision, 20*, 625–628.

*Phillips, W. S. (1935). *An analysis of certain characteristics of active and prospective teachers* (Contributions to Education No. 161). Nashville, TN: George Peabody College.

*Piper, M. K., & O'Sullivan, P. S. (1981). The National Teacher Examination: Can it predict classroom performance? *Phi Delta Kappan, 62*, 401.

*Popham, W. J. (1965). Predicting student teachers' instructional behavior from a structured and an unstructured test of professional knowledge. *California Journal of Educational Research, 16*, 7–13.

Porter, A. C., Young, P., & Odden, A. (2001). Advances in teacher assessments and their uses. In V. Richardson (Ed.), *Handbook of research on teaching* (4th ed., pp. 259–297). Washington, DC: AERA.

*Pyle, W. H. (1928). The relation between intelligence and teaching success: A supplementary study. *Educational Administration and Supervision, 14*, 257–267.

Quirk, T. J., Witten, B. J., & Weinberg, S. F. (1972). *The National Teacher Examinations: An annotated bibliography 1940–1971* (Research Memorandum 72-4). Princeton, NJ: Educational Testing Service.

Quirk, T. J., Witten, B. J., & Weinberg, S. F. (1973). Review of studies of the concurrent and predictive validity of the National Teacher Examinations. *Review of Educational Research, 43*(1), 89–113.

Reynolds, A., Tannenbaum, R. J., & Rosenfeld, M. (1992). *Beginning teacher knowledge of general principles of teaching and learning: A national survey.* Princeton, NJ: Educational Testing Service. (ERIC Document Reproduction Service No. ED385570)

*Riggs, I. M., & Riggs, M. L. (1990). Predictors of student success in a teacher education program: What is valid, what is not. *Action in Teacher Education, 7*(4), 41–46.

*Riggs, I. M., Riggs, M. L., & Sandlin, R. A. (1992). *An assessment of selection criteria validity for a teacher education program.* Paper presented at the annual meeting of the American Educational Research Association, San Francisco. (ERIC Document Reproduction Service No. ED353291)

*Ritter, E. L. (1918). Rating of teachers in Indiana. *Elementary School Journal, 18*, 740–756.

*Rolfe, J. F. (1945). The measurement of teaching ability. Study Number Two. *Journal of Experimental Education, 14*, 52–74.

Rosenthal, R. (1994). Parametric measures of effect size. In H. Cooper & L. V. Hedges (Eds.), *Handbook of research synthesis* (pp. 231–244). New York: Russell Sage Foundation.

*Rostker, L. E. (1945). The measurement of teaching ability. Study Number One. *Journal of Experimental Education, 14*, 6–51.

*Ryans, D. J. (1951). The results of internal consistency and external validation procedures applied in the analysis of test items measuring professional information. *Educational and Psychological Measurement, 11*, 549–560.

*Salzman, S. A. (1989). *The PPST and NTE as predictors of student teacher performance.* Paper presented at the annual meeting of the Northern Rocky Mountain Educational Research Association, Jackson, WY. (ERIC Document Reproduction Service No. ED314475)

*Salzman, S. A. (1991). *Selecting the qualified: Predictors of student teacher performance.* Paper presented at the annual meeting of the Association of Teacher Educators, New Orleans, LA. (ERIC Document Reproduction Service No. ED330672)

Sandefur, J. T. (1985). *State assessment trends.* Washington, DC: American Association of Colleges of Teacher Education.

*Sandiford, P., Cameron, M. A., Conway, C. B., & Long, J. A. (1937). *Forecasting teaching ability* (University of Toronto Educational Research Bulletin No. 8). Toronto, Canada: University of Toronto.

*Schick, G. J. (1957). *The predictive value of a teacher judgment test.* Unpublished doctoral dissertation, University of Wisconsin.

*Schwartz, A. N. (1950). A study of the discriminating efficiency of certain tests of the primary source personality traits of teachers. *Journal of Experimental Education, 129,* 63–93.

*Seagoe, M. V. (1945). Prognostic tests and teaching success. *Journal of Educational Research, 38,* 685–690.

*Seagoe, M. V. (1946). Prediction of inservice success in teaching. *Journal of Educational Research, 39,* 658–663.

Shaddish, W. R., & Haddock, C. K. (1994). Combining estimates of effect size. In H. Cooper & L. V. Hedges (Eds.), *Handbook of research synthesis* (pp. 261–281). New York: Russell Sage Foundation.

*Shea, J. A. (1955). *The predictive value of various combinations of standardized tests and subtests for prognosis of teaching efficiency.* Doctoral dissertation. Washington, DC: Catholic University of America Press.

*Short, J. R. (1971). *An analysis of the criteria used in hiring teachers in relationship to a follow-up indicator of teacher success.* Unpublished doctoral dissertation, University of Alabama.

Shulman, L. S. (1987). Knowledge and teaching: Foundations of the new reform. *Harvard Education Review, 57,* 1–22.

*Siegel, W. G. (1969). *A study of the relationship between selected undergraduate academic achievement variables and teaching success.* Unpublished doctoral dissertation, Washington State University.

*Somers, G. T. (1923). *Pedagogical prognosis: Predicting the success of prospective teachers* (Contributions to Education No. 140). New York: Bureau of Publications, Teachers College, Columbia University.

*Southern Regional Education Board. (1982). *Teacher testing and assessment: An examination of the National Teacher Examinations (NTE), the Georgia Teacher Certification Test (TCT), and the Georgia Teacher Performance Assessment Instrument (TPAI) for a selected population.* Atlanta, GA: Author. (ERIC Document Reproduction Service No. ED229441)

*Stephens, J. M., & Lichtenstein, A. (1947). Factors associated with success in teaching Grade Five arithmetic. *Journal of Educational Research, 40,* 683–694.

*Stewart, M. L. (1940). A study of success and failure in eleven years of rural teacher training. *Educational Administration and Supervision, 26,* 372–378.

*Stoelting, G. J. (1955). The selection of candidates for teacher education at the University of Wisconsin. *Journal of Experimental Education, 24,* 120–132.

Strauss, R. P., & Sawyer, E. A. (1986). Some new evidence on teacher and student competencies. *Economics of Education Review, 5,* 41–48.

*Stuit, D. B. (1937). Scholarship as a factor in teaching success. *School and Society, 46,* 382–384.

*Thacker, J. A. (1964). *A study of the relationship between principals' estimates of teaching efficiency and scores on National Teacher Examinations, academic averages, and supervisors' estimates of potential for selected teachers in North Carolina.* Unpublished doctoral dissertation, University of North Carolina at Chapel Hill.

*Tiegs, E. W. (1928). *An evaluation of some techniques of teacher selection.* Bloomington, IL: Public School Publishing Company.

*Tudhope, W. B. (1942). A study of the training college final teaching mark as a criterion of future success in the teaching profession. Part 1. *British Journal of Educational Psychology, 12,* 167–171.

*Ukpolo, F. T. (1998). *Classroom success and the National Teacher Examination core battery scores of first year teachers.* Unpublished doctoral dissertation, Tennessee State University, Nashville.

*Ullman, R. R. (1930). The prediction of teaching success. *Educational Administration and Supervision, 16*, 598–608.

*Ullman, R. R. (1931). *The prognostic value of certain factors related to teaching success.* Ashland, OH: A. L. Garber.

*Veal, R., & Hulme, G. (1981). *Assessing the writing skill of prospective English teachers.* Paper presented at the annual meeting of the International Reading Association, New Orleans, LA. (ERIC Document Reproduction Service No. ED205986)

*Wagenhorst, L. H. (1930). Relation between ratings of student teachers in college and success in first year of teaching. *Educational Administration and Supervision, 16*, 249–253.

*Walberg, H. J. (1967). Scholastic aptitude, the National Teacher Examinations, and teaching success. *Journal of Educational Research, 61*, 129–131.

*Watkins, R. M. (1987). *Competency testing, administrative evaluation, self-assessment, and student achievement as measures of teacher effectiveness.* Unpublished doctoral dissertation, East Texas State University.

*Webster, W. J. (1984). *Five years of teacher testing: A retrospective analysis.* Paper presented at the Annual Meeting of the American Educational Research Association, New Orleans, LA. (ERIC Document Reproduction Service No. ED276769)

*Whitney, F. L. (1922). *The intelligence, preparation, and teaching skill of state normal school graduates in the United States.* Minneapolis: University of Minnesota.

*Whitney, F. L. (1924). The prediction of teaching success. *Journal of Educational Research Monograph, 6.*

*Whitney, F. L., & Frasier, C. M. (1930). The relation of intelligence to student teaching success. *Peabody Journal of Education, 8*, 3–6.

Wilson, S., & Youngs, P. (2005). Research on accountability processes in teacher education. In M. Cochran-Smith & K. M. Zeichner (Eds.), *Studying teacher education: The report of the AERA Panel on Research and Teacher Education* (pp. 591–643). Mahwah, NJ: Lawrence Erlbaum.

Manuscript received February 21, 2007
Revision received June 20, 2008
Accepted June 22, 2008

American Educational Research Journal
March 2009, Vol. 46, No. 1, pp. 183–202
DOI: 10.3102/0002831208323274
© *2009 AERA. http://aerj.aera.net*

How Teachers Respond to Children's Inquiry

Susan Engel
Kellie Randall
Williams College

This study examined how teachers respond when children engage in inquiry-based deviations from a planned task. Thirty-one teachers each completed a brief science activity and accompanying worksheet with a student confederate. Teachers were given one of two goals for the study: help the students complete a worksheet or help the students learn more about science. The instructions had a significant effect on the teachers' responses to students' deviations. Teachers in the worksheet condition tended to discourage deviation and draw the students back to the task at hand, whereas teachers in the learn more condition were more likely to encourage and expand on the deviation. Apart from their responses to students' deviations, nearly all teachers were classified as encouraging, suggesting that an articulated goal for the activity has a particular effect on the response to deviations. Implications for the role of teachers in the development of children's curiosity are considered.

KEYWORDS: child development, science education, teacher characteristics

Curiosity and Learning

Although most people believe curiosity is essential to learning, it is not clear that children express much curiosity when they are at school. Tizard and Hughes (1984) found that British toddlers who asked many questions when with their parents asked almost no questions when they were at school, leading the researchers to suggest that something about the school was not conducive to the development of what they called "intellectual search." In a recent naturalistic study of the expression of curiosity in elementary

SUSAN ENGEL *is a senior lecturer in psychology and director of the Program in Teaching in the Department of Psychology, Williams College, Williamstown, MA 01267; e-mail: Susan.L.Engel@williams.edu. Her research interests include narrative development, the development of autobiographical memory, play, and the development of curiosity.*

KELLIE RANDALL *is currently teaching high school social studies through Teach for America; e-mail: 07KGR@williams.edu.*

classrooms, very few instances of verbal or gestural inquiry were identified (Engel, 2007). Although some research shows a waning of curiosity during middle childhood, other studies have shown that at least in some circumstances and with some children, curiosity is alive and well during that period (Henderson, 1994; Henderson, Charlesworth, & Gamradt, 1982; Henderson & Moore, 1979; Loewenstein, 1994).

The apparent infrequency with which children ask questions and engage in exploratory behavior in their classrooms is worth learning more about, given the common intuition that curiosity is an important part of education. In one study, for instance, over 70% of teachers surveyed circled *curiosity* as one of the five top characteristics they strive to encourage in their students (Engel & Hackmann, 2002). Developmental research confirms the idea that curiosity drives intellectual development. For instance, Piaget's theory of intellectual development is premised on children's natural urge to understand their environment—he defined curiosity as the need to explain the unexpected, whereas Jerome Kagan defined it as the need to resolve uncertainty (Kagan, 1972; Piaget, 1969).

In one of the first experiments to look at curiosity, Berlyne (1960) asked participants long lists of questions about invertebrates. He also asked the participants to rate how surprising and interesting each question was. The participants were then provided with a long and randomly organized list of answers to the questions. Finally, they were given the original questionnaire a second time. Just as Berlyne predicted, the participants were better able to answer those questions they had rated as surprising or engaging. The surprising and engaging questions caused arousal. Information gathering was then aimed at reducing that arousal by finding answers to those questions.

Research has also linked curiosity to heightened cognitive ability. Alberti and Witryol (1994) tested third- and fifth-grade students to determine their preference for familiar versus unfamiliar stimuli. They found the students who showed the greatest preference for new and unfamiliar stimuli were those who had previously scored highly on an achievement test. Maw and Maw (1972) tested fifth-graders' abilities to detect verbal absurdities. Students who had been rated as highly curious outperformed their low-curiosity counterparts in identifying the absurdities. The researchers argued that this was because highly curious children gather more information when they read and therefore achieve greater comprehension. In a subsequent study, Maw and Maw (1975) found that children who rated themselves as highly curious performed better on a mental abilities test. More recently, Chouinard (2007) has provided evidence that preschoolers' questions are a key component of their cognitive development. Recent research in science education demonstrates the educational value of discovery and exploration in the school setting (Kuhn, 2005).

Because curiosity is both a state and a trait (Henderson & Moore, 1979), a curious child might also be an academically competent child—which says little about the causal relationship between the two. However, research has also shown that when a situation is designed to arouse curiosity, children display improved academic performance. Mittman and Terrell (1964) assigned first and second graders into one of three groups: low, moderate, or high curiosity. The high- and moderate-curiosity groups were presented with dot drawings, the content of which could only be determined after the 30th and 9th dot had been connected, respectively. The low-curiosity group also viewed a dot drawing but was shown the completed drawing before beginning the task. They therefore knew the content of drawing from the start. The children were then asked a series of questions that required them to learn to distinguish between three-dimensional geometric objects based on form and size. Each correct answer allowed them to make one connection in their dot drawing. Students in the high-curiosity group gave significantly fewer wrong answers than those in the moderate- and low-curiosity groups; they were also more likely to report the experiment as fun and to be disappointed when it ended. The authors reasoned that uncertainty about the content of the drawing motivated the children to perform better so that they could connect the dots and reduce the arousal.

Situational Influences

Recent work on the development of interest and its relationship to academic achievement provides a new dimension to our understanding of curiosity by demonstrating the educational value of a child's engagement with particular materials or topics. Although interest and curiosity constitute somewhat different psychological constructs, they are clearly linked and share certain central properties (Silvia, 2008). Interest, like curiosity, is a motivating force that leads children to greater involvement with an object, class of objects, or topic. Researchers have defined individual interest as "interest built on stored knowledge about and value for a class of objects or ideas which leads to a desire to be involved in activities related to that topic" (Boekaerts & Boscolo, 2002, p. 378). Research on the development of interest has focused on individuals' sustained involvement with an object or class of objects over time (Hidi & Renninger, 2006; Renninger, Hidi, & Krapp, 1992), whereas *curiosity* usually refers to a transitory state or behavior directed at a given object or event in a particular setting. However, some researchers have suggested that interest is often precipitated by curiosity (Bergin, 1999). A child who is curious about some unexpected aspect of an object may explore the object, which can lead to sustained interest in that group of objects. The relationship might also work in the other direction. Henderson (Henderson et al., 1982; Henderson & Moore, 1979) has shown that although some children are more curious than others across situations, individual differences are mediated by situational factors. Interest in particular objects or activities might constitute one such situational factor. Children may express more curiosity about things in which they have a prior interest.

Renninger and Wozniak (1985) found that children were better able to recall objects to which they had shown a prior interest. Another study found that fifth and sixth graders had superior comprehension of reading passages written on high-interest topics (Hidi, 1990). As with curiosity, interest leads to a more intrinsically motivated engagement with ideas and materials, and across age groups, eliciting interest spurs learning (Bull & Dizney, 1973; Fransson, 1977). Lowry and Johnson (1981) put elementary school students into small groups to learn about a topic in social studies. In the first condition, children were encouraged to focus on controversy and uncertainty in the domain, whereas in the second condition children were encouraged to work together to learn the facts. Children in the controversy condition were more interested in their topic than their counterparts in the noncontroversy group. Their interest in the topic led the children in the controversy group to learn more information; they were also more eager to forgo a recess to watch a film on the topic after the unit was over.

As Alexander points out, situational interest can lead to the kind of individual interest that is linked with mastery of a domain (Ainley, Hidi, & Berndorff, 2002; Alexander, 1997; Renninger, Ewen, & Lasher, 2002). Taken together, these studies suggest that when children are drawn to spend time exploring specific materials or topics, they are more likely to learn about them. Research on interest underscores the situational nature of such engagement and complements similar findings from studies on the situational nature of curiosity.

Since Berlyne's (1960) and Mittman and Terrell's (1964) early work, research has identified a number of components of the social and physical environment that influence a child's level of curiosity. For instance, Coie (1974) showed that children's exploratory behavior was highly influenced by the number and kind of interesting and unfamiliar objects that were available. The nature of the curiosity-evoking situation influenced how children responded: Box tasks, chemical tasks, inclined plane tasks, and other displays each caused different curiosity behaviors in the same child. One child might be very interested in and explore a display on birds but then show little to no interest in completing a chemistry task. All children displayed some form of curiosity, although not every situation was interesting to every child. Renninger (1990) has shown that even toddlers exhibit a wider range of exploratory behaviors and explore for longer when they have shown a prior interest in those objects. This research highlights individual differences between children in terms of the objects and topics in which children are interested. Individual differences in the objects and topics that elicit curiosity seem to be equally strong. Although the objects children interact with are an important influence on the expression of curiosity, people also play a role in suppressing or eliciting a child's curiosity.

Role of Adults in Fostering Curiosity

Although we tend to think of curiosity as a solitary experience, in fact, children often express curiosity in the company of others. Teachers and parents in particular seem to influence a child's expression of curiosity. For instance, children who receive answers to questions, rather than "I don't know" responses, are more likely to ask subsequent questions (Endsley & Clarey, 1975).

Henderson et al. (1982) observed children, either in peer groups or with a parent, in a natural science museum. Children accompanied by their parents explored exhibits more thoroughly, inspected and touched objects more frequently, and asked more questions than children who attended with peers. Adults do not always positively influence curiosity or the kinds of exploratory behavior associated with curiosity. Coie (1974) examined children's exploratory behavior in relation to the social cues they received from adults. Children were invited into a room that contained interesting objects, and they were asked to wait there on their own. Those children who were urged by the experimenter to explore did in fact exhibit much higher levels of exploratory behavior than those children who were left in the room with no explicit direction to explore.

However, the relationship between adult behavior and children's curiosity is not a simple one. Henderson (1984) found that parents of high-exploratory children offered more information when playing in a room filled with many different types of toys than did parents of low-exploratory children. Low-exploratory children explored less with a passive experimenter than with their mothers, suggesting that adult influence is not the same for all children— some children may require more encouragement or input from an adult in order to express curiosity. Clearly, adults play an important role in determining a child's expression of curiosity, whether directly, through modeling and encouragement, or indirectly, via the activities and materials they provide.

Although research has shown that adults *can* encourage children's curiosity, it is not clear that they typically *do* encourage it. The few studies that have looked at teachers' actual response to curiosity in real classrooms are not very encouraging. Tizard and Hughes (1984) found that British toddlers who asked many questions with their parents asked almost no questions when they were at school, leading the researchers to suggest that something about the school was not conducive to the development of what they called "intellectual search."

Observations from preschool classrooms find that teachers often do not modify their questions to the ability level of the individual and instead tend to ask mainly low-level questions to all children, questions that simply ask children to label or produce previously learned information rather than engage in higher-level cognitive processes (Hestenes, Cassidy, & Niemeyer, 2004). Few questions required students to synthesize information, speculate cause-and-effect relationships, search for similarities between subjects, evaluate consequences, or plan further action. The expression of curiosity in classrooms seems to dwindle even more as children get older.

In a naturalistic study of the expression of curiosity in a classroom setting, very few instances of verbal or gestural inquiry in kindergarten and fifth-grade classrooms were identified. Teachers asked many more questions than students did, and they already knew the answers to most of the questions they asked. Few questions were asked (by teachers or students) that sought new information. In quite a few cases, teachers subtly discouraged their students from exploration and inquiry, for instance by suggesting a child stick to her work or by reminding a student that he had little time left for a task (Engel, 2007). Although some might argue that school-age children simply do not exhibit much curiosity, studies have shown that kindergarten and fifth-grade children do, under certain circumstances, inquire and explore (Coie, 1974; Engel & Hackmann, 2002; Henderson, 1984). One possibility is that during the elementary school years, teachers are doing something to discourage children's inquiry. Perhaps the highly structured school day causes teachers to focus primarily on completing certain well-defined tasks to the exclusion of other kinds of learning. Given the time and task constraints put on teachers, there might be little incentive for them to encourage curiosity in their classrooms. Emphasizing the completion of assignments, sticking to a curriculum, and meeting narrowly defined educational goals may lead teachers to view a child's curiosity as taking the child off track.

Teachers' Response to Curiosity

We know that specifying a goal induces people to develop a representation of the problem and ways to resolve it; the perceived purpose or goal of an activity imposes a specific program for reaching the solution. Thus, when problems are framed even slightly differently so that the goals are changed, people may choose a different course of action (Zukier, 1986). Teachers are certainly not exempt from having their behavior shaped by articulated goals. A longitudinal study by Osborn, McNess, and Broadfoot (2000) in England found that the introduction of assessments and standardized curriculums changed the way teachers approached teaching in their classrooms. Teachers reported that they felt unable to prioritize the "affective and creative" aspects of a curriculum. Additionally, due to the pressures placed on them as teachers, they felt they were unable to give students any choices or control over the material they learned. Teachers are likely to have goals set for them by principals and administrators. Another study found that teachers with performance-oriented goals were likely to have principals who encouraged a performance-oriented approach to teaching (Roeser, Marachi, & Gehlbach, 2002). Social psychologists have long known that people strive to comply with authority (Milgram, 1983), although this dynamic has not yet been explored in the context of teachers' responses to children's inquiry and curiosity. Is it possible that when it comes to encouraging or discouraging the kind of inquiry associated with curiosity, teachers' responses are influenced by their perceptions of goals or by the voice of authority?

The present study was designed to learn more about the role of the teacher in children's expression of curiosity in a classroom setting. Previous research has documented the impact of an adult's discouraging or encouraging feedback in a laboratory setting, but in those experiments a researcher rather than a teacher was influencing the child's behavior. Thus, the focus was on the child. This tells us little about whether teachers actually do encourage children's spontaneous expressions of inquiry or what might influence a teacher's response to such inquiry. A teacher who believes the goal of an activity is to complete a worksheet (a common goal in U.S. classrooms) might go about a learning activity very differently than a teacher who believes the goal is to help the child learn more about a given domain (science, literature, etc.). More specifically, we hypothesized that if we emphasized the worksheet in our instructions, teachers would be more likely to discourage the child's inquiry-based deviations in an attempt to keep the student focused on the task at hand. We speculated that if, instead, we emphasized the goal of learning about a domain, teachers would be more willing to allow the student to go off task (but not off topic) and initiate their own steps in the activity.

Method

Each teacher was asked to help an elementary-age student with a learning activity called Bouncing Raisins. The activity, designed to illustrate the effects of carbonation, involved mixing baking soda, vinegar, and water together and then observing what happened when raisins were dropped into the mixture. In the first condition, teachers were encouraged to "help children finish a worksheet," whereas in the second condition, teachers were encouraged to "help the child learn more about how things float, sink, and the interaction of the elements." During the activity, the student, who was a confederate, deviated from the worksheet by showing curiosity about various items in the room. We were interested in how teachers responded to students' exploratory behavior. We also wanted to know whether the teachers' sense of the goal of the task would influence their responses.

Participants

Thirty-one school teachers were recruited through newspaper ads and flyers distributed to local schools in a rural/suburban county in western Massachusetts. The ads asked for teachers to participate in a study to be conducted at a nearby college in exchange for $20. When participants replied to the flyers, they were told the study was about "how children learn," that they would be asked to complete a brief learning activity with a student, and that the session would be videotaped. Once the teachers agreed to participate, a time was scheduled for them to come into the laboratory.

Twenty-two of the teachers worked primarily with elementary-age students, and 7 of the 9 teachers who worked primarily at the middle and high school levels reported previous experience working with elementary students. On average, the teachers had 17 years of experience. There were 24 women and 7 men in the study.

In addition to the teachers, the study also required the use of student confederates, who were recruited through word of mouth. To facilitate scheduling, six students were used (three boys and three girls), all between the ages of 10 and 12. Before participating in any trials, the students first met with the experimenter, who explained their role. Students then ran through the activity once with the experimenter so they were familiar with it and then with a college student playing the role of a teacher so they were comfortable with their role. Students were paid $10 for each session they completed.

Materials

The experiment took place in a small pleasant room in a psychology department of a liberal arts college. The room was set up with a table, chairs, and a couch. On the table were all the materials required for the learning activity: a glass, a measuring cup, water, baking soda, white vinegar, raisins, and colored chocolate candies (M&Ms). Also on the table were materials not required for the activity, including snack foods (colored candies called Skittles, Cheerios, Goldfish crackers, marshmallows, and mints), juice boxes, straws, spoons, cotton balls, and marbles. A video camera, set up on a table across the room, was used to record the sessions.

Procedure

The teachers were each invited into the room where the experiment would take place. They were provided with a packet of materials to read through that included an initial consent form, the instruction sheet, a sheet outlining the science behind the activity Bouncing Raisins, and two copies of the worksheet (Appendices A–D).

All of the teachers were told, "We are interested in how children learn. Please help the student who will join you here with the science activity set out on the table. Do whatever you normally would when helping a student with this kind of activity." All teachers were also told they would have 11 minutes to complete the task with the child. The time limit was chosen so as to give them barely enough time to complete the task without any interruptions. Thus, the teachers would face a trade-off between finishing the task and allowing the student to deviate. In order to make the time limit salient, we chose the nonstandard period of 11 minutes.

Teachers were randomly assigned to one of two conditions. In the worksheet condition, the instructions told the teacher "to help the child complete the task and accompanying worksheet." In the learn more condition, the instructions told the teacher to "help the student learn more about how things float and sink, and the interaction of elements." The experimenter read the instructions aloud and then gave the teacher a written copy (Appendix A). Teachers were then left alone in the room and given 3 minutes to read through the materials.

Once the teacher had finished going through the written information, the experimenter came back into the room with the student confederate. The student and teacher were introduced and led over to the table where the experiment was set up. In the center of the table all of the materials necessary to complete the activity were provided. Off to the sides of the table were the snack foods and other various objects. Once the student and teacher sat down, the experimenter prepared to leave the room. Here we strengthened the two conditions by having the experimenter say either "Have fun learning about science" or "Have fun with the worksheet," depending on the condition. The experimenter then turned on the camera and left the room.

At some point during the task, students deviated from the task by dropping an item not mentioned in the worksheet into the solution (a small brightly colored candy called a Skittle). Students were told that they should deviate openly so the teacher could see what they were doing. If the teachers reprimanded or questioned the deviation, the students were instructed to say, "I just wanted to see what would happen." This was to help ensure that the deviations were done in such a way that they would be interpreted as curious behavior driven by a need to seek information rather than as off-task misbehavior.

The experimenter watched the activity through a one-way mirror. After at least 11 minutes passed, the experimenter waited for the teacher and student to get to a stopping point before interrupting. All of the written materials were collected. The teacher was then given a questionnaire to fill out that asked about his or her teaching background, impressions of the student, and impressions of the task. The experimenter left the room with the student, allowing the teacher to complete the questionnaire alone. When the teacher finished the forms, the experimenter came back in and collected the worksheet. At this point, the teacher was debriefed about the true nature of the experiment, told that the student was working with the researchers and was supposed to deviate from the task, and offered an opportunity either to discard the data from the session or to sign a second consent form describing the actual experiment. Each teacher was then given $20 for participation. No teachers requested that their sessions be discarded.

Coding Scheme

Two observers who were blind to the experimental condition of the sessions coded the first 11 minutes of each videotape. Every comment the teachers made throughout the task was coded as encouraging, neutral, or restrictive. The teachers' responses to the deviation were coded separately as encouraging, neutral, or restrictive. Interrater reliability on both of these measures was .98.

Teaching style. Teaching style describes the kind and quantity of comments made throughout the session.

Encouraging—offering extra information, asking new questions, giving positive feedback to the student: "Good job." "I think that is an excellent explanation." "*Dancing*—that is a great word to describe the raisins. Let's write down they are dancing."
Neutral—reading directly from the worksheet, directing the child through the steps of the activity.
Restrictive—correcting or criticizing the child: "The procedure says to add 8 raisins. Make sure you are adding exactly 8; count them out first." "No, no, wait, let's read through this first."

Response to deviation. Response to deviation is how the teacher responded when the child did something not explicitly asked on the worksheet.

Encouraging—asking questions to follow up the deviation, incorporating the deviation into the lesson, and showing approval of the child's action: "Was that a Cheerio?" "What a good idea!"

Neutral—ignoring, pretending not to have seen, making no comment, and showing no interest in what happens.

Restrictive—correcting or scolding; attempting to bring the focus back to the worksheet without discussing the deviation: "It didn't ask you to do that. You have to stick to the directions." "Let's just follow the procedure outlined."

Results

Overall Teaching Style

In order to examine the specific effect of condition on teachers' responses, we measured their overall response to children during the activity. Each teacher's comments made prior to the deviation were counted, and a ratio of encouraging to restrictive comments was calculated for each teacher. Teachers who had a ratio above 70:30 were categorized as encouraging. Ratios of 70:30 or below were categorized as restrictive. With the exception of 2 teachers, all of the teachers were categorized as encouraging. Teachers on average made 24.7 comments prior to the deviation. The range was 13 to 40, and the mode was 27. One of the 2 that fell below the 70:30 ratios responded restrictively to the deviation. A chi-square test showed that instructions had no significant effect on teacher style of interaction prior to the deviation, $\chi^2(1, N = 31) = 1.10, p = .294$.

Response to Deviation

In order to ensure that no factors other than instructions influenced the teacher's response to the deviation, we looked for differences as a function of the teacher's gender, student's gender, and years of teacher experience.

A chi-square revealed that teacher's gender did not have an effect on the type of response, $\chi^2(2, N = 31) = 0.189, p = .910$.

Teachers who had taught 3 or fewer years were categorized as low experience, and those who had taught more than 3 years were categorized as high experience. A chi-square revealed there was no difference between low- and high-experience teachers in their reactions to the deviation, $\chi^2(2, N = 31) = 0.717, p = .699$.

Finally, the gender of the student did not influence the teachers' responses either, $\chi^2(2, N = 31) = 0.994, p = .608$.

The instructions, however, did have a significant effect on teachers' responses to the deviation. A chi-square test showed that teachers in the worksheet condition were significantly more likely to respond restrictively than teachers in the learn more condition, $\chi^2(2, N = 31) = 17.349, p < .001$ (see Figure 1). The effect of the condition was large (Cramer's $V = .75$). In the learn more

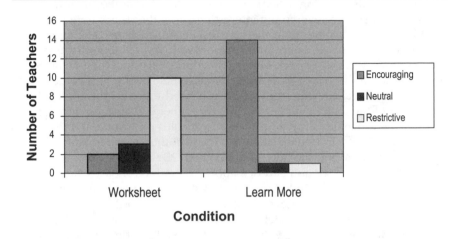

Figure 1. **Teachers' reactions to deviation by condition.**

condition, 88% of teachers encouraged the students' deviations, compared to only 13% of teachers in the worksheet condition. Teachers' understanding of the goal significantly influenced the way in which they responded to a student's deviation. Moreover, the finding that most of the teachers were encouraging prior to the deviation suggests that the condition seemed to exert a specific influence on the teachers' responses to deviation from a task.

Discussion

The teachers in our study were, by and large, friendly and encouraging. All of them made more encouraging comments than restrictive comments, and 65% never made a restrictive comment. However, when it came to the way they responded to the children's deviations to the task, teachers were influenced by the instructions they were given. When teachers were directed to focus on completing a worksheet, they were more likely to discourage inquiry-based deviations than those who were directed to help the children learn more about the domain. We interpret this to mean that when it comes to responding to children's unplanned inquiries, teachers are sensitive to the instructions they receive. These teachers may differ from the larger population of teachers in that they volunteered to be in a study. They may be more comfortable with their teaching styles, happier to be observed, and more eager to interact with children than those teachers who do not volunteer for such a study. Thus, their overall encouragement of children before the deviation may not be representative of the whole population of teachers. In some ways, this makes the finding even more striking. Even the friendliest and most encouraging teachers (e.g., the ones willing to be observed in an experiment) can be influenced to discourage children's exploration of materials. However, it remains for future studies to explore whether a wider range of teachers would respond in a similar fashion.

Although the coding scheme was useful for testing the main hypothesis, it did not capture everything interesting about the data. There was quite a bit of individual variation in the way teachers approached the task. Some teachers read through all the information with the students first, so they would know what to expect. Others chose to explain as they went. Some teachers sat on the couch with the students, whereas others chose to sit off to the side in a chair. One teacher even elected to sit on the floor, on the other side of the table, with her back to the camera. One teacher took some Skittles and a marshmallow to model a molecule of carbon dioxide to help convey the science behind the activity. Another teacher stopped and explained why carbon dioxide is abbreviated CO_2.

Teachers who encouraged deviations also added their own questions, going beyond those provided on the worksheet: "Do you think it would be different if we had added the ingredients in a different order?" "Do you think it would have worked if we left out one of the steps?" "Do you know any other uses for carbon dioxide?" Teachers displayed a wide variety of encouraging reactions to the deviation. Some simply laughed and acknowledged the deviation: "It'll be interesting to see what happens to those!"

Some pushed the issue further, inviting the children to think more about the results: "Wow, what's happening with the Skittle?" "Do you think the water is going to turn orange now?"

Many teachers went on to suggest their own deviations and extra steps: "We have so many things here, we might as well try out all of them." "What else can we add?"

A wide range of restrictive responses was observed as well. Most teachers were gentle when redirecting the students: "Let's finish this part first." "Wait; let's see what happens with the raisins before we do anything else."

Many of the teachers referred to the directions when trying to refocus the students. In one case, however, the teacher was somewhat harsh: "You were not supposed to do that. Show me where it said to put that in there. It didn't."

When children deviated, some of the teachers who responded restrictively also asked the children why they did so. Children, as instructed, answered, "I just wanted to see what would happen." This elicited a range of responses. One teacher smiled and said, "Well, curiosity is the beginning of all scientific knowledge. What do you think is going to happen?" Some of the teachers still responded restrictively, even after the students explained they were just curious: "Well, curiosity is a very good thing, but probably we should stick to the directions."

Teacher–Student Rapport

All of the young confederates did an excellent job playing model students. They were pleasant and well behaved; they also acted engaged and interested in the experiment, no matter how many times they had already been through it. Answers to the postactivity questionnaire made it clear that the students' acting had been successful. All the teachers positively evaluated the students with whom they worked. Some representative examples of words used to describe the students were "polite," "interested," "curious," "intelligent," "smart," "eager to learn," "inquisitive," "motivated," and "a pleasure."

Similarly, the students' evaluations of the teachers were generally positive as well. After the students left the lab room, while the teachers were filling out the questionnaire, they were asked how they felt it had gone. Students almost always had positive things to say about the teachers: "She didn't want me to drop extra things in, but it was still fun." "She looks like a witch, but she was actually really nice." "He was so much fun; we added everything in." Only once did a student report feeling uneasy about deviating.

Teachers' Reactions to Debriefing

Most of the teachers were surprised when they were debriefed and learned the true nature of the study. Only one teacher believed that she had been the true subject, and not the student, but she thought the purpose was to see if teachers allowed the students to eat the "junk food" on the table. After being debriefed, most of the teachers went on to say how their sessions had gone and how they responded. Almost every one of them, including those who had discouraged the deviation, said they had let the student deviate and emphasized how important curiosity is in the classroom. One teacher said, "Oh, I'm not very good at enforcing rules and following exact instructions like that. That just is not the way I am in my classroom. I hope that doesn't hurt your results at all." That same teacher had responded restrictively and had even gone so far as to fish the extra object out of the mixture. Most of the teachers believed they had done a good job encouraging the students' curiosity. This suggests that teachers are either not that accurate or not very straightforward with their self-appraisals. It also means that, regardless of their responses, they all believe that encouraging children's inquiry is the right thing to do.

It might be the case that in actual classrooms one would not find the predominance of friendly, encouraging teachers found in these data. Perhaps those teachers who volunteered for our study were more confident (happy to be observed) and generally more engaged in teaching (willing to participate in research that might contribute to education) or might in some other way differ from the general population of teachers. Future work in naturalistic settings is needed to find out how common it is for teachers to respond as they did in the present study. In addition, future work needs to discover how teachers respond to children's domain-relevant deviations from a task when they are among a group of peers. We were eager, in this first study, to attain a more precise picture of the interactions between an individual child and a teacher. Naturally, it will be important to follow up by finding out whether the effects we found generalize to situations that more closely resemble real classrooms. This would seem to be a promising avenue for future research.

Although characteristics such as a teacher's gender and level of experience or the gender of the student did not interact with the condition, it is possible that such characteristics might cumulatively interact with condition. For example, perhaps inexperienced female teachers respond more restrictively to boys than to girls when encouraged to finish the worksheet. Future research is needed to assess possibilities such as this.

Conclusion

If curiosity is as important to cognitive development and academic achievement as research has indicated, why is there so little of it in classrooms? One part of the answer may be that various forces keep teachers from encouraging it. The goal of the present study was to find out more about how teachers do in fact respond when children inquire. Given the realities of classroom management, we were particularly interested in what teachers do when children deviate from a planned activity, not to disrupt or distract but to find out more about the underlying domain. The trade-off we created, between finishing a task and encouraging inquiry, seemed to capture at least one kind of conflict many teachers face each day. The instructions we gave approximate the different kinds of direction that teachers must respond to from principals and state mandates.

The results suggest that teachers who encourage children while working on a school-related task can be quite responsive to the directions they receive regarding the focus of the activity. Teachers who are otherwise encouraging can be influenced to respond less encouragingly to children's explorations. When they feel obligated to achieve a specific concrete goal, they may sacrifice the chance to foster a child's curiosity. This means that students' likelihood of receiving encouragement for their curiosity and exploration may depend less on the individual characteristics of their teachers than on the goals their teachers are trying to achieve and on the very human tendency teachers have to comply with the goals articulated by those in authority.

This study provides a first step in understanding the dynamics that influence children's expression of curiosity in school. Although these results do not offer a definitive explanation for why there seems to be so little curiosity in classrooms, the data do provide us with a piece of the puzzle and lead to three different sets of questions for further research. First, more work is needed to find out how well the present findings generalize to a wider range of teachers and whether the same dynamic can be found when the inquiring child is in a classroom of others. In-depth interviews and observations will be useful to explore individual differences in how teachers respond to unscripted exploration in their classrooms. This will help us find out how the present findings map onto the responses of real teachers responding to children who are spontaneously and genuinely expressing curiosity. Second, more information is needed about how teachers' behavior affects children's curiosity over long periods of time (e.g., the school year). When teachers promote curiosity, does it actually lead to greater knowledge, enjoyment, and investment in learning? A recent study underscores the power of teachers' responses in determining children's educational outcomes (Mashburn et al., 2008). Does this influence also shape the development of curiosity over the long run? A third set of questions concerns how to train, induce, or lead teachers (those who volunteer for this kind of study and those who do not) to encourage curiosity in students. One step along that route is to use teachers' expertise in science education as an independent variable. Do teachers who know more about science respond in a unique way when students explore objects and materials in unplanned ways? What can be learned from those teachers that might be used in helping new teachers? If we are to nurture the development of curiosity in school-age children, we need to know more about the conditions under which it thrives or diminishes.

Appendix A
Initial Consent Form Signed by Teachers

How Children Learn

I agree to participate in the ----- College study on How Children Learn, in which I will help an elementary school student work on a brief science activity. I give my permission for the video recording of the session to be included in this research. I understand that these data will be used for research purposes only and that the material will not be accessible to anyone other than the researchers. My identity will be confidential, and will not appear on any of the data analyses or subsequent descriptions of the research. I accept $20.00 for my participation.

Name and Date

Appendix B
Instructions Given to Teachers

"Learn More" Condition

Dear Teacher,

Please help the student who will join you here with the science activity set out on the table. Do whatever you normally would when helping a student with this kind of activity. You have 11 minutes to work on this activity and help the child learn more about how things float, sink, and the interaction of elements. When the time is up the experimenter will come back in the room to alert you. Thank you again for your time.

"Worksheet" Condition

Dear Teacher,

Please help the student who will join you here with the science activity set out on the table. Do whatever you normally would when helping a student with this kind of activity. There is a worksheet that asks the child to answer some questions and record the results of the activity. Please help them fill out the worksheet. You will have 11 minutes to complete the task and corresponding worksheet with the child. When the time is up, the experimenter will come back in the room to alert you and collect the completed worksheet. Thank you again for your time.

Appendix C
Information Given to Teachers Explaining the Science Behind the Activity

Bouncing Raisins

Carbon dioxide is a colorless gas that is comprised of one carbon atom and two oxygen atoms. Carbon dioxide is the gas that is used in carbonated soda drinks. Chemical leaveners, such as baking powders and baking soda, release carbon dioxide when exposed to acids. The white vinegar in this experiment is an acid, so when it is combined with the baking soda bubbles of carbon dioxide are created. These bubbles attach to the raisins and lift them to the top. Once the raisins reach the surface, the bubbles escape and the raisins sink. Once they sink, new bubbles collect again and the whole process begins again. The raisins will continue to bounce up and down.

Appendix D
The Worksheet

Chemistry Worksheet

Name: _____
Date: _____

Gather the following materials:

*4 tablespoons (60 milliliters) of vinegar
*3 tablespoons (45 milliliters) of baking soda
*1 tall, clear glass or jar
*Enough water to fill half the glass or jar
*8 or more raisins
*8 or more peanuts

Now follow these steps:

1. Add the vinegar and baking soda to the water.

2. What happened? _____

_____

_____

(continued)

Appendix D (continued)

3. Drop the raisins in one at a time into the mixture.

4. What happened? _____

_____

_____

5. Can you come up with an explanation? _____

_____

_____

6. Now try the procedure with peanuts.

7. Did the same thing happen? _____

8. Why or why not? _____

_____

_____

Appendix E
Consent Form Signed by Teachers After Debriefing

Teachers' Responses When Children Deviate From a Task

Having participated in the study, the real nature of this research has been explained to me. I understand that the research actually focuses on how teachers respond when children deviate from a task, and that the child in the study was not the real subject but instead, working with the researchers. Having learned the actual nature of the work, I give my permission for the video recording of the session to be included in the data analyses. I understand that these data will be used for research purposes only and that the material will not be accessible to anyone other than Susan Engel and Kellie Randall. My identity will be confidential, and will not appear on any of the data analyses or subsequent descriptions of the research. I accept $20.00 for my participation.

_____   _____

I agree to have the videotape included   Name and Date

_____   _____

I do not agree to have the videotape included   Name and Date

Appendix F
Postactivity Questionnaire Given to Teachers

Name:

Date:

How long have you been teaching? (Note: If you are currently in school for your degree in education, please share what year you are in and briefly discuss time you have spent in a classroom working with children.)

What age group do you normally work with?

What age groups do you have experience working with?

What subjects do you most enjoy teaching?

What were your impressions of the task?

What were your impressions of the child?

Was there anything you felt hindered your ability to help the child with the task?

Is there anything you would suggest to improve the task?

Note

This research was supported by a grant from the Spencer Foundation.

References

Ainley, M., Hidi, S., & Berndorff, D. (2002). Interest, learning and the psychological processes that mediate their relationship, *Educational Psychology, 94,* 545–561.

Alberti, E., & Witryol, S. (1994). The relationship between curiosity and cognitive ability in third- and fifth-grade children. *Journal of Genetic Psychology, 155,* 129–146.

Alexander, P. (1997). Mapping the multidimensional nature of domain learning: The interplay of cognitive, motivational and strategic forces. *Advances in Motivation and Achievement, 10,* 213–250.

Bergin, D. (1999). Influences on classroom interest. *Educational Psychologist, 34,* 87–98.

Berlyne, D. (1960). *Conflict, arousal and curiosity.* New York: McGraw Hill.

Boekaerts, M., & Boscolo, P. (2002). Interest in learning, learning to be interested. *Learning and Instruction, 12,* 375–382.

Bull, S. G., & Dizney, H. F. (1973). Epistemic curiosity-arousing prequestions: Their effect on long-term retention. *Journal of Educational Psychology, 65,* 45–49.

Chouinard, M. (2007). Children's questions: A mechanism for cognitive development. *Monographs of the Society for Research in Child Development, 72*(1), 1–129.

Coie, J. D. (1974). An evaluation of the cross-situational stability of children's curiosity. *Journal of Personality, 42,* 93–116.

Endsley, R. C., & Clarey, S. A. (1975). Answering young children's questions as a determinant of their subsequent question-asking behavior. *Developmental Psychology, 11,* 863.

Engel, S. (2007). *Open Pandora's box: Curiosity in the classroom* (Sarah Lawrence College Occasional Papers). Sarah Lawrence College, New York.

Engel, S., & Hackmann, H. (2002). *Curiosity in context: The classroom environment examined.* Paper presented at the Society for Research in Child Development, Biennial Meetings, Tampa, FL.

Fransson, A. (1977). On qualitative differences in learning: IV Effects of intrinsic motivation and extrinsic test anxiety on process and outcome. *British Journal of Educational Psychology, 47,* 244–257.

Henderson, B. (1984). Parents and exploration: The effect of context on individual differences in exploratory behavior. *Child Development, 55,* 1237–1245.

Henderson, B. (1994). Individual differences in experience-producing tendencies. In H. Keller, K. Schneider, & B. Henderson (Eds.), *Curiosity and exploration* (pp. 213–225). Berlin: Springer-Verlag.

Henderson, B., Charlesworth, W. R., & Gamradt, J. (1982). Children's exploratory behavior in a novel field setting. *Ethology and Sociobiology, 3,* 93–99.

Henderson, B., & Moore, S. G. (1979). Measuring exploratory behavior in young children: A factor-analytic study. *Developmental Psychology, 15,* 113–119.

Hestenes, L., Cassidy, D. J., & Niemeyer, J. (2004). A microanalysis of teachers' verbalizations in inclusive classrooms. *Early Education and Development, 15,* 23–38.

Hidi, S. (1990). Interest and its contribution as a mental resource for learning. *Review of Educational Research, 60,* 549–571.

Hidi, S., & Renninger, K. (2006). The four-phase model of interest development. *Educational Psychologist, 41,* 111–127.

Kagan, J. (1972). Motives and development. *Journal of Personality and Social Psychology, 22,* 51–66.

Kuhn, D. (2005). *Education for thinking.* Cambridge, MA: Harvard University Press.

Loewenstein, G. (1994). The psychology of curiosity: A review and reinterpretation. *Psychological Bulletin, 116,* 75–98.

Lowry, N. J., & Johnson, D. W. (1981). Effects of controversy on epistemic curiosity, achievement, and attitudes. *Journal of Social Psychology, 115,* 31–43.

Mashburn, A. J., Pianta, R. C., Hamre, B. K., Downer, J. T., Barbarn, O. A, Bryant, D., et al. (2008) Measures of classroom quality in prekindergarten and children's development of academic, language, and social skills. *Child Development, 79,* 493–513.

Maw, W. H., & Maw, E. W. (1972). Differences between high- and low-curiosity fifth-grade children in their recognition of verbal absurdities. *Journal of Educational Psychology, 63,* 558–562.

Maw, W. H., & Maw, E. W. (1975). Note on curiosity and intelligence of school children. *Psychological Reports, 36,* 782.

Milgram, S. (1983). *Obedience to authority.* New York: Harper Perennial.

Mittman, L. R., & Terrell, G. (1964). An experimental study of curiosity in children. *Child Development, 35,* 851–855.

Engel, Randall

Osborn, M., McNess, E., & Broadfoot, P. (2000). *What teachers do: Changing policy and practice in primary education.* New York: Continuum.

Piaget, J. (1969). *The psychology of intelligence.* New York: Littlefield, Adams.

Renninger, K. A. (1990). Children's play interests, representation, and activity. In R. Fivush & J. Hudson (Eds.), *Emory cognition series: Vol. 3. Knowing and remembering in young children.* New York: Cambridge University Press.

Renninger, K., Ewen, L., & Lasher, A. (2002). Individual interest as context in expository text and mathematical word problems. *Learning and Instruction, 12,* 474–491.

Renninger, K. A., Hidi, S., & Krapp, A. (Eds.). (1992). *The role of interest in learning and development.* Mahwah, NJ: Lawrence Erlbaum.

Renninger, K. A., & Wozniak, R. H. (1985). Effect of interest on attentional shift, recognition, and recall in young children. *Developmental Psychology, 21,* 624–632.

Roeser, R. W., Marachi, R., & Gehlbach, H. (2002). A goal theory perspective on teachers' professional identities and the contexts of teaching. In C. Midgley (Ed.), *Goals, goal structures, and patterns of adaptive learning* (pp. 205–242). Mahwah NJ: Lawrence Erlbaum.

Silvia, P. (2008). Interest—The curious emotion. *Current Directions in Psychological Science, 17,* 57–60.

Tizard, B., & Hughes, M. (1984). *Young children learning.* Cambridge, MA: Harvard University Press.

Zukier, H. (1986). The paradigmatic and narrative modes in goal-guided inference. In R. M. Sorrentino & E. T. Higgins (Eds.), *Handbook of motivation and cognition: Foundations of social behavior* (pp. 503–549). New York: Guilford.

Manuscript received November 2, 2007
Revision received March 4, 2008
Accepted July 2, 2008

American Educational Research Journal
March 2009, Vol. 46, No. 1, pp. 203–231
DOI: 10.3102/0002831208323368
© *2009 AERA. http://aerj.aera.net*

The Preparation of Students From National Science Foundation–Funded and Commercially Developed High School Mathematics Curricula for Their First University Mathematics Course

Michael Harwell
Thomas R. Post
Arnie Cutler
University of Minnesota
Yukiko Maeda
Purdue University
Edwin Anderson
University of Minnesota
Ke Wu Norman
University of Montana
Amanuel Medhanie
University of Minnesota

The selection of K–12 mathematics curricula has become a polarizing issue for schools, teachers, parents, and other educators and has raised important questions about the long-term influence of these curricula. This study examined the impact of participation in either a National Science Foundation–funded or commercially developed mathematics curriculum on the difficulty level of the first university mathematics course a student enrolled in and the grade earned in that course. The results provide evidence that National Science Foundation–funded curricula do not prepare students to initially enroll in more difficult university mathematics courses as well as commercially developed curricula, but once enrolled students earn similar grades. These findings have important implications for high school mathematics curriculum selection and for future research in this area.

KEYWORDS: mathematics education, postsecondary education, achievement

There is widespread agreement among teachers, parents, school administrators, mathematics educators, mathematicians, and others of the importance of providing K–12 students with rigorous instruction that promotes mathematical understanding, but there is less agreement on how to achieve this goal. A manifestation of the lack of agreement is the "math wars" that have pitted defenders of commercially developed (CD) mathematics curricula against those advocating curricula supported by the National Science Foundation (NSF; Schoenfeld, 2004). In general, CD mathematics curricula stress traditional algorithms and procedures, while National Science Foundation–funded (NSFF) curricula focus to a greater degree on problem solving and other higher order thinking skills such as synthesis, generalization, and evaluation. Specifically, NSFF curricula refer to those curricula that were funded from a solicitation of proposals (RFP NSF 91-100) through the NSF in the early 1990s (Senk & Thompson, 2003) that were designed to be aligned with the National Council of Teachers of Mathematics' (NCTM; 1989) *Curriculum and Evaluation Standards for School Mathematics.*

MICHAEL HARWELL is a professor at the University of Minnesota, Department of Educational Psychology, 250 Education Sciences Building, 56 East River Road, Minneapolis, MN 55455-0364; e-mail: *harwe001@umn.edu*. His research interests include the relationship between socioeconomic status and student achievement and applications of propensity scores in education.

THOMAS R. POST is a professor at the University of Minnesota, Department of Curriculum and Instruction, 175 Peik Hall, 157 Pillsbury Drive SE, Minneapolis, MN 55455; e-mail: *postx001@umn.edu*. His research interests focus on middle-grades mathematics and in particular the teaching and learning of rational number concepts.

ARNIE CUTLER (deceased) was a research associate for the Minnesota Mathematics Assessment Project at the University of Minnesota. His research interests focused on K–12 mathematics instruction.

YUKIKO MAEDA is an assistant professor at Purdue University, Department of Educational Studies, Beering Hall of Liberal Arts & Education, 100 N. University Street, West Lafayette, IN 47907-2098; email: *ymaeda@purdue.edu*. Her research interests are the validity and reliability of educational tests, the methodology of meta-analyses, and the robustness of hierarchical linear models in educational research.

EDWIN ANDERSON is a research associate for the Minnesota Mathematics Assessment Project, 175 Peik Hall, 157 Pillsbury Drive SE, Minneapolis, MN 55455; email: *ander630@umn.edu*. His research interests focus on K–12 mathematics instruction.

KE WU NORMAN is an assistant professor in the Department of Mathematical Sciences, Mathematics Building, University of Montana, Missoula, MT 59812; email: *ke@mso.umt.edu*. Her research interests focus on the impact of high school mathematics curricula on college mathematics performance and the use of college mathematics placement tests.

AMANUEL MEDHANIE is a graduate student in the Department of Educational Psychology, 250 Educational Sciences Building, 56 East River Road, Minneapolis, MN 55455; email: *medha001@umn.edu*. His research interests are the use of propensity scores in educational research and longitudinal data analysis.

Disagreement over which mathematics curriculum is most appropriate can be linked indirectly to the introduction of the NCTM (1989) standards and directly to curricula that have been designed to conform to those standards. It is important to emphasize that the 1989 standards were the result of the efforts of hundreds of professionals and received near unanimous acceptance and acclaim from all sectors of academia and society. In 2000 the NCTM published a revised document, *Principles and Standards for School Mathematics*, that expanded upon and updated the 1989 NCTM document and again involved literally hundreds of professionals in its development. Endorsees of the 2000 document voiced their support for the "quality mathematics curricula and assessment criteria" and included 15 major mathematical societies such as the Mathematical Association of America and the American Mathematical Society.

In a very real sense these two NCTM documents, although widely supported, challenged the hegemony of CD mathematics curricula in U.S. schools. In response to this challenge, advocates of CD curricula have taken their case to a variety of constituencies, especially parents. The advocates have argued that teaching mathematics using NSFF curricula leads to poor mathematics performance with potentially dire consequences such as poor student performance on the mathematics portions of standardized tests taken by college-bound students (Wu, 1997) or that these curricula do not adequately prepare students for calculus and other mathematically oriented courses as taught at the university level.

On the other hand, proponents of NSFF curricula often point to published reports of disappointing mathematics achievement of students, most of whom completed a CD curriculum (Hiebert, 2000; Schoen, Fey, Hirsch, & Coxford, 1999), and argue that large-scale changes in the way we think about, develop, implement, and assess school mathematics programs are needed. For example, results from the Trends in International Mathematics and Science Study (1996) indicated that U.S. 8th grade and 12th grade students performed below international averages. The *National Assessment of Educational Progress Report* (Braswell et al., 2001) indicated that 17% of high school seniors in the United States were proficient in mathematics in terms of reaching a minimum level of competency. The report of the Senior Assessment Panel of the International Assessment of U.S. Mathematical Sciences (1998) characterized U.S. K–12 mathematics instruction as weak and pointed out that this has several adverse effects, including the fact that the majority of mathematics PhD students at U.S. universities hail from other countries.

Regional evidence of problems are reflected in a 1999 report by the Minnesota State College and University System that found only 38% of students entering a postsecondary institution in the State College System, almost all of whom would have completed a CD curriculum, were considered ready to begin postsecondary mathematics at the level of college algebra. The corresponding figure for 2-year colleges was 18%. Moreover, fewer than 7% of eighth-grade students will take 4 full years of college-intending mathematics coursework in high school. Similar findings have been reported in many states, including Wisconsin, Iowa, Illinois, North and South Dakota, and Washington.

These findings challenge the assumption that CD curricula, which have dominated K–12 mathematics instruction in Minnesota and elsewhere in the United States for many years, have adequately prepared students for university-level mathematics. However, little is known about the preparation of students who completed an NSFF mathematics curriculum in high school for university mathematics.

Theoretical Models Underlying NSFF Curricula

The 1989 and 2000 NCTM *Standards* documents incorporated components of various cognitively oriented theories about the development of mathematics knowledge and the nature of student learning. There is also reason to believe that the fundamental principles that underpin the development of the NSFF curricula should promote mathematics learning for a diverse population of student learners.

Until recently, principles of behavioral (Skinner, 1938) and neobehavioral (Gagne, 1963, 1985) psychology have dominated curriculum development and evaluation in school mathematics. Widespread use of behavioral objectives, task analysis, stimulus response theory, and operant conditioning are artifacts of this psychological perspective. More recently, cognitive psychological perspectives (Bruner, 1960; Dienes, 1960; Dienes & Golding, 1971; Piaget, 1960; Piaget & Inhelder, 1958) have received considerable attention as psychologists and educators realized that learning is primarily internal to the individual and its measurement involves more than documenting a series of observable behaviors that may be related only to the mastery of isolated skills and procedures.

Research on student conceptual development during the 1970s and beyond (e.g., Bruner, 1964; Bruner, Olver, & Greenfield, 1966; Dienes, 1960; Lesh, 1979; Shulman & Sparks, 1992) has been strongly influenced by these cognitive perspectives. The NCTM *Standards* documents (1989, 2000) were also influenced by these perspectives. This in turn had a decided impact on the direction of the development of NSFF curricula because the NSF required that each proposal document specify how the planned project would reflect the principles espoused in the 1989 *Standards* document.

Development of NSFF Mathematics Curricula

Fearing for the future levels of technological literacy in this country and for the future of our ability to lead in this area, the NSF funded 13 full mathematics programs (3 elementary, 5 middle grades, and 5 at the high school level) at a cost of approximately US$100 million, beginning in the early 1990s. Within each program, 30 to 40 persons (mathematics educators, mathematicians, teachers, etc.) worked to complete the writing and pilot testing of each of these curricula, which generally took 5 or 6 years. At the high school level, all programs were committed to considering algebra, geometry, probability, statistics, and topics in discrete mathematics every school year. This was a radical departure from the traditional Algebra 1, Geometry, Algebra 2, Precalculus (college algebra) sequence.

The NSFF curricula were for the most part problem centered, focusing on problems embedded in realistic settings that took several class periods to explore and resolve. The mathematical content and its development were in part motivated by the problems considered. Small group and cooperative student activities, along with a de-emphasis on the teacher lecture format, were strongly encouraged and considered fundamental to the success of the programs. Extensive teacher support materials and professional development opportunities, also funded by the NSF, were provided to school districts adopting these programs.

Although no curriculum can ever be totally supported by research, these materials were the most "researched" school mathematics curriculum materials of any in history. They represent the "best practices" of the time and in general reflect accumulated research results as to the nature of student mathematical conceptualization and learning. Thus, these new curricula reflect, for the most part, contemporary cognitive approaches to mathematics teaching, learning, and assessment. These curricula are also consistent with a broader school reform movement emphasizing the role of students as active participants in a learning process that involves problem solving, small group work, and connections to the world outside the classroom (Newmann, Marks, & Gamoran, 1996; Schoenfeld, 2004). Last, these curricula correspond to the positions of the NCTM, the main professional organization in the field.

Evidence of the Performance of Middle School and High School Students in NSFF Curricula

Research on the achievement of students learning from NSFF curricula in Grades K–12 provides evidence of the levels of student learning (Senk & Thompson, 2003). In general, students who completed an NSFF curriculum do as well as or better than students who completed a CD curriculum on nonstandardized achievement measures that typically consist of classroom problem sets (Cichon & Ellis, 2003; Huntley, Rasmussen, Villarubi, Sangtong, & Fey, 2000; Lott et al., 2003; Schoen & Hirsch, 2003; Webb, 2003).

Research has also indicated that NSFF curricula appear to satisfactorily prepare students to succeed on standardized tests, including the Stanford Achievement Test (Abeille & Hurley, 2001; Harwell et al., 2007; Post et al., 2008), the Iowa Test of Educational Development Ability to Do Quantitative Thinking (Abeille & Hurley, 2001), the Iowa Test of Basic Skills (Schoen & Hirsch, 2003), the Scholastic Assessment Test Mathematics subtest (Webb, 2003), the Comprehensive Test of Basic Skills (Webb, 2003), and the Preliminary Scholastic Aptitude Test (Cichon & Ellis, 2003; Lott et al., 2003).

The performance of students completing an NSFF curriculum on standardized tests is in many ways surprising because such tests are not aligned with the content or focus of NSFF curricula, suggesting that these students are at a disadvantage. Despite strong encouragement in the literature to link mathematics content and assessment in new ways (Le et al., 2006; National Research Council, 1998; NCTM, 2000; Pellegrino, 2006), the evidence is that tests sensitive to NSFF curricula such as the New Standards Reference Examination in Mathematics (New Standards, 1997) are used far less often than their standardized counterparts.

Research of NSFF high school mathematics curricula has also shown that students completing these curricula generally fare as well as or better than students who completed a CD curriculum on a variety of nonachievement outcomes related to educational success. These outcomes have included the tendency of students completing an NSFF curriculum to take more mathematics classes in high school than students studying from CD mathematics curricula (Cichon & Ellis, 2003; Webb, 2003), report higher ratings in their confidence and the usefulness of mathematics, and display more positive attitudes toward mathematics (Schoen & Pritchett, 1998).

Another factor that has been shown to be related to mathematics achievement in middle school and high school is socioeconomic status (SES; Coleman et al., 1966; Reys, Reys, Lapan, Holliday, & Wasman, 2003; Riordan & Noyce, 2001; Sirin, 2005), a relationship that appears to be unaffected by participation in an NSFF curriculum (Harwell et al., 2007; Post et al., 2008). Teacher professional development (Schoen, Cebulla, Finn, & Fi, 2003) and fidelity of implementation of an NSFF mathematics curriculum (Schoen et al., 2003) have also been shown to be related to mathematics achievement. The impact of teacher quality on student achievement is often cited as an important factor to consider, but the literature is mixed on key contributors to this impact or the magnitude of the effect (Wayne & Youngs, 2003).

The data across different geographical areas and various curricula show that middle school and high school students studying from NSFF curricula perform similarly on standardized measures of mathematics achievement and on the mathematics portions of nonstandardized tests when factors that can affect mathematics performance are taken into account. Some of these factors are wholly or partly under the control of schools (e.g., fidelity of implementation of NSFF curricula and teacher professional development), while others, like prior mathematics achievement and SES, are not. This in turn suggests that these factors need to be taken into account in examining the preparation of students completing NSFF and CD high school mathematics curricula for university-level mathematics.

Evidence of the Effectiveness of NSFF Mathematics Curricula to Prepare Students for University-Level Mathematics

Despite evidence of success, NSFF curricula have come under intense criticism from Web-based sources[1] and other venues. Much of the criticism claims that students completing an NSFF curriculum are poorly prepared to succeed in calculus and other university-level mathematics courses. Since 70% of the students who were eighth graders in 1988 attended some type of postsecondary institution by 1994 (National Center for Education Statistics [NCES], 1998), the preparation of students completing NSFF and CD high school mathematics curricula for university-level mathematics is important (Kuenzi, Matthews, & Mangan, 2006; Riley, 1998). Students who enroll at a university underprepared often must first take courses they should have completed in high school, and about one quarter of all freshmen enroll in at least one postsecondary remedial mathematics course (Parsad & Lewis, 2003). Documenting the preparation of students for university-level mathematics as a function of their high school mathematics curriculum is essential to remedying the problem of underprepared students.

Somewhat surprisingly, disappointing results on national and international assessments and the low percentage of high school graduates ready to begin their college mathematics careers with college algebra or calculus have not prompted much research on how well NSFF or CD high school mathematics curricula prepare students for university-level mathematics. In fact, we are aware of only two peer-reviewed published research studies addressing the relationship between high school mathematics curricula and student success in university-level mathematics.

Schoen and Hirsch (2003) examined the grade point averages (GPAs) of students from two similar high schools who later enrolled in Calculus I and above at the University of Michigan. Graduates of the NSFF Contemporary Mathematics in Context (Core-Plus) curriculum had a higher overall GPA in Calculus I and other more advanced mathematics courses when compared with students in a CD curriculum. Hill and Parker (2006) used a sample of more than 3,000 to study student performance in university mathematics coursework and reported findings that were critical of NSFF curricula. In particular, these authors reported that students who completed the NSFF Core-Plus mathematics curriculum in high school began their university mathematics coursework with less difficult courses and subsequently completed even less difficult mathematics courses than a group of students who did not complete Core-Plus in high school. One important difficulty with this study was that the specific mathematics curriculum completed by these students was, as acknowledged by the authors, in question and could have included students who completed other NSFF curricula, University of Chicago School Mathematics Project (UCSMP) curricula, or even a CD curriculum.

O'Neil (2002), in an unpublished thesis, studied the relationship between high school mathematics curriculum (CD and NSFF) and grade in the first college mathematics course for a small sample of students ($N = 48$) who had completed 4 years of the NSFF math curriculum Math Connections. Completion of a CD or NSFF curriculum (Math Connections) did not have a statistically significant relationship with the grade a student earned in the first college mathematics course.

In response to the sparseness of this literature, the Mathematical Sciences Education Board (2004) has called for formal studies of this relationship. The current study examined the preparation of students for university-level mathematics as a function of the high school mathematics curriculum they completed. The research question addressed was as follows:

> Do university students who completed at least three levels of high school mathematics in an NSFF curriculum differ from those who had similar exposure to a commercially developed curriculum in the difficulty level of their first university mathematics course or in the grade they earned in that course, when taking into account background factors such as prior mathematics achievement, ethnicity, and gender?

A high school level was defined to be the content equivalent of a year-long course taught 1 hour per day and has been commonly referred to as a Carnegie unit (Boyer, 1983). Addressing this question should lead to a better understanding of the similarity or differences in the preparation of students who completed an NSFF or a CD curriculum in high school for university-level mathematics.

Method

The methodology in this study was informed in part by *On Evaluating Curricular Effectiveness: Judging the Quality of K–12 Mathematics Evaluations* (Mathematical Sciences Education Board, 2004). This document provides criteria for effective evaluation of curriculum material, and several of its recommendations were incorporated into this research.

Research Design

This study employed a quasi-experimental design for cross-sectional data (Pedhazur & Schmelkin, 1991) in which the high school mathematics curriculum (group) a student completed was the independent variable of most interest. Difficulty of students' first university-level mathematics course and the grade earned in that course served as dependent variables.

This quasi-experimental design allowed effects corresponding to the research question to be examined but did not automatically permit strong causal inferences because of the absence of random assignment (Pedhazur & Schmelkin, 1991). As a result, our goal was to statistically control for important differences between the two curriculum groups that could bias our inferences.

Sampling

Two populations were of interest. The target population consisted of post-secondary students in a midwestern state in the United States who had graduated from 1 of the more than 325 high schools in the state. Our sampled population, on the other hand, consisted of students enrolled at a single large public university in a midwestern state in the United States during the fall of 2002 or fall of 2003 terms who had graduated from 1 of 85 high schools for which at least 10 students enrolled at the university, which helped to ensure reasonable high school–based statistical estimates. The fall of 2002 was chosen as the first term to study postsecondary performance because it allowed for significant numbers of students to be sampled who had completed at least three levels of an NSFF high school mathematics curriculum. The fall of 2002 term was also the point at which fairly extensive student admission information was available in an electronic form, greatly simplifying data collection. Student data for two consecutive semesters were available: fall of 2002 and spring of 2003 for one cohort and fall of 2003 and spring of 2004 for a second cohort.

Data

Archival data from three sources were collected.

State. Data for the state-mandated Basic Skills Test (BST) for mathematics (Minnesota Department of Education, 1998) administered in eighth grade served as a measure of prior mathematics achievement. This test covers mathematics content up through and including pre-algebra, and its development followed traditional procedures for establishing psychometric criteria of validity and reliability and for ensuring that different forms of the test offered from one year to the next possessed items of the same difficulty. However, its use resembles a criterion-referenced test since students must exceed a predetermined cutoff to be eligible for high school graduation (students falling below the cutoff can retake the test). The percentage of students eligible for a free or reduced-price lunch at a high school when the sampled students were high school seniors was also obtained from the Minnesota Department of Education and was used as a high school–level measure of SES.

University. Information on a student's application to the university was also tapped, including a student's transcript data reflecting his or her high school coursework. Among the variables extracted from these records were ACT Mathematics score, GPA in high school mathematics courses, overall high school GPA, high school percentile rank, number of levels of high school mathematics completed (three, four, or five), sex, SES (eligibility for a free or reduced-price lunch), and ethnicity (Native American, African American, Asian, Hispanic, or White). Other variables collected from the university included when a student enrolled (fall of 2002 or fall of 2003) and mathematics grade and course-taking information.

Altogether, 5,410 university student records were available initially. Because BST scores resided in an external data file, it was necessary to match records electronically to link each student's BST score with his or her university record, a process that was successful for 70% (3,788) of the students but unsuccessful for 1,622 students. Among students for whom records could not be matched, there was evidence that some ethnic subgroups were disproportionately affected. Among African American students in the original sample, 52% did not have BST scores, followed by Asian (40.4%), Hispanic (35.1%), and White (24.6%) students. Further examination of the ethnic subgroups showed that students for whom BST scores were not available on average showed slightly lower mathematics achievement. For example, average ACT Mathematics scores for African American and White students for whom BST scores were not available were 17.7 (*SD* = 4.61) and 25.1 (*SD* = 4.16), respectively, but among students with BST scores ACT Mathematics means for these two ethnic subgroups were 18.8 (*SD* = 4.35) and 25.6 (*SD* = 4.58), respectively.

Among students for whom BST Mathematics scores were available (*N* = 3,788), a total of 32% (1,225) did not take a mathematics course in their first year of university study and therefore provided no difficulty or grade data. Among the 1,225, 81.7% had completed a CD curriculum in high school, quite similar to the percentage of students completing a CD curriculum in the original sample (82.1%). While the tendency of students who completed NSFF and CD curricula to enroll in a mathematics course during their first year of university study was similar (67.1% and 65.6%, respectively), the group of 1,225 consistently showed slightly lower average prior mathematics achievement compared to those who enrolled for a mathematics course.

Missing data further reduced the pool of available students and was most pronounced for the ethnicity and ACT Mathematics variables. There were too few Native American students in our sample with sufficient data to ensure credible estimation of parameters connected to this ethnic group, and these students were omitted. Similarly, two students who classified themselves as international students were also omitted.

We further restricted the sample to students from high schools offering a single curriculum, all of which offered a CD curriculum, and to students who completed an NSFF curriculum in a high school offering both NSFF and CD curricula. The result was that the 513 students who completed a CD curriculum and graduated from a high school offering both NSFF and CD curricula were omitted from the analyses. This was done to allow mathematics curriculum (NSFF and CD) to be a high school–level variable; that is, all students from a particular high school in the sample completed an NSFF or a CD mathematics curriculum.

In sum, many students from the original sample of 5,410 were omitted because (a) BST Mathematics scores were not available, (b) students completed a CD mathematics curriculum in a high school offering both CD and NSFF mathematics curricula, (c) there were too few Native American students, or (d) students did not enroll in a mathematics course during their first year of university study. In addition, missing data on variables such as ACT Mathematics and ethnicity reduced the pool of available students in some analyses; these students were slightly more likely to be non-White and to have slightly lower scores on variables reflecting academic success such as high school percentile rank and high school GPA. With these omissions, the remaining sample consisted of 371 students who completed an NSFF curriculum and 1,296 students who completed a CD curriculum.

The net effect of the reduction in sample size was to limit inferences to a population of students (a) whose prior mathematics achievement was less variable and slightly higher than that of the original sample and (b) who enrolled in at least one mathematics course in their first year of university study. Still, the resulting 1,667 students from 85 high schools used in the analyses ensured good precision of estimation and adequate statistical power to detect effects of interest.

High schools. Another important source of data were the high schools, which provided information about the kind of mathematics curriculum a student completed in high school (i.e., had successfully completed at least three levels). Although the university maintains electronic records of the high school courses taken by each applicant and the associated grades, we quickly detected discrepancies in how particular mathematics courses were coded in university records and the correct descriptors in the data collection. For example, some schools reported "Integrated 1, 2, 3, and 4" as their high school mathematics courses, information that the university then recorded. We use the descriptor *integrated* to denote detailed study of algebra, geometry, probability, and statistics each year. This is sometimes used interchangeably with *Standards-based*, the term sometimes used to denote NSFF curricula. In some cases the courses recorded as integrated were actually a traditional publisher's text series that had a subtitle with the word integrated in it.

These initial experiences confirmed our pre-study expectation that accurate categorizations of students as having completed an NSFF or a CD mathematics curriculum in high school required us to contact each high school to independently obtain descriptions of their mathematics programs, including the mathematics courses offered and the textbooks used. Although labor intensive, this was necessary to ensure credible inferences about the NSFF and CD groups. Among the sampled high schools, 32 offered both an NSFF and a CD mathematics curriculum and 53 offered a CD curriculum exclusively, the latter including students exposed to the UCSMP curriculum (none of the high schools offered an NSFF curriculum exclusively). NSFF curricula in our sample of high schools were the Interactive Mathematics Program, Mathematics: Modeling Our World, and Core-Plus, which, given our research questions, were not differentiated in the data analyses.

The maximum number of students from a single high school in our sample was 77, with a median of 16 students, and these students were assumed to be representative of a population that completed at least one university mathematics course. Evidence that mathematics achievement patterns frequently differ among urban, suburban, and rural high schools (Finn, Gerber, & Wang, 2002; NCES, 2004) led us to obtain information on high school location. An examination of the sample showed that large urban and suburban high schools were well represented and smaller, typically rural high schools less so.

Variables

Independent variables. The high school mathematics curriculum a student completed (NSFF or CD) was the independent variable of major interest. Other independent variables in the data analyses that served as control variables were sex; ethnicity; BST Mathematics score; ACT Mathematics score; high school percentile rank; high school mathematics GPA; overall high school GPA; high school location; size of graduating high school class, which served as a proxy for high school size; and the proportion of students eligible for a free or reduced-priced lunch at each high school, which was a proxy for SES. When a student enrolled at the university and when he or she enrolled in the first university mathematics course also served as independent variables. The latter was used to take into account the possibility that students who waited to enroll in a mathematics course in the spring might perform differently because they had the benefit of a semester's experience.

Dependent variables. The dependent variables were the difficulty level of a student's first mathematics course and the grade earned in that course. If completion of a particular high school curriculum better prepares students mathematically, those students would be expected to initially enroll in more difficult (advanced) mathematics courses and to have better grades. Examining mathematics course descriptions at the university led to the construction of a 4-point Likert scale to capture the level of course difficulty:

Level 1: This level includes courses that should have been completed in high school. They often do not carry college credit. Students do enter the university without the required or recommended high school background, and these courses are designed to provide a foundation for students to be successful in future mathematics courses.

Level 2: This level includes courses for students who satisfactorily completed four levels of college-intending mathematics in high school. Courses at this level could be categorized in general as college algebra and precalculus mathematics.

Level 3: This is the typical entry level for well-prepared high school students who begin postsecondary mathematics coursework with beginning calculus (several types of calculus are available at the university, such as short calculus, Calculus I, or calculus with a biological emphasis).

Level 4: This level is considered an extension of beginning calculus. Titles include Calculus II, Differential Equations, Linear Algebra, Multivariable Calculus, and Sequences and Series.

University Mathematics Placement Tests and Mathematics Teaching

In studying the difficulty of the first university mathematics class a student enrolls in and his or her grade in that class, it is important to consider the role of mathematics placement tests. Other things being equal, we might expect students who completed a particular mathematics curriculum in high school to perform well on a placement test whose content and structure tend to match the high school mathematics curriculum, but there appears to be little evidence one way or the other. O'Neill (2002) reported a significant difference favoring students who completed a CD curriculum over those who completed an NSFF curriculum on the College Board's Accuplacer Test, whose content is generally consistent with that of CD curricula.

The university uses three mathematics placement tests; one is administered by a campus unit designed for students who are not yet ready to succeed academically in college-level mathematics coursework and the other two by academic units with significant instructional service functions. Two of the exams test for general readiness for postsecondary mathematics, and the other focuses on readiness for calculus. A perusal of these exams showed that they concentrate on algebraic manipulation, with only a few items on trigonometry and probability.

Once a student has taken one or more of these placement tests, he or she meets with an academic counselor, who may also be the student's advisor. The exact structure of the advising process varies across academic units at the university but in general involves the counselor using placement test information along with other relevant information, such as ACT Mathematics score, high school grades, and Advanced Placement Calculus scores if available, to advise a student on which mathematics class to enroll in initially. Any such recommendation is nonbinding, although previous analyses indicated that approximately 88% of freshmen in our sample followed the placement recommendation. The variability in the counseling process and the way that mathematics placement information is used can mean different initial course placement recommendations for identical student profiles. For example, a student could be advised to begin with calculus but opt to enroll in a precalculus course or vice versa, and both cases could impact the difficulty and grade dependent variables. Significant difficulties with obtaining credible placement data led us to omit this information from our analyses, and this is an important limitation of the study.

Variation across university mathematics instructors was curtailed somewhat by the university mathematics department's policy of standardizing course syllabi, using common student assignments and examinations, and using a single course-specific distribution of scores for assigning grades. Still, we had no data capturing the impact of teacher quality on student achievement, and this too is an important limitation of the study.

Data Analyses

Initially, descriptive analyses were performed to explore patterns in the data, followed by two-level hierarchical linear modeling (HLM; Raudenbush & Bryk, 2002) that treated students as nested within high schools. To control for compounding of Type I error rates, we used an adjusted Type I error rate attributed to Sidak (1967) of the form $\alpha' = 1 - (1 - \alpha)^{1/k}$, where α is the unadjusted Type I error rate, k is the number of statistical tests, and α' is the adjusted Type I error rate. We chose to compute adjusted Type I error rates for each table of statistical test results that we report based on an overall α = .10, which resembles a family-wise error rate strategy often associated with planned comparisons in ANOVA. For example, Table 1 reports 28 statistical test results for four student-level background variables. Based on α = .10, each of the 28 statistical hypotheses are tested at α' = .0037.

Results

Descriptive Analyses

Several descriptive analyses were performed to explore patterns in the data, and a representative subset of these results is reported. First, data for students who entered the university in the fall of 2002 (N = 1,075, 49.3%) and the fall of 2003 (N = 1,105) were examined. The percentage of students who completed an NSFF curriculum entering in the fall of 2002 and the fall of 2003 increased slightly, from 21.3% to 23%, respectively, while the corresponding CD percentages were 78.7% and 77%, respectively.

Descriptive statistics reflecting students' academic achievement and background variables like SES and ethnicity are reported in Table 1. A number of these relationships were found to be statistically significant, and the variance in a dependent variable explained by an independent variable was used as an index of effect size, with larger effects associated with stronger relationships. Following Cohen's (1988) guidelines, the effects in Table 1 ranged from quite weak (.02) to large (.16).

Correlations among several student variables are reported in Table 2 and show that the relationships between first university mathematics grade and other variables range from weak to moderate. Among the strongest correlations are those involving the number of levels of high school mathematics, overall high school GPA, ACT Mathematics scores, and the correlation between BST and ACT scores.

Table 3 reports high school mathematics achievement, difficulty of the first university mathematics course by curriculum group, and the number of levels of high school mathematics completed. As expected, increasing numbers of levels of high school mathematics were associated with higher average mathematics grades for both curriculum groups.

HLM Analyses

HLM was used to examine the effect of high school mathematics curriculum on the difficulty level of the first university mathematics course a student enrolled in and the grade earned in that course. The two dependent variables were analyzed separately. Students were treated as clustered within high schools to permit within–high school dependency among students to be estimated. If present, modeling this dependency with HLM should ensure more credible statistical test results than would ordinarily be possible with traditional regression modeling. The difficulty of a student's first university mathematics course was analyzed assuming an ordinal scale of measurement.

Table 1
Descriptive Results for Student Socioeconomic Status (SES), Sex, Ethnicity, and High School Location

Variable	ACT Math	BST Math	High School GPA	High School Math GPA	High School Percentile Rank	First University Math Grade	Difficulty of First University Math Course
SES	$\hat{\eta}^2 = .02^*$	$\hat{\eta}^2 = .05^*$	$\hat{\eta}^2 = .02^*$	$\hat{\eta}^2 = .02^*$	$\hat{\eta}^2 = .01^*$		$\hat{\eta}^2 \leq .01^*$
Low (6.3%)							
M	22.5	83.5	3.23	3.10	70.8	2.50	1.97
SD	5.6	14.3	0.60	0.76	20.2	1.21	0.99
n	100	104	104	97	99	104	104
High (93.7%)							
M	25.4	91.9	3.51	3.45	78.9	2.74	2.44
SD	4.7	8.1	0.47	0.58	16.9	1.02	0.87
n	1,519	1,558	1,551	1,424	1,523	1,558	1,558
Sex	$\hat{\eta}^2 = .09^*$	$\hat{\eta}^2 = .05^*$	$\hat{\eta}^2 = .10^*$	$\hat{\eta}^2 = .08^*$	$\hat{\eta}^2 \leq .01^*$	$\hat{\eta}^2 = .016^*$	$\hat{\eta}^2 = .06^*$
Female (45.1%)							
M	23.8	89.2	3.53	3.4	79.9	2.70	2.18
SD	4.5	10.2	0.48	0.58	16.8	1.05	0.77
n	735	751	747	682	733	751	751
Male (54.9%)							
M	26.5	93.1	3.47	3.43	77.4	2.75	2.60
SD	4.6	7.1	0.49	0.58	17.5	1.04	0.93
n	887	913	910	841	900	913	913
Ethnicity	$\hat{\eta}^2 = .12^*$	$\hat{\eta}^2 = .16^*$			$\hat{\eta}^2 = .06^*$		$\hat{\eta}^2 = .06^*$
African American (4.7%)							
M	19.2	77	2.87	2.73	62	2.15	1.53
SD	4.1	16.8	0.56	0.72	19	1.19	0.66
n	77	79	79	75	76	79	79
Asian American (15.1%)							
M	23.8	88.8	3.49	3.42	77.2	2.77	2.34
SD	4.9	10.9	0.47	0.61	18.2	1.04	0.96
n	244	256	256	235	253	256	256

(continued)

217

Table 1 *(continued)*

Variable	ACT Math	BST Math	High School GPA	High School Math GPA	High School Percentile Rank	First University Math Grade	Difficulty of First University Math Course
Hispanic (3.1%)							
M	21.9	87.6	3.21	3.12	70.6	2.65	2.04
SD	4.9	9.7	0.64	0.73	21.7	0.99	0.95
n	49	52	50	50	51	52	52
White (76.8%)							
M	26.1	92.9	3.54	3.48	80.1	2.75	2.49
SD	4.4	6.3	0.44	0.54	16.1	1.02	0.84
n	1,254	1,280	1,275	1,166	1,256	1,280	1,280
	$\hat{\eta}^2 = .026^*$	$\hat{\eta}^2 = .057^*$	$\hat{\eta}^2 = .027^*$	$\hat{\eta}^2 = .032^*$	$\hat{\eta}^2 = .014^*$	$\hat{\eta}^2 \leq .01^*$	$\hat{\eta}^2 = .016^*$
High school location							
Rural (16.8%)							
M	25.7	92.6	3.57	3.51	81.3	2.58	2.42
SD	4.5	7	0.43	0.55	15.4	1.0	0.83
n	268	273	273	248	270	273	273
Suburban (65.8%)							
M	25.5	92.1	3.52	3.45	78.4	2.79	2.47
SD	4.5	7.5	0.46	0.56	17.3	1.01	0.88
n	1,039	1,066	1,060	981	1,054	1,066	1,066
Urban (17.4%)							
M	23.5	86.6	3.30	3.21	74.3	2.58	2.58
SD	5.8	13.1	0.59	0.71	18.4	1.13	1.13
n	272	282	281	255	260	282	282

Note. BST = Basic Skills Test; GPA = grade point average; M = mean; SD = standard deviation; n = sample size; $\hat{\eta}^2$ = percentage of variance in a dependent variable (e.g., ACT Mathematics) explained by an independent variable (e.g., SES). *Indicates statistically significant at $\alpha' = 1 - (1 - \alpha)^{1/k} = .0037$, where $\alpha = .10$ is the unadjusted Type I error rate, k is the number of statistical tests = 28, and α' is the adjusted error rate. To investigate the relationship between the background variables and the difficulty of a first university mathematics course, a Kruskal-Wallis test for ordered contingency tables was performed; for all others an F test was used. Difficulty of first university mathematics course was coded on a 4-point scale (1 = *courses that would typically have been completed in high school;* 4 = *beyond Calculus I*). The value in parentheses for each subgroup reports the relative size of that subgroup; for example, 6.3% of the sample was categorized as eligible for a free/reduced-price lunch.

Table 2
Correlations Among Student Variables

Variable	1	2	3	4	5	6	7	8	9
1. ACT Math score	—								
2. High school math GPA	.506*	—							
3. BST Math (% correct)	.643*	.469*	—						
4. High school math levels	.564*	.417*	.394*	—					
5. High school percentile rank	.439*	.764*	.393*	.366*	—				
6. High school overall GPA	.493*	.878*	.451*	.423*	.860*	—			
7. Sex	−.291*	−.002	−.204*	−.143*	.062	.063	—		
8. Difficulty of first university math course	.719*	.521*	.486*	.593*	.512*	.534*	−.237*	—	
9. Grade of first university math course	.270*	.276*	.173*	.212*	.204*	.270*	−.023	.131*	—

Note. Listwise N = 1,455. BST = Basic Skills Test; GPA = grade point average.
*Indicates statistically significant at $\alpha' = 1 - (1 - \alpha)1/k = .0029$, where $\alpha = .10$ is the unadjusted Type I error rate, k is the number of statistical tests = 36, and α' is the adjusted error rate.

All analyses were performed with the HLM6 software (Raudenbush, Bryk, & Congdon, 2005).

Difficulty data. A generalized hierarchical proportional odds model for ordinal data was fitted to difficulty (1 = *courses ordinarily completed in high school;* 2 = *courses up to but not including Calculus I,* such as college algebra and precalculus; 3 = *Calculus I;* 4 = *beyond Calculus I).* Analysis of ordinal data is typically done by reexpressing the m categories of the ordinal variable in the form of $m - 1$ cumulative logits, represented by the log of the cumulative odds of each level of the variable (Raudenbush & Bryk, 2002, pp. 317–322). For example, for the first category of the difficulty variable, the corresponding logit had the form $\log\{[Prob(R_{ij} = 1)]/[1 - Prob(R_{ij} = 1)]\}$, where $Prob(R_{ij} = 1)$ represents the probability that the ith student from the jth high school enrolled in a university mathematics course of Level 1 difficulty and $1 - Prob(R_{ij} = 1)$ is the probability that a student enrolled in a more difficult mathematics course. For the second category of mathematics courses up to but not including Calculus I, the corresponding logit had the form $\log\{[Prob(R_{ij} \leq 2/[1 - Prob(R_{ij} \leq 2)]\}$, and so on.

We began by fitting an unconditional model to the logits that produced a statistically significant between-school variance of .61, indicating that students from different high schools tended to enroll in initial mathematics courses of varying difficulty.

Next, a model was fitted with the student-level control variables BST (eighth-grade BST in mathematics); number of levels (full-year equivalents) of high school mathematics completed (three, four, or five); GPA in high school mathematics classes; overall high school GPA; high school percentile rank; ACT Mathematics score; sex; ethnicity as captured by dichotomous

Table 3
High School and University Mathematics Achievement by Number of Levels of Mathematics Completed in High School and Curriculum Group

High School Math Levels Completed	Curriculum Group	ACT Math	BST Math	High School GPA	High School Math GPA	Grade of First University Math Course	Difficulty of First University Math Course
3	CD						
	M	21.1*	84.7*	3.11	2.86	2.34	1.68*
	SD	4.1	12.3	0.6	0.75	1.12	0.6
	n	190	194	194	175	194	194
3	NSFF						
	M	18.7	78.2	2.91	2.81	2.33	1.35
	SD	3.3	15.4	0.6	0.75	1.13	0.51
	n	65	68	68	62	68	68
4	CD						
	M	24*	90.6*	3.44*	3.31	2.56	2.06*
	SD	3.9	8.3	0.44	0.56	1.05	0.57
	n	626	641	639	587	641	641
4	NSFF						
	M	21.3	87.7	3.31	3.27	2.53	1.76
	SD	3.7	10.2	0.56	0.68	1.07	0.57
	n	150	153	153	142	153	153
5	CD						
	M	28.1*	94.2*	3.66	3.6	2.91	2.99*
	SD	3.9	6.3	0.35	0.45	0.99	0.79
	n	943	974	965	903	974	974
5	NSFF						
	M	26.3	92.8	3.61	3.54	2.92	2.73
	SD	4.3	6.8	0.36	0.46	0.94	0.85
	n	146	150	149	134	150	150

Note. M = mean; SD = standard deviation; n = sample size; CD = commercially developed high school mathematics curriculum; NSFF = National Science Foundation–funded high school mathematics curriculum. Difficulty of first university mathematics course was coded on a 4-point scale (1 = *courses that would typically have been completed in high school*; 4 = *beyond Calculus I*). To investigate the relationship between curriculum group and difficulty of first university mathematics course, a Kruskal-Wallis test for ordered contingency tables was performed; for all others an F test was used.
*Indicates statistically significant at $\alpha' = 1 - (1 - \alpha)^{1/k} = .0058$, where $\alpha = .10$ is the unadjusted Type I error rate, k is the number of statistical tests = 18, and α' is the adjusted error rate. The largest $\hat{\eta}^2$ values were for ACT (.10) and BST (.07) for three high school math levels completed and ACT for four levels (.09); the remaining $\hat{\eta}^2$ values were .03.

predictors for African American (yes, no), Asian, and Hispanic students; year a student enrolled at the university (fall of 2002, fall of 2003); and whether the student took a mathematics course in the first semester.

The school-level model included the curriculum offered at a high school (CD or NSFF) as a predictor in the random intercepts model in which average school logits served as the outcome. Other predictors added to the random

Table 4
**Hierarchical Linear Modeling Fixed Effects for
University Mathematics Course Difficulty Data**

Fixed Effect	Coefficient
Threshold1	4.72*
Threshold2	7.08*
Level 2: high schools	
Intercept	−3.598*
Size	0.001
Rural	−0.219
Suburban	0.183
Socioeconomic status	1.977
High school curriculum	0.717*
Between-school variance	0.611*
Level 1: students	
Year enrolled	−0.079
ACT Math score	−0.078*
High school percentile rank	−0.012
High school math GPA	−0.026
Female	0.970*
BST Math	−0.065*
High school overall GPA	−2.165*
TookFall	0.218
High school math level	−1.560*
African American	−0.284
Asian	0.115
Hispanic	−0.086

Note. High school size = size of high school graduating class; High School Location 1: 0 = *nonrural*, 1 = *rural*; High School Location 2: 0 = *nonsuburban*, 1 = *suburban*; high school socioeconomic status = percentage of high school students eligible for a free/reduced-price lunch; high school curriculum: 0 = *CD*, 1 = *NSFF*; year enrolled: 0 = *fall of 2002*, 1 = *fall of 2003*; sex: 0 = *males*, 1 = *females*; BST Math = Basic Skills Test in Mathematics; TookFall = took first mathematics course in the fall term: 0 = *no*, 1 = *yes*; high school math level = number of high school mathematics levels completed (three, four, or five); African American: 0 = *non-African American*, 1 = *African American*; Asian: 0 = *non-Asian*, 1 = *Asian*; Hispanic: 0 = *non-Hispanic*, 1 = *Hispanic*.
*Indicates statistically significant at $\alpha' = 1 - (1 - \alpha)^{1/k} = .0050$, where $\alpha = .10$ is the unadjusted Type I error rate, k is the number of statistical tests = 21, and α' is the adjusted error rate.

intercepts model to serve as control variables were size of graduating class (*Mdn* = 380), location (urban, suburban, or rural), and percentage of students eligible for a free/reduced lunch (SES; *Mdn* = 18%). All predictors were grand mean centered.

High school–level random effects were assumed to be normally distributed, and modest evidence of nonnormality did not appear to be large enough to distort the results. The HLM results for difficulty are reported in Table 4.

With respect to our first research question, the key result in Table 4 is the significant slope for curriculum group (.717), meaning that curriculum is

Table 5
**Hierarchical Linear Modeling Fixed Effects for
University Mathematics Course Grade Data**

Fixed Effect	Coefficient
Level 2: high schools	
Intercept	2.661*
Size	0.000
Rural	0.088
Suburban	-0.119
Socioeconomic status	-0.445
High school curriculum	0.068
Between-school variance	0.047*
Level 1: students	
Year enrolled	0.006
ACT Math score	0.010
High school percentile rank	0.001
High school math GPA	-0.004
Female	-0.071
BST Math	0.012*
High school overall GPA	0.807*
TookFall	-0.138
High school math level	0.182*
African American	-0.162
Asian	-0.010
Hispanic	0.075
Difficulty Level 4 vs. Level 1	1.348*
Difficulty Level 3 vs. Level 1	-0.018
Difficulty Level 2 vs. Level 1	0.544

Note. High school size = size of high school graduating class; High School Location 1: 0 = *nonrural*, 1 = *rural*; High School Location 2: 0 = *nonsuburban*, 1 = *suburban*; high school socioeconomic status = percentage of high school students eligible for a free/reduced-price lunch; high school curriculum: 0 = *CD*, 1 = *NSFF*; year enrolled: 0 = *fall of 2002*, 1 = *fall of 2003*; sex: 0 = *males*, 1 = *females*; BST Math = Basic Skills Test in Mathematics; TookFall = took first mathematics course in the fall term: 0 = *no*, 1 = *yes*; high school math level = number of high school mathematics levels completed (three, four, or five); African American: 0 = *non-African American*, 1 = *African American*; Asian: 0 = *non-Asian*, 1 = *Asian*; Hispanic: 0 = *non-Hispanic*, 1 = *Hispanic*; Difficulty Level 4 vs. Level 1: 0 = *Level 1*, 1 = *Level 4*; Difficulty Level 3 vs. Level 1: 0 = *Level 1*, 1 = *Level 3*; Difficulty Level 2 vs. Level 1: 0 = *Level 1*, 1 = *Level 2*.
*Indicates statistically significant at $\alpha' = 1 - (1 - \alpha)^{1/k} = .0048$, where $\alpha = .10$ is the unadjusted Type I error rate, k is the number of statistical tests = 22, and α' is the adjusted error rate.

related to the difficulty level of a student's first university mathematics course. Exponentiating the curriculum slope $\exp(.717) = 2.04$ means that with other predictors held constant, a student who completed an NSFF curriculum in high school and who is "average" on all predictors is twice as likely to enroll in less difficult courses as not, compared to an average student who completed a CD curriculum in high school. None of the other high school–level predictors of intercepts were significant.

Following Raudenbush and Bryk (2002, pp. 317–325), the model-implied probabilities of a student enrolling in a mathematics course of a given difficulty can be estimated. Specifically, for an average student who completed a CD curriculum in high school, the model-implied probabilities of enrolling in a university mathematics course of Difficulty 1 (least difficult), 2, 3, or 4 (most difficult) are .03, .72, .24, and .01, respectively; for an average student who completed an NSFF curriculum in high school, these probabilities are .05, .81, .13, and .01, respectively. These probabilities suggest that average students completing a CD or an NSFF curriculum are about equally likely to enroll in the least difficult mathematics courses (.03 vs. .05, respectively). Students who completed an NSFF curriculum are somewhat more likely to enroll in a mathematics course of Level 2 difficulty (e.g., precalculus) than those completing a CD curriculum (.81 vs. .72, respectively), but both curriculum groups have large model-implied probabilities that an average student will enroll in a course that should have been completed in high school. The major difference in the model-implied probabilities between the two curriculum groups is for enrolling in a mathematics course of Level 3 difficulty, where students who completed a CD curriculum are almost twice as likely to enroll in a course of the difficulty of Calculus I compared to students who completed an NSFF curriculum (.24 vs. .13, respectively).

Other statistically significant effects reported in Table 4 included the number of levels of high school mathematics (−1.56), with students completing fewer high school mathematics levels more likely to enroll in less difficult courses, and sex (.97), with male students who were average on all predictors 2.63 times more likely to enroll in more difficult courses as not, compared to female students. The significant slope for ACT Mathematics $\exp(−.078) = .92$ reflects the change in the log odds of a student enrolling in a less difficult mathematics course relative to a more difficult mathematics course for a one-unit increase in ACT Mathematics. Put another way, for higher levels of mathematics achievement, as defined by the ACT, students are increasingly likely to enroll in more difficult university mathematics courses relative to enrolling in less difficult courses. A similar interpretation can be given to the significant and large effect for overall high school GPA.

Grade data. An unconditional model was first fitted to the grade data to estimate variation between and within high schools on this variable and the dependency of grades for university students who graduated from the same high school. The average grades that students earned in their first university mathematics course varied significantly across the sample of high schools, producing an estimated between-school variance of .047. The associated intraclass correlation of .054 means that the dependency among students' first university grade in a mathematics course who had attended the same high school was relatively small. However, if such dependency is not modeled, estimates can be biased (Raudenbush & Bryk, 2002); therefore, we continued to use HLM. There was evidence of moderate nonnormality, but refitting the model after omitting cases that appeared to be responsible did not substantially impact the findings, and the results reported below are based on all available cases.

Next, the models including student- and high school–level predictors used for mathematics course difficulty were fitted to the grade data. The only difference was that dummy-coded predictors capturing mathematics course difficulty were added as student-level predictors to control for this variable. The fixed-effects HLM results are reported in Table 5.

With respect to our first research question, the key result in Table 5 is that the slope for curriculum group in the intercept model is not significant (.068, p = .418), meaning that with the other predictors held constant, the mathematics curriculum a student who was average on other predictors completed while in high school was not related to the grade earned in the first university mathematics course. The significant slope for the dummy-coded predictor for Level 4 versus Level 1 difficulty (1.348) means that students enrolling in more difficult mathematics courses tended to obtain higher grades on average than those enrolling in the least difficult courses, and the significant slope for number of high school mathematics levels completed (.182) means that students who completed more levels tended to get higher grades.

In sum, the HLM results provided evidence that students completing a CD mathematics curriculum are more likely to begin their university mathematics work in a more difficult mathematics course than students who completed an NSFF curriculum once various background factors were taken into account. However, there was no relationship between the high school mathematics curriculum a student completed and the grade earned in that course.

Discussion

There is abundant evidence that many students are not adequately prepared for university mathematics in the United States, with approximately one quarter of all U.S. students completing at least one mathematics course that should have been completed in high school. Concerns about the preparation of students for university-level mathematics have focused attention on high school mathematics.

For decades, high school mathematics has been dominated by CD curricula, which stress traditional algorithms and procedures in which students tend to be passive learners. Beginning in the 1990s, standards-based curricula that were informed by cognitive principles of learning were developed with the support of the NSF. These curricula emphasized problem solving and small group work and treated students as active participants in the learning process. Despite the investment in NSFF curricula, little is known about their ability to prepare students for university mathematics. This study adds two primary findings to this literature.

First, there was no relationship between a student's high school mathematics curriculum and the grade that student earned in the first university mathematics course, suggesting that the two curricula prepare students equally in terms of proficiency attained in a university mathematics course. Our grade results are consistent with findings reported by O'Neill (2002) but differ from those reported by Schoen and Hirsch (2003), who found that students completing an NSFF curriculum had higher grades.

Second, CD curricula appeared to do a better job of preparing students to initially enroll in a more difficult mathematics course than NSFF curricula, for example, Calculus I. However, the model-implied probabilities that students will enroll in a mathematics course of Level 2 difficulty, reflecting courses that should have been completed in high school, are large regardless of the high school mathematics curriculum a student completed.

The model-implied probabilities also differ substantially from the NCES (Parsad & Lewis, 2003) finding that approximately 25% of all U.S. students take at least one college mathematics course that should have been completed in high school. However, in comparing these results it is important to recognize that the NCES finding is based on the definition of adequate preparation for college mathematics used by each of the more than 1,100 sampled institutions. We defined adequate student preparation for college mathematics as initially enrolling in Calculus I or higher, but it is likely that some and perhaps many of the institutions sampled by the NCES employed a different definition. Different definitions of adequate mathematics preparation will impact the percentage of students identified as needing remedial college mathematics coursework and the interpretation of related findings. For example, had we chosen to treat students who were ready to begin their college mathematics work with college algebra or precalculus as adequately prepared, the interpretation of our course-taking findings would be quite different.

In short, our results suggest that if the focus of high school mathematics for college-bound students is to prepare them to begin their college work with Calculus I, the percentage of students in need of remedial mathematics in college may be higher (and perhaps much higher) than suggested by the NCES finding.

It is also important to emphasize that the tendency of students who completed an NSFF curriculum to enroll in a less difficult university mathematics course emerged in our findings after statistically controlling for several variables, including high school mathematics achievement. Thus, explanations for this finding do not appear to include students' mathematical proficiency but may include factors at the high school level, the university level, or both.

High School Factors

An important high school factor to consider in framing our grade and difficulty results is that students in the fall of 2002 or fall of 2003 cohorts who completed NSFF curricula were likely taught by high school teachers with limited experience with these materials, in many cases only 1 to 2 years.

Effective instruction in any curriculum requires that the teacher know what content students have already been exposed to and ideally where the elaboration of various topics will appear in the future. The relatively limited experience of teachers with these curricula may have impacted our findings, but we had no data with which to explore this possibility.

A second high school factor that may be relevant to understanding our findings is the fidelity with which teachers using NSFF curricula implemented these materials in terms of both content and method. We did not have access to students' high school teachers or administrators; thus, we were unable to ascertain with certainty the fidelity with which teachers of these students implemented these curricula. However, we are optimistic about the fidelity with which NSFF curricula were implemented because of previous experiences with the NSF Local System Change (LSC) Project at the University of Minnesota (1997–2001). This project provided 130 or more hours of targeted professional development to over 1,100 middle-grade and secondary mathematics teachers. As part of the 130 hours, teachers received 20 hours of mentor on-site assistance based on mentor impressions. We were satisfied that most of the teachers implemented new NSFF curricula with fidelity. These experiences provide indirect evidence that high school mathematics teachers who taught students who completed NSFF curricula, an unknown number of whom also participated in the LSC Project, implemented these materials with fidelity. Still, limited resources precluded our ability to make credible assessments of this important variable.

University-Level Factors

One university-level factor that may help to explain the tendency of graduates of NSFF curricula to enroll in less difficult mathematics courses initially relates to the content of the mathematics placement tests. The first mathematics course a student enrolls in is guided by the results of a mathematics placement test and input or recommendations from the student's academic advisor, but for students in our sample these are not binding. Thus, students may have elected to enroll in more or less difficult mathematics courses, and available data suggest that about 12% of our sample did so.

Still, students for whom the content of these tests is consistent with their high school mathematics curriculum would be expected to perform better than students for whom the content of these tests does not match their high school mathematics curriculum particularly well. Our experience with university mathematics placement tests suggests that their content generally favors students completing a CD curriculum because of its emphasis on traditional algorithms and procedures and represents a significant obstacle for students who completed an NSFF curriculum in which traditional algorithms and procedures were not emphasized. A mismatch between the content of the university mathematics placement tests and that of NSFF curricula may help to explain the tendency of these students to start with less difficult university mathematics courses.

Another factor that may be related to the tendency of students from NSFF curricula to start with less difficult mathematics courses is the familiarity (or unfamiliarity) of university academic counselors with these curricula. For example, a counselor examining the high school transcript of a student who completed a CD curriculum and who saw the label "Precalculus" would likely be more familiar with the content of this course, compared to seeing the label "Core-Plus 3" on the transcript of a student who completed an NSFF curriculum. It seems plausible that counselors unfamiliar with the high school mathematics courses a student completed might tend to recommend a less difficult university mathematics course.

A second university factor to consider in framing our findings is the orientation of mathematics instruction in examining the grade a student earned in the first university mathematics course. Students for whom instructional content and method in a university mathematics course are similar to that which they experienced in high school may be predisposed to perform better. At the university from which students were sampled, it is fair to say that in general mathematics instruction is much closer in content and practice to that in CD curricula than NSFF curricula, a common phenomenon (Steen, 1987). This similarity may help students who experienced a CD curriculum in high school, but we had no data to shed light on this important factor.

In sum, one or more high school– and university-level factors may have influenced our results, and our inability to control for these factors in our statistical models is a clear limitation, in particular the role of university mathematics placement tests and academic counselors. Moreover, student-oriented factors such as motivation and self-confidence may have impacted our findings. Our findings about the efficacy with which the high school mathematics curricula prepare students for their first university mathematics course need to be framed against these limitations.

Implications for Future Curricular Decisions and Future Research

These results should advance the ongoing debate regarding the adequacy of NSFF curricula in helping students prepare for subsequent university-level mathematics. Curricular decisions by school districts toward CD mathematics curricula and away from NSFF curricula that appear to be occurring in many states, including Minnesota, need to be guided by credible research evidence. Our findings add to this evidence but certainly do not provide a sufficient basis for such decisions.

As evidence of the ability of these curricula to prepare students for university mathematics increases, teachers, administrators, counselors, researchers, and the public must engage in discussions concerning CD and NSFF high school mathematics curricula and which option is more appropriate for their schools. Such discussions will almost inevitably identify several questions in nccd of furthcr study, such as (a) What are the patterns in student performance, course taking, and persistence in later university science, technology, engineering, and mathematics courses, and where do students end their university mathematics course taking? (b) Do these results generalize to 2-year colleges and less selective 4-year institutions? (c) Do these results generalize to students from small high schools where they are less likely to have competing types of high school mathematics curricula? and (d) What is the nature and role of university mathematics placement tests and academic counselors on students' university mathematics course taking?

Notes

This research was supported by the National Science Foundation under Grant ESI-9618741. Any opinions, findings, conclusions, or recommendations expressed in this material are those of the authors and do not necessarily reflect the views of the National Science Foundation.

[1]For example, see Mathematically Correct at http://www.mathematicallycorrect.com and New York City HOLD at http://www.nychold.com.

References

Abeille, A., & Hurley, N. (2001). *Final evaluation report: Mathematics modeling our world*. Retrieved October 18, 2003, from http://www.comap.com/high-school/projects/mmow/FinalReport.pdf

Boyer, E. L. (1983). *High school: A report on secondary education in America*. New York: Harper & Row.

Braswell, J. S., Lutkus, A. D., Grigg, W. S., Santapau, S. L., Tay-Lim, B., & Johnson, M. (2001). *The nation's report card: Mathematics 2000*. Washington, DC: National Center for Education Statistics.

Bruner, J. S. (1960). *The process of education*. Cambridge, MA: Harvard University Press.

Bruner, J. S. (1964). The course of cognitive growth. *American Psychologist, 19*, 1–15.

Bruner, J. S., Olver, R. R., & Greenfield, P. M. (1966). *Studies in cognitive growth*. New York: John Wiley.

Cichon, D., & Ellis, J. G. (2003). The effects of mathematics connections on student achievement, confidence, and perception. In S. L. Senk & D. R. Thompson (Eds.), *Standards-based school mathematics curricula: What are they? What do students learn?* (pp. 345–374). Mahwah, NJ: Lawrence Erlbaum.

Cohen, J. (1988). *Statistical power analysis for the behavioral sciences* (2nd ed.). New York: Academic Press.

Coleman, J. S., Campbell, E. Q., Hobson, C. J., McPartland, J., Mood, A. M., Weinfeld, F. D., et al. (1966). *Equality of educational opportunity* (OE-38001 and supp.). Washington, DC: U.S. Department of Health, Education, and Welfare, Office of Education.

Dienes, Z. P. (1960). *Building up mathematics*. London: Hutchinson Educational.

Dienes, Z. P., & Golding, E. W. (1971). *Approach to modern mathematics*. New York: Herder & Herder.

Finn, J. D., Gerber, S. B., & Wang, M. C. (2002). Course offerings, course requirements, and course taking in mathematics. *Journal of Curriculum and Supervision, 17*, 336–366.

Gagné, R. M. (1963). Learning and proficiency in mathematics. *Mathematics Teacher, 51*, 620–626.

Gagné, R. M. (1985). *The conditions of learning and theory of instruction* (4th ed.). New York: Holt, Rinehart & Winston.

Harwell, M. R., Post, T. P., Maeda, Y., Davis, J. D., Cutler, A. L., Andersen, A. E., et al. (2007). Standards-based mathematics curricula and secondary students' performance on standardized achievement tests. *Journal of Research in Mathematics Education, 38,* 71–101.

Hiebert, J. (2000). *National Education Longitudinal Study of 1988 Eighth Graders.* Washington, DC: National Center for Educational Statistics, U.S. Department of Education. Retrieved November 7, 2007, from http://nces.ed.gov/quicktables /Detail.asp?Key=63

Hill, R. O., & Parker, T. H. (2006). A study of Core-Plus students attending Michigan State University. *American Mathematical Monthly, 113,* 905–921.

Huntley, M. A., Rasmussen, C. L., Villarubi, R. S., Sangtong, J., & Fey, J. T. (2000). Effects of Standards-based mathematics education: A study of the Core-Plus Mathematics Project algebra and functions strand. *Journal for Research in Mathematics Education, 31,* 328–361.

Kuenzi, J. J., Matthews, C. M., & Mangan, B. F. (2006). *Science, technology, engineering and mathematics (STEM) education issues and legislative options. Report of the Congressional Research Service* (Library of Congress No. RL33434). Retrieved November 7, 2007, from http://media.umassp.edu/massedu/stem/ CRS%20Report%20to%20Congress.pdf

Le, V., Stecher, B. M., Lockwood, J. R., Hamilton, L. S., Robyn, A., Williams, V., et al. (2006). *Improving mathematics and science education: A longitudinal investigation of the relationship between reform-oriented instruction and student achievement.* Santa Monica, CA: RAND.

Lesh, R. (1979). Mathematical learning disabilities: Considerations for identification, diagnosis, and remediation. In R. Lesh, D. Mierkiewicz, & M. G. Kantowski (Eds.), *Applied mathematical problem solving* (pp. 111–180). Columbus, OH: ERIC/SMEAR.

Lott, J. W., Hirstein, J., Allinger, G., Walen, S., Burke, M., Lundin, M., et al. (2003). Curriculum and assessment in SIMMS Integrated Mathematics. In S. L. Senk & D. R. Thompson (Eds.), *Standards-based school mathematics curricula: What are they? What do students learn?* (pp. 399–424). Mahwah, NJ: Lawrence Erlbaum.

Mathematical Sciences Education Board. (2004). *On evaluating curricular effectiveness: Judging the quality of K–12 mathematics evaluations.* Washington, DC: National Academies Press.

Minnesota Department of Education. (1998). *Basic Skills Test.* Retrieved December 15, 2007, from http://education.state.mn.us/mde/index.html

National Center for Education Statistics. (1998). *National Education Longitudinal Study of 1988 Eighth Graders: National Education Longitudinal Study.* Retrieved January 27, 2008, from http://nces.ed.gov/quicktables/Detail.asp?Key=63

National Center for Education Statistics. (2004). *Digest of education statistics.* Washington, DC: Author. Retrieved November 3, 2006, from http://nces.ed.gov/ programs/digest/d04/tables/dt04_115.asp

National Council of Teachers of Mathematics. (1989). *Curriculum and evaluation standards for school mathematics.* Reston, VA: Author.

National Council of Teachers of Mathematics. (2000). *Principles and standards for school mathematics.* Reston, VA: Author.

National Research Council. (1998). *Measuring what counts: A conceptual guide for mathematics assessment.* Washington, DC: National Academies Press.

Newmann, F. M., Marks, H. M., & Gamoran, A. (1996). Authentic pedagogy and student performance. *American Journal of Education, 104,* 280–312.

New Standards. (1997). *1996 New Standards Reference Examination technical summary.* Pittsburgh, PA: University of Pittsburgh, Learning Research and Development Center.

O'Neill, C. T. (2002). *The effect of an NCTM Standards-based curriculum on student performance in college mathematics courses.* Unpublished master's thesis, Central Connecticut State University, New Britain.

Harwell et al.

Parsad, B., & Lewis, L. (2003). *Remedial education at degree-granting postsecondary institutions in fall 2000* (NCES 2004010). Washington, DC: National Center for Education Statistics. Retrieved January 27, 2008, from http://nces.ed.gov/pubsearch/pubsinfo.asp?pubid=2004010

Pedhazur, E. J., & Schmelkin, L. P. (1991). *Measurement, design, and analysis: An integrated approach.* Hillsdale, NJ: Lawrence Erlbaum.

Pellegino, J. W. (2006). *Rethinking and redesigning curriculum, instruction, and assessment: What contemporary research and theory suggests. A paper commissioned by the National Center on Education and the Economy.* Retrieved November 7, 2007, from http://www.skillscommission.org/pdf/commissioned_papers/Rethinking%20and%20Redesigning.pdf

Piaget, J. (1960). *The psychology of intelligence.* Littlefield, NJ: Adams.

Piaget, J., & Inhelder, B. (1958). *The growth of logical thinking from childhood to adolescence* (A. Parsons & S. Seagrin, Trans.). New York: Basic Books.

Post, T. P., Harwell, M. R., Davis, J. D., Maeda, Y., Cutler, A., Anderson, E., et al. (2008). Standards-based mathematics curricula and middle grade students' performance on standardized achievement tests. *Journal of Research in Mathematics Education, 38,* 71–101.

Raudenbush, S. W., & Bryk, A. S. (2002). *Hierarchical linear models: Applications and data analysis methods* (2nd ed.). Newbury Park, CA: Sage.

Raudenbush, S. W., Bryk, A. S., & Congdon, R. (2005). HLM 6.02: Hierarchical linear and nonlinear modeling [Computer software]. Lincolnwood, IL: Scientific Software International.

Reys, R., Reys, B., Lapan, R., Holliday, G., & Wasman, D. (2003). Assessing the impact of Standards-based middle grades mathematics curriculum material on student achievement. *Journal for Research in Mathematics Education, 34,* 74–95.

Riley, R.W. (1998). The state of mathematics education: Building a strong foundation for the 21st century. Speech delivered at the annual meeting of the American Mathematical Society and the Mathematical Association of America, Baltimore. *Notices of the American Mathematical Society, 45,* 487–490. Retrieved January 27, 2008, from http://www.ams.org/notices/199804/riley.pdf

Riordan, J. E., & Noyce, P. E. (2001). The impact of two Standards-based mathematics curricula on student achievement in Massachusetts. *Journal for Research in Mathematics Education, 32,* 368–398.

Schoen, H. L., Cebulla, K. J., Finn, K. F., & Fi, C. (2003). Teacher variables that relate to student achievement when using a Standards-based curriculum. *Journal for Research in Mathematics Education, 34,* 228–259.

Schoen, H. L., Fey, J. T., Hirsch, C. R., & Coxford, A. F. (1999). Issues and options in the math wars. *Phi Delta Kappan, 80,* 444–453.

Schoen, H. L., & Hirsch, C. R. (2003). The Core-Plus Mathematics Project: Perspectives and student achievement. In S. L. Senk & D. R. Thompson (Eds.), *Standards-based school mathematics curricula: What are they? What do students learn?* (pp. 311–344). Mahwah, NJ: Lawrence Erlbaum.

Schoen, H. L., & Pritchett, J. (1998). *Students' perceptions and attitudes in a Standards-based high school mathematics curriculum.* Paper presented at the annual meeting of the American Educational Research Association, San Diego, CA. (ERIC Document Reproduction Service No. ED420518)

Schoenfeld, A. H. (2004). The math wars. *Educational Policy, 18,* 253–286.

Senior Assessment Panel of the International Assessment of U.S. Mathematical Sciences. (1998). *Report of the Senior Assessment Panel of the International Assessment of U.S. Mathematical Sciences.* Retrieved June 1, 2006, from http://www.nsf.gov/pubs/1998/nsf9895/nsf9895.pdf

Senk, S. L., & Thompson, D. R. (2003). Middle school mathematics curriculum reform. In S. L. Senk & D. R. Thompson (Eds.), *Standards-based school mathematics curricula: What are they? What do students learn?* (pp. 181–192). Mahwah, NJ: Lawrence Erlbaum.

Shulman, L., & Sparks, D. (1992). Merging content knowledge and pedagogy: An interview with Lee Shulman. *Journal of Staff Development, 13*, 1, 14–16.

Sidak, Z. (1967). Rectangular confidence regions for the means of multivariate normal distributions. *Journal of the American Statistical Association, 62*, 626–633.

Sirin, S. R. (2005). Socioeconomic status and academic achievement: A meta-analytic review of research. *Review of Educational Research, 75*, 453.

Skinner, B. F. (1938). *The behavior of organisms.* New York: Appleton-Century-Crofts.

Steen, L. A. (1987). Introduction. In L. A. Steen (Ed.), *Calculus for a new century* (pp. 11-13). Washington, DC: Mathematical Association of America.

Trends in International Mathematics and Science Study. (1996). *Pursuing excellence: A study of U.S. eighth-grade mathematics and science teaching, learning, curriculum, and achievement in international context: Initial findings from the Third International Mathematics and Science Study.* Retrieved February 10, 2007, from http://nces.ed.gov/pubsearch/pubsinfo.asp?pubid=97198

Wayne, A. J., & Youngs, P. (2003). Teacher characteristics and student achievement gains: A review. *Review of Educational Research, 73*, 89–122.

Webb, N. L. (2003). The impact of the Interactive Mathematics Program on student learning. In S. L. Senk & D. R. Thompson (Eds.), *Standards-based school mathematics curricula: What are they? What do students learn?* (pp. 375–398). Mahwah, NJ: Lawrence Erlbaum.

Wu, H. (1997). The mathematics education reform: Why you should be concerned and what you can do. *American Mathematical Monthly, 104*, 946–954.

Manuscript received February 28, 2007
Revision received July 2, 2008
Accepted July 7, 2008

American Educational Research Journal
March 2009, Vol. 46, No. 1, pp. 232–274
DOI: 10.3102/0002831208323938
© 2009 AERA. http://aerj.aera.net

Educational Computer Use in Leisure Contexts: A Phenomenological Study of Adolescents' Experiences at Internet Cafés

Sebnem Cilesiz
The Ohio State University

Computer use is a widespread leisure activity for adolescents. Leisure contexts, such as Internet cafés, constitute specific social environments for computer use and may hold significant educational potential. This article reports a phenomenological study of adolescents' experiences of educational computer use at Internet cafés in Turkey. The purposes of the study were to understand and describe the phenomenon in depth and arrive at the essence of adolescents' experiences with the phenomenon. Data were collected through series of in-depth phenomenological interviews with six adolescents and analyzed using phenomenal analysis. The results include potential benefits of Internet cafés as specific social leisure contexts of educational computer use for adolescent development. Implications for designing and studying computer-based informal learning environments are presented.

KEYWORDS: phenomenology, computer use, informal learning, context, adolescence, Internet café, Turkey

Educational research has placed increasing emphasis on the place and context of educational experiences (Gruenewald, 2003a, 2003b; Vadeboncoeur, 2006), building on the insight that learning experiences and outcomes are shaped by the contexts in which they are embedded (Brown, Collins, & Duguid, 1989; Resnick, 1987). Likewise, experiences of using computers are embedded in the social and cultural context in which computer use takes place (e.g., Mumtaz, 2001; Sutherland, Facer, Furlong, & Furlong, 2000; Zhao & Frank, 2003). Indeed, any human behavior, including computer use, is so embedded

SEBNEM CILESIZ is an assistant professor of cultural foundations, technology, and qualitative inquiry in the School of Educational Policy and Leadership, The Ohio State University, 29 West Woodruff Avenue, 301 Ramseyer Hall, Columbus, OH 43210; e-mail: *cilesiz.1@osu.edu*. Her research interests include social and cultural contexts of technology use and qualitative research methodology. Her previous work has been published in *Qualitative Inquiry*.

in and constrained by its social and cultural contexts that to construe such behavior as independent would be misleading (Granovetter, 1985). Adolescents use computers and the Internet in different contexts, including schools, libraries, homes, and public access points such as Internet cafés (Becker, 2000; DeBell & Chapman, 2003). Although the social and cultural contexts of computer use are critical to understanding adolescents' experiences with using computers, little research has investigated those experiences with respect to their contexts. Furthermore, despite the fact that computer use is a widespread leisure activity for adolescents (Roberts, Henriksen, & Foehr, 2004; Subrahmanyam, Kraut, Greenfield, & Gross, 2000) and despite the importance of leisure time and activities during adolescence (Eccles & Barber, 1999; Verma & Larson, 2003), little research has focused on computer use in leisure contexts as informal learning environments.

Formal, nonformal, and informal learning environments are three broad contexts (Maarschalk, 1988; Reed & Loughran, 1984; Smith, 1988) that afford different types of experiences with computer use. Central characteristics of informal learning environments are high participant autonomy and a lack of formal structure. Informal learning involves the process of acquiring attitudes, values, skills, and knowledge through participation in everyday social activities (Maarschalk, 1988; Smith, 1988; Vadeboncoeur, 2006). In using and learning to use computers in informal settings, social interaction is vital (Mitra & Rana, 2001; Sawchuk, 2003; Selwyn, 2005). Internet cafés—businesses that offer access to computers and the Internet on a drop-in basis for hourly fees—are a kind of informal learning environment where social interaction is at the heart of computer use. They represent a specific social and cultural context—affording virtually full autonomy and prolonged social interactions characteristic of *third places* (Liff & Steward, 2003; Uotinen, 2003)—that mediates the experiences of adolescents with computers and promotes specific adolescent cultures (Laegran, 2002).

Although Internet cafés are a widespread phenomenon in many countries, particularly popular among adolescents[1] (Bolukbas, 2003; Laegran, 2002), their educational potential has not been studied to date. The present study was a phenomenological investigation (Husserl, 1969, 1970a, 1970b; Moustakas, 1994) of adolescents' experiences of educational uses of computers at Internet cafés in Turkey. Its purpose was to understand and describe in depth the phenomenon of educational uses of computers at Internet cafés and to arrive at the *essence* (Husserl, 1969; Moustakas, 1994) of these experiences. This study was a response to calls for research on specific contexts of computer use (Hall & Israel, 2004), on particular contexts of education (Vadeboncoeur, 2006), and on adolescents' leisure experiences outside formal educational and family settings (Eccles & Barber, 1999). It builds on and contributes to the literature on computer use in informal learning environments as well as the literature on Internet cafés.

The remainder of this article is structured as follows. First, I provide a review of the literature on computer use within three broad contexts. Then, I describe the context and methodology of this study, followed by a presentation of the results. I conclude the article with a discussion of the results and implications.

Contexts of Education and Computer Use

The place and context of educational experiences are increasingly recognized as important (Gruenewald, 2003a, 2003b; Vadeboncoeur, 2006); learning experiences and outcomes are shaped by the settings in which learning activities are embedded (Brown et al., 1989; Resnick, 1987). A context is a constellation of factors such as location, relationships, content, pedagogy, assessment, control, supervision, organization, and schedules (Vadeboncoeur, 2006; Wellington, 2001). Increasing emphasis on contexts is reflected in recent studies focusing on educational experiences in particular learning spaces (Barton, Tan, & Rivet, 2008; Nespor, 2000). Like all educational experiences, computer use is embedded in and shaped by the social and cultural attributes of the environment in which it takes place (e.g., Nicolopoulou & Cole, 1993; Sutherland et al., 2000; Zhao & Frank, 2003).

An important framework for conceptualizing contexts of educational experiences distinguishes formal, nonformal, and informal learning environments (Maarschalk, 1988; Reed & Loughran, 1984; Smith, 1988, 2006; Vadeboncoeur, 2006), each comprising a range of micro-contexts that are constellations of different attributes (e.g., Cole, 1996; Nicolopoulou & Cole, 1993; Zhao & Frank, 2003). In the present article, I focus on reviewing the relationship between context and the experience of computer use in the three broad contexts—formal, nonformal, and informal—prior to describing the specific context of the present study, Internet cafés.

Learning Environments as Contexts of Education

Formal learning environments are constituted by recognized educational institutions, primarily the planned and hierarchically organized, graded system from elementary school through university (Maarschalk, 1988; Smith, 1988, 2006). Nonformal learning environments are planned but highly adaptable organized settings (such as after-school programs, in-service training, self-help groups, and educational television and radio) in which an intentional effort is made to influence people for learning that fills specific needs (Maarschalk, 1988; Reed & Loughran, 1984). Informal learning environments are integrated with everyday life and social activities (Greenfield & Lave, 1982; Vadeboncoeur, 2006), whereby individuals acquire values, attitudes, skills, and knowledge in spontaneous situations, from peers, family, and neighbors; work and play; and marketplace, library, and mass media (Maarschalk, 1988; Smith, 1988).

Informal learning is driven and enabled by conversation, involves exploring and enlarging experience, and can take place in any setting (Smith, 1988). In informal learning environments, individuals choose and pursue the content of learning (Dierking & Falk, 2003), mainly through social interactions such as observation, imitation, and receiving demonstration (Greenfield & Lave, 1982; Reed & Loughran, 1984). Informal learning forms the largest part of educational experiences, has long-lasting results (Dierking & Falk, 2003; Reed & Loughran, 1984), occurs over time (Vadeboncoeur, 2006), and is highly effective (Illich, 1971; Resnick, 1987). Informal learning environments differ from nonformal learning environments in their structure.[2] The former allow participants spontaneity and high autonomy over their participation and activities, whereas the latter are designed to fulfill certain objectives and are structured accordingly, for example, in the form of membership or enrollment, adult supervision, and institution-defined roles.

Computer Use in Formal Learning Environments

Formal educational institutions constitute a prominent context of educational experiences that affords a range of activities and outcomes. Research has shown the shaping influence of school space, school culture, range of legitimate activities, and pedagogy on educational experiences and learning in formal learning environments (Barton et al., 2008; Brown et al., 1989; Nespor, 1987, 2000). The largest body of literature on computer use in formal contexts focuses on academic, cognitive, and attitudinal outcomes (e.g., Cradler, 1994; Kozma, 1991; Kulik, Bangert, & Williams, 1983; Papert, 1993) as well as effective pedagogy (e.g., Becker, 2000; Cuban, 1993; Cuban, Kirkpatrick, & Peck, 2001; Pea, 1997; Sandholtz, Ringstaff, & Dwyer, 1997) associated with the use of computers in teaching and learning curricular content.

Few studies on computer use in formal learning environments have focused on context, highlighting the importance of school culture (Clark, 2006) and the role of teacher dispositions (Vannatta & Fordham, 2004) in the effective implementation of technology. For example, Zhao and Frank (2003) conceptualized schools and their social contexts as ecosystems in which certain uses of computers emerge and live. They argued that similar to species' adapting to an ecosystem, only certain uses of computers survive in a school ecosystem, depending on key contextual factors such as the hierarchical organization of the environment and teachers' interactions with it, available technologies, and teachers' perceptions of computer uses. In addition, the use of computers for instruction is mediated by teachers' beliefs about learners, the role of technology, and the institutional culture of good teaching (Windschitl & Sahl, 2002). The organization and logistics of schools and classrooms, supervision and intervention, curricula, and teachers' practices and attitudes are other contextual factors shaping the way computers are used in schools (Wellington, 2001).

These studies thus suggest that contextual factors of formal learning environments shape the way computers are used, enabling certain uses and obstructing others. For example, while adolescent computer users can be characterized into seven types on the basis of their patterns of use—hacker, game player, game creator, eager tool user, reluctant tool user, luddite, and sporadic user—each classroom activity involving computers accommodates only certain types of users (Upitis, 1998); those who are excluded may lose their interest in and change their attitudes toward computer use in formal learning environments (Mumtaz, 2001). Additionally, because adolescents spend a large portion of their time outside of school, there is increasing attention to their activities and potential educational opportunities in nonschool settings (Dierking & Falk, 2003; Vadeboncoeur, 2006), so it is essential to explore their use of computers in a variety of contexts.

Computer Use in Nonformal Learning Environments

Nonformal learning environments are organized settings, such as youth clubs and after-school programs, in which an intentional effort is made to foster learning in specific areas (Maarschalk, 1988; Reed & Loughran, 1984). They differ from formal learning environments in their structure (e.g., mixed-age groups, flexible schedules), which may shape experiences with and outcomes of using computers (Hall & Israel, 2004). Research on computer use in nonformal learning environments has focused on program evaluation and academic outcomes in computer-based after-school and out-of-school programs,[3] reporting that participation in those environments can lead to positive academic outcomes, such as computer literacy, linguistic and thinking skills, and academic achievement (Blanton, Moorman, Hayes, & Warner, 1997; Hall & Israel, 2004; Mayer, Schustack, & Blanton, 1999; Schustack, Strauss, & Worden, 1997).

In addition to academic results, after-school computer programs may generate outcomes such as positive social-emotional, academic, and technical attitudes associated with the use of computers (Gallagher, Michalchik, & Emery, 2006); indeed, in some instances other outcomes such as community service by designing Web pages, self-expression through digital media, and long-term culture change, were observed, although the set learning goals of the programs were not accomplished (Gallego & Cole, 2000; Zhao, Tan, & Mishra, 2000). More generally, research points to the potential of nonformal learning environments to offer positive developmental outcomes for adolescents, such as exploring their senses of self and future opportunities, the development of creativity and expression, and exposure to multiple perspectives and diversity (Eccles, 1999; Heath, 2001; Nocon & Cole, 2006; Smith, 2006; Vadeboncoeur, 2006). These benefits are more likely to surface when adolescents are given a choice of activities and opportunities for discussion and interaction (Eccles & Barber, 1999; Hall & Israel, 2004).

Conversely, if the degree of independence offered does not meet adolescents' desire for autonomy, they may develop negative views of these contexts as well as low levels of interest and engagement (Eccles & Barber, 1999; Liu et al., 2002). Paradoxically, it has been noted that nonformal learning environments are becoming more structured (Bekerman, Burbules, & Silberman-Keller, 2006), perhaps because their funding is contingent on the fulfillment of (academic) program goals (Gallagher et al., 2006; Mahoney & Zigler, 2006; Nocon & Cole, 2006). A common challenge for nonformal learning environments is to provide activities that are engaging to participants while maintaining their school-like norms and structure, because the choice of activity and engagement may lead to tensions between program staff members and participants (Bruce & Bruce, 2000; Nicolopoulou & Cole, 1993). Indeed, despite the organizers' intentions, within the structure of after-school computer programs operated by schools, it was not possible to create a true clubhouse spirit whereby students would have the means and freedom to decide how and when to use technology to achieve their own goals (Zhao, Mishra, & Girod, 2000). Thus, the structure inherent in nonformal learning environments facilitates a bounded range of experiences with computer use; to understand the full spectrum of experiences and outcomes with computer use, I turn to the literature on computer use in informal learning environments.

Computer Use in Informal Learning Environments

Computer use in informal learning environments is by definition not structured or planned, allowing a high level of individual autonomy. Studies on computer use in informal learning environments tend to focus on the context of home; a smaller body of research on everyday computer use implies the existence of characteristics of informal settings (e.g., spontaneity) without reference to context. At home, adolescents' experiences with computers include recreational (e.g., playing games, e-mail) and academic (e.g., completing school assignments, word processing) elements (Becker, 2000; DeBell & Chapman, 2003). A wealth of literature focuses on the relationship between home computer use and academic achievement, reporting positive relationships between general home computer use and academic achievement, in subject areas as well as overall grades (e.g., Attewell & Battle, 1999; Jackson et al., 2006; Subrahmanyam et al., 2000). Certain uses of computers at home, such as word processing and video games, were found to be positively related to the development of critical thinking, spatial, and visual skills (Becker, 2000; Pillay, 2003; Subrahmanyam et al., 2000). Finally, home computer use was found to be related to long-term positive attitudes toward computers and interest in advanced computer courses (Selwyn, 1998, 2005) as well as positive developmental outcomes for young children (psychological reasoning and feelings of accomplishment) and for adolescents (identity development) (Turkle, 1984).

Parental influence and perspectives constitute an important contextual element of home computer use; adolescents' activities at home are shaped by parental authority, even when parents are not physically present (Downes, 2002; Facer, Sutherland, Furlong, & Furlong, 2001; Sutherland et al., 2000). In comparison with formal learning environments, home may be considered a less structured and thus more suitable setting to explore the power of computing (Wellington, 2001). However, it is a unique informal learning environment, which provides less than full autonomy (because of parental influence) and induces largely solitary uses of computers for adolescents (Roberts et al., 2004; Subrahmanyam, Greenfield, Kraut, & Gross, 2001).

A few other studies on computer use in informal learning environments have investigated the processes of everyday and leisure use of computers. For example, an investigation of the uses of computers located in outdoor kiosks in slums in India by children (aged 5–16 years) without guidance or instruction demonstrated children's ability to master basic computer operations within a few days by self-instruction, forming impromptu classes, and seeking help from peers, emphasizing the importance and potential of free exploration on the computer (Mitra & Rana, 2001). Social interaction in everyday computer use, such as mentoring by social contacts during the initial stages of computer use, was also found to be important for adults (Selwyn, 2005). Learning to use computers within everyday peer networks is a gradual process consisting of isolated, emergent learning moments in the ongoing activity of computer use (Sawchuk, 2003; Selwyn, 2005); it demonstrates a specific form of peer interaction that is distinct from the pedagogy of formal learning and from informal conversation that resembles peripheral participation in a community of practice (Sawchuk, 2003).

Communities of practice are groups of individuals who share a concern or a passion for an experience in a common domain, share knowledge and learn from one another aspects of their practice as they interact regularly, and consequently increase their knowledge as individuals and as a group through sustained interaction (Wenger, 1999). Learning, particularly developing expertise in the practice itself, is inherent in communities of practice. Participation in communities of practice not only enables the individuals and the group to develop expertise and learn, but it also fosters the building of identity (Wenger, 1999). Defining the self and building identity in social groups formed around the interest of computer use were also highlighted by others (Sawchuk, 2003; Turkle, 1984, 1997). Desire for affiliation with a community was found to be a major incentive of highly committed leisure computer users (Rheinberg & Tramp, 2006). Specifically, adolescents' interest in computer use has to do with the construction of identities and reproduction of peer group culture; computer use and expertise can also serve as an arena for conversation in peer groups and thus function as a currency by which friendship is constructed (Facer et al., 2001; Roberts et al., 2004).

Internet Cafés as Informal Learning Environments

Internet cafés are a distinct kind of informal learning environment that affords sustained social interaction and leisure use of computers with virtually full user autonomy, enabling users to choose their activities on the computer to the extent allowed by a country's laws (which may, for instance, prohibit access to certain kinds of Web sites). Internet cafés are businesses that offer public access to computers and the Internet on a drop-in basis for hourly fees (e.g., Liff & Laegran, 2003; Liff & Steward, 2003). The defining characteristic of Internet cafés is having a number of Internet-capable computers in a café-like environment (Laegran & Stewart, 2003; Liff & Steward, 2003; Wakeford, 2003). Internet cafés exist in many countries[4] and are especially prevalent where computers or Internet subscription rates are not affordable for large parts of the population (Sairosse & Mutula, 2004). However, distinct from other public computer access points, such as libraries and computer business centers (Liff & Laegran, 2003), Internet cafés are not mere sites for computer access. They are "technosocial spaces" (Laegran & Stewart, 2003, p. 360) where attributes of a café context enhance and complement the experience of leisurely computer use (Liff & Laegran, 2003). Socializing and making friends are important functions of Internet cafés, particularly for adolescents (Bolukbas, 2003; Laegran, 2002; Sairosse & Mutula, 2004).[5] For instance, in rural Norway, Internet cafés replace the function of gas stations as spaces for youth cultures that allow adolescents to belong to a certain lifestyle as well as to extend their repertoire of identities and network in the local community (Laegran, 2002).

Studies of various Internet cafés have found that Internet cafés resemble third places, affording a particular form of sociality (Liff & Steward, 2003; Uotinen, 2003). Third places are social gathering places where conversation is a major attraction and activities are largely unplanned, unscheduled, unorganized, and unstructured (Oldenburg, 1999, 2001). They provide common ground for people to socialize regularly and form a community without formal criteria for membership and exclusion, enabling sustained and prolonged social relationships; regularity and trust are important factors for community acceptance (Oldenburg, 1999).

Education and Internet Cafés in Turkey

Turkey is a country located in southeastern Europe and southwestern Asia, with a population of 70.5 million (Central Intelligence Agency, 2008). The country's education system includes a structure of college admissions that is governed by a centralized comprehensive test and is preceded by 3- and 4-year high schools.[6] Many adolescents pursue additional skills, such as foreign languages or computer-related competencies, to gain advantage in a competitive labor market. Because of a relatively low purchasing power—Turkey's gross domestic product per capita is $8,900 (Central Intelligence Agency, 2008)—owning a personal computer is not feasible for a large portion of the population. For example, in 2003, there were 40.7 personal computers per 1,000 people in Turkey; this figure was 625 in the United States (The World Bank, 2003, p. 300). A scarcity of resources also impairs the use of educational technology in many schools (Akbaba-Altun, 2006; Bayram & Seels, 1997; Yedekcioglu, 1996). Additionally, given the relatively low hourly charges for computer use at Internet cafés in Turkey (approximately $0.50, according to Daub, 2004), many adolescents turn to Internet cafés to use computers (Tor & Erden, 2004), which makes their educational potential worthy of investigation. While the state acknowledges the benefits of computer and Internet access for children and adolescents, it controls Internet cafés strictly (Altintas, Aydin, & Akman, 2002; Yesil, 2003). Access to Web sites that are illegal by the country's laws, such as those with pornographic or separatist content, is banned, and the operations of Internet cafés are restricted[7] and enforced by police raids (Moore, 2001; Yesil, 2003).

The Present Study

The study reported in the remainder of this article was a phenomeno-logical investigation. The phenomenon studied was adolescents' *educational uses of computers at Internet cafés*, which I hereafter refer to as *the phenomenon*. The purposes of the study were to understand and describe in depth the phenomenon of educational uses of computers at Internet cafés and to arrive at the essence of these experiences. The study was conducted in a city of 250,000 in Turkey, referred to here as Yesildere (all names of places, persons, and institutions used throughout this article are pseudo-nyms, and any identifying information has been altered or removed). According to a member of the local Internet café union, there are approximately 180 Internet cafés in Yesildere; data were collected in the two largest Internet cafés in the downtown area.

Methods

Methodological Framework

I used a phenomenological framework and methodology (Husserl, 1969, 1970a, 1970b; Moustakas, 1994) to study adolescents' lived experiences of educational uses of computers at Internet cafés. A phenomenon is the object of a conscious subject's experience as it presents itself (Moustakas, 1994). Phenomenology dates back to the beginning of the 20th century and includes *transcendental, existential,* and *hermeneutic* traditions (Audi, 2001; Schwandt, 1997). This study uses the transcendental phenomenological framework developed by Edmund Husserl, which I hereafter refer to as *phenomenology*. Phenomenology was a suitable methodology for the purposes of this study for two reasons. First, it is concerned with lived experiences and seeks reality in individuals' narratives of their experiences of and feelings about specific phenomena, producing their in-depth descriptions. Second, phenomenology is the study of the *lifeworld (Lebenswelt)*, defined as "what we know best, what is always taken for granted in all human life, always familiar to us in its typology through experience" (Husserl, 1970a, pp. 123–124). Everyday experiences of educational uses of computers at Internet cafés are embedded in the partici-pants' lifeworlds. Phenomenology is a systematic attempt to come in direct contact with these worlds, uncover and describe the meaning structures of lived experiences, and arrive at a deeper understanding of the nature or mean-ing of everyday mundane experience of phenomena (Lauer, 1965; van Manen, 1990). In doing so, it is concerned with the a priori or intuitive basis of knowl-edge (Crotty, 1998; Husserl, 1969). "An epistemological investigation that can seriously claim to be scientific must satisfy the principle of freedom from sup-positions" (Husserl, 1970b, p. 263). This is accomplished by engaging in *epoche* (or bracketing), meaning disciplined, systematic efforts to suspend one's natural standpoint and prejudgments regarding the phenomenon being investigated (Husserl, 1969; Moustakas, 1994).

Phenomenology aims to obtain direct descriptions of experience without considering its cause or attempting to ascertain whether these descriptions are in agreement with an independent reality (Husserl, 1969; Kvale, 1996; Polkinghorne, 1989). The only evidence phenomenology seeks and accepts is that offered by consciousness itself (Lauer, 1965); "pure essential truths do not make the slightest assertion concerning facts" (Husserl, 1969, p. 57). Thus, the truth value of a description of experience is epistemically irrelevant to the phenomenological enterprise. Furthermore, phenomenology does not allow for empirical generalizations, the establishment of functional relationships, or the development of theory with which to predict or control; instead, "it offers us the possibility of plausible insights that bring us in more direct contact with the world" (van Manen, 1990, p. 9). The alternative to generalizability is to present in-depth descriptions for readers' inspection and exploration (American Educational Research Association, 2006; Lincoln & Guba, 1985; Seidman, 1991).

Phenomenology is founded on a Cartesian dualist ontology of realism and idealism (Beyer, 2004). Realism maintains that a world exists without humans' consciousness of it, whereas idealism maintains that the external world is not independent of cognizant minds. Conscious subjects and their objects are separate, yet they interact; meaning is to be found in this relationship (Crotty, 1998). Every psychical experience consists of two dimensions: *noesis* and *noema* (Husserl, 1969; Moustakas, 1994). Noesis is the act of experience, such as perceiving, feeling, thinking, remembering, or judging. Noema is the object of action, such as the perceived, the felt, the thought, the remembered, or the judged. Any existing noesis corresponds to a noema, and vice versa; this essential relationship between noesis and noema is referred to as *intentionality* (Audi, 2001; Crotty, 1998), indicating that a subject intends toward an object (Kockelmans, 1994). This study was concerned with the phenomenon of educational uses of computers at Internet cafés (noema) as a group of participants experienced it (noesis); neither of these dimensions can exist without the other.

The goal of phenomenological research is to uncover the essence of the experience of a specific phenomenon. Essence is the condition or quality of an experience commonly shared by studied subjects; it is what makes an experience what it is and without which an experience would not be what it is (Husserl, 1969; Moustakas, 1994; van Manen, 1990). Every experience is a manifestation of its essence. As such, every experience consists of textures (varying appearances) and structures (what might account for or underlie the manifestation). The essence of the experience of a phenomenon can be described through an investigation of the structures that underlie the instances of that essence, focusing on the commonalities of the nature of the experience (Polkinghorne, 1989; van Manen, 1990).

Selection of Participants

Adolescent high school students who regularly used computers educationally at Internet cafés constituted the participant pool. This age group was chosen for a number of reasons: first, studying the out-of-school activities of adolescents is important (Dierking & Falk, 2003; Eccles & Barber, 1999; Vadeboncoeur, 2006); second, adolescents make up the largest group of Internet café users in Turkey[8] (Bolukbas, 2003); and third, among Internet café patrons (who legally must be aged 12 years or older), high school–age adolescents are better suited for a phenomenological study than younger ones. Older adolescents are more likely to have the capacity to reflect on and provide full and sensitive descriptions of their lived experiences, which is essential for in-depth phenomenological interviews (Creswell, 2007; Polkinghorne, 1989).

A phenomenological framework requires a relatively homogeneous group of participants (Creswell, 2007), so flyers were posted in two Internet cafés with similar features: Ephesus and Cappadocia. Individuals selected to participate in a phenomenological study must have significant and meaningful experiences of the phenomenon being investigated (Creswell, 2007; Harrist, 2006; Polkinghorne, 1989). Thus, criterion sampling—selecting individuals who fulfill certain criteria as participants—works well with phenomenological studies, particularly when the criteria are indicative of having significant experiences of the phenomenon (Creswell, 2007). I made contact visits to screen volunteers according to predetermined criteria to determine if they qualified as participants (Seidman, 1991). The first criterion was attending Internet cafés regularly, at least twice a week, to ensure that the phenomenon was a part of the adolescent's lifeworld. The second criterion was having experiences of certain uses of computers that are indicative of educational use. This criterion was evaluated using an inclusive list of educational uses of computers based on the International Society for Technology in Education's (2000) *National Educational Technology Standards for Students*. In a phenomenological study, "the important reality is what people perceive it to be" (Kvale, 1996, p. 52), so it is essential to allow participants to illustrate their experiences of phenomena rather than imposing definitions on them (Ashworth, 1999). Thus, during the contact visit, rather than using a standard measure, I asked volunteers to briefly describe if and how they used computers educationally at Internet cafés (without providing any information of what constituted educational uses). Those who referred to two or more items on the list of educational uses in their descriptions were considered qualified to participate in the study; participants referred to four to eight items. (For an example of similar participant selection in a phenomenological study, see Mastain, 2006.)

Treating what constitutes education or educational uses of computers in this open-ended way is particularly meaningful considering the challenges and disagreements about what constitutes education (or educational computer use) in informal learning environments (Alexander & Wade, 2000; Vadeboncoeur, 2006). Indeed, Alexander and Wade (2000) concluded that "perhaps, the students themselves should define what learning is in these informal settings" (p. 351). Other criteria to qualify as a participant included being a high school student, agreeing to participate in a series of audiotaped interviews, and having written parental or guardian consent to participate. Consistent with recommendations for sample size in the phenomenological literature (Creswell, 2007; Polkinghorne, 1989), six adolescents were recruited as participants.

Data Collection

Data were collected through series of three open-ended, in-depth phenomenological interviews, following Seidman (1991). Phenomenological interviews were consistent with the framework and suitable for the purposes of this study because of their focus on "the experienced meanings of the subjects' life world" (Kvale, 1996, p. 53). Seidman explained,

> The first interview establishes the context of the participants' experience. The second allows participants to reconstruct the details of their experience within the context in which it occurs. And the third encourages the participants to reflect on the meaning their experience holds for them. (p. 17)

Accordingly, in this study, the first interview covered the participant's overall experiences of the phenomenon as well as its history up to the present time. The second interview covered the details of participant's lived experiences by focusing on experiences that stood out, feelings associated with them, and their meaning. The third interview consisted of open reflection on the meaning of experiences as well as revisiting the previous two interviews. The first two interviews were semistructured, while the third one was unstructured (Kvale, 1996; see Appendix C for the interview guide). A brief survey was administered prior to the interviews to collect demographic and background information about the participants to put the findings into context and interpret the data (see responses in Appendix B).

Interviews were conducted at public places, mainly in quiet corners of Internet cafés, and were audiotaped. The lengths of the interviews varied between 40 and 90 minutes, consistent with Seidman's (1991) recommendation for nonadult participants. Interviews were transcribed verbatim (Poland, 2002), and the transcriptions of the three interviews were merged into one document for each participant, which constituted the raw data for this study.

Data Analysis

Data were analyzed using *phenomenal analysis*, following Moustakas (1994). In the first step of phenomenal analysis, I *horizonalized* the data by ascribing equal value to every statement and selecting statements relevant to the phenomenon. I translated the relevant statements into English as literally as possible; I subjected both my selections and translations to peer review to ensure validity (details follow below). In the second step, I transformed the data into statements representing *meaning units* by splitting statements whenever there was a transition in meaning. In the third step, I crafted profiles (Seidman, 1991) for each participant, constituted by his or her verbatim statements representing meaning units rearranged in narrative form, with my

insertions placed within brackets.[9] Each statement by an individual expressing a meaning unit, either shared with other participants or unique to that
individual, was included in his or her profile. Profiles are coherent narratives
having a beginning, a middle, and an end, following the general structure of
the interviews (Seidman, 1991); in the present study, this profile structure
comprised history of computer use and early experiences at Internet cafés,
current experiences of the phenomenon and the meaning of Internet cafés,
and reflections on the overall experience. These profiles are called *individual textural descriptions*; they represent a participant's description of his or
her experiences of the phenomenon and consist of the textures: the particular appearances of an individual manifestation of the essence. In the fourth
step, I engaged in *imaginative variation* to interpret participants' descriptions
represented in the textural descriptions, to investigate the structures that might
underlie the individual manifestations. Then, I crafted *individual structural
descriptions* of each participant's experience that reflected my re-presentation
of the participant's own understandings (Titchen & Hobson, 2005).

In the fifth step, I identified the similarities in the textures of participants'
experiences. Six meaning units were shared by five participants, constituting
the textural similarities, and are called the *shared meaning units* (shown by participant in Table 1). In the sixth step, I integrated all individual textural descriptions around the shared meaning units to create one textural description
representing the group as a whole, called *composite textural description*. In the
seventh step, I integrated the individual structural descriptions along essential
structural elements, arriving at the *composite structural description*. In the final
step of phenomenal analysis, I synthesized the composite textural description
into the composite structural description to create a general description of the
phenomenon called the *textural-structural synthesis*. The synthesis consists of
an elaboration of *essential structural elements* and supporting textural elements
and represents the essence of the experience of the phenomenon. The essence
of an experience is never completely exhausted, so this essence does not represent a universal truth but the essence at a specific time and place, as manifested in a specific collection of individuals' experience and as seen from the
perspective of an individual researcher (Moustakas, 1994).

Validity

In this study, I took several measures to address some of the traditional
(Guba & Lincoln, 1982; Merriam, 1995) as well as alternative notions of validity (Lather, 1986a, 1986b; Lincoln, 1995). In phenomenological research, a
high level of objectivity is required on the part of researchers to produce
valuable knowledge (Husserl, 1969, 1970b; Moustakas, 1994; Titchen &
Hobson, 2005). First, to ensure phenomenological validation, I engaged in
the *epoche* (bracketing) process, to identify and set aside throughout the
study my presuppositions from previous encounters or experiences with the
phenomenon (Ashworth, 1999; Moustakas, 1994). I began by articulating a
subjectivity statement to capture and bracket my subjectivity regarding the

phenomenon (Peshkin, 1988) and continued the *epoche* process by abstaining from making judgments throughout the study.

Second, to reduce the impact of my subjectivity on the findings (Merriam, 1995; Wolcott, 1990), I used two forms of peer review provided by a scholar of educational technology fluent in Turkish and English. First, at the horizonalization stage of data analysis, this colleague reviewed my selection of participants' statements on the basis of their relevance to the phenomenon to ensure that my judgment did not misrepresent the relevant data. Second, my colleague reviewed my translations of these statements from Turkish into English to ensure that meanings were not distorted. On the basis of this peer review, I revised the selected statements and their translations.

Third, I used member checks (Lather, 1986a, 1986b; Lincoln & Guba, 1985; Merriam, 1995). Prior to the second and third interviews, I asked the participants to verify my initial understandings of the major points from the preceding interview(s); moreover, the third interview was dedicated to reflection and member check (Seidman, 1991). This process ensured that the participants' voices, rather than my own, are represented in the findings (Lincoln, 1995).

Fourth, I responded to calls for transparency of the research process (American Educational Research Association, 2006; Ragin, Nagel, & White, 2004). I disclose my subjectivity statement (Wolcott, 1990) in Appendix A to enable readers to put findings into context and to understand how the data were interpreted (Merriam, 1995). I provide detailed accounts of how decisions such as participant selection were made and how data were collected and analyzed; report the limitations of the study; include the complete textural and structural descriptions of some participants, thus presenting both negative and positive points (Lincoln & Guba, 1985); and provide a detailed description of the study context and present information about each participant. This transparency facilitates readers' evaluations of how closely their situations match that of this study and judgments of the transferability of the findings (American Educational Research Association, 2006; Guba & Lincoln, 1982; Lincoln & Guba, 1985; Merriam, 1995; Seidman, 1991; Wolcott, 1990).

Fifth, I heeded calls for reciprocal relationships with participants rather than unilaterally beneficial ones (Lather, 1986b; Lincoln, 1995). For example, sharing personal information cannot be appropriately compensated financially. Thus, in addition to compensating the participants for their time with 6 hours of access at the Internet café of their choice, I offered to share some perquisites of my privilege—that of being an educated person (Lincoln, 1995). Even after data collection was completed, I made myself available to participants to provide information and advice on matters related to college admissions and studying abroad.

Results

The phenomenon investigated in this study is educational uses of computers at Internet cafés. As described earlier, no definition of educational uses was imposed on the participants; rather, it was derived from the data. In summary, the meaning of educational uses from the participants' point of view includes learning curricular subjects and content; developing computer, language, and social skills; expanding extracurricular interests; developing emotionally and maturing; developing values and multicultural awareness; and learning about careers and physical development.

Data analysis resulted in 15 narratives: textural and structural descriptions for each of the six participants, a composite textural description, a composite structural description, and a textural-structural synthesis representing the essence of the experience. Within the space limitations of this article, I present the results by providing a table and a brief description of shared meaning units to demonstrate textural commonalities, individual textural and individual structural descriptions of three selected participants to demonstrate in-depth examples of participants' meanings and experiences of the phenomenon, and the textural-structural synthesis describing the essence of the experience of the phenomenon.

A meaning unit was designated as a shared meaning unit when five or more participants' statements included it. The three informants represented in detail—Mehmet, Emir, and Aylin—were selected on the basis of the textures of their experiences relative to those of the group. Emir, with fewest (four) of the shared meaning units, was selected as least representative of the group. Mehmet, with all six of the shared meaning units, was selected as most representative of the group. The statements of each of the remaining four participants included five shared meaning units. Among them, Aylin was selected as most representative: one of three female respondents, one of three who had been preparing for the university entrance test, and one of two whose use of computers was framed by their studies in English. Appendix B contains information about the participants, and Table 1 contains the shared meaning units by participant.

History as a game player refers to a participant's descriptions of his or her past experiences of playing computer games prior to educational uses of computers. Learning from the Internet refers to a participant's statements about learning a specific topic from activities on the Internet, such as learning German from Web pages. Gaining "general cultural" knowledge refers to statements about gaining general intellect, for example, on world politics and literature. Incidental learning refers to statements that involve learning facts or skills while using computers for a different purpose (usually over a sustained period), for example, improving English-language and keyboard skills. Being in control refers to a participant's statements about having choice and control over activities at the Internet café (usually in contrast to school). Experiences as lifestyle refers to a participant's statements about his or her experiences as his or her way of life, preferences, and habits, such as reading online newspapers daily instead of reading paper copies.

As explained in the "Methods" section, a textural description represents a participant's description of his or her experience of the phenomenon, and a structural description reflects my re-presentation of the participant's own

Table 1
Shared Meaning Units by Participant

	Emir	Amber	Mehmet	Aylin	Leyla	Deniz
History as game player	x	x	x	x		x
Learning from the Internet	x		x	x	x	x
Gaining "general cultural" knowledge		x	x	x	x	x
Incidental learning	x	x	x	x	x	
Being in control		x	x	x	x	x
Experiences as lifestyle	x	x	x		x	x

understanding; whether these descriptions correspond to an independent reality has not been ascertained. The textural-structural synthesis is an in-depth description of the participants' experiences of the phenomenon and represents the essence. These results reflect the experiences of the participants of this study, hence no generalization beyond the participants and context studied is intended; transferability of the findings to other settings may be judged by readers (American Educational Research Association, 2006; Seidman, 1991).

Textural Description of Mehmet's Experiences

There was a computer [in our home] before I was born. I started going to Internet cafés to play [the game] Counter Strike. I have been going for 10 years. I am getting bored of games; [it] is like a transition period; you first play games, then you get bored and move on to the Internet. [In] high school[10] I started using the Internet to learn German. I used to surf the Internet a lot [and] search anything that comes to my mind in Google, but I started getting tired of the Internet. I used to chat [but] never grew fond of chat anyway; I found out that one could not learn anything from it. I played with 3D Studio Max, Excel, Front Page, Delphi, Visual Basic, Visual C++. I made Web pages for my friends [and] [my school's] Web site. I search [the Web] about fixing computers and programming; I explore [their codes and] try to develop codes in the same way. I can do pretty advanced things within my limits, creat[ing] applications in Delphi.

I believe computers to be the most useful tools [in education]. Computers helped me very much in becoming like this; I gained a lot of information about programming [and] related to my coursework. I could say that I learned everything about schoolwork from the Internet. I make a lot of use of the Internet in solv[ing] science problems, for example, [by posting] university entrance test preparation questions [and] answers [on] a forum. Maybe I could not have found these resources from books or libraries. I would not have so much knowledge without computers. When I studied German [on the Web] my grades were increasing. My English is [now] very advanced. [In] MS-DOS, everything was in English [and] now most applications are in English; I learned [English] while playing with those programs. [Using computers also] develops our general cultural knowledge. For example, I am very good at [solving] crossword puzzles; I believe computers helped. On the one hand, [Internet café] distances you from school, on the other hand it makes you closer to school. There is the possibility that you will cut classes to come here, but there is also the possibility that you will go to school after studying here. Of course it depends on what kind of a person you are.

[Using computers at Internet cafés] is more a social act; it is more fun to be with friends. I believe Internet cafés are geared for this purpose—uniting people who understand this business [computers]. If everyone would sit at home, they could not exchange information with each other. Even a small child can come [to] an Internet café and learn something. At home you only develop yourself, here you can also teach your friends or people who sit by you; it benefits not just you but others too. [They learn] by watching me, [or] maybe I explain or show [something] to them, have them do things. I taught someone Flash for a month, [because] I want them to develop too, so that there are people around me who understand me regarding computers. [Internet cafés] have a large place in my life. Because I have spent a long time in my life with [them], I would feel that something is missing if I did not have them. There would be a large void in my life. I come every day; I spend most of my time at the Internet café. After a while it becomes a need. It feels as though you cannot do without it. It is like addiction in some respects. Maybe it should not be called addiction, but it is a habit, for some reason we feel like coming here. When I first started going to Internet cafés, I used to play truant; I would play [games] from morning until evening. [This habit] distances you from school. It does not distance one from life though, it makes you closer to life. I mean you learn more things about life. For example, it develops social skills. I am a very unsociable person; I have difficulty in making friends. I had not had a real friend until the end of middle school. I thought computers could help me overcome this, [that] I would perhaps become more sociable by using chat because [I] feel more confident [in a chat room]. When I started high school, I made several friends. It was exactly the year that I had begun using chat. I believe it had an impact. I am more sociable compared to the past; there is a lot of difference. If I had not come to the Internet café maybe I could not even talk to you.

I believe [using Internet cafés] increased my general cultural knowledge. I learned so much; I am proud of myself. [I arrived at] a place most people cannot reach. I feel successful, more important, [and] in the upper level of society [by] doing things no one can do. I have always seen myself lower than the society [but now] I have confidence in myself because I know more than any child who sits here. [Now I] tell people about myself. They look at you with a different eye, as if you are bigger than them. [In] society, there are those who know computers and those who do not. They hire people who know computers, not those who do not. Society is split in knowledge, intellect, English, computers, everything. Leaders are those [who use computers] and others are the lower class, this is how everyone sees it. I see it that way too. I see myself in the level of those who know well. I would rather work at a computer than being a factory worker. My dream since childhood was to work with computers. I feel there is a future profession for me even if I cannot pass the university entrance test; at least I will not be unemployed. It gives me confidence. I feel ready for life, as if there are no barriers in front of me.

Structural Description of Mehmet's Experiences

For Mehmet, educational uses of computers have utility, both short and long term. He believes that as a result of his activities, he became one of the most knowledgeable individuals at that Internet café; he is sought after for his computer knowledge and skills. These skills make him feel confident and socially competent. His feelings of increased social skills are an example of perceived short-term utility. The long-term utility Mehmet perceives of his experiences is future employment security and quality. He is very confident in his knowledge and skills of computers and is optimistic about having future job security in desirable positions. He associates computers with high-status jobs and perceives himself to be a good fit for them; this reflects his feelings of superiority and entitlement as well as his imagination of a future self as a knowledgeable and worthy adult. Mehmet emphasizes that these privileges are earned self-accomplishments. Thus, all the resources he spent (time, money, even truancy) toward educational uses of computers at Internet cafés are well justified as investments in the future.

Mehmet conveys a constant desire for progress as well as an ambition for superiority and competitiveness. While he feels gratified about his social distinction, he also emphasizes a need for company. He cites the latter as his motive to teach others, but teaching others might be a way to enact his perceived superiority to others. This exemplifies his folding his accomplishments into a developing sense of self. His experiences of educational uses of computers have become a significant part of his identity. He thinks that his life would be empty without them. While attributing a high level of significance to his Internet café experiences, Mehmet feels differently about school. He supplements his formal schooling at the Internet café by learning academic topics and preparing for the university entrance test, yet he plays truant to go to the Internet café to "learn more things about life." This may reflect a view that self-education at Internet cafés enables an alternative career path.

Textural Description of Emir's Experiences

> I was in fifth grade. A computer was my dream. I saw a computer game at my friend's and admired it so much. As a surprise, my father brought [a computer] home; I was very happy. We would only play games on the computer. Later, I was connecting [to] the Internet at home and visiting a few sites. My Internet café habit started in sixth grade. I was always wondering [how] they play games there together. One day we went to an Internet café. There was a 15-year age restriction then; they did not let us in. The second day, they did not let us in. The third day, I said "O brother, I wonder very much. Let me play this game with everyone." He let me in for an hour. My first experience was very nice. We would go to play games with friends. [Later I visited Web] pages that I would hear on television [and] was curious about. I started searching [the Web] on arabul.com[11]; I also got my first e-mail account then. In seventh grade, I wanted to share with others the fun fiction stories I wrote to develop my creativity. I only had the chance to share them with a few people I was exchanging e-mails with. Someone told

me "Emir, there is chat, you can enter a room and talk to everyone interested in it." I entered, and I was stunned.

I came up to here by myself. In middle school[12] we had a computer course, but I think there was no education, because they would teach Word, Excel, some Internet applications. Of course I knew computers better than that. For example, on mIRC [a chat program], I was a wizard; I showed users the commands they did not know. Then I started making my own amateur [Web site]. I learned important things about hardware by looking at articles on the Internet. This Internet and computers support me very much with my assignments and [learning] on other topics. Even when you search a word, millions of results come up. [Once] I was researching [for] a term paper about genetics on the Internet. There are tons of encyclopedias in our house, but none had anything about genetics; I found it on the Internet. It was my first term paper; it was the best [in class]. [On the Internet] I look at anything that gets my attention, just to learn. I can download videos of artificial insemination, microscope images of cell membrane. I even learned [about] the reproduction of ants, I was curious. Genetics is my favorite topic and biology my favorite course. Here we [I and two friends] who are interested in biology founded a [online] biology fan club. I thought of pursuing genetic engineering; I am researching if I can become a genetic engineer in Turkey. I have [online] friends interested in animations. I [also] communicate with my brother, who is studying physics at a university in [Major City] [and] I get his help [with] science and math problems. [The Internet café] gives me many benefits, [for example when] searching a topic with my friends. If I do not find [information for] my term paper, they could find or show resources. When they cannot find an assignment, I will find it. We reciprocate, we support each other. So it is like education with each other.

[My interests] change every day; I expand [them] constantly. I research a topic I am curious [about] whenever it crosses my mind. My curiosity will end [only] after 10 to 15 questions. If I would ask [these] on the streets or shops, the man [shopkeeper] would be sick; at least the computer cannot attack me. Thanks to Google, I call it "Google father." Of course I do not believe everything [on the Internet]—for example parapsychology. I search for the origin. I do not trust amateur sites. Because computer is now [my] lifestyle, if I need to research, I research from the Internet. I usually do not read newspapers but I enter news sites and [news] portals send me e-mails. I do not have flowers at home, but I grow a cyber flower. I researched about diets and it helped; I [lost] weight. I learned about cooking omelets. Thanks to the Internet; it supports me on any matter. I translated games into Turkish, and [now] I watch CNN news, I listen to music in English online. My vocabulary capacity and pronunciation are almost very good now. I express myself [and] my imagination very well in writing. I publish my fun fiction stories and animations on the Internet. This animation culture contributed to developing my imagination. I would like to expand myself [further], I certainly cannot continue with this identity until I am 20. I would like to become a programmer. There is a need in Turkey; everyone should have learned and used computers 10 years from now. I start building the groundwork now.

[For me Internet café is] a place [to] hang out, meet my friends, [and] wait for each other comfortably without being bored. There are chess, tea, and stuff [to do] to use time—I [read] my e-mails, download and organize my files, practice some online programs, visit [some] sites and forums, take care of my cyber flower. I enjoy [myself], I feel happy, entertained, and peaceful. [The owner] trusts and [lets us] pay later if we do not have any money. Ephesus [is] the best place because people are typically good—[apparent in their] economic status, attire, speaking style. We all have a place; we are all smart, well-behaved, well-dressed, clean kids. Vagabonds cannot enter here; they feel excluded. When they look around, it is as if the well-dressed, clean kids look down on them. [Even] if they have [money] to stay for five hours, they leave; they cannot even stay half an hour. This pleases me. The thing I like most is [that] I usually sit in this small room[13] of mine [with] a few friends, comfortable [and] happy. There are very few [people I make friends with] in Yesildere. I do not enjoy a monotonous life. I select my friends accordingly; being interested in computers, having a wide imagination, listening to me very carefully are the most important factors for me. I elevate and develop myself [by] researching on the computer. It helps my education so much. I learned everything from the computer. I can talk [to] smart people who think like this. [My classmates] cannot think what I think, they see everything differently. I come here all the time like an addicted customer; they come less [often] but they usually play games. The computer has thousands of uses; those who see [it] as a game tool are inferior. I do not like to have conversations with those monotonous people.

Internet Café is a part of my life; it is like an organ, a life and death matter. I see it like a need; like eating, it is impossible for me to be without computers. It helped me in this way: when my parents got divorced, I almost [had] depression. I turned to computers; [they] became a source of livelihood and peace for me. The computer was like a medicine [cure]. [It] makes me forget, I begin not to care. I see there are tons of people around me—teachers, friends, my mother— they come shouting and yelling at me. As soon as I turn on the computer, it is as if a glass wall around me rises. I can see them hitting the glass, trying to make me hear their voices, but I cannot hear them. It is a completely distinct world. If my mood is zero or even negative, when I sit at the computer it will go up to 100 percent. It helps me a lot. I say "thanks to the computer," otherwise I would lose it. Of course this is better for me. If the computer had not supported me, I would have become a vagabond; started smoking, alcohol, and drugs. I might have even stabbed someone. I would be an insecure boy. The computer increased my self-confidence. It moved me to a very high level. It made me cool, thoughtful, [and] gave an experience in everything in my life. Now I think I am 25 or so, in terms of intelligence. Computers, the Internet café distinguished me from my peers. Those who are interested [in computers] tend to be this monotonous mass. In Yesildere there is not one person like me, who does the things that I do.

Structural Description of Emir's Experiences

Emir follows his curiosity to pursue a range of interests, from academic areas to computer applications to life improvement. Exploring these interests freely helps him refine his interests and his developing self. He speaks of himself as someone whose lifestyle is tied to computers, who is interested in the use of computers to pursue other interests and advanced applications. His current experiences and future aspirations are intertwined: he explores his interest around biology and genetics in his everyday uses of computers and considers genetic engineering as a future profession. This is a path to identity building. Emir is confident in his knowledge, his abilities to gain and use it, and the benefits it has for him. He believes that using and learning from computers has personal benefits—learning about his interests, becoming self-sufficient, relieving from problems, and avoiding potential bad habits—and collective benefits such as educating society and solving social problems. On the basis of his positive experiences with and strong attachment to computers, Emir built faith that they are universally good and have the capacity to solve any problem, if put to educational uses.

Emir describes being in an altered state when he engages with the computer and cuts contact with the outside world. His metaphor of the glass wall indicates that he lives in a society without being integrated in it. This is apparent in his physical separation from the crowds at Ephesus by sitting in a small room alone with his headphones on or with a few close friends. His using computers educationally unlike the "monotonous mass" and aspiring to become a computer programmer are two ways in which he attempts to establish his difference from others: building his current identity as an exceptional (educational) computer user and developing his future identity as a computer professional. He feels that he is superior to and more intelligent than his peers and trusts himself to become a leader rather than a follower, which gives him confidence. Indeed, his feeling of superiority and desire for detachment may be in retaliation for being rejected in the past; Emir did not have friends, because others "looked down on people with split parents." He turned to the Internet, where people are more "frank."

Computers have been a major remedy for Emir's problems. Consequently, he experiences at once dependence and independence in his use of computers. On the one hand, his ability to access information and learn independently enhances his self-sufficiency and reduces his need for his parents, teachers, brother, and friends. Emir can get answers to his many questions—even on intimate or sensitive topics such as losing weight and reproduction—without being concerned about appropriateness or being a bother. Furthermore, computers prevent him from engaging in addictions such as smoking, drinking, and consuming drugs, contributing to his independence. Thus, Emir feels empowered by the computer. On the other hand, Emir's faith in and emotional attachment to computers signals a dependency relationship; he has feelings of belonging, peace, and comfort at the Internet café. Educational use of computers is his lifestyle, a "life and death matter"; he attaches high importance to computers, substitutes them with social contacts, and believes in their far-reaching benefits. These experiences seem to have redefined Emir's social relationships; he now depends on computers while avoiding other addictions and dependencies. The Internet café occupies a large space in Emir's life; it even enters the domain of his formal education, leading him to question the sufficiency of school instruction, emphasizing his ability to learn independently. This may be related less to the actual respective contributions of school and the Internet café to his education and more to his perceived fit in these environments. He feels welcome, belonging, and in harmony with the social environment of the Internet café, whereas he feels dissonance with the social environment (teachers and other students) of the school.

Textural Description of Aylin's Experiences

We had a computer [at home] for 2 years before I started going to Internet cafés. There were only some games [on it]; I would fiddle around. I have been using Internet cafés regularly for five years, [and] have accumulated great knowledge. Because [of my] interest in English, I started with games in English. I would chat with foreigners in the game. I was very interested in games that develop intelligence too. That's how it started. Later, when I met the Internet, everything fell in its place. You can find English in any form on the Internet. I [exchanged] e-mails with an e-mail pal. I was always wondering how daily talk occurs, because it is not written [in textbooks]. The best way to find out was to chat with a person from that country. I chatted with people [from the USA] and learned their daily talk; even daily writing is very different. I [also] learned a lot from comics on foreign Web sites because they reflect the culture, signs, ways of communicating, and conceptions of humor.

You first start out superficially. [Educational use] begins with playing games, [then] it is up to the individual. If one does not want to research, she cannot keep herself from games [and] will not get anything out of it. Curiosity is a must; a person without curiosity will lose time [at Internet cafés]. Also friendships at Internet cafés are very good. People can help each other and develop an exchange. I used to ask myself: how can I find different Web sites on this topic? I did not know about search engines, I would type "www" but didn't know what [to type] next. Then a friend of mine suggested search engines; I [saw] it is a mass of information, like an archive in front of my eyes. You want to reach everywhere [and] try everything. If you are a curious person, you search for more, you get interested in more things. They follow each other; this way you learn a whole lot and consequently develop yourself.

I learned [much] by always being at an Internet café. For example, I was interested in poetry and literature; I found nice writings and stories by searching. Because I am a student, everything is educational [for me]. You cannot think of anything else when you are in school. [Using] Internet cafés is helping with the university entrance test. I took practice tests and searched for resources. Internet is ideal for [locating] various resources. If there were no Internet, I would lose my time searching for stuff at libraries. Although books are arranged, it is still difficult to search because there are so many. I do not think people could expand their interests this way. Without Internet cafés, or Internet, our areas of interest would be very narrow. And we would know only about our vicinity; there would be no interaction between cultures. Your interaction with different cultures increases [on the Internet]; you [can] learn about other cultures and be reflective [about] yours.

I have pursued other interests as well, [like] music and sports. [When] I wanted to lose weight, I learned it from the Internet. I am very interested in history [so] I was wondering how to [obtain] a tourist guide certificate. Just by reading the information on [the Internet], I learned [about the procedure] and started preparing to get the tourist guide certification. Also, I practiced various programs like Word, Excel, and Photoshop. I learned the basics, in case I need to use them in the future. It was very enjoyable. I would like to learn all of the software packages. I want to be a person who is good at computers. I want to become an English teacher, I believe it will contribute to my [profession] too. I am sure it will contribute to every area of my life; I just need to learn and it will help.

[Internet café helps] my development. For example, I am interested in writing, [but] I needed help with put[ting] it on paper. I learned [from the Internet about experiences of] successful authors [who] initially could not write [because] they were afraid of making mistakes. Now I can write; I realized my hidden writing skills. I believe my imagination has developed, my perspective expanded, and my self-confidence increased. I discovered my aptitudes and what I can do; I gained a wide perspective [in] thought, worldview, emotion; I [became] more mature and conscientious. I was shocked when I saw pictures of starving people in Africa; seeing how hungry some people are and how much some countries consume is emotional development.

Research [and] learning on the Internet enhances participation in society. If you have accumulated information, you can have a say everywhere; it means power, [and] your self-confidence increases. What if you did not search, wonder about things? In order for you to comment on a topic in a social group, you need to have knowledge. The simplest, easiest, and fastest way to develop yourself is [by using] Internet cafés; you can find one in every corner. At Internet cafés, as an individual you have the right [and] the ability to make choices. One understands that she can direct her own life, your confidence increases as you learn. For me, Internet café means a place like school, another institution that educates me. Unlike at school, there is no one to tell you "you are to learn this, you are to do that" as a teacher imposes on you. The Internet café provided me the opportunity to choose [my] education. You can become an individual [and] establish your difference from others. I am going through a transition now [from being taught to learning] because there will not always be someone to teach me. [My experiences] mean maturation in every sense.

Structural Description of Aylin's Experiences

Aylin's description reflects a consciousness of learning in several domains: academic (linguistic and writing skills), everyday knowledge (nutrition), adult learning (exploring careers), as well as development (emotional development, multicultural awareness). She masters computer skills incidentally and purposefully. Her curiosity and beliefs about computers seem to guide her experiences. Aylin considers curiosity essential to learning and attributes her sustained curiosity to having made positive learning experiences. It seems these experiences enabled her to discover her skills, to identify her interests, and to project these onto potential future professions. Aylin has two major beliefs. First, she believes that her way of using computers at Internet cafés makes her knowledgeable in many areas. She observes progress of becoming knowledgeable and cultured in her ability to converse with others on a range of topics, which makes her feel respected, powerful, and thus confident. Second, she believes that computer skills will be useful for her in the future. Accordingly, she is optimistic about materializing her image of her future self as "a person who is good at computers," a mature adult, and a teacher. Powered by her optimism, she is vested in fulfilling that future self. She appears to take more responsibility for her education as she nears graduation from high school; using computers at Internet cafés educationally serves that purpose well. As part of the transition from being an adolescent to becoming an adult, she emphasizes her freedom to choose what to learn and to identify her interests. She feels ready to assume the role and responsibility of an independent adult learner. She is glad to establish her difference from others, thereby asserting her identity. She perceives this transition as maturation and emancipation from the authority of schooling.

Textural-Structural Synthesis: The Essence of the Experience

The following synthesis describes the essence of the experience of the phenomenon of adolescents' educational uses of computers at Internet cafés in Turkey. It explains how the essential structural elements underlie the various manifestations of the experience. This textural-structural synthesis represents the essence at a particular time and place, as manifested in the participants' experiences, as seen from the perspective of an individual researcher as a result of an intuitive and reflective study of the phenomenon (Moustakas, 1994).

The essence of the experience of the phenomenon of educational uses of computers at Internet cafés for these adolescents is building identities as educational computer users, which distinguish them from those who do not use computers educationally, through engaging in activities they perceive to have current utility or anticipate to have future utility, in an environment that gives them control over their experiences through its structure that is essentially unlike school. Thus, three interrelated structural elements constitute the essence of the experience of the phenomenon: building an identity linked to aspects of the experience, experiencing current and anticipating future utility of educational computer use, and contrasting Internet café experiences to formal schooling. I describe these elements essential to the experience of the phenomenon below.

Identity building. For the participants, the experience of the phenomenon is closely related to identity building. Identities are built and communicated in relation to prominence and ways of computer use, comparison of oneself with

255

others, and future aspirations. Experiences of the phenomenon are profound; association with Internet cafés is vital—"like an organ," (Emir), "my third eye" (Leyla), "a bond that ties me to life" (Leyla)—constituting a habit, routine, need, or "addiction" (Mehmet, Emir). Indeed, connection to the body is an identity statement. It seems that these adolescents have so internalized their experiences that they ascribe physical connection to them. Without them, they would be crippled; they would feel "as if my arms were taken off . . . as if I did not have arms or legs (Amber), "not sufficient" (Deniz), that "there would be a large void in my life" (Mehmet). However, it is not just computer use that is important; participants' ways of using computers (educationally) make up an important aspect of their identity building. These adolescents define themselves as individuals who use computers regularly in ways that educate and develop their selves, who are experts in using computers and accessing information, who use their free time for intellectual ventures at Internet cafés, who belong to a distinguished group that is knowledgeable and cultured.

In particular, participants believe that they became learned, cultured, and sophisticated individuals through using computers at Internet cafés. Those who use computers and the Internet "like those who read books [can] become knowledgeable" (Deniz). The availability of information and the facility of accessing it, going beyond the sphere of knowledgeable others in their social circles (outside the Internet café), can be empowering. It can make one feel "cool, thoughtful" (Emir), knowledgeable, cultured—only through certain uses of computers. These adolescents use the versatility and power of computers to "learn" (Mehmet, Emir, Amber), "develop myself" (Deniz, Amber, Emir), "do my work" (Emir), "research" (Aylin, Emir), "enhance my culture and knowledge" (Deniz), "increase my intellect" (Amber), and "expand my worldview" (Leyla), not "just to play games" (Deniz). Playing games is history, it happens when one is "not very knowledgeable" (Deniz) yet; going to Internet cafés to play games is a "transition period" (Mehmet). These adolescents ascribe some elitism to educational uses of computers. For them, playing games is elementary and passé, those who see the computer "as a game tool are inferior" (Emir) and "superficial" (Aylin), whereas educational computer users feel "superior," "elevate[d]" (Emir), "privileged" (Amber), and exceptional. Participants prefer to dissociate themselves from games and those who play games, to "establish your difference" (Aylin) from other users of Internet cafés. This way they can separate from the "monotonous mass" (Emir) and "become an individual" (Aylin). Distinction from others is an important part of becoming an individual and building an identity. Also, games belong to childhood, whereas these adolescents are "building the groundwork" for the future (Emir), feeling "mature" (Aylin, Amber, Deniz) and "ready for life" (Mehmet). They have future aspirations: to become college-educated professionals (e.g., genetic engineer, computer engineer, English teacher), professionals in computer-related positions not requiring college degrees (e.g., computer programmer, hardware specialist, digital designer), and computer-savvy and cultured adults. The present experiences of the phenomenon are located between elementary uses of computers in the past and an image of the self as a sophisticated computer user in the future. Central to the experience of building an identity is the perception of making progress from the past to the present and into the projected future. Although these participants are on a progressive trajectory, those who underuse computers by "unconsciously play[ing] games" (Deniz) or "chatting for 8 hours" (Deniz) do not make progress, they will "have to depend on games" (Amber). "They won't get anything out of it" (Aylin), missing out on the potential advantages of educational uses of computers.

Experiencing and anticipating utility. The experience of the phenomenon is also closely related to experiencing current and anticipating future utility. Participants experience current utility in the form of respect and meeting like-minded people as well as in feelings of maturity, distinction, prestige, and sophistication, which in turn increase their self-confidence. Knowledge, manners, and social skills acquired at Internet cafés can be displayed in social situations, functioning as a currency to generate social returns such as respect and connections. It can afford them "the benefit of being able to talk to people" (Leyla), and consequently "your self-confidence will increase" (Aylin). "Friends and grown-ups ask for help. When I can help them . . . I am pleased. . . . Then you have prestige, as you help people, and get a social environment" (Deniz). Seeing themselves as central knowledgeable figures in the Internet café's social environment is a token of pride and self-confidence.

Future utility is anticipated because of the potential of acquired knowledge and skills to increase prospects of future employment, enhance facility in future jobs, and lead to high test scores, which enables college admission. Participants' anticipation of these utilities is linked to strong beliefs in the positive effects of educational uses of computers: that they will provide skills that will be necessary in the future, that they can make one cultured, that they will solve individual and/or social problems. Accordingly, educational uses of computers are an investment for the future for participants; some make this investment intentionally, for example, by learning computer applications (Aylin, Deniz, and Mehmet), while others expect their regular experiences will return utility (Emir, Amber, Leyla).

Contrasting Internet cafés with school. Participants make sense of their experiences of educational computer use at Internet cafés by contrasting them with their experiences in school. This contrast results in three qualities of the experiences at Internet cafés in relation to schooling. First, experiences of educational uses of computers at Internet cafés are seen as *supplementing* schoolwork, by completing school assignments, preparing for the university entrance test, further exploring academic interests (history, genetics, programming), and establishing academic initiatives (biology fan club). Second, these experiences are seen as helping overcome restraints of schooling, thus *complementing* school education, by exploring areas not covered in school (e.g., nutrition [Emir, Aylin]), pursuing lifelong skills school may

257

not address (e.g., sociability [Mehmet], multicultural awareness [Aylin], expanded worldview [Leyla]), making up for what is seen as insufficient (e.g., knowing more than "Word, Excel" [Emir], staying abreast of developments in technology [Deniz]). Third, these experiences are seen as *competing with* formal educational organizations. As participants see utilities of their experiences at Internet cafés, they compare these functions with those of schooling, at times treating them as alternative means to their goals (e.g., secure employment). An Internet café is "an educational venue, just like school" (Deniz), it is "very important. . . . It comes right after school. Sometimes it can be equivalent to school" (Amber).

The content of school subjects appears agreeable to these adolescents; it is the structure and authority of schooling that they seem to harbor resentment against. Internet café "does not limit me" (Amber), it does not have "rules [or] things that restrict you" (Leyla). Consequently, they challenge the dominance of formal schooling. For them, Internet cafés are another place for education; "unlike at school, there is no one to tell you you are to learn this, you are to do that" (Aylin). "Education does not only take place in school . . . we cannot call a person uneducated or illiterate because he did not go to school" (Leyla). Along with considering alternative paths to education comes the responsibility over their own education; education is "not limited to school and the teachers . . . [it] is up to the individual to develop himself" (Deniz), because "there will not always be someone to teach me" (Aylin).

Discussion

Computer Games as a Stepping-Stone

An important insight from the present study is that initial experiences at Internet cafés with playing games are a shared textural element of the experience; this suggests that games had an *intermediary* function in the path of developing from nonusers into educational users of computers. This is consistent with Clark's (2003) finding that initial experiences with computers focus on games and entertainment. Indeed, Selwyn (1998, 2005) found that sustained interest in learning and computer use can be traced back to earlier computer game play. Therefore, apart from learning advantages derived from playing computer games, such as increased visual skills (Subrahmanyam et al., 2000) and problem-solving skills (Pillay, 2003), experience with playing computer games may be an important ingredient in adolescents' development of educational uses of computers in informal social contexts.

Internet Cafés as Sites for Communities of Practice

Internet cafés as third places allow people to build sustained relationships around the common interest of computer use. A major purpose for adolescents' patronage of Internet cafés is to make friends and socialize (Bolukbas, 2003; Laegran, 2002; Sairosse & Mutula, 2004). According to their descriptions, participants' experiences with the phenomenon, including their history, are shaped by and interrelated with their participation in the social context of Internet cafés. They indicated that they learned and developed their intellect "by always being at an Internet café" (Aylin) around like-minded people and by aspiring role models and more capable peers. Deniz stated,

> When I began going to Internet cafés, when I was 12 or so, I only came to play games. I saw that some people older than I were doing things like [Web design] . . . . I thought they were cool things. . . . I admired them. . . . They did not tell me [what to do, but] I would observe them. . . . I said, why not, I can also do these things.

Mehmet indicated teaching others at the Internet café in order to have people to interact with.

Although adolescents and young adults dominate Internet cafés in Turkey, patrons come from a wide range of ages, levels of education, and occupations (Bolukbas, 2003). Diversity of individuals in knowledge, skills, and interests is a major resource for learning in social settings (Lave & Wenger, 1991; Sawchuk, 2003). Additionally, such settings are ideal for fulfilling adolescents' need to exchange ideas with nonfamilial adults (Eccles, 1999). At Internet cafés, other customers are peers who may serve as "the more capable peer" (Vygotsky, 1978, p. 86) to adolescents. The studied adolescents indicated the existence of impromptu teaching and observation at Internet cafés as well as learning from others about possible computer uses (e.g., Aylin's learning about search engines, Emir's learning about chat rooms about fiction writing, and Leyla's learning about e-mail when her friend casually said "my mailbox is full"). Thus, they were socialized and assimilated into the practice of educational uses of computers.

Similar to Sawchuk's (2003) finding regarding adults' experiences of learning how to use computers in their everyday lives, this process of modeling and learning in a social setting at Internet cafés can be explained by the concept of legitimate peripheral participation; it is a process by which novices or newcomers become part of a community of practice by gradually moving from peripheral participation in the sociocultural activities of the community to a more central participation in them (Lave & Wenger, 1991). The results of this study suggest the existence of communities of practice of educational users of computers at Internet cafés; participants' descriptions of their experiences pointed to three aspects that characterize a community of practice: mutual engagement, joint enterprise, and shared repertoire (Wenger, 1999). *Mutual engagement* is demonstrated by regularly attending an Internet café, by conversing and interacting while engaging in computer activities, as well as by articulating reputation and identity in relation to others. Examples of mutual engagement include Leyla's writing e-mails together with her friends, acquaintances' and grown-ups' going to Deniz for help at the Internet café, and Mehmet's and Deniz's considering themselves the most skilled in certain applications at their Internet café. *Joint enterprise* is demonstrated by developing meaning and criteria and judging experiences by tastes and criteria of the community. Participants' seeing utility in their practice, associating their experiences with progress, and (negative) judgments and evaluation of those who play computer games are examples of a joint enterprise. *Shared repertoire* is demonstrated by history, routines, and ways of doing things. Examples of shared repertoire include the habit of Emir and his friends to sit together in the same place every time; Deniz, Mehmet, and their friends' common knowledge of highly advanced computer applications; and Amber and Emir's expectation to see each other and habit of waiting for each other at the Internet café before school.

Internet Cafés as Contexts for Identity Building

Adolescence is a time of strong attachment to causes and peers (Eccles, 1999; Erikson, 1968), and "a computer center or a computer club can become the focus of their [adolescents'] social life" (Turkle, 1984, p. 138). Computer expertise is a means by which adolescents build their identities within their peer group cultures (Facer et al., 2001; Turkle, 1984). Learning (with computers) can also serve as a specific interest for adolescents, with which to build an individual identity with related future aspirations (Krapp, 2002).

According to the findings of this study, identity building is an essential component of the experience of educational uses of computers at Internet cafés for adolescents. The informal learning environments constituted by Internet cafés enable access to a range of "examples of the types of people that it is possible for participants . . . to become" (Hull & Greeno, 2006, p. 83) as well as opportunities for adolescents to practice and experience identities they imagine. Participants' descriptions of their experiences reflected all three aspects of identity as conceptualized by Hull and Greeno (2006): interpersonal, epistemic, and discoursal. *Interpersonal identity* refers to identity in relation to others, such as the image of the self as a valued social participant. This aspect of identity was present in participants' comparisons of themselves with others and affiliations with a (peer) group. Being sought after and/or respected by peers and others at Internet cafés, being superior to game players, being privileged in comparison with those who did not use computers were among the arguments by which participants made sense of and experienced their identities interpersonally. *Epistemic identity* is defined as identity regarding a person's increasing expertise and understanding, such as a valued sense of self as a knowledgeable participant in the community. This was present in these adolescents' references to being educational users of computers. For example, they reported learning and gaining knowledge in intellectual domains, academic topics, and computer skills as well as building social skills through their experiences at Internet cafés. Participants built their senses of self as knowledgeable individuals with associated feelings of being sophisticated, prestigious, exceptional, distinguished, mature, and superior. *Discoursal identity* is identity as narrated in stories about the selves we were, are, want to become, and imagine it possible to be. Participants' descriptions of their experiences contained their past selves as game players and novices to the world of computers; their current selves as educational computer users, for whom it is a lifestyle or necessity to use computers in this way; and their imagined and desired future selves as educated professionals, cultured adults, and computer experts.

Wenger (1999) pointed to the role of communities of practice in supporting identity building. Adolescents in this study expressed signs of belonging to a community of practice of educational users of computers, while openly dissociating themselves from game players; indicating that they used to play games in the past, they emphasized that they no longer do so. They belittled games as useless and regular game players as inferior, boring, or unable to make progress. No longer being a game player appears to be an important part of building an identity as an educational computer user. We build our identities through the practices we engage in as well as those we do not engage in (Wenger, 1999). Thus, dissociating from one form of computer use (games) serves the same purpose as associating with another (educational uses): identity building (Turkle, 1984; Wenger, 1999).

As a matter of fact, adolescence is an important period of identity building; experiences in this period can have far-reaching influence in a person's life (Erikson, 1968; Verma & Larson, 2003). Developing a sense of one's social location, reflecting on one's own competence and knowledge (and resulting self-confidence), and imagining and committing to future careers are major tasks of identity building for adolescents (Erikson, 1968). These three tasks correspond to the three aspects of identity (i.e., interpersonal, epistemic, and discoursal, respectively) demonstrated by the adolescents in this study in relation to their experiences of the phenomenon. These results suggest that Internet cafés are important places for these adolescents' accomplishment of a significant developmental pursuit (the development of identity); they may facilitate this development by providing for adolescents the templates (i.e., role models) to envision potential identities as well as by making it possible to exercise those imagined identities. To sum up, Internet cafés provide adolescents with an extended repertoire of identities (Laegran, 2002) and a leisure environment where adolescents are afforded the choice of activity, thus potentially contributing to their identity development, particularly as it relates to success, social location, peer associations around shared interests, and future aspirations (Eccles & Barber, 1999).

The Charm of Internet Cafés as Educational Contexts

Informal and formal learning environments have differing purposes, features, and outcomes; both are essential for the development of well-rounded adults with competencies in various aspects of their lives (Resnick, 1987). Participants interpreted their experiences of educational uses of computers at Internet cafés by relating them to their formal education, pointing to their experiences of functions of Internet cafés as supplementing, complementing, and competing with formal educational organizations. Furthermore, they considered the informal learning environments of Internet cafés to be more aligned with their developing selves as self-directed learners and mature and autonomous individuals, contrasting them to the structure and authority in school, which they perceived to be limiting.

Schools and similarly structured learning environments may be experienced by adolescents as being at odds with their learning and development needs (Bekerman et al., 2006; Halpern, 2002; Zhao, Mishra, et al., 2000); even home may not afford sufficient opportunities for freedom and exploration (Sutherland et al., 2000). A mismatch between these structures and adolescents' desire for more autonomy and independence may cause tensions and conflicts (Bruce & Bruce, 2000), reducing adolescents' interest and motivation (Liu et al., 2002) and increasing their propensity to develop negative views of these settings (Eccles, 1999). It is perhaps for this reason that adolescents prefer social settings, peer groups, and other informal learning environments outside home to formal and organized activities (Eccles, 1999; Heath, 2001), just as Internet cafés were the preferred educational settings for adolescents in this study.

Learning in informal environments—in the presence of self-control and autonomy and the absence of structure, adult control, and supervision—can be as effective as it is in formal settings (Illich, 1971; Resnick, 1987). Indeed, some of the experiences of the participants in this informal learning context fall into areas determined essential to healthy youth development (Dierking & Falk, 2003) and are more likely to occur in informal settings (Dewey, 1938; Illich, 1971; Reed & Loughran, 1984). Furthermore, informal learning environments may provide adolescents with specific benefits, such as the development of creativity and expression, exposure to multiple perspectives and diversity, and the development of identity (Eccles & Barber, 1999; Heath, 2001; Nocon & Cole, 2006; Smith, 2006; Vadeboncoeur, 2006), provided that adolescents are given choices and autonomy as well as opportunities for discussion and interaction (Eccles & Barber, 1999; Hall & Israel, 2004). The results of this study suggest that Internet cafés provide such a context.

Limitations of the Study

The requirement to obtain parental or guardian consent for participation in this study limited the participant pool to adolescents whose parents knew and approved of their attending Internet cafés. There are adolescents who use Internet cafés without the knowledge and/or consent of their parents. It would have been informative to explore the experiences of those adolescents as well, because parental involvement may affect and contribute to particular experiences. Another limitation of the study was the need to translate the interview data. Because adolescents living in Turkey had limited English-speaking skills, in-depth phenomenological interviews could not be conducted in English. Thus, I conducted the interviews in Turkish, translated them, and had them verified by a second person; this study could not have been conducted otherwise.

Delimitations of This Study and Suggestions for Further Research

Representativeness of participants. This study focused on the experiences of adolescents who used computers educationally at Internet cafés. On the basis of the purpose of the study and consistent with the phenomenological framework, generalization of the findings and the degree to which participants are representative of the general population of adolescents was not a concern (Creswell, 2007; Seidman, 1991; van Manen, 1990). Indeed, a relatively homogeneous group of participants was sought to identify the essence of the experiences of this group and describe it in depth (Creswell, 2007). Only some information about the participants—such as their ages, locations of computer access, and length of time of using Internet cafés—was collected to understand their experiences better. Neither this information nor the literature on Internet cafés in Turkey allows the judging of participants' representativeness, particularly in terms of the way they use computers at Internet cafés. Participants stated that they are a minority among adolescents and the Internet café clientele in their use of computers, but empirical verification of this point was beyond the purpose of this study. Future research should consider focusing on the range of experiences adolescents have at Internet cafés.

Process of development of educational uses of computers. Although the results of this study indicate that playing computer games may be an important ingredient in the development of adolescents' educational computer uses at Internet cafés, I did not investigate actual practices of computer use, how the process of transition from games to educational uses may occur, or how other ingredients, coupled with experiences of playing games, may contribute to becoming an educational computer user. Understanding the role of playing computer games and the process of developing educational uses of computers may have important implications for designing learning environments and interventions for the benefit of adolescents; thus, these would be important areas for future research to pursue.

Implications

Although Internet cafés are specific contexts, they are instances of informal learning environments. Therefore, the implications of this study may apply to other informal learning environments sharing contextual characteristics with Internet cafés (i.e., affording a third-place type of sociability combined with minimal levels of structure, authority, and supervision). As discussed in the "Methods" section, from the vantage point of phenomenology, it is ultimately up to readers to make connections to their own experiences and judge the applicability of the results of this study to their empirical settings of interest.

This study focused on the experiences of adolescents who use computers *educationally* at Internet cafés. As such, the results have implications for promoting educational uses of computers at Internet cafés and in other informal learning environments. Understanding adolescents' experiences and meanings of educational computer use may help educators, policy makers, and researchers design interventions and steer adolescents toward uses of computers deemed desirable. In Turkey and in other countries where Internet cafés are prevalent, many adolescents use them regularly; at the same time, resources are often scarce, and many adolescents have only limited access to computers in schools and at home. In these contexts, teachers at high schools may be able to capitalize on existing resources outside of schools and homes, most notably at Internet cafés, by giving students information about how to better use these resources. They may offer information sessions or theoretical courses that require only one or even no computer at all, to instruct students on topics including conducting Internet searches, obtaining career related information, available mailing lists and chat rooms on academic interests, and learning how to use specific computer applications. Similarly, state and/or local authorities may require Internet cafés to make available for patrons information sheets on how to accomplish certain computer tasks or containing lists of useful Web sites, thus potentially stimulating educational experiences of using computers at Internet cafés.

This study suggests that adolescents may choose educational experiences in leisure settings when afforded free exploration and virtually full autonomy. Their experiences may lead to important developmental outcomes such as recognizing, identifying, and pursuing their own interests as well as exploring future paths, thus contributing to their identity development. The findings of this study suggest further that coalescence of computer use and socializing may have additional advantages for adolescents such as benefiting from positive peer influence and participating in an educational community of practice. However, such benefits may fade away in formal as well as highly structured nonformal learning environments (Bruce & Bruce, 2000; Eccles, 1999; Liu et al., 2002). Therefore, organizations that operate nonformal learning environments, such as after-school computer programs, should consider providing reduced structure and authority and higher independence and autonomy for adolescents, like Internet cafés providing mere access to computers, rather than being an extension of school.

In the United States, third places such as the Internet cafés investigated in this study are scarce (Oldenburg, 1999), so using computers and socializing are usually separate activities competing for adolescents' time (Roberts et al., 2004; Subrahmanyam et al., 2001). This raises concerns about the impact of computer use on adolescents' social relationships and psychological well-being (Subrahmanyam et al., 2001). Thus, policy makers and local governments may consider operating, funding, or subsidizing Internet cafés or computer-based learning environments that are similar to Internet cafés in structure, as is done in Finland (Uotinen, 2003) and Norway (Laegran & Stewart, 2003). Accordingly, future research in the United States, and other countries where third places are rare, should consider examining the effects of adolescents' use of computers in these settings. In so doing, researchers should consider designs that allow for the inclusion of outcomes that may be characteristic of informal learning environments.

Finally, interventions into informal learning environments should consider not increasing their structure, thereby formalizing the environment. The findings of this study imply, consistent with previous literature (Eccles, 1999; Nocon & Cole, 2006), that the formalization of informal learning environments may have disadvantages. Instead, this study pronounces the importance of social context and positive peer influence in choosing educational uses of computers. As one participant indicated, for educational uses of computers to flourish, "there must be a social context. . . . Someone at an Internet café can learn useful things because there are people he can model . . . and admire. . . . Admiration is a major factor I believe" (Deniz). Interest in education and identity as a learner are fostered in social relationships and communities (Crick & Wilson, 2005; Greenfield & Lave, 1982) and can affect how effectively existing resources are used to facilitate learning (Barton et al., 2008). Fostering learning-related identities may evoke *educational* uses of computers in social settings in which computers are available. As a result, policy makers interested in steering adolescents toward educational uses of computers should consider promoting an adolescent culture in which educational computer use is desirable. The promotion of role models on television, in teen magazines, on the Internet, at school, and in teen hangout places such as malls may inspire adolescents to use computers educationally in leisure contexts.

Appendix A
Subjectivity Statement

I am a young Turkish woman, who was born and raised in western Turkey. My family placed much emphasis on education. Throughout my education, and particularly as an adolescent, I was fortunate to have ample access to resources such as libraries, foreign-language labs, science labs, computer labs, and sports facilities at school. In college, I also had a home computer; by the time I graduated from college, I was a proficient computer user. Even though I have experiences with different activities on the computer, I have been primarily an instrumental user. In other words, I have not regularly played games, chatted, or entertained myself on the computer, but I have used computers mainly to search for specific information and to do assignments. Currently, I use computers for doing work, collecting information, and communicating with friends.

During my adolescence, Internet cafés were yet unknown in Turkey, and later I used them rarely to check e-mail while traveling. However, in my adult life, I became familiar with people who were "regulars" at Internet cafés or other public access points. Some were not good in school but were considered computer geniuses in their peer groups. They proved to me that even playing multiuser domain role-playing games could help one gain important skills, that being in a community of computer users can be very useful, and that one could learn to use computers in creative ways if he or she had enough exposure to them. Some of those people eventually made careers out of their unique computer skills, leading me to see how computers could be means for economic opportunity and upward social mobility.

(continued)

Appendix A (continued)

My perception of educational uses of computers is broad and general. I believe that anything that contributes to one's learning, education, and development (mental, physical, and emotional) is an educational use of computers. This includes learning content matter, practical skills (e.g., cooking), emotional skills (e.g., conflict resolution), social skills (e.g., table manners), intellectual development (e.g., scientific developments, current events), and information technology skills (e.g., programming, e-mailing, and graphics design). It is with this background and beliefs that I investigated the phenomenon of adolescents' educational uses of computers at Internet cafés. I made every effort to keep these beliefs aside (i.e., bracket them) throughout the study.

Appendix B
Participants

The following information is based on the participants' responses to the background information survey administered prior to the interviews.

Emir is a 16-year-old male ninth grade student. He owns a computer with Internet access. He uses the Internet café (Ephesus) for 2 to 3 hours every day and has done so for the past 5 years. He considers himself an advanced computer user. His parents are divorced; Emir lives with his single father but frequently visits his mother, who lives in the same city.

Amber is a 17-year-old female 10th grade student. She is Emir's close friend. She does not own a computer, but she can use the family computer at home or the one at her father's business. Everyone in her family uses computers. She uses the Internet café (Ephesus) for about 2 hours every day and has done so for 7 years. She considers herself an advanced computer user.

Mehmet is an 18-year-old male 11th grade student. He is Amber's brother and knows Emir too. He does not own a computer, but he can use the family computer at home, the one at his father's business, or the computers at school. Everyone in his family uses computers. He uses the Internet café (usually Ephesus) for 3 hours every day. He considers himself a "super" computer user.

Aylin is an 18-year-old female 11th grade student. She is preparing to study English in college. She owns a computer and can also use the one at her parents' shop. Her father also uses computers. She uses the Internet café (Cappadocia) for 4 to 5 hours a week and has done so for the past 5 years. She thinks that she is good at computers.

Leyla is an 18-year-old female 11th grade student. She is Aylin's friend. She is also preparing to study English in college. She does not own a computer but can use one at school. She uses the Internet café (Cappadocia) for 4 to 6 hours a week. She considers herself an average computer user.

Deniz is a 17-year-old male 11th grade student at a vocational school in the computer hardware area. He owns a computer, but he does not have Internet access at home. He also has ample access to computers at school. His younger brother also uses computers. Deniz uses Internet cafés (mostly Ephesus and Cappadocia) for 3 hours every day and has done so for the last 5 years. He thinks that his computer skills are "enough" but can be developed further.

Appendix C
Interview Guide

The first two interviews were semistructured. While the questions in the interview guide were used to provide a structure, the interviews were customized according to each participant's responses and the flow of the interview. The third interview was unstructured (Kvale, 1996), with no preset questions.

Interview 1

- Tell me about your experiences of educational uses of computers at Internet cafés. What kinds of educational activities do you engage in on the computer?
- How did you learn about Internet cafés? How did you start going to Internet cafés?
- How did you start using computers at Internet cafés? How did you come to use computers in this way?
- Describe some purposes of using computers for education at the Internet café.
- Is there anything you would like to add?

Interview 2

- Revisiting the first interview; new questions that arose.
- Tell me about your educational experiences of using computers at Internet cafés that stand out for you. How do you feel about them (those experiences that stand out for you)?
- What does using computers (in this way) at Internet cafés mean for you? How important is using computers (in this way) at Internet cafés for you?
- How has using computers (in this way) at Internet cafés changed you or your life? How do you feel about this change?
- Is there anything you would like to add?

Interview 3

- Discussion and participants' feedback and clarification on my preliminary findings and interpretations of the first two interviews (member check).
- New questions that arose on the basis of the first two interviews.
- Any additional thoughts or opinions participants might have.
- Further reflections on the meaning and significance of experiences.

Notes

I thank Thomas Greckhamer for his thorough reviews and valuable comments on earlier drafts of this article. I am grateful to Associate Editor Patricia Alexander and anonymous reviewers of the *American Educational Research Journal* for their detailed and constructive comments on earlier drafts of this article.

[1]Turkey is one such country, accommodating almost 19,000 Internet cafés in 2006 (Intel Corporation, 2006); more than 41% of Internet users in the country access it at Internet cafés (Turkey State Statistics Institute, 2004). Adolescents constitute approximately half of Internet café users in the country (Bolukbas, 2003).

[2]Some literature uses the terms *informal, nonformal,* and *out-of-school* synonymously to refer to the negation of schooling (e.g., Dierking & Falk, 2003; Heath, 2001;

Resnick, 1987). However, I follow a distinction between nonformal and informal education (Smith, 2006) because the dichotomous formulation of in- and out-of-school environments does not fully capture the emphasis on the importance of context (Bekerman, Burbules, & Silberman-Keller, 2006; Vadeboncoeur, 2006) on which this study focused. Vadeboncoeur (2006) referred to nonformal learning environments such as after-school programs as "*structured* informal" (p. 240).

[3]While they may be called informal learning environments in the original literature, according to the framework used in this article, they are nonformal learning environments.

[4]See, for example, The Cybercafe Search Engine (http://cybercaptive.com) for a list.

[5]Similarly, Michaels (1993) found video game parlors to be a place for adolescents to meet old friends and make new ones, with teens entering and leaving in groups as well as continuing their interactions through cooperative and competitive game play or normal conversation during game play.

[6]The length of instruction at vocational schools and English-medium schools (such as Anatolian High Schools), which admit on the basis of centralized aptitude test scores, is 4 years; at all other high schools, it is 3 years.

[7]Internet cafés are prohibited from operating near schools and mosques.

[8]Forty-eight percent of Internet café users in Turkey are between the ages of 16 and 20 (Bolukbas, 2003).

[9]Each profile is written in the participant's voice, rearranging his or her statements to form a coherent narrative. Some sentences in the profile are a combination of two or three clauses or phrases. I do not indicate the breaks or combination points in the text so as not to interrupt flow. Occasionally, I changed word order within a sentence to maintain correct grammar and sentence structure, paying attention to preserving the meaning of the original statements and context.

[10]Anatolian High Schools (one of which Mehmet attended) are highly selective public schools with English as the medium of instruction; German as a foreign language is often part of the curriculum.

[11]Arabul.com is a Turkish search engine.

[12]Middle school covers Grades 6 to 8 in Turkey.

[13]Ephesus (the Internet café Emir uses regularly) is organized into rooms. He and his good friends usually sit in the same place in a small room with three computers.

References

American Educational Research Association. (2006). Standards for reporting on empirical social science research in AERA publications. *Educational Researcher, 35*(6), 33–40.

Akbaba-Altun, S. (2006). Complexity of integrating computer technologies into education in Turkey. *Educational Technology & Society, 9*(1), 176–187.

Alexander, P., & Wade, S. (2000). Contexts that promote interest, self-determination, and learning: Lasting impressions and lingering questions. *Computers in Human Behavior, 16*, 349–358.

Altintas, K., Aydin, T., & Akman, V. (2002). Censoring the Internet: The situation in Turkey. *First Monday, 7*(6). Available at http://www.firstmonday.org/issues/issue7_6/altinta/index.html

Ashworth, P. (1999). "Bracketing" in phenomenology: Renouncing assumptions in hearing about student cheating. *International Journal of Qualitative Studies in Education, 12*(6), 707–721.

Attewell, P., & Battle, J. (1999). Home computers and school performance. *The Information Society, 15*(1), 1–10.

Audi, R. (Ed.). (2001). *The Cambridge dictionary of philosophy* (2nd ed.). New York: Cambridge University Press.

Barton, A. C., Tan, E., & Rivet, A. (2008). Creating hybrid spaces for engaging school science among urban middle school girls. *American Educational Research Journal, 45*, 68–103.

Bayram, S., & Seels, B. (1997). The utilization of instructional technology in Turkey. *Educational Technology Research and Development, 45*(1), 112–121.

Becker, H. J. (2000). Who's wired and who's not: Children's access to and use of computer technology. *Future of Children: Children and Computer Technology, 10*(2), 44–75.

Bekerman, Z., Burbules, N., & Silberman-Keller, D. (Eds.). (2006). *Learning in places: The informal education reader.* New York: Peter Lang.

Beyer, C. (2004). Edmund Husserl. In E. N. Zalta (Ed.), *The Stanford encyclopedia of philosophy.* Retrieved February 8, 2007, from http://plato.stanford.edu/archives/fall2004/entries/husserl/

Blanton, W. E., Moorman, G. B., Hayes, B. A., & Warner, M. L. (1997). Effects of participation in the fifth dimension on far transfer. *Journal of Educational Computing Research, 16*(4), 371–396.

Bolukbas, K. (2003, April 18). *Internet cafelere sosyolojik bir yaklasim* [A sociological approach to Internet cafés]. Paper presented at the Internet and Society Symposium, Diyarbakir, Turkey.

Brown, J. S., Collins, A., & Duguid, P. (1989, January-February). Situated cognition and the culture of learning. *Educational Researcher*, pp. 32–42.

Bruce, S. P., & Bruce, B. C. (2000). Constructing images of science: People, technologies, and practices. *Computers in Human Behavior, 16*, 241–256.

Central Intelligence Agency. (2008, March 20). Turkey. In *The world factbook.* Retrieved March 28, 2008, from https://www.cia.gov/library/publications/the-world-factbook/geos/tu.html

Clark, K. (2003). Using self-directed learning communities to bridge the digital divide. *British Journal of Educational Technology, 34*(5), 663–665.

Clark, K. (2006). Practices for the use of technology in high schools: A Delphi study. *Journal of Technology and Teacher Education, 14*(3), 481–499.

Cole, M. (1996). *Cultural psychology: A once and future discipline.* Cambridge, MA: Belknap.

Cradler, J. (1994). *Summary of current research and evaluation findings on technology in education.* San Francisco, CA: Far West Laboratory.

Creswell, J. W. (2007). *Qualitative inquiry and research design: Choosing among five approaches* (2nd ed.). Thousand Oaks, CA: Sage.

Crick, R. D., & Wilson, K. (2005). Being a learner: A virtue for the 21st century. *British Journal of Educational Studies, 53*(3), 359–374.

Crotty, M. (1998). *The foundations of social research: Meaning and perspective in the research process.* London: Sage Ltd.

Cuban, L. (1993). Computers meet classroom: Classroom wins. *Teachers College Record, 95*(2), 185–210.

Cuban, L., Kirkpatrick, H., & Peck, C. (2001). High access and low use of technologies in high school classrooms: Explaining an apparent paradox. *American Educational Research Journal, 38*, 813–834.

Daub, T. C. (2004, July/August). Cost of cyberliving. *Foreign Policy*, p. 92.

DeBell, M., & Chapman, C. (2003). *Computer and Internet use by children and adolescents* (No. NCES 2004-014). Washington, DC: National Center for Education Statistics.

Dewey, J. (1938). *Experience and education.* New York: Macmillan.

Dierking, L., & Falk, J. (2003, Spring). Optimizing out-of-school time: The role of free-choice learning. *New Directions for Youth Development, 97*, 75–88.

Downes, T. (2002). Blending play, practice and performance: Children's use of the computer at home. *Journal of Educational Enquiry, 3*(2), 21–34.

Eccles, J. (1999, Fall). The development of children ages 6 to 14. *The Future of Children*, pp. 30–44.

Eccles, J., & Barber, B. (1999). Student council, volunteering, basketball, or marching band: What kind of extracurricular involvement matters? *Journal of Adolescent Research, 14*(1), 10–43.

Erikson, E. H. (1968). *Identity: Youth and crisis.* New York: W. W. Norton.

Facer, K., Sutherland, R., Furlong, R., & Furlong, J. (2001). What's the point of using computers? The development of young people's computer expertise in the home. *New Media & Society, 3*(2), 199–219.

Gallagher, L., Michalchik, V., & Emery, D. K. (2006). *Assessing youth impact of the computer clubhouse network.* Menlo Park, CA: SRI International.

Gallego, M. A., & Cole, M. (2000). Success is not enough: Challenges to sustaining new forms of educational activity. *Computers in Human Behavior, 16,* 271–286.

Granovetter, M. (1985). Economic action and social structure: The problem of embeddedness. *American Journal of Sociology, 91*(3), 481–510.

Greenfield, P., & Lave, J. (1982). Cognitive aspects of informal education. In D. Wagner & H. Stevenson (Eds.), *Cultural perspectives on child development* (pp. 181–207). San Francisco, CA: W. H. Freeman.

Gruenewald, D. A. (2003a). The best of both worlds: A critical pedagogy of place. *Educational Researcher, 32*(4), 3–12.

Gruenewald, D. A. (2003b). Foundations of place: A multidisciplinary framework for place-conscious education. *American Educational Research Journal, 40*(3), 619–654.

Guba, E. G., & Lincoln, Y. S. (1982). Epistemological and methodological bases of naturalistic inquiry. *Educational Communications and Technology Journal, 30,* 233–252.

Hall, G., & Israel, L. (2004). *Using technology to support academic achievement for at-risk teens during out-of-school time.* Wellesley, MA: National Institute on Out-of-School Time.

Halpern, R. (2002). A different kind of child development institution: The history of after-school programs for low-income children. *Teachers College Record, 104*(2), 178–211.

Harrist, S. (2006). A phenomenological investigation of the experience of ambivalence. *Journal of Phenomenological Psychology, 37*(1), 85–114.

Heath, S. B. (2001). Three's not a crowd: Plans, roles, and focus in the arts. *Educational Researcher, 30*(7), 10–17.

Hull, G., & Greeno, J. (2006). Identity and agency in nonschool and school worlds. In Z. Bekerman, N. Burbules, & D. Silberman-Keller (Eds.), *Learning in places: The informal education reader* (pp. 77–97). New York: Peter Lang.

Husserl, E. (1969). *Ideas: General introduction to pure phenomenology* (W. R. B. Gibson, Trans., 5th ed.). London: Allen & Unwin.

Husserl, E. (1970a). *The crisis of European sciences and transcendental phenomenology* (D. Carr, Trans.). Evanston, IL: Northwestern University Press.

Husserl, E. (1970b). *Logical investigations* (J. N. Findlay, Trans.). New York: Humanities Press.

Illich, I. (1971). *Deschooling society.* New York: Harper & Row.

Intel Corporation. (2006). Intel, Internet ve bilgisayar kullanim oranini artirma amaciyla yeni gelistirdigi Intel® Ag Yönetim Platformu'nu, Avrupa, Ortadogu ve Afrika cografyasinda ilk olarak Türkiye'de uygulamaya sundu. Retrieved February 19, 2006, from http://www.intel.com/cd/corporate/pressroom/emea/tur/archive/2006/266622.htm

International Society for Technology in Education. (2000). *National educational technology standards for students.* Washington, DC: Author.

Jackson, L. A., vonEye, A., Biocca, F. A., Barbatsis, G., Zhao, Y., & Fitzgerald, H. (2006). Does home Internet use influence academic performance of low-income children? *Developmental Psychology, 42*(3), 429–435.

Kockelmans, J. (1994). *Edmund Husserl's phenomenology.* West Lafayette, IN: Purdue University Press.

Kozma, R. (1991). Learning with media. *Review of Educational Research, 61*(2), 179–211.

Krapp, A. (2002). Structural and dynamic aspects of interest development: Theoretical considerations from an ontogenetic perspective. *Learning and Instruction, 12,* 383–409.

Kulik, J. A., Bangert, R., & Williams, G. W. (1983). Effects of computer-based teaching on secondary school students. *Journal of Educational Psychology, 75*(1), 19–26.

Kvale, S. (1996). *InterViews.* Thousand Oaks, CA: Sage.

Laegran, A. S. (2002). The petrol station and the Internet cafe: Rural technospaces for youth. *Journal of Rural Studies, 18,* 157–168.

Laegran, A. S., & Stewart, J. (2003). Nerdy, trendy, or healthy? Configuring the Internet cafe. *New Media & Society, 5*(3), 357–377.

Lather, P. (1986a). Issues of validity in openly ideological research: Between a rock and a soft place. *Interchange, 17*(4), 63–84.

Lather, P. (1986b). Research as praxis. *Harvard Educational Review, 56*(3), 257–277.

Lauer, Q. (1965). Introduction. In E. Husserl (Ed.), *Phenomenology and the crisis of philosophy.* New York: Harper & Row.

Lave, J., & Wenger, E. (1991). *Situated learning: Legitimate peripheral participation.* New York: Cambridge University Press.

Liff, S., & Laegran, A. S. (2003). Cybercafes: Debating the meaning and significance of Internet access in a cafe environment. *New Media & Society, 5*(3), 307–312.

Liff, S., & Steward, F. (2003). Shaping e-access in the cybercafe: Networks, boundaries and heteropian innovation. *New Media & Society, 5*(3), 313–334.

Lincoln, Y. S. (1995). Emerging criteria for quality in qualitative and interpretive research. *Qualitative Inquiry, 1*(3), 275–289.

Lincoln, Y. S., & Guba, E. G. (1985). *Naturalistic inquiry.* Beverly Hills, CA: Sage.

Liu, M., Russell, V., Chaplin, D., Raphael, J., Fu, H., & Anthony, E. (2002). *Using technology to improve academic achievement in out-of-school-time programs in Washington, D.C.* Washington, DC: Urban Institute.

Maarschalk, J. (1988). Scientific literacy and informal science teaching. *Journal of Research in Science Teaching, 25*(2), 135–146.

Mahoney, J. L., & Zigler, E. F. (2006). Translating science to policy under the No Child Left Behind Act of 2001: Lessons from the national evaluation of the 21st-century community learning centers. *Journal of Applied Developmental Psychology, 27,* 282–294.

Mastain, L. (2006). The lived experience of spontaneous altruism: A phenomenological study. *Journal of Phenomenological Psychology, 37*(1), 25–52.

Mayer, R. E., Schustack, M. W., & Blanton, W. E. (1999). What do children learn from using computers in an informal, collaborative setting? *Educational Technology, 39*(2), 27–31.

Merriam, S. (1995). What can you tell from an N of 1? Issues of validity and reliability of qualitative research. *PAACE Journal of Lifelong Learning, 4,* 51–60.

Michaels, J. W. (1993). Patterns of video game play in parlors as a function of endogenous and exogenous factors. *Youth & Society, 25*(2), 172–289.

Mitra, S., & Rana, V. (2001). Children and the Internet: Experiments with minimally invasive education in India. *British Journal of Educational Technology, 32*(2), 221–232.

Moore, M. (2001, February 3). Internet sparks culture clash among Turks. *The Washington Post,* p. A17.

Moustakas, C. (1994). *Phenomenological research methods.* Thousand Oaks, CA: Sage.

Mumtaz, S. (2001). Children's enjoyment and perception of computer use in the home and the school. *Computers & Education, 36,* 347–362.

Nespor, J. (1987). The construction of school knowledge: A case study. *Journal of Education, 169*(2), 34–54.

Nespor, J. (2000). School field trips and the curriculum of public spaces. *Journal of Curriculum Studies, 32*(1), 25–43.

Nicolopoulou, A., & Cole, M. (1993). Generation and transmission of shared knowledge in the culture of collaborative learning. In E. Forman, N. Minick, & A. Stone (Eds.), *Contexts for learning: Sociocultural dynamics in children's development* (pp. 283–314). New York: Oxford University Press.

Nocon, H., & Cole, M. (2006). School's invasion of "after-school": Colonization, recolonization, or expansion of access? In Z. Bekerman, N. Burbules, & D. Silberman-Keller (Eds.), *Learning in places: The informal education reader* (pp. 99–121). New York: Peter Lang.

Oldenburg, R. (1999). *The great good place: Cafes, coffee shops, bookstores, bars, hair salons, and other hangouts at the heart of a community.* New York: Marlowe.

Oldenburg, R. (Ed.). (2001). *Celebrating the third place.* New York: Marlowe.

Papert, S. (1993). *Mindstorms: Children, computers, and powerful ideas* (2nd ed.). New York: Basic Books.

Pea, R. D. (1997). Teaching and learning with educational technologies. In H. J. Walberg & G. D. Haertel (Eds.), *Psychology and educational practice* (pp. 274–296). Berkeley, CA: McCutchan.

Peshkin, A. (1988). In search of subjectivity—One's own. *Educational Researcher, 17*(7), 17–21.

Pillay, H. (2003). An investigation of cognitive processes engaged in by recreational computer game players: Implications for skills of the future. *Journal of Research on Technology in Education, 34*(3), 336–350.

Poland, B. D. (2002). Transcription quality. In J. F. Gubrium & J. A. Holstein (Eds.), *Handbook of interview research: Context and method* (pp. 629–649). Thousand Oaks, CA: Sage.

Polkinghorne, D. (1989). Phenomenological research methods. In R. Valle & S. Halling (Eds.), *Existential-phenomenological perspectives in psychology* (pp. 41–60). New York: Plenum.

Ragin, C. C., Nagel, J., & White, P. (2004). *Workshop on scientific foundations of qualitative research.* Arlington, VA: National Science Foundation.

Reed, H., & Loughran, E. (Eds.). (1984). *Beyond schools: Education for economic, social, and personal development.* Hadley, MA: Common Wealth Company.

Resnick, L. (1987). Learning in school and out. *Educational Researcher, 16*(9), 13–20.

Rheinberg, F., & Tramp, N. (2006). Analysis of the incentive for intensive leisure-time use of computers. *Zeitschrift für Psychologie, 214*(2), 97–107.

Roberts, D. F., Henriksen, L., & Foehr, U. G. (2004). Adolescents and media. In R. M. Lerner & L. Steinberg (Eds.), *Handbook of adolescent psychology* (2nd ed., pp. 487–521). Hoboken, NJ: John Wiley.

Sairosse, T. M., & Mutula, S. M. (2004). Use of cybercafes: Study of Gaborone City, Botswana. *Electronic Library and Information Systems, 38*(1), 60–66.

Sandholtz, J., Ringstaff, C., & Dwyer, D. (1997). *Teaching with technology: Creating student-centered classrooms.* New York: Teachers College Press.

Sawchuk, P. (2003). *Adult learning and technology in working-class life.* New York: Cambridge University Press.

Schustack, M. W., Strauss, R., & Worden, P. E. (1997). Learning about technology in a non-instructional environment. *Journal of Educational Computing Research, 16*(4), 337–351.

Schwandt, T. A. (1997). *Qualitative inquiry: A dictionary of terms.* Thousand Oaks, CA: Sage.

Seidman, I. (1991). *Interviewing as qualitative research.* New York: Teachers College Press.

Selwyn, N. (1998). The effect of using a home computer on students' educational use of IT. *Computers & Education, 31*, 211–227.

Selwyn, N. (2005). The social processes of learning to use computers. *Social Science Computer Review, 23*(1), 122–135.

Smith, M. (1988). *Developing youth work: Informal education, mutual aid and popular practice.* Milton Keynes, UK: Open University Press.

Smith, M. (2006). Beyond the curriculum: Fostering associational life in schools. In Z. Bekerman, N. Burbules, & D. Silberman-Keller (Eds.), *Learning in places: The informal education reader* (pp. 9–33). New York: Peter Lang.

Subrahmanyam, K., Greenfield, P., Kraut, R. E., & Gross, E. F. (2001). The impact of computer use on children's and adolescents' development. *Applied Developmental Psychology, 22*, 7–30.

Subrahmanyam, K., Kraut, R. E., Greenfield, P., & Gross, E. F. (2000). The impact of home computer use on children's activities and development. *The Future of Children: Children and Computer Technology, 10*(2), 123–144.

Sutherland, R., Facer, K., Furlong, R., & Furlong, J. (2000). A new environment for education? The computer in the home. *Computers & Education, 34*, 195–212.

Titchen, A., & Hobson, D. (2005). Phenomenology. In B. Somekh & C. Lewin (Eds.), *Research methods in the social sciences* (pp. 121–130). London: Sage Ltd.

Tor, H., & Erden, O. (2004). A research about primary school students level who takes advantage from information technology. *Turkish Online Journal of Educational Technology, 3*(1). Available at http://www.tojet.net/articles/3116.htm

Turkey State Statistics Institute. (2004). *Turkey's statistical yearbook.* Retrieved February 19, 2007, from http://www.tuik.gov.tr/yillik/yillik_2004.pdf

Turkle, S. (1984). *The second self: Computers and the human spirit.* New York: Simon & Schuster.

Turkle, S. (1997). *Life on the screen: Identity in the age of the Internet.* New York: Simon & Schuster.

Uotinen, J. (2003). Involvement in (the information) society—The Joensuu Community Resource Centre Netcafé. *New Media & Society, 5*(3), 335–356.

Upitis, R. (1998). From hackers to luddites, game players to game creators: Profiles of adolescent students using technology. *Journal of Curriculum Studies, 30*(3), 293–318.

Vadeboncoeur, J. (2006). Engaging young people: Learning in informal contexts. *Review of Research in Education, 30*, 239–278.

van Manen, M. (1990). *Researching lived experience.* Albany: State University of New York Press.

Vannatta, R., & Fordham, N. (2004). Teacher dispositions as predictors of classroom technology use. *Journal of Research on Technology in Education, 36*(3), 253–271.

Verma, S., & Larson, R. (2003). Editors' notes. *New Directions for Child and Adolescent Development, 99*, 1–7.

Vygotsky, L. S. (1978). *Mind in society: The development of higher psychological processes.* Cambridge, MA: Harvard University Press.

Wakeford, N. (2003). The embedding of local culture in global communication: Independent Internet cafes in London. *New Media & Society, 5*(3), 379–399.

Wellington, J. (2001). Exploring the secret garden: The growing importance of ICT in the home. *British Journal of Educational Technology, 32*(2), 233–244.

Wenger, E. (1999). *Communities of practice: Learning, meaning, and identity.* New York: Cambridge University Press.

Windschitl, M., & Sahl, K. (2002). Tracing teachers' use of technology in a laptop computer school: The interplay of teacher beliefs, social dynamics, and institutional culture. *American Educational Research Journal, 39*, 165–205.

Wolcott, H. (1990). On seeking—and rejecting—validity in qualitative research. In E. Eisner & A. Peshkin (Eds.), *Qualitative inquiry in education* (pp. 121–152). New York: Teachers College Press.

The World Bank. (2003). *World development indicators.* Washington, DC: Author.

Yedekcioglu, O. (1996, January). Use of computers at high schools in Turkey. *Technological Horizons in Education.* Available at http://www.thejournal.com/articles/12380

Yesil, B. (2003). Internet cafés as battlefield: State control over Internet cafés in Turkey and the lack of popular resistance. *Journal of Popular Culture, 37*(1), 120–127.

Zhao, Y., & Frank, K. (2003). Factors affecting technology uses in schools: An ecological perspective. *American Educational Research Journal, 40,* 807–840.

Zhao, Y., Mishra, P., & Girod, M. (2000). A clubhouse is a clubhouse is a clubhouse. *Computers in Human Behavior, 16,* 287–300.

Zhao, Y., Tan, S. H., & Mishra, P. (2000). Teaching and learning: Whose computer is it? *Journal of Adolescent & Adult Literacy, 44*(4), 348–354.

Manuscript received March 14, 2007
Revision received June 16, 2008
Accepted July 13, 2008

American Educational Research Journal
March 2009, Vol. 46, No. 1, pp. 275–314
DOI: 10.3102/0002831208324517
© 2009 AERA. http://aerj.aera.net

Sources of Middle School Students' Self-Efficacy in Mathematics: A Qualitative Investigation

Ellen L. Usher
University of Kentucky

According to A. Bandura's (1986) social cognitive theory, individuals form their self-efficacy beliefs by interpreting information from four sources: mastery experience, vicarious experience, social persuasions, and physiological or affective states. The purpose of this study was to examine the heuristics students use as they form their mathematics self-efficacy from these and other sources. Semistructured interviews were conducted with eight middle school students who reported either high or low self-efficacy and with students' parents and mathematics teachers. Students relied on information from all four hypothesized sources, which were combined according to various heuristics. Teaching structures, course placement, and students' self-regulated learning also emerged as important factors related to self-efficacy. Results refine and extend the tenets of social cognitive theory.

KEYWORDS: motivation, mathematics education, self-efficacy, sources of self-efficacy

As a fundamental part of his social cognitive theory, Bandura (1986) posited that unless people believe they can produce desired outcomes, they have little incentive to act. Although ample research attests to the predictive power of academic self-efficacy—the beliefs students hold about their academic capabilities—on academic achievement, there have been few efforts to investigate the sources underlying these self-beliefs (Pajares & Urdan, 2006). In the social cognitive theoretical framework, human functioning is viewed as the product of the reciprocal influences of personal, behavioral, and environmental determinants (Bandura, 1986). Humans rely on cognitive, vicarious, self-regulatory, and self-reflective processes, all of which

ELLEN L. USHER *is an assistant professor of educational psychology in the Department of Educational and Counseling Psychology at the University of Kentucky, 249 Dickey Hall, Lexington, KY 40506-0017; e-mail: Ellen.Usher@uky.edu. Her research focuses on clarifying the origins and correlates of academic self-efficacy.*

play a central role in people's adaptation and change. Self-efficacy beliefs develop as the result of emotional, cognitive, or motivational processes; behavioral indicants; or the social environments in which people live and work. In school, for example, students' self-efficacy beliefs can be enhanced when students alter their emotions and thoughts (personal factors), when their teachers use effective classroom structures (environmental factors), and when students improve their self-regulatory practices (behavior).

Bandura (1997) hypothesized that students form their self-efficacy by selecting and interpreting information from four primary sources, the most powerful of which is the result of their own previous performance, or *mastery experience*. Students also build their self-efficacy beliefs through the *vicarious experience* of observing the actions of others. It is for this reason that models can play a powerful role in the development of self-efficacy. The third source of self-efficacy information comes from the *social persuasions* that individuals receive from others. Students often depend on parents, teachers, and peers to provide evaluative feedback, judgments, and appraisals about their academic performance. Finally, self-efficacy beliefs are informed by *emotional and physiological states* such as arousal, anxiety, mood, and fatigue.

The bulk of the research that has addressed the hypothesized sources of self-efficacy has been quantitative in nature and has targeted the self-efficacy beliefs of high school and college-aged students in predominantly White settings (e.g., Hampton & Mason, 2003; Lent, Lopez, & Bieschke, 1991; Lent, Lopez, Brown, & Gore, 1996). Researchers have typically investigated the sources by seeking students' responses to four self-report measures, each presumably tapping a source of self-efficacy, and subjecting them to correlational analyses (Usher & Pajares, in press). Empirical evidence supports Bandura's (1997) contention that mastery experience is the most influential source of efficacy information, but the predictive value of the other sources has been inconsistent, likely because of methodological limitations. For example, items from quantitative measures designed to assess vicarious experience have consistently shown poor internal consistency, obscuring the relationship between this source and self-efficacy (Usher & Pajares, in press). Likewise, the use of anxiety measures as a proxy for students' physiological arousal fails to capture other forms of physiological or affective arousal that may affect self-efficacy.

Contextual and demographic factors may also have played a role in research outcomes in this area. Researchers investigating the sources of middle and high school students' self-efficacy beliefs have reported that students may rely differently on the sources of self-efficacy as a function of their gender, ethnic background, and learning domain. For example, boys report stronger mastery experiences and lower anxiety in the area of mathematics (Lent et al., 1996) and science (Britner & Pajares, 2006), but girls report greater mastery experiences and lower anxiety in writing (Pajares, Johnson, & Usher, 2007). Researchers have also detected mean differences favoring girls on social persuasions and vicarious experiences in mathematics (Lopez,

Lent, Brown, & Gore, 1997). Others have found that social persuasions accounted for 4 times more variance than did mastery experience in middle school girls' academic self-efficacy, suggesting that girls rely more on information gained from their relationships with others than on their own accomplishments (Usher & Pajares, 2006).

Researchers have also examined whether the formation of self-efficacy differs for students of diverse ethnicity. For example, Usher and Pajares (2006) found that only mastery experience and social persuasions predicted the academic self-efficacy beliefs of African American middle school students, whereas all four hypothesized sources predicted the self-efficacy of White students. African American students also reported greater physiological arousal than did their White peers. In another study, Indo Canadian immigrant middle school students reported receiving more information from vicarious influences and social persuasions than did their Anglo Canadian peers, which may have reflected a cultural emphasis on *other-oriented* rather than on *self-oriented* messages as indicative of one's capabilities (Klassen, 2004).

Comparatively few qualitative investigations of the sources have been undertaken, and all of the existing studies have been conducted with college students and adults. Zeldin and Pajares (2000) asked women who excelled at careers in mathematics, science, and technology to describe the people, events, and situations that influenced their career paths. Vicarious experience and social persuasions powerfully influenced women's confidence in these male-dominated fields. The messages women received from those whose opinions they held in high regard served as important contributors to women's personal efficacy beliefs. In a follow-up investigation, Zeldin, Britner, and Pajares (2007) investigated the sources of men's self-efficacy beliefs in these domains and found that men tended to rely on their personal accomplishments when describing the basis for their confidence in mathematics, science, and technology. In particular, they spoke of their natural abilities, inclinations, or talents in these domains. The modeling experiences men reported were informative to their careers but were not as persuasive as they had been for women interviewed earlier (i.e., Zeldin & Pajares, 2000). Although vicarious experiences helped show men *how* to approach mathematics-related careers, these experiences did little to convince men of their capabilities to succeed. Men also recalled passing moments when they received support from significant others, but these persuasions were less influential for the self-efficacy beliefs of men. Participants in both studies, however, referenced experiences that took place during their adolescence as having had a profound effect on their self-efficacy.

Other researchers have examined the sources of self-efficacy qualitatively by asking college students to list what makes them feel confident in their coursework. One group of researchers asked undergraduate engineering students to list and rank the factors that influenced their confidence that they would be successful in an introductory course (Hutchison, Follman, Sumpter, & Bodner, 2006). Students generally reported that mastering course content increased their confidence, though women were more likely than men to report that availability of help in the class made them more confi-dent. Lent, Brown, Gover, and Nijjer (1996) reported similar findings from college undergraduates whom they asked to list what affected their mathe-matics self-efficacy. Students in these studies primarily listed mastery expe-riences and rarely vicarious experiences, social persuasions, or physiological arousal as central to their self-efficacy, which may have been a function of the open-ended nature of the measures used.

Qualitative inquiry can provide a better understanding of the genesis of self-efficacy beliefs by revealing the heuristic techniques younger students use to evaluate their academic capabilities (see Pajares & Schunk, 2005). In particular, an interview approach offers a phenomenological lens through which the development of efficacy beliefs can be viewed and enables researchers to examine the different conditions under which students process and appraise their experiences at particular junctures in their schooling.

This study features eighth-grade students who, at the cusp of their tran-sition to high school, have already accumulated a rich history of academic performance and feedback. Researchers have documented that students often experience a decline in academic motivation and self-efficacy during important school transitions (e.g., Wigfield, Eccles, Mac Iver, Reuman, & Midgley, 1991). Most have pointed to a mismatch between adolescents' changing developmental needs and the school environment as a likely cause (Eccles, 2004; Eccles & Midgley, 1989). Giving voice to middle school stu-dents who are old enough to reflect articulately on their own learning could provide new insights about how self-efficacy develops.

The purpose of this study was to use qualitative methods to investigate the rules or heuristics these students use to select and interpret information related to their mathematics self-efficacy. I also sought to examine whether other factors might be related to students' self-efficacy in mathematics. Of particular interest was students' *self-regulation*, which refers to "the self-directive process by which learners transform their mental abilities into aca-demic skills" (Zimmerman, 2002, p. 65). Bandura (1986) hypothesized a reciprocal relationship between self-regulation and self-efficacy, both of which are driven by individuals' capacity to self-reflect. This reciprocity has also been empirically documented (Zimmerman & Schunk, 2008). Students who view themselves as capable tend to set higher learning goals for them-selves and to plan their work and monitor their progress more effectively (see Schunk & Ertmer, 2000, for a review). Likewise, when students increase their repertoire of self-regulated learning skills, their academic self-efficacy is enhanced (e.g., Zimmerman & Bandura, 1994; Zimmerman & Kitsantas, 1999). Hence, I aimed to see whether and how participants discussed self-regulation within the context of the sources of mathematics self-efficacy. Of course, I remained open to the possibility that participants would describe other sources as well.

Three questions guided the investigation: (a) How do students with high or low mathematics self-efficacy interpret and weigh efficacy-relevant infor-mation, and do these interpretations seem to differ for boys and girls or for

African American and White students? (b) What insights can teachers and parents provide about the sources of their students' and children's mathematics self-efficacy beliefs? (c) What additional factors, such as self-regulated learning, might be related to the development of students' mathematics self-efficacy beliefs?

Method

Participants and Setting

Interviews were conducted in March and April of 2006 with eight students selected from a group of public middle school (Grades 6–8) students who had participated in a larger quantitative study in February of 2006 (N = 824). All participants were attending Grade 8 of their middle-class, suburban school located in the southeastern United States. The school student body was 66% White, 21% African American, 6% Hispanic, 4% Asian, and 3% mixed ethnic origin.

Interviewees were selected from four subgroups of interest: African American girls, White girls, African American boys, and White boys. Students in each subgroup were first rank ordered by their mean response scores on four quantitative self-efficacy measures that they had completed several weeks earlier. Following the guidelines set forth by Bandura (2006), these measures assessed self-efficacy at four levels, ranging from most to least specific: mathematics skills self-efficacy (e.g., I can successfully solve math exercises involving inequalities), self-efficacy for self-regulated learning in mathematics (e.g., How well can you organize your math work?), grade self-efficacy (e.g., How confident are you that you will pass math with a grade higher than 70%?), and self-efficacy to complete a variety of mathematics-related courses (e.g., I am confident that I will make a final grade of A or B in geometry). Mean scores reflected the six points of the Likert-type response scale and ranged from 1 (lowest self-efficacy level) to 6 (highest self-efficacy level). Two participants, one ranked highest in self-efficacy and one ranked lowest in self-efficacy, were then selected from each of the four subgroups of interest. In cases in which a student declined or was not permitted to participate, "runners-up" were invited. Three such cases occurred, but this did not in any way compromise the aim of selecting students with either low or high self-efficacy, as all participants met this criterion. Interviews took place during noncore instructional hours in the school's media center.

At the beginning of the school year, students had been placed in one of four mathematics courses according to their achievement, ability, and preference: prealgebra, on-level algebra, advanced algebra, or honors geometry. In this particular setting, placement and performance in one's eighth-grade mathematics course is considered "high stakes" because it largely determines the mathematics track a student will follow in high school, which in turn has important implications for the student's admission to college. Table 1 provides general information about participants, including each student's mathematics course placement.

Table 1

Description of Phase 3 Study Participants[a]

Student's Name	Gender Age	Ethnicity	Self-Efficacy Mean Score[b]	Math Teacher Math Course	Mother's Occupation (M) Father's Occupation (F)
Students with high self-efficacy					
Brandy Palmer	Female 14	African American	5.83	Ms. Wheeler Algebra	M: shipping agent for computer company F: police investigator
Hannah Murphy	Female 13	White	5.98	Ms. Barkley Honors Geometry	M: high school math teacher F: lawyer
Jamaal Haines	Male 14	African American	5.12	Ms. Barkley Honors Geometry	M: hospital bill collector F: military contractor
Zach Bettino[c]	Male 13	White	5.90	Ms. Barkley Honors Geometry	M: certified public accountant F: criminal defense investigator
Students with low self-efficacy					
Tanisha Jones[c]	Female 13	African American	2.57	Ms. Matthews Prealgebra	M: housekeeping manager for a governmental agency
Arden Cramer	Female 14	White	2.12	Ms. Matthews Algebra	M: part-time emergency room nurse F: corporate employee for beverage company
Xavier Relaford	Male 14	African American	3.66	Ms. Matthews Prealgebra	M: disabled
Chris Simmons	Male 14	White	2.20	Ms. Matthews Algebra	M: homemaker F: commercial construction owner

[a]Participants were given the option of selecting a pseudonym to be used to identify them in the study. If no selection was made, a pseudonym was assigned in an effort to preserve the ethnic and semantic origin of each participant's given name and surname.

[b]Mean score obtained by students' responses on a 6-point Likert-type scale.

[c]Zach's and Tanisha's mothers have different surnames because of remarriage: Ms. Kaiser and Ms. Wilson, respectively.

Interviews were subsequently conducted with the mathematics teachers of each student participant and with one of the student's parents. In all cases, the parent who volunteered to be interviewed was the mother. The eight teacher interviews took place during planning periods in teachers' classrooms. The parent interviews took place at a location specified by the parent so as to ensure each participant's comfort and convenience. One parent (Brandy's mother) who had agreed to participate in the study later withdrew because of a family emergency. Participants were given the option of selecting a pseudonym to be used to identify them in the study. If no selection was made, a pseudonym was assigned in an effort to preserve the ethnic and semantic origin of each participant's given name and surname. All interviews were conducted and transcribed by the author, who had no prior relationship with any of the study participants apart from having previously administered a survey in students' mathematics class.

Interview Protocol

A semistructured interview protocol adapted for middle school students from Zeldin and Pajares (2000) was used to gain information about the four sources of efficacy information believed to underlie students' self-efficacy beliefs in mathematics. A semistructured interview format does not lend itself to a one-to-one matchup between theoretical constructs and the interview questions asked. As Merriam (1998) pointed out, this format "allows the researcher to respond to the situation at hand, to the emerging worldview of the respondent, and to new ideas on the topic" (p. 74). For this reason, I crafted questions general enough to allow participants the freedom to answer in whatever direction they chose, and I used probes to seek more detail, clarification, or examples (Merriam, 1998). Global questions (e.g., "Tell me about yourself as a math student") permitted lengthy or complex responses that often demonstrated the dynamic processes through which self-efficacy beliefs are modified. These methods also enabled me to gather information related to other factors potentially associated with students' self-efficacy.

Table 2 provides the semistructured interview protocol used with students. Parent and teacher protocols were similarly structured but crafted with the goal of probing how students appraise efficacy-relevant information (e.g., "Tell me about how Hannah views herself as a math student"). Questions on the protocol are organized categorically, but changes in ordering during the interview helped to maintain conversational flow. An interview checklist utilized during each interview ensured that all theoretical constructs were addressed. I concluded each student interview with a question explicitly targeting sources of self-efficacy in mathematics (e.g., "What could make you feel more confident about yourself in mathematics?"). This question prompted students to state, emphasize, or reiterate what they believed were the sources of their confidence.

Each interview was scheduled to last approximately 45 minutes. Interviews were digitally recorded and were transcribed by the author. To

Table 2
Student Interview Protocol

Background
1. Tell me about where you have previously gone to school.
2. Tell me a little bit about your family.
3. Tell me little bit about yourself.
   a. What sort of personality do you have?
   b. What sorts of things do you enjoy doing outside of school?
   c. Tell me about your friends.
   d. Tell me about the people you most admire.
4. Describe yourself as a student.
   a. What would you say is your best subject in school? Why? What is your favorite subject? Why?
   b. What subject do you feel is your weakest? Why? Which subject is your least favorite? Why?
   c. Tell me about the grades you typically make in school. Do you agree with the grades you are given?

Mathematics experiences and self-efficacy
5. I am going to ask you several questions about a specific subject you study in school. I want you to think hard about all the math classes you've ever taken as well as other experiences you've had involving math. First, tell me about yourself as a math student.
   a. What sort of work habits do you have in math?
   b. If you were asked to rate your ability in math on a scale of 1 (lowest) to 10 (highest), where would you be? Why? How would you rate your confidence that you will do well on the upcoming state math test?
   c. What do you like to do related to math outside of school? [mastery experiences]
   d. Tell me about a time you experienced a setback in math. How did you deal with it?
6. Tell me a story that explains to me something about the type of student you are in math. In other words, share with me something that happened to you that involves this subject and perhaps your parents, teachers, or friends.

Mathematics learning environment
7. Tell me about the math class you are in.
   a. Does your school group students according to their abilities in math? If so, which group are you in?
   b. How would you say you compare to the rest of your classmates in your math abilities? How about to the rest of the students in your grade?
8. Tell me about the math teachers you've had.
   a. What sorts of things do your teachers tell you about your performance in math?
   b. What do you think your teacher(s) would tell your parents about how you do in math?
   c. How does your teacher make you feel about your ability in math?
   d. Describe the best teacher you've had in math. What made her (or him) so good?
   e. What could your teachers do to help you feel more confident in your math abilities?
9. Under what conditions do you perform well in math? Under what conditions do you perform less well? Why?

(continued)

Table 2 **(continued)**

Mathematics and others
10. Have you ever been recognized for your ability in math? Explain.
11. Tell me about your family and math.
    a. What do members of your family do that involves math?
    b. What do your parents tell you about math?
    c. How are your siblings in math?
    d. What would you parents tell your teachers about you as a math student?
12. Tell me about your friends (not necessarily your classmates) and math.
    a. Describe how most of your friends do in math.
    b. What do your friends say about math? What do they say about those who do well?
    c. How do you think your friends would describe you in math?
13. Do you think the people you admire would be good at math? Why?

Affective and physiological response to mathematics
14. I want to ask you to think about how math makes you feel. You probably haven't been asked to think about that before. When you are given a math test, how does that make you feel? How do you feel when you are given a math assignment?

Sources of self-efficacy in mathematics
15. Earlier you rated your math ability on a scale of 1 to 10. How would you rate your *confidence*? Why? What could make you feel more confident about yourself in math?

---

mirror the informality of discussions with students, teachers, and parents, the terms *math* and *mathematics* are used interchangeably.

Analysis

Interview data were transcribed, coded, and analyzed according to the guidelines set forth by Miles and Huberman (1994) and using the NVivo 7.0 software program. A start list of codes was developed to mirror the study's theoretical framework and guiding questions, and first-level codes were added for other variables that emerged from the data as warranted. For example, first-level codes were created to represent *curiosity, teaching structures*, and *readiness* as factors that may be related to students' self-efficacy. Because of the semistructured protocol design, some questions (e.g., "Tell me a story that explains to me something about the type of student you are in math") elicited a response that lasted several minutes and addressed several constructs. As a result, responses often required multiple codes.

Reliability checks (described below) were conducted on first-level codes. Revisions to these codes were made as needed so as to reflect the data accurately. Ancillary annotations were added to data that were ill-fitting to the original codes assigned. This helped to capture surprising patterns that emerged that were not easily tapped by a single code.

After assigning first-level codes to all transcripts, I listened to each interview again while reviewing individual transcripts and codes. This process enabled me to verify the accuracy and internal consistency of the coding system, to combine similar codes when redundancies occurred (e.g., *self-talk* with *self-modeling*), to reduce the number of first-level codes by collapsing related categories, and to remove codes assigned to passages that were tangential to the study. Next I combined categories with similar codes in a higher-level, "tree-node" format. This permitted me to sort through larger chunks of information more efficiently and to see general trends and patterns in the data, both within and between participants. For example, the first-level codes for *vicarious experiences from peers, vicarious experiences from adults,* and *self-modeled experiences* were combined in a higher-level node labeled *vicarious experience.*

The data were next organized on four conceptually clustered matrices. On each matrix, rows were labeled with the codes reflecting the various sources of self-efficacy (e.g., mastery experience). Columns on the first matrix were labeled *High Self-Efficacy* and *Low Self-Efficacy.* Cells on that matrix represented the intersection of mathematics efficacy information and self-efficacy level (e.g., mastery experiences for students with high self-efficacy; failure experiences for students with low self-efficacy). Subsequent matrices were created by gender, ethnicity, and participant type (i.e., student, parent, or teacher), respectively. Investigating the data in this basic way helped identify cross-case and intergroup patterns and differences.

Reliability and Validity

Merriam (1998) outlined several means by which researchers can establish reliability and show that results drawn from qualitative data analysis are consistent. This study's design enabled me to compare the self-efficacy judgments students made on earlier quantitative measures at the time of our interview. Although interview questions were kept general enough to invite students to express their perceived mathematics capabilities however they might view them, students' responses reflected both task- and domain-specific efficacy beliefs in a manner congruent with their responses to quantitative measures. For example, Chris noted that "when it comes to like percents and stuff, I can't do it. And fractions. But like equations and like geometry, like, I can do that well." As illustrated in Table 1, his quantitative self-efficacy scores mirrored this modest belief in his capabilities. This symmetry offers evidence for the internal validity of students' self-efficacy reports and demonstrates that students' quantitative and qualitative self-efficacy judgments, though not identical, were generally consistent.

Data collected from parents and teachers in response to similar questions (e.g., "Tell me about how [child's name] views himself/herself as a math student") were used to complement students' views of their own mathematics capabilities and thereby offered triangulation of the data that also enhanced internal validity. Member checks were conducted with participants to give them an opportunity to modify, clarify, or expand information they shared during the initial interview. Such checks help ensure that the study's results are an accurate reflection of participants' beliefs at the time of the interview (Merriam, 1998).

According to Miles and Huberman (1994), working toward a high degree of intercoder reliability permits researchers to present "an unequivocal, common vision of what the codes mean" (p. 64). Although I coded all transcripts independently, it was important to verify that the codes assigned were meaningful, logical, and consistent with those that other readers would assign. To this end, two graduate students familiar with social cognitive theory and self-efficacy were asked to code three complete interview transcripts comprising 44 pages (14% of total transcript pages). Coding cross-checks were conducted by tallying the number of agreements and disagreements between the graduate students and the researcher. The ratio of the number of agreements to the number of agreements plus disagreements was used as a measure of intercoder reliability (Miles & Huberman, 1994). We obtained an intercoder reliability of 93%. Disagreements in coding were resolved by returning to Bandura's (1997) theoretical description of the sources of self-efficacy for clarification. I also invited an expert in social cognitive theory to code an additional (unique) 10-page section of an interview transcript. Interrater reliability for this cross-check was 96%.

An audit trail was created by maintaining a detailed record of how and when data were collected and by labeling the data gathered and the revisions made during each step of the analysis. The NVivo software program enables researchers to create and maintain a digital filing system that hyperlinks all relevant materials—in this case audio files, coded interview transcripts, journal notes made at each interview site, annotations made during coding, coding lists, and data matrices and queries. This careful system of organization increased the likelihood that the conclusions drawn here would match those drawn by researchers following the same methodology.

The use of a research methodology previously designed for use in an empirical investigation of the sources of self-efficacy (i.e., Zeldin & Pajares, 2000) enhances the contribution this work makes to existing qualitative findings on the sources. External validity is further enhanced when participants and settings are described with sufficient detail to enable readers to assess similarities among study participants and people learning in other contexts (Miles & Huberman, 1994). Working within the well-defined theoretical framework of social cognitive theory also permits me to look for connections between participants' responses and theoretical constructs.

Results and Discussion

In this section, I begin by offering background information about the eight students who participated in the study, their interests, and their academic record in mathematics (see Figures 1–3). Next I present students' interpretations of information related to their mathematics self-efficacy that appears to be related to the four sources hypothesized by Bandura (1997). I then turn to students' descriptions of their self-regulatory skills, a factor they

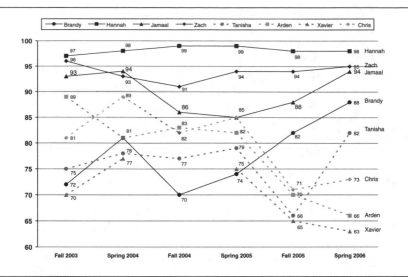

Figure 1. **Student grade point averages in middle school mathematics: Grades 6–8.**
Note. Grade point averages can range from 0 to 100. Scores for students with low self-efficacy are plotted along dotted lines.

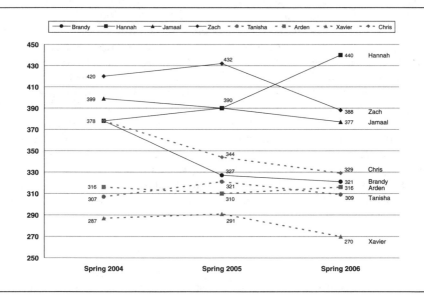

Figure 2. **Student scores on state criterion-referenced competency tests, 2004–2006: Mathematics Total.**
Note. Scores on this measure can range from 150 to 450. Scores for students with low self-efficacy are plotted along dotted lines.

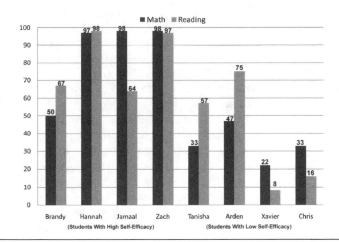

Figure 3. **Student scores on the Grade 8 (fall 2005) Iowa Test of Basic Skills: Mathematics and Reading.**
Note. Scores on this measure are reported as percentiles and are norm referenced.

often mentioned with regard to their competence in mathematics. Parent and teacher perspectives provide additional context for students' remarks. Throughout this section I first present results for students who reported high mathematics self-efficacy and then for those with low self-efficacy because the stories that emerged from these two groups differed most dramatically. I follow each section with a summary and a brief discussion of general trends and other group differences.

Background of Participants

Students With High Self-Efficacy

Brandy described herself as an aspiring Alvin Ailey professional dancer who loves music, is outgoing, and, in math class, tends to be a "loud mouth." Through her calm, cool demeanor and reflective disposition, Brandy explained that she planned to move in with her grandmother for ninth grade to attend a special high school of the arts in an inner-city district. Her grandmother, she beamed, was one of the first African American women to work in a barber shop and was someone Brandy admired for being a steady figure in times of stress. Brandy has two older siblings—a sister who did not finish high school and a brother who worked as a disc jockey in a local club. She described mathematics as her best subject and largely attributed this to the teachers she had who made math interesting and fun.

287

Usher

Hannah arrived promptly and eagerly for her interview and carefully placed on the table before her a neatly organized binder notebook with color-coded tabs for each subject area. In a frenetic cadence, the curly haired adolescent managed to explain within the first several minutes of our talk that she held a long and shining record as an exceptional math student, belonged to the Jewish faith, enjoyed reading and playing the flute more than doing things her younger sister liked (such as soccer or partying), and was "sort of obsessive about school."

Described by his teacher as one of the most well-liked boys at school, *Jamaal*, who characterized himself as "real laid back," wore a glowing smile and spoke in a calm and mature manner. With handsome features and self-declared athletic prowess, Jamaal drew frequently on his opportunity as a middle school student to play cornerback for the high school football team when describing the competitive edge he felt in math class. Jamaal was the oldest man in his household since his father, to whom he talked on the phone daily, had left to work for a year as a contractor in the Middle East.

Zach, a tidy, thin student who spoke in a quick and to-the-point manner, expressed his affinity for golf, tennis, baseball, and video games. Zach's mother portrayed her son as notoriously curious and inquisitive about everything: "We have a joke in our family. 'Now that's a Zach question.'" Zach was eager to point out that he was in "four-serve TAG" (i.e., placed in gifted-track classes in all four core subjects) but referred to himself as "a terrible writer." His math achievement record, he assured me, had always been near perfect.

Students With Low Self-Efficacy

An only child for 12 of her 13 years and an aspiring psychiatrist, *Tanisha* seemed comfortable talking about herself and her experiences. Petite, well-groomed, and perhaps a tad behind the developmental curve for average 13-year-old girls, Tanisha explained that she enjoyed "playing," watching television, and talking on the phone with friends. Her mother noted that Tanisha had been distracted from schoolwork earlier in the year by her romantic interests. Math, Tanisha squirmed, had always been a challenge for her, and middle school math was increasingly difficult. Nevertheless, she was beginning to regain some confidence in her ability to handle her math coursework.

Arden, a blonde-haired student whose passion was singing, dancing, and acting in the school play, arrived for our interview with an enthusiastic but nervous smile and clutching a teen novel. She began by offsetting her aversion to math with her passion for reading and writing. Self-described as talkative, spontaneous, and social, Arden was characterized by her mother as someone who is creative and imaginative but who "swallows a lot of her stuff." The day before our interview, Arden had received her interim report card, on which was the lowest math grade she had ever earned—a 54.

Xavier spent his afternoons, evenings, and weekends playing video games, basketball, football, and just "hanging out." Although he appeared to feel slightly awkward in his overweight body, Xavier's endearing smile and eager-to-please demeanor made him agreeable to talk with. His mother described him as "a follower," which she said was likely why Xavier wound up in alternative school for several months after handling a friend's pellet gun at Carlyle Middle School (CMS) during seventh grade. Xavier said he had always struggled with mathematics and held a borderline-passing grade point average across middle school.

With a wry sense of humor and dirty blonde bangs draped across his eyes, *Chris* proudly declared that he did not fit the "preppy" or popular-kid mold at his middle school. Chris denied any association with "gothic freaks" but admitted that he and his friends, whom he described as "dorks," enjoyed doing "weird stuff" such as dressing up as ninjas and frightening people. A budding guitarist, Chris felt it important to point out that he hated feeling as if he had "a collar on" at school and at home, and he appreciated people who had a sense of humor and were willing on occasion to overlook his wrongdoings. Chris never felt that mathematics was his strong subject, despite having managed to do well in math during elementary school.

It seems important to point out that when Brandy, Jamaal, and Tanisha entered Grade 6, they began voluntarily taking a 40-mile bus ride twice each day to attend CMS. The school system's voluntary majority-to-minority (called "M-to-M") desegregation program, currently being phased out, permits students who are in the racial majority at their home schools (in this district, typically African American students who live in the southern end of the district) to receive free transportation to attend schools where they would be in the racial minority (typically at the northern end of the district). Because schools in the northern half of this district outperform schools from the southern half on standardized achievement tests and other measures, many parents opt to send their children north for the opportunity of a better education. For Brandy, Jamaal, and Tanisha, this arrangement meant an average daily bus commute of 3 hours.

Interpretations of Performance Experiences

Mastery Experiences of Students With High Self-Efficacy

Bandura (1997) noted that "performance situations contain constellations of factors that convey efficacy information" (p. 85). Brandy, Hannah, Jamaal, and Zach described how several factors related to their mathematics performance served as indicants of their capabilities in math. These mastery experiences were typically evoked by interview questions that invited students to talk about themselves as math students or to tell a story explaining the type of math student they are. For all students, strong academic performance seemed to go hand-in-hand with confidence. Zach and Hannah were quick to point out that they had never earned below a high A average in math. Each beamed about having outperformed others on standardized tests.

Zach noted that he scored in the 97th percentile of the Iowa Test of Basic Skills; Hannah remarked that she earned a higher score on the math portion of the Scholastic Aptitude Test than had many high school students. Jamaal also pointed out his stellar performance on standardized tests and noted that, were he to improve his study habits, he would certainly be capable of earning top grades in math. Brandy interpreted her high scores in her current math class as a powerful source of confidence. She was quick to recognize how instrumental her math teacher, Ms. Wheeler, had been in helping her to be successful.

For Jamaal and for Zach, performing well in math was a direct result of how easy math had always been. Jamaal admitted, "I don't push myself. Like, it just comes naturally. I'm just real confident at it because I never study for tests and I make good grades." Zach noted matter-of-factly that "math always comes easy to me more than any other thing." Coincidentally, their mothers told me that in their respective elementary schools, both boys had been so mathematically advanced in first grade that their teachers sent them to second-grade classes for math instruction. Both boys drew on this early experience of mastery to explain their self-assurance in geometry. The perception they held that math work was easy accompanied a belief that they possessed a natural aptitude for math. In fact, both boys' mothers spoke in awe of their precocious sons' giftedness. "Honestly, I don't know where Jamaal gets his gift from," noted Ms. Haines. Zach's mother attributed her son's success to an inborn trait: "You know, some people are just *so* not math. Either you have it or you don't in math. I'm a CPA [Certified Public Accountant], so, you know, obviously that's where they got their math."

Hannah recalled the boredom and ease of her math classes when she used to receive "on-level" instruction (i.e., not specialized for gifted students) in elementary school. She seemed less inclined than did her male counterparts to boast about how easy middle school math came to her, however. Rather, she took pride in the meticulous methods she used to ensure that her mathematics performances were always masterful: "I always show my work. And then I always, usually I always go back to check." Hannah's mother believed her daughter "put that 'work harder' on herself. Because she has really good study habits, and I think that helps her, you know, make the higher marks she has. And she's confident and comfortable with herself and what she knows." Ms. Barkley, who taught both Hannah and Zach, commented on the differences between these two students.

> I think it comes naturally to Hannah, but I think she works harder at it than Zach does. . . . She works a little harder to ensure that she has everything there. Where Zach would be more like, "I've got it. Here it is." . . . Zach can make 100s also, but Hannah would be more likely to have a 100 average.

Their academic records indicated that Zach and Hannah were equally able mathematics students. Hannah, however, seemed prone to attribute her success—and her confidence—to her diligence and effort rather than to an inborn capacity for math, which her male counterparts flaunted. These highly confident boys held what Dweck (2000, 2006) has called an *entity* or *fixed view* of mathematics ability, whereas Hannah tended toward an *incremental* or *growth view*, believing that her ability in math was largely due to effort and hard work—factors she controlled.

Brandy began Grade 8 placed in a prealgebra class after having nearly failed math in Grade 7, but she quickly earned such high marks in Ms. Wheeler's class that her teacher promoted her to algebra. Brandy described her feeling of surprise and praised the skills of her math teacher, Ms. Wheeler, in making math seem effortless.

> Last year my highest grade in math was like a 71, and I had, like, Fs for most of the year and Cs for some parts. I was getting it, but I wasn't really *getting* it. And for this year, to make nothing less than a 90 . . . me and my parents started realizing that it wasn't me. It was the teacher.

Brandy attributed so much of her confidence to her teacher's skills that she worried math might again become difficult for her when she changed schools. "I don't know if all my teachers will be like Ms. Wheeler and make it as easy for me. That kind of scares me."

It was clear that Ms. Wheeler frequently sent Brandy messages that she was capable, but these messages were natural consequences of the routine opportunities for success that Ms. Wheeler structured for her students. What did she do to help students such as Brandy feel confident?

> I try to pace the subject so that it's simple. Little steps. But the thing about teaching math is it's got to be very sequential so that you go from here to here to here. All of a sudden you're way up here and they don't even know it. They'll say, "Oh, this is easy." That's the best compliment they can give me, especially in a high-level class, "That's easy." Because I will say to them, "No, that wasn't easy. You're just smart."

Such a teaching approach is no doubt what Bandura (Evans, 1989) had in mind when he emphasized that "in addition to convincing children they have the capabilities to perform well, one can also structure challenges for them in such a way that they will experience a high level of success" (p. 61). Such an approach was vital in helping Brandy to interpret her successes in math in a way that enhanced her efficacy beliefs.

(Non)Mastery Experiences of Students With Low Self-Efficacy

Unlike their counterparts with high self-efficacy, Tanisha, Arden, Xavier, and Chris described a struggle with mathematics that began or worsened during middle school. For these students, low grades in math and perceived difficulty of math were factors that undermined their beliefs in their capabilities. Arden's low math average at the time of the interview made her aware of the growing conceptual challenge of middle school math, particularly algebra.

> Now it's just all different, and it's so much harder. . . . You, like, have to be perfect on all the fundamentals. Otherwise you won't get anything else. And that kind of stinks because I didn't get some of them.

Arden's mother agreed and added that Arden had struggled with math since elementary school. She blamed a weak third-grade teacher for loosening the already shaky foundation her daughter had in math: "I knew that was a pivotal year. I had heard third grade was, like, a really strong important year, and she had a horrible math teacher." Ms. Matthews, Arden's eighth-grade teacher, also attributed Arden's present difficulties in algebra to the large gaps in Arden's understanding of mathematics: "She has a terrible time with basic skills. I mean, if we ever do anything with fractions, she's lost."

Tanisha recalled the shock of her low math grades: "I never got a C before in my life. That was surprising." Unlike her low-confidence peers, however, Tanisha had experienced a turnaround in eighth grade that both her mother and teacher described as "night and day." But Tanisha believed that any improvement in her math performance was a result of "learning the steps and taking time, because like with other stuff, you can't just *get* math like that. You have to actually take the time and like sit down and like. Mostly everything was quick for me, but math it wasn't like that." Tanisha seemed convinced: "I've always done something wrong in math."

Xavier earned his first F on his report card when he was in seventh-grade math, after which "I just shut down. I just quit believing in myself." For him, the difficulty of math seemed overwhelming and success beyond reach. Note his view of his mathematics ability as a fixed entity. "It's just so hard. I, I don't think I'm smart enough for it or something." His mother sadly recalled the younger Xavier who "used to run in and show me, 'Look Mom, I got a 90 on my math test'" and who now tells himself "'I can't do it.'"

As noted above, math course placement in Grade 8 seemed to communicate important information to students about their mathematics capabilities. At the start of the school year, Arden and Tanisha were placed in algebra and Chris in honors algebra. All earned failing grades. Ms. Matthews, their teacher, recommended that each student move back a level—Arden and Tanisha to prealgebra and Chris to on-level algebra. Tanisha and Chris accepted the recommendation and expressed relief in the higher grades they earned and the better understanding they had of math concepts. As Chris explained, "In the beginning of the year I was in honors. And I flunked it. Like bad. I was in the 40s. But I switched and brought that up." Although he admitted having gaps in his understanding of certain mathematical concepts, such as percentages, he felt he was handling math better than he did initially. Tanisha felt similarly.

Arden, on the other hand, had missed several weeks of school during the first semester because of illness and attributed her failure to her absence. Discouraged and angered by her teacher's suggestions that she move back a level in math, she elected to remain in her algebra class. Ms. Cramer, afraid of crushing her daughter's hope, supported Arden's decision. Ms. Matthews dreaded the long-term consequences this would have for Arden in math:

> I told her mom, "You know, you can leave her in algebra, but I think you're playing games with what kind of confidence she's going to have in the future for math." Just 'cause the age that they're at right now, you know? They're so impressionable. And if Arden decides that she can't do math right now, then she'll probably think that forever.

Arden, nearly in tears, even admitted, "I'm just not doing good. Like since I've not been doing good and not understanding then there's like no confidence. Because I don't think I'm ever going to, like, get it." Though she claimed to put forth great effort in math, her efforts met little success. She longed for a classroom environment that was paced to provide her with frequent mastery opportunities: "I need to take it really slow. Like, I just need to like, you know, step-by-step understand the first concept so that I can understand the fifth one." Unlike the switch that Tanisha and Chris made from their more- to less-advanced math classes, which may have helped them salvage what confidence remained, Arden's choice to continue in algebra left her with skills inadequate for increasingly difficult task demands. Pajares (2006) observed that "academic work should be hard enough that it energizes, not so hard that it paralyzes" (p. 344). The repeated failures Arden described having in algebra may have had a paralyzing effect on her confidence.

Summary of Performance Experiences

Brandy, Hannah, Jamaal, and Zach called on a history of successful performances and their facility with math when describing their self-assuredness. Teachers and parents confirmed the mathematical abilities that these students possessed. Unlike her peers, however, Brandy attributed her recent successes in math to the learning environment provided by her math teacher, Ms. Wheeler, who Brandy maintained was the reason math had become manageable. Whether these students attributed their successes to internal or external, stable or unstable causes, their interpretations of their performances were favorable and self-affirming. Tanisha, Arden, Xavier, and Chris expressed few recollections of past success in math and felt that the increasing rigor of their math coursework revealed their weaknesses. They seemed to interpret the amount of effort math required of them as a sign of their inefficacy. Transferring to another math course level enabled Tanisha and Chris to salvage the belief that they could better handle math; remaining in a math class that was too difficult, on the other hand, left Arden with a crushed sense of efficacy. For Xavier, even the lowest math class seemed to afford few opportunities for success.

Interpretations of Vicarious Experience

Vicarious Experiences of Students With High Self-Efficacy

Vicarious experience from adults. Brandy, Hannah, Jamaal, and Zach each boasted their good fortune to have parents who not only pushed them in math but modeled an interest in the subject themselves. Hannah spoke of how much her mother, a high school algebra and geometry teacher, had helped her with math over the years and mentioned how excited she felt in those rare moments when she caught her mother in error. Brandy's father, an elementary mathematics teacher turned police officer, was fond of setting up math "quizzes" for his daughter at every occasion, particularly when they went shopping. Zach also spoke of his mathematically inclined parents, acknowledging that his mom "used math like every day" and his dad was "a human calculator." Jamaal credited his father with having helped him learn math at a very young age, but he explained that "math's not [my dad's] thing." In fact, Jamaal disclosed, "when my dad was in college, I used to help him with his homework." Although one might assume that seeing his father struggle with math would diminish Jamaal's belief in his own capabilities, just the opposite seemed to happen. Consider how Jamaal made sense of this:

> No one in my family has a math brain that I know of. No one. And I mean, I like to be the one. I would like to be the first one to break the barrier. And that's a little bit of more why I feel confident in it. Because I know that I can, and I have the mind for it.

Comparing his abilities to those of his family members made Jamaal feel more confident that he was (and could be) different.

Vicarious experience from peers. The students with strong confidence in their mathematics abilities made many more comments in reference to peers than to adults. In line with Bandura's (1997) theorizing that people typically compare themselves "to particular associates in similar situations, such as classmates, work associates, competitors, or people in other settings engaged in similar endeavors" (p. 87), all four seemed keenly aware of how their own performances compared with those of their classmates. Brandy noted, "I think I'm one of the people who gets it the easiest in math, 'cause at my table I'm always the first, and like my other partners are like, 'What's the answer? How'd you get that?'" She also spoke of her delight in outperforming her tenth-grade brother in math. Zach hesitated to rate his math confidence as a 10 out of 10 because he was aware of "some people in my class that always get everything. We'll just be starting it, and they can get it in, like, a second." Although he viewed himself as "better than most eighth graders" at math, being able to think of students who were more capable was enough to temper Zach's estimation of his own abilities.

Of all the students interviewed, Jamaal seemed to rely most on vicarious information from peers when evaluating his self-efficacy in math. He described himself as highly competitive, noting that he and his math class-mates often compared test grades to see who scored the highest. As if to indicate how much this fueled the competitive thrill, Jamaal reminded me that he was "in some pretty tough classes with some pretty smart people." In fact, Hannah and Jamaal, who were in the same class, both mentioned the remarkable performance of one particular fellow competitor, Stacey, who scored 100% on an important statewide test.

> I was real mad when Stacey had got a 100. I wasn't really mad, but I was kind of jealous. Like I envied it. Like I wished I was that one that got 100. I mean sometimes, now that, *that's* one of the things that give me the extra drive. That gives me the extra determination to work harder in math to get good grades like everyone else. (Jamaal)

Ms. Barkley, Jamaal's math teacher, pointed out the extraordinary degree to which Jamaal was "aware of the people around him. I think that's just the nature of him." And Jamaal's mother, who was no doubt even more aware of this nature, emphasized that the main reason she and her husband enrolled Jamaal in the district's M-to-M bussing program was to expose him to the challenge of learning alongside more accomplished peers. She explained, "I want him to compete. I want him to know that there's somebody out there that knows a lot more than you. Get with them. Ask them how do they do that." Jamaal's mother seemed to echo the observation made by William James (1899) more than a century ago that "the deepest spring of action in us is the sight of action in another" (p. 27).

Vicarious experience from self. Individuals often rely on personal comparative information or on cognitive self-modeling when forming beliefs about their capabilities (Bandura, 1997). Several such modeling experiences were important to Brandy, Hannah, and Jamaal. Hannah's beliefs about her math capability seemed directly tied to her internal standards. For instance, in an off-hand but telling remark, she recalled how sad she felt when she once earned an 89% on a math test. Her teacher, Ms. Barkley, referred to Hannah as a "perfectionist," someone likely to always say to herself convincingly, "Certainly I can do a little bit better." Hannah's mother echoed this observation and described her daughter as someone who placed a great deal of pressure on herself to excel in everything she set out to do.

Brandy was able to recite the internal dialogue she often had about her math work, specifying that one of the sources of her confidence was "my own conscience telling me that I can do it." She feared that students her age "put more pressure on ourselves than we actually need to. Like, we always thinking of the down side of things. Like on tests, 'What if I fail?' not, 'I can do this. I am going to pass.'" Jamaal took similar refuge in his internal dialogue:

> I'll be like, "Come on." I'll be thinking about different ways to solve problems and stuff like that. I'll be saying, "Come on, Jamaal, you can do this," and stuff like that. . . . I don't know what it does, but it's just like extra comfort to me.

Vicarious Experiences for Students With Low Self-Efficacy

Vicarious experience from adults. The students who reported low mathematics self-efficacy each characterized their own mothers (and sometimes both parents) as being deficient in math. Arden reported feeling frustrated when her parents could not help her understand math homework problems. Her mother confessed her own poor performance in and distaste for middle and high school math: "You know, when I was in school, I thought the same thing [as my daughter]. Especially algebra." Similarly, Xavier noted that his mom "said she even had problems with math. She said math was her worst subject." Ms. Relaford, Xavier's mother, admitted frustration in guiding her son mathematically: "I don't know how to do algebra. That was not my forte." Tanisha, who said her mother "was probably like me in school," added that her aunt sometimes tried to encourage her by recounting her own struggle in math. And although Chris made clear his admiration of his older brother and his father, neither was available to Chris as a role model in mathematics. Overall, these students were in want of people at home who could model for them the skills and strategies they needed to succeed in math.

Vicarious experience from peers. Though Tanisha, Arden, Xavier, and Chris reported fewer peer-referential self-judgments, they generally compared themselves unfavorably with more-capable peers. Arden, who remained in the on-level algebra class all year despite her failure, confessed that she often realized how much better her classmates were doing at math than she was. Watching classmates who were more competent made her feel "shamed . . . because, like, if they get it, I should get it." She was chagrined by how quickly her friends grasped new concepts and, by contrast, how long it took her to understand. Ms. Cramer, Arden's mother, recalled the turn for the worse Arden's self-efficacy took when, in Grade 4, Arden was one of only two students in her class who did not qualify for the school's talented and gifted program. For Arden this meant being left in her regular classroom one day a week while her talented and gifted classmates went on enrichment excursions elsewhere. Bandura (1997) has observed that such "evaluative school practices quickly impose comparative appraisals whether children like it or not" (p. 92). Indeed, Ms. Cramer marked this as the time when Arden began referring to herself as "the dumb one."

After Tanisha moved back from algebra to prealgebra in the early part of the school year, her teacher noticed that she continued making referential comparisons to her *former* algebra classmates, and this seemed to be the measuring stick by which Tanisha judged her own competency in math. Researchers have noted that people tend to look to individuals who are similar or slightly higher in ability when making self-comparative evaluations (Bandura, 1997; Wheeler & Suls, 2005). Tanisha listened carefully to what these more advanced students had to say about their experiences in the algebra class, believing that it would help her determine how well equipped she was to face algebra again in ninth grade.

> Some of my friends tell me about [algebra], and, you know, some of their tests that they told me about, they said it was hard. But, you know, that's kind of what makes me feel like I'm not going to do good in it. Because, like, if they can't do it, then I probably can't do it.

Likewise, Chris compared himself negatively to his classmates. His teacher, Ms. Matthews, noted that he often grumbled in class, "I don't get it. I'm the only one in here who doesn't get it." Xavier indicated that he felt similarly in ability to the students in his prealgebra class, but he lowered his estimate when asked how he compared to all students in eighth grade. "I probably would take myself down to like 2 to 4 [out of 10] 'cause there's a lot of kids that's in TAG and like honors algebra and stuff." He added that most of his friends were better at math than he was.

Vicarious experience from self. Of the four students with low self-efficacy, only Arden and Chris identified using cognitive self-modeling strategies to shore up their math confidence. Arden said that she "just kind of keep[s] telling myself that I'll do OK" as a way of "keeping my confidence up." Unfortunately, this strategy did little to ensure a better performance in math, which often shocked her. "I get [my work] back, and it's like, all wrong."

By his own admission, Chris often became angry with himself and others when he encountered difficulty in math. He made an effort to describe his internal dialogue. "I batter myself a lot. I tell myself, 'Why don't you do this crap? Why don't you study?'" Toward the end of our interview, a puzzled look came over his face as he struggled to explain this source of his confidence in math. Evaluating his math confidence was based

> more [on] what I tell myself. It's not as much as, you know, my grades and what teachers tell me, it's more like, you know, me saying, "Okay, I messed this test up, but you know, I can study and do better on the next one," instead of, you know, "What the heck is this?"

He realized that his tendency to select and to replay negative experiences was central, and detrimental, to his sense of efficacy in math. This cognitive reframing may be adaptive for Chris in that it serves to protect his self-esteem by allowing him to attribute his poor performance to external, changeable factors such as poor study skills or lack of effort (Dweck, 2006). In this way, Chris may be psychologically reserving space for his self-efficacy beliefs to return.

Summary of Vicarious Experience

Students were able to shed light on the relative importance of the multiple forms vicarious experiences can take. They relied on modeled information from parents, peers, and self to inform their confidence judgments. The heuristics students described using when interpreting this information makes evident the danger inherent in relying solely on observed or self-rated experience when assessing vicarious experience. Though, in general, exposure to incompetent math models at home lowered youngsters' sense of efficacy, this was not always the case. Jamaal was able to construe his parents' inaptitude for math in a way that boosted his belief that he could be different. This observation is consistent with social cognitive theory and Bandura's (1997) admonition that "a host of personal, social, and situational factors affect how direct and socially mediated experiences are cognitively interpreted" (p. 79). Talking to Jamaal revealed that his appraisal of his family members' struggles with math coupled with his own successes provided him with evidence that he was different, and quite capable.

Each of the eight students interviewed seemed particularly attentive to how their peers were faring in mathematics and used this information as a basis by which to gauge their own math capabilities. Interestingly, however, only those students with high self-efficacy reported a competitive drive to outperform others. The four with low self-efficacy seemed convinced of their relative inferiority in mathematics, particularly when comparing themselves with slightly more capable peers.

The rare glimpses Brandy, Jamaal, Arden, and Chris were able to offer of what they say and think to themselves when doing mathematics indicated that the mental models students create may serve to nourish (or undermine) beliefs about their own capabilities. Purkey (2000) contended that "positive and realistic self-talk contributes to human dignity and personal efficacy" (p. 2) and that the responsibility of ensuring that students talk to themselves about themselves in positive ways rests not only with the student but with the family and school as well. Sadly, if negative self-messages are not properly redirected, they may chip away at the potential beneficial effects of even the smallest academic victory.

Interpretations of Social Persuasions

Social Persuasions for Students With High Self-Efficacy

Social persuasions from adults. Brandy, Hannah, Jamaal, and Zach each mentioned that encouragement from their teachers and parents helped them feel confident in math. Brandy and Jamaal held their current math teachers in highest esteem and viewed them as vital to their success. In fact, Brandy credited Ms. Wheeler's frequent support with having abolished Brandy's own negative view about her math capabilities and with having altered her outlook about math itself.

> Ms. Wheeler always says, "You can do this, guys. You can do this." Every time you tell somebody they can do it, they're going to start to believe it, and they're going to start to want to do it more and want to be better than what they are.

Ms. Wheeler described Brandy as someone who did not "fit the mold" of students in her algebra class because "she doesn't act like she has a brain in her head at times, and then the next thing you know, she's aced the test." She added that Brandy was in an ethnic minority and that, because of this, she viewed Brandy's success in a different light. "It's very unusual to find a child like that in a higher-level class getting an A. So she sticks [out] . . . there it is. I'm looking at that going, 'there's a kid I could help get a scholarship.'"

Early in the school year, when Ms. Wheeler taught Brandy in prealgebra, she noticed a student in need of "refinement"; she believed she saw a diamond in the rough. She quickly placed Brandy in a higher-level math class and began to interact with Brandy in a way that served as a powerful social persuasion. Researchers have long contended that the expectations teachers hold for their students influence a number of classroom practices, such as verbal and nonverbal communication, differentiated instruction, level of challenge, classroom climate, and grading procedures (Good, 1987; Rosenthal, 2002). Having been handpicked by her teacher for refinement during eighth grade may well have been for Brandy a social persuasion that changed her academic trajectory.

Ms. Barkley had a similar, though less explicit, view about helping Jamaal in math. She was afraid that a well-behaved student such as Jamaal could easily "get lost in the shuffle. At the very beginning of the year I don't think I knew how smart Jamaal was because he wasn't showing it until I learned him." She lamented the fact that many teachers do not take the harder road of "learning" their students, which for her entailed paying closer attention to them and enabling them to give all that they are able to give. It was this personal attention that Jamaal said made Ms. Barkley "one of my favorite math teachers that I've ever had in my whole life." He heralded his teacher as someone who was natural to talk to and who always structured lessons in a way that guaranteed each student's understanding. Ms. Barkley, a highly respected teacher and chair of the mathematics department at CMS, described her goal to help all students feel capable. First and foremost, she identified the perils of a fixed-ability mindset.

> How many times do you hear people say, "I was never good at math. I don't understand it." If you can get them to think, "Hmm. I can understand this," then you've probably raised their confidence level by 50% just by thinking they can.

I asked Ms. Barkley what she thought was the best way to raise math confidence. "I guess you just try to keep making successful situations until they feel like Zach and Hannah."

To be sure, for Zach and Hannah, social persuasions from Ms. Barkley came as a natural product of the students' masterful math performances. Their many achievements meant that they were no strangers to external recognition from other sources too. Not only did both students mention the good feeling of being praised by their teachers in class; Hannah received the top school-wide academic honor at CMS in Grade 7, and Zach received a $50 monetary award from his parents each time he earned all As on his report card.

Brandy and Jamaal also expressed the importance of their parents' persuasions, although these messages carried a different tenor. Brandy noted that her mother's encouragement often contained the message that "everything's not going to be easy and not going to get handed to you every time you need it. You're gonna have to get your head on your shoulders and know what you want and go for it." She said that her mom had been through many challenges of her own and wanted Brandy to learn how to handle her struggles well. Jamaal's mother, who gave birth to Jamaal while herself a junior in high school, also spoke of how she and her husband urged their son toward a better path—one that would present obstacles that he must overcome.

> Well we're telling him that in this society, and I'm not going to say that racism is, it's still alive, but it's hidden. So being a Black man, you have to go that extra mile. You have to prove yourself. You have to prove a point. You have to prove that you want this and you're good at it. You're good at everything that you do. Whatever you touch is golden. So you have to believe that. And you have to go that extra mile to prove that.

Jamaal seemed particularly attentive to the messages from his father:

> [My dad] tells me all the time he lives his life vicariously through me. So he wants me to do things that he wasn't able to do, like play sports and be good at math, 'cause he's smart, but math's not his thing. And he also don't want me to make some of the mistakes that he made when he was young, so he tries to keep me out of trouble a lot.

Encouragement from his family was one source that gave Jamaal "that extra push," he told me, "but not enough to do my homework," he added parenthetically with a grin.

Some researchers have observed that African American students' academic self-efficacy beliefs in particular have profited from the persuasive messages sent by members of the African American community—teachers and parents in particular (e.g., Usher & Pajares, 2006). Walker (2000) noted that, historically, African American schools were driven by forms of interpersonal and institutional caring that conveyed to students that they were capable of achieving, despite the negative messages those students received in the larger world (see also Hughes et al., 2006). In other words, the positive social persuasions operating at a local level may have served to immunize African American students against some of the negative messages they received from the broader culture. The stories told by Brandy and Ms. Wheeler and by Jamaal, his parents, and Ms. Barkley suggest that, though these African American students may have received the same quantity of positive feedback for their academic work as did their White peers, the *quality* of that feedback was quite different, and its influence was more pervasive.

300

Social persuasions from peers. Brandy, Hannah, Jamaal, and Zach reported that they were often solicited for help by their classmates and peers, which gave them a psychological boost. Hannah recalled being asked during homeroom, "Why do you have to be so smart?" Brandy and Jamaal described friends who were envious of their success, and both mentioned that some peers called them names or otherwise tried to bring them down. Jamaal's mother remembered how much Jamaal was teased during elementary school because "it was not cool to be smart down south [in the district's lower-achieving schools]." Jamaal and Brandy felt that setting high personal goals protected them from feeling bothered by the taunting. "I know being smart will help me in the long run," said Brandy. "I'm keeping [my grades] up for college and scholarships. And just going forward in life."

Social Persuasions for Students With Low Self-Efficacy

Social persuasions from adults. Tanisha, Arden, Xavier, and Chris recounted tales of social persuasions from adults that ranged from empowering to demoralizing. Tanisha made significant progress in math during eighth grade and felt the accompanying pride of her teacher and family. Her mother was thrilled with Tanisha's improvement but noted that her daughter remained more attuned to her teacher's praise than to her family's. Indeed, Tanisha attributed her new-found confidence in math to the evaluative feedback she received on her work. Arden, on the other hand, expressed anger at her algebra teacher, Ms. Matthews, for having suggested early in the school year that she drop back to a prealgebra class. Her mother explained that Ms. Matthews's recommendation became to Arden like a looping vote of no confidence made more salient with every passing day. Consequently, her mother added, Arden had to pay the psychological cost of always feeling that "Ms. Matthews thinks I shouldn't be in here."

Chris expressed frustration that neither his parents nor his math teacher understood his needs. Although he was careful to point out that Ms. Matthews, his teacher, did not overtly discourage him, her impatience with his questions made him "feel low about what I can do." Pajares (2006) observed that "successful persuaders cultivate young people's beliefs in their capabilities while ensuring that the envisioned success is attainable" (p. 349). It seemed that the approach Ms. Matthews thought best fell short of enabling Chris to envision his own success. Instead, he became more convinced of his own inadequacy.

But Ms. Matthews was not the only person who fell short in persuading Chris that he was capable in math. He was aggravated by his parents' "theory that I'm a prodigy 'cause I did good in elementary school and I do good on big standardized tests. I wouldn't say I'm dumb, but I'm not a genius. I can't do everything right all the time." For him, the burden of his parents' high expectations coupled with their rare words of encouragement also diminished his belief that he could ever be successful in math.

Discouraging comments seemed to be the most consequential source of Xavier's low self-efficacy. When I asked him to describe what led him to "shut down" in math a year earlier, he explained,

> I just quit believing in myself. I just felt like no one was believing in me. And at that point my brother, he wasn't there. He was in college. And I just didn't think no one was believing in me, so I was just thinking, why would I, why should I believe in myself when no one was, you know, believing in me?

Xavier confided that a week prior to our interview, his mother told him that she did not understand why he was spending time studying for the state standardized math exam. He was overcome with emotion as he struggled to repeat his mother's words to me: "'You ain't gonna pass it anyway,' she said." His teacher, Ms. Matthews, also believed Xavier's low confidence stemmed from home and that "when he comes [to school] it's kind of like a self-fulfilling prophecy. He just assumes that he can't do it, so he just doesn't do it." Paradoxically, Ms. Matthews seemed to have long since thrown in the proverbial towel with Xavier. She made her own frustration and despair toward her student clear when I asked her to describe how she envisioned Xavier's future. She chuckled,

> Jail. I mean, I hate to say that, but I don't think that he'll go anywhere. I mean, there's some kids that you just can't save. For me, Xavier is that kid. I mean there is nothing that I say to him that seems to matter.

Though he made no mention of discouraging remarks from his teacher, Xavier said he yearned for someone who would take a more active role in his learning to ensure that he was grasping each concept. These multiple perspectives reveal how unaware each person was of the other.

Social persuasions from peers. Unlike their counterparts with high self-efficacy, Tanisha, Arden, Xavier, and Chris made few comments about messages that their age-mates sent them about their mathematics capabilities, and these comments were mixed. For example, Arden believed that support from her peers helped her feel better about her prospects in math. She often mentioned a few close friends who encouraged her in math. Xavier, on the other hand, received negative messages from peers about his math performance. "I thought I was good in math, but then people was telling me that I wasn't good. They would be like, 'You ain't good at math. I don't even know why you're doing it.'"

Summary of Social Persuasions

The persuasive messages that almost always accompany school success seemed to be noticeable and beneficial to students with high self-efficacy. Students with low self-efficacy rarely reported hearing such messages and instead remarked that receiving little or no positive feedback curtailed their beliefs about their own capabilities. Brandy and Jamaal were fueled by their parents' persuasive coaching that they could reach their goals and even surpass the achievements of others. An equally important social injunction accompanied these messages of encouragement. The opposite was true for Xavier, who had become convinced that his mother did not believe that he could ever be successful in math. Unlike any other student I interviewed, Xavier seemed particularly bothered by the negative comments peers made about his math performance.

Construal of Physiological and Affective Information

Physiological and Affective States of Students With High Self-Efficacy

Brandy, Hannah, Jamaal, and Zach generally felt content in math, even eager to attend math class each day. They otherwise described their physiological arousal in math in terms of the discomfort they felt when confronting the unknown. Note how Jamaal described feeling when his math teacher introduced a new topic.

> Whenever we change subjects, I always start confused. And whenever I get confused, I get real tense. When we first started learning circles, I was so lost and confused I got hives and started sweating. I couldn't think straight. But other than that, I feel, I mean, I'm happy in math class. Math makes my day a lot of times.

Despite his occasional disequilibrium, Jamaal said he never doubted his capability to understand a math concept. Nor did tests arouse particular anxiety. "I take tests real good, so I don't get, like, tensed up. But it's just, I'm very curious before I take the test because I want to know what's on it." Perhaps the most palpable irritation Ms. Barkley conveyed during our interviews was with Zach's insatiable need to rectify immediately any discrepancy between what he understood and what was being presented to him. In fact, by Zach's and his mother's admission, Zach's intense anticipation and curiosity made him prone to quick frustration when his questions were not answered at once or when he did not understand what he missed on a test.

Brandy expressed a tendency to feel nervous before a test, particularly before standardized math tests used to determine course placement or promotion. She said she had to calm herself down before undertaking such evaluations—until she met her teacher, Ms. Wheeler, who had a clever way of reducing students' apprehension prior to tests.

> It makes it easy. Ms. Wheeler doesn't call it a test. She says, "It's a quiz, it's a worksheet, it's whatever you want it to be. Just make sure you do your best. It's a puzzle, it's a game. Just do your best." And [on] most tests she doesn't even put the word "Test" on it, or she doesn't tell us it's a test. It takes the pressure off so you can think about what you're doing more.

As a consequence, Brandy felt able to approach math tests unruffled, with the simple aim of doing her best rather than beset by doubts that she would fail. She described her math class as "a fun place to be."

Physiological and Affective States of Students With Low Self-Efficacy

The physiological and affective states that Tanisha, Arden, Xavier, and Chris experienced in math ranged from depression and apathy to anger and stress. Xavier's mother referred to his academic "depression," which she said was a result of having failed time and time again. Indeed, by his own account, depression seemed to dominate his approach to math. "I got self-esteem issues I think. 'Cause sometimes I think I can do it, and then, like another time I just be like totally down. 'I can't do this.'" Ms. Matthews proclaimed that Xavier showed extreme fatigue in her class, often putting his head down and sleeping when faced with material he felt was too confusing. During the week of our interview, Xavier reportedly slept through most of the standardized tests being given in school.

By all accounts, Chris approached his difficulties in math with impatience, agitation, and rage. He said that doing poorly in math made him "want to, like, throw the desk across the room," and that when he got angry, "I kind of shut down." Chris also vented his frustration with Ms. Matthews: "I get really, really, really, irritated with teachers when they won't help." When he became angry, he said he would purposefully skip help sessions or would not complete his homework. His mother described how Chris bunched up paper or slammed his book shut when he experienced difficulty. "He just gets really stressed out. You can just see. He gets angry. Chris has a temper." I happened to be standing outside Chris's math class as he finished a test the day of our interview. Clearly distressed, he had erased a hole in his paper and had to exchange his test for a new copy. I asked his teacher about this. Ms. Matthews explained that this was a typical test-taking experience for Chris, likely prompted because "he's pissed off at himself that he doesn't know how to do it. Or that he's not sure about it." Chris's agitation seemed to portend the negative performances he dreaded.

Arden depicted herself as having always had a negative attitude toward math. To those with whom she was completely honest, she said she described math this way: "'I hate it. It's horrible. I don't understand it. Ms. Matthews isn't doing it right. Or, I'm just falling short.' Or like, 'I don't understand it at all and I hate it and it's boring.'" She felt "extremely pressured" by the high-stakes standardized tests on which failure meant retention. She also described how difficult it was for her to remain focused in math.

After Tanisha did what her teacher called "a 180," she stopped laying her head down on her desk and started paying attention in math class. The only worry that Tanisha expressed about math was in regard to ninth-grade algebra. Her difficulty understanding algebra concepts at the beginning of eighth grade invoked a dread that she would "freak out" when encountering the concepts again the next year.

Summary of Construal of Physiological and Affective States

All students expressed at least brief moments of heightened physiological and affective arousal in mathematics. Only the students with low self-efficacy, however, interpreted this as a sign of incompetence. This is likely because of the degree of arousal students experienced. Bandura (1997) noted that "as a general rule, moderate levels of arousal heighten attentiveness and facilitate deployment of skills, whereas high arousal disrupts the quality of functioning" (p. 106). The uncomfortable cognitive dissonance described by students with high self-efficacy likely facilitated the acquisition of new skills. The arousal subsided as soon as students were able to reach a firmer understanding of new material or dissonant feedback. For the students with low self-efficacy, however, and particularly for the boys, their construal of physiological information left them with less confidence and impaired functioning. As Bandura observed, "By conjuring up aversive thoughts about their ineptitude and stress reactions, people can rouse themselves to elevated levels of distress that produce the very dysfunctions they fear" (p. 106).

Self-Regulated Learning

As each interview was analyzed, it became evident how much students with high and low self-efficacy differed in the degree to which they felt able to (and perhaps were urged to) regulate their own learning. For most students, the ability to self-regulate one's own learning was directly related to self-efficacy and to its sources—mastery experience and physiological arousal in particular.

Self-Regulated Learning for Students With High Self-Efficacy

Of the eight students interviewed, none was as self-regulated as Hannah, who described her "obsessive" need to rewrite her math notes until they were perfect. Hannah approached her math work in a systematic manner, always well in advance of her next class. "I'm, like, dedicated to do my math homework," she explained, adding that she completed problems from easiest to most difficult, showing her work at every step, and rechecking each problem after she had reached the end of the assignment. Ms. Barkley characterized Hannah as "a very meticulous math student. Every step written down neatly, explicitly, and usually correctly." Ms. Murphy, Hannah's mother, mentioned that in the summer Hannah would complete packets of enrichment math work, wait a month, and then review them all again before school started to be sure she remembered the skills she acquired. Such habits helped Hannah approach her math class with confidence. Hannah added that when she encountered a math concept that posed any difficulty for her, she would face the challenge directly by finding similar problems to work through. Self-regulated learning was a means of equilibrating her confidence, reducing her anxiety, and ensuring her own mastery of the material.

Zach described a systematic approach to completing his homework, which he did "before anything else" each afternoon. His mother added that "it is just a given in our house. It's just a given. When they were little, they would come home, have a snack, do their homework." Until they were older, she explained, her children would be required to sit at the table until homework was complete. She said this habit had become so ingrained in them that she never needed to check for homework completion anymore. Hannah's mother described a similar expectation in her household. Brandy had a habit of completing her math homework at school to avoid having to do it late in the evening after her long bus ride. Each of these strategies helped students approach math class prepared to face new lessons.

Unlike his high self-efficacy counterparts, Jamaal admitted that his work habits were deficient. Both he and his mother described him as "lazy" with his academic work. An avid athlete, Jamaal acknowledged that he often viewed math homework as an unnecessary review and that, as long as his grades were high, he need not waste much time on it. As his interest grew in football and social activities, completing math homework came at an increasingly high cost. This shift in values likely led Jamaal to minimize time spent on math outside school (Wigfield, Hoa, & Klauda, 2008). When I asked him whether he felt he was capable of being the top math student in his school, Jamaal assured me that, but for his poor self-regulation, he was certain he could. And his work habits, he was sure, were within his control.

Self-Regulated Learning for Students With Low Self-Efficacy

Tanisha, Arden, Xavier, and Chris expressed having great difficulty regulating their work in mathematics. Arden described her difficulty staying focused in class when the material did not make sense to her. "I just kind of block it out, I guess. And like, I take notes and stuff, but when you go back and read those, those don't help at all." Although she and her mother claimed she attended extra help sessions offered by her teacher, Ms. Matthews had not seen Arden after school for several months. Arden's involvement in the school play had required her to considerably reduce the time she spent on schoolwork. Her trouble attending to lectures, her poor note taking, and the fact that she had missed extra help sessions meant a shaky foundation for Arden in math.

Chris also found more appealing ways to spend his time than doing math homework. He explained that the good intentions he had of doing his homework each day were usually thwarted by e-mail, computer games, and his guitar, activities that were more valuable to him. Ms. Matthews was aware of the problem.

> He just needs to get his organization together because that would help him study. I really think that's where, that's like the missing piece with him. So if he could just fall in line with his homework, and practice it the way that it needs to be practiced, then when he gets to the test he would say, "Oh, I've done this five times. I know how to do it now."

Similarly, Tanisha and her mother and teacher blamed Tanisha's early failure in math on her poor study habits during the first semester of the school year. Her mother was encouraged to see Tanisha's gradual improvements.

Xavier's work habits had only worsened, however. His mother complained of having to punish her son to motivate him to complete any of his work. She was also uncertain as to whether Xavier was attending math help sessions or the school's free Saturday math tutorial. According to Xavier, his "slacking off" was the reason that he did not make it into algebra in eighth grade. His teacher agreed. "I would say 70–80% of [Xavier's trouble in math] is due to work habits, because I think that he could do it if he tried." His poor study habits were a part of the self-fulfilling prophecy she felt she was witnessing.

Summary of Self-Regulatory Information

The relationship between self-efficacy beliefs and self-regulatory processes has been shown to be reciprocal in nature, such that altering students' self-regulatory processes can change their self-perceptions and vice versa (Zimmerman, 2008; Zimmerman & Cleary, 2006). Students' ability to self-regulate their mathematics learning may have supported their mathematics self-efficacy beliefs. Those who struggled to maintain a habitual study place and time, who lacked organizational skills, and who had difficulty following material covered in class were those whose self-efficacy beliefs also suffered. To the contrary, the strong self-regulatory skills that most students with high self-efficacy displayed may have helped them approach math with greater confidence. As theorized by Bandura (1997), students are unlikely to implement self-regulatory learning strategies unless they possess a belief that they will be successful in doing so. The increase of competing demands for students' time and attention may encroach on the time students spend and the value they place on math. Additional research should target the sources of students' beliefs in their efficacy to manage these interfering factors.

Conclusions

The central goal of this study was to use qualitative methods to investigate the rules or heuristics that students with high and low self-efficacy use to select and interpret information related to their mathematics self-efficacy. The study's findings demonstrate that students with high mathematics self-efficacy also reported having high levels of achievement in mathematics, and students with low self-efficacy recounted their poor performance and struggles. This observation is consistent with Bandura's (1997) social cognitive theory, which posits that the interpretations students make of their past successes and failures serve as an important source of information about their efficacy. Mastery experience has also emerged as a powerful source of self-efficacy in both quantitative and qualitative investigations in this academic domain (e.g., Lent et al., 1996; Lopez, Lent, Brown, & Gore, 1997; and see

Usher & Pajares, in press). When students feel they have mastered requisite subskills, when they have accomplished difficult tasks, when they interpret performances as successful, they develop a robust belief in their personal efficacy (Bandura, 1997). If this is the case, teachers of mathematics should take care to deliver instruction in such a way as to maximize the opportunity for "*authentic* mastery experiences," however small (Pajares, 2006, p. 344). Helping students acquire a sense of mastery often requires ingenuity, patience, and perseverance and should not be confused with artificial attempts to boost students' self-esteem by assigning work that provides little challenge or satisfaction.

Results from this study also reveal that students do not uniquely rely on their own experiential repertoire in mathematics to refine their efficacy judgments. Models provide opportunities for vicarious learning. Recall that Jamaal interpreted his parents' failures in mathematics as compelling evidence that he could be different, that he had what it takes to succeed. Quantitative methods that have typically been used to investigate the sources (e.g., correlational/regression analyses that assume the successful experiences of social models are positively related to self-efficacy) would not have revealed why or how students such as Jamaal interpret the unsuccessful experiences of others in such a way as to *enhance* self-efficacy. As this and other qualitative studies have demonstrated, people often rely on the experiences of others to refine beliefs in their own capabilities (e.g., Zeldin & Pajares, 2000). With careful thought, quantitative methods could be designed that may permit a better understanding of these relationships on a larger scale.

Similarly, qualitative inquiry revealed that Brandy credited her teacher's ability to provide her with opportunities for successive attainments as essential to improving her mathematics competency. As Brandy explained, Ms. Wheeler provided both the skill transmission and the social validation that were instrumental in building her own sense of competence during eighth grade. Although quantitative and qualitative findings would have likely converged on this point, the perspective gained from conversing with Brandy and her teacher enables outsiders to catch a glimpse of the ways in which a teacher's pedagogical approach nurtured her student's perceptions of mastery in a manner that was maximally persuasive.

One new and potentially important finding emerged from students' interpretations of their physiological and affective arousal in math. Students with high self-efficacy framed their bouts of heightened arousal in ways that were motivating; those with low self-efficacy experienced a level of distress that left them feeling disheartened and often paralyzed. This observation underscores the complexity of physiological and affective arousal as a source of self-efficacy and calls into question findings from quantitative research that have shown no relationship between arousal and self-efficacy. As Bandura (1997) asserted, the relationship between physiological arousal and self-efficacy may not always be negative or linear and therefore may need to be modeled more flexibly in quantitative research.

Qualitative inquiry also clarified links between self-efficacy and self-regulation. It may come as little surprise that most students with high self-efficacy proactively rely on a stock of self-regulatory skills when learning math. Those with low self-efficacy struggled to manage their math work and rarely sought help from teachers. Self-efficacious students are more likely to use cognitive and metacognitive strategies in the classroom than are those who doubt their competence (Zimmerman & Schunk, 2008). Likewise, helping students become better self-regulators of their learning can increase their self-efficacy perceptions (e.g., Schunk & Lilly, 1984; Schunk & Swartz, 1993; Zimmerman & Bandura, 1994; Zimmerman & Kitsantas, 1999).

Several interviews in this study revealed that, consistent with theorists' contentions, the message students send themselves—the internal dialogues—are related to their beliefs about their mathematics capabilities (Bandura, 1997; Purkey, 2000). Bandura (1997) included *cognitive self-modeling*—visualization of one's own self coping in diverse situations and under challenging circumstances—as a part of vicarious experiences. He argued that individuals find satisfaction and confidence when they "visualize themselves repeatedly confronting and mastering progressively more challenging or threatening situations" (p. 95). Self-talk and self-modeling may be part of a student's larger repertoire of self-regulatory skills. Both Brandy and Jamaal were able to coach themselves through difficulties. Having a stock of such self-regulatory strategies served to put into place for some students what Zimmerman and Kitsantas (2005) called a *self-empowering cycle* that enhances both confidence and competence in mathematics. The preliminary findings in this study pave the way for future efforts to investigate the benefits that students might gain from envisioning their own success.

Findings from this study point to the significance of contextual influences in the formation of self-efficacy beliefs, in this case, course placement and assignment. Parents, teachers, and students alike noted this importance. Such designations can carry with them information from all four hypothesized sources of self-efficacy. Being enrolled in geometry in eighth grade and the talented and gifted program served as a boost and a confirmation to Hannah, Jamaal, and Zach that they were ahead of most students their age. Jamaal seemed to thrive on the competitive environment in his geometry class. Brandy was promoted from prealgebra to algebra during the school year, which sent her a powerful persuasive message that she was capable. Chris and Tanisha moved back a level in mathematics after experiencing difficulty at the beginning of the year. The move left them able to review concepts that they would need for mastery of more-complex skills and hence provided them with more opportunities for mastery. For Arden, however, remaining in algebra despite her teacher's plea that she move back a level only reinforced her sense of inefficacy. If Arden's mother was correct, this self-doubt traced back to when Arden did not qualify for placement in the school's talented and gifted program in elementary school.

Interviews with teachers and parents provided a unique look at the complex environments in which self-efficacy beliefs take root. One implication to emerge from these interviews is that teachers and parents should become more aware of the messages—both explicit and implicit—that they send to students, for these messages might travel with students for the rest of their lives, framing their interpretations of information related to their academic competence. Indeed, college students and adults have illustrated the lingering, potent effects of the messages significant others sent them during their childhood and adolescence about their academic capabilities (Pajares, 1994; Zeldin & Pajares, 2000).

Other conversations served as a reminder that praise can have unintended effects. Recall Zach's mother, the CPA who praised her son for his good fortune in being born with an ability for math. "Either you have it or you don't in math," she claimed. Parents who communicate a belief to their children that mathematics (or any other) ability is a fixed entity and that success reflects ability simultaneously send the message that failure reflects a *lack* of ability, a message that can have problematic consequences for motivation (Molden & Dweck, 2006). These students may tend to frame difficulties as evidence that they lack natural ability (Dweck & Leggett, 1988). Consequently, this fixed-ability mindset makes "confidence and motivation more fragile" (Dweck, 2006, p. 205). Helping all students believe that academic competencies can be improved through effort and perseverance enables them to interpret efficacy-relevant information adaptively, thereby safeguarding their self-efficacy (Schunk, 2008).

An additional aim of this study was to examine whether students appear to interpret the sources of self-efficacy differently as a function of their gender or race. Few qualitative differences in boys' and girls' remarks about their sense of competence in mathematics emerged, though girls generally reported being better self-regulators than did boys. This is in contrast to interview results with women and men who pursued careers in mathematics, science, or technology and who interpreted the sources of self-efficacy quite differently (Zeldin et al., 2007; Zeldin & Pajares, 2000). Women interpreted vicarious experience and social persuasions as the most influential sources of self-efficacy, whereas men attended more to their mastery experiences. Interestingly, teachers and parents of the eighth-grade students in this study were more likely to attribute girls' successes in mathematics to hard work than to ability. They spoke of girls' conscientiousness in mathematics, which often manifested in girls' expressed fear of failure. Teachers and parents rarely questioned boys' mathematics ability but emphasized their surprise that boys could get by in mathematics despite their substandard work habits. It is difficult to conclude how these messages might be transmitted to children and what, if any, long-term effects they might have, but, as already noted, teachers and parents should closely examine the messages they may be sending to these youngsters. As all of the adults in this study were women, future research might target male perspectives on these issues.

I also analyzed the data for possible differences in the way African American and White students talked about their self-beliefs in mathematics.

The greatest distinction I observed in participants' comments was the emphasis that Jamaal, Brandy, and Xavier placed on the social persuasions they received from their parents and teachers. Quantitative findings have also indicated that social persuasions are an important source of academic self-efficacy for African American middle school students (Usher & Pajares, 2006). Both Ms. Wheeler and Ms. Haines underscored their belief that encouragement is central to fostering African American students' beliefs in their academic capabilities. It remains less clear whether African American students receive the messages sent to them in qualitatively different ways, though this would be an important question to examine further.

Limitations

I made every effort to select the design, methodology, and analyses in this study so as to maximize the study's potential contribution to an understanding of how mathematics efficacy beliefs take hold during middle school. I have tried to craft a compelling narrative of each student based on the data to provide what Eisner (1998) would call "a confluence of evidence that breeds credibility" (p. 110). Nevertheless, several limitations deserve mention.

The conclusions I have drawn are situated within the framework of social cognitive theory and may differ from those drawn by researchers from other theoretical homes. Some may ask whether the open-ended nature of the interview questions invited judgments that more closely reflect students' mathematics self-concept than self-efficacy. To be sure, the present methodological approach may blur these conceptual lines, but the focus of this study was on *sources* of self-efficacy beliefs, which themselves likely undergird higher-order self-concept beliefs (see Bong & Skaalvik, 2003).

This study relied on interviews conducted with 23 participants who were asked to reconstruct experiences with respect to their own (or to their student's or child's) mathematics competence at a single point in time. Such a design prohibits a causal analysis of the development of mathematics self-efficacy. The hypothesized reciprocity between personal, environmental, and behavioral determinants suggests that reverse causal ordering is also plausible. To address this question of causal ordering, future designs may incorporate interviews over the course of a school year with simultaneous self-efficacy assessment. For example, Zimmerman (2008) has proposed such a model for integrating the assessment of self-efficacy, self-regulated learning strategies, and achievement. Finally, the interviews here are representative of students in a specific context (e.g., students with high and low mathematics self-efficacy in Grade 8 at a selected suburban school) and do not represent all middle school students. I urge readers to determine for themselves the transferability of the data presented here and to use the present account as what Lee Cronbach (1975) called "a working hypothesis, not a conclusion" (p. 125) as they examine the formation of self-efficacy in other contexts.

Note

I would like to express my appreciation to Frank Pajares, Samuel Candler Dobbs Professor of Education at Emory University, for his helpful comments and suggestions on an earlier version of this article. I would also like to thank the students, parents, and teachers who graciously agreed to participate in this study.

References

Bandura, A. (1986). *Social foundations of thought and action: A social cognitive theory*. Englewood Cliffs, NJ: Prentice Hall.

Bandura, A. (1997). *Self-efficacy: The exercise of control*. New York: Freeman.

Bandura, A. (2006). Guide for constructing self-efficacy scales. In F. Pajares & T. Urdan (Eds.), *Adolescence and education: Vol. 5. Self-efficacy and adolescence* (pp. 307–337). Greenwich, CT: Information Age.

Bong, M., & Skaalvik, E. M. (2003). Academic self-concept and self-efficacy: How different are they really? *Educational Psychology Review, 15*, 1–40.

Britner, S. L., & Pajares, F. (2006). Sources of science self-efficacy beliefs of middle school students. *Journal of Research in Science Teaching, 43*, 485–499.

Cronbach, L. (1975). Beyond the two disciplines of psychology. *American Psychologist, 30*, 116–127.

Dweck, C. S. (2000). *Self-theories: Their role in motivation, personality, and development*. Philadelphia: Psychology Press.

Dweck, C. S. (2006). *Mindset: The new psychology of success*. New York: Random House.

Dweck, C. S., & Leggett, E. L. (1988). A social-cognitive approach to motivation and personality. *Psychological Review, 95*, 256–272.

Eccles, J. S. (2004). Schools, academic motivation, and stage-environment fit. In R. Lerner & L. Steinberg (Eds.), *Handbook of adolescent psychology* (2nd ed., pp. 125–153). Hoboken, NJ: Wiley.

Eccles, J. S., & Midgley, C. (1989). Stage-environment fit: Developmentally appropriate classrooms for young adolescents. In C. Ames & R. Ames (Eds.), *Research on motivation in education* (Vol. 3, pp. 139–186). San Diego, CA: Academic Press.

Eisner, E. (1998). *The enlightened eye: Qualitative inquiry and the enhancement of educational practice*. New York: Macmillan.

Evans, R. I. (1989). *Albert Bandura: The man and his ideas—a dialogue*. New York: Praeger.

Good, T. L. (1987). Two decades of research on teacher expectations: Findings and future directions. *Journal of Teacher Education, 4*, 32–47.

Hampton, N. Z., & Mason, E. (2003). Learning disabilities, gender, sources of self-efficacy, self-efficacy beliefs, and academic achievement in high school students. *Journal of School Psychology, 41*, 101–112.

Hughes, D., Rodriguez, J., Smith, E. P., Johnson, D. J., Stevenson, H. C., & Spicer, P. (2006). Parents' ethnic-racial socialization practices: A review of research and directions for future study. *Developmental Psychology, 42*, 747–770.

Hutchison, M. A., Follman, D. K., Sumpter, M., & Bodner, G. M. (2006). Factors influencing the self-efficacy beliefs of first-year engineering students. *Journal of Engineering Education, 95*, 39–47.

James, W. (1899/2001). *Talks to teachers on psychology*. Mineola, NY: Dover.

Klassen, R. (2004). A cross-cultural investigation of the efficacy beliefs of South Asian immigrant and Anglo non-immigrant early adolescents. *Journal of Educational Psychology, 96*, 731–742.

Lent, R. W., Brown, S. D., Gover, M. R., & Nijjer, S. K. (1996). Cognitive assessment of the sources of mathematics self-efficacy: A thought-listing analysis. *Journal of Career Assessment, 4,* 33–46.

Lent, R. W., Lopez, F. G., & Bieschke, K. J. (1991). Mathematics self-efficacy: Sources and relation to science-based career choice. *Journal of Counseling Psychology, 38,* 424–430.

Lent, R. W., Lopez, F. G., Brown, S. D., & Gore, P. A. (1996). Latent structure of the sources of mathematics self-efficacy. *Journal of Vocational Behavior, 49,* 292–308.

Lopez, F. G., Lent, R. W., Brown, S. D., & Gore, P. A. (1997). Role of social-cognitive expectations in high school students' mathematics-related interest and performance. *Journal of Counseling Psychology, 44,* 44–52.

Merriam, S. B. (1998). *Qualitative research and case study applications in education.* San Francisco: Jossey-Bass.

Miles, M. B., & Huberman, A. M. (1994). *Qualitative data analysis* (2nd ed.). Thousand Oaks, CA: Sage.

Molden, D. C., & Dweck, C. S. (2006). Finding "meaning" in psychology: A lay theories approach to self-regulation, social perception, and social development. *American Psychologist, 61,* 192–203.

Pajares, F. (1994). Inviting self-efficacy: The role of invitations in the development of confidence and competence in writing. *Journal of Invitational Theory and Practice, 3,* 13–24.

Pajares, F. (2006). Self-efficacy beliefs during adolescence: Implications for teachers and parents. In F. Pajares & T. Urdan (Eds.), *Adolescence and education: Vol. 5. Self-efficacy beliefs of adolescents* (pp. 339–367). Greenwich, CT: Information Age.

Pajares, F., Johnson, M. J., & Usher, E. L. (2007). Sources of writing self-efficacy beliefs of elementary, middle, and high school students. *Research in the Teaching of English, 42,* 104–120.

Pajares, F., & Schunk, D. H. (2005). Self-efficacy and self-concept beliefs: Jointly contributing to the quality of human life. In H. Marsh, R. Craven, & D. McInerney (Eds.), *International advances in self research* (Vol. 2, pp. 95–121). Greenwich, CT: Information Age.

Pajares, F., & Urdan, T. (Eds.). (2006). *Adolescence and education: Vol. 5. Self-efficacy beliefs of adolescents.* Greenwich, CT: Information Age.

Purkey, W. W. (2000). *What students say to themselves: Internal dialogue and school success.* Thousand Oaks, CA: Corwin Press.

Rosenthal, R. (2002). The Pygmalion effect and its mediating mechanisms. In J. Aronson (Ed.), *Improving academic achievement: Impact of psychological factors on education* (pp. 25–36). New York: Academic Press.

Schunk, D. H. (2008). Attributions as motivators of self-regulated learning. In D. H. Schunk & B. J. Zimmerman (Eds.), *Motivation and self-regulated learning: Theory, Research, and Applications* (pp. 245–266). New York: Erlbaum.

Schunk, D. H., & Ertmer, P. A. (2000). Self-efficacy and academic learning: Self-efficacy enhancing interventions. In M. Boekaerts, P. R. Pintrich, & M. Zeidner (Eds.), *Handbook of self-regulation* (pp. 631–650). San Diego, CA: Academic Press.

Schunk, D. H., & Lilly, M. W. (1984). Sex differences in self-efficacy and attributions: Influence of performance feedback. *Journal of Early Adolescence, 4,* 203–213.

Schunk, D. H., & Swartz, C. W. (1993). Goals and progress feedback: Effects on self-efficacy and writing achievement. *Contemporary Educational Psychology, 18,* 337–354.

Usher, E. L., & Pajares, F. (2006). Sources of academic and self-regulatory efficacy beliefs of entering middle school students. *Contemporary Educational Psychology, 31,* 125–141.

Usher, E. L., & Pajares, F. (in press). Sources of self-efficacy in school: Critical review of the literature and future directions. *Review of Educational Research*.

Walker, V. S. (2000). Valued segregated schools for African American children in the South, 1935–1969: A review of common themes and characteristics. *Review of Educational Research, 70*, 253–285.

Wheeler, L., & Suls, J. (2005). Social comparison and self-evaluations of competence. In A. J. Elliot & C. S. Dweck (Eds.), *Handbook of competence and motivation* (pp. 566–578). New York: Guilford.

Wigfield, A., Eccles, J., Mac Iver, D., Reuman, D., & Midgley, C. (1991). Transitions at early adolescence: Changes in children's domain-specific self-perceptions and general self-esteem across the transition to junior high school. *Developmental Psychology, 27*, 552–565.

Wigfield, A., Hoa, L. W., & Klauda, S. L. (2008). The role of achievement values in the regulation of achievement behaviors. In D. H. Schunk & B. J. Zimmerman (Eds.), *Motivation and self-regulated learning: Theory, research, and applications* (pp. 169–195). New York: Erlbaum.

Zeldin, A., Britner, S. L., & Pajares, F. (2007). A comparative study of the self-efficacy beliefs of successful men and women in mathematics, science, and technology careers. *Journal of Research on Science Teaching*. Advance online publication. Retrieved November 7, 2007. doi: 10.1002/tea.20195.

Zeldin, A. L., & Pajares, F. (2000). Against the odds: Self-efficacy beliefs of women in mathematical, scientific, and technological careers. *American Educational Research Journal, 37*, 215–246.

Zimmerman, B. J. (2002). Becoming a self-regulated learner: An overview. *Theory Into Practice, 41*, 64–70.

Zimmerman, B. J. (2008). Investigating self-regulation and motivation: Historical background, methodological developments, and future prospects. *American Educational Research Journal, 45*, 166–183.

Zimmerman, B. J., & Bandura, A. (1994). Impact of self-regulatory influences on writing course attainment. *American Educational Research Journal, 31*, 845–862.

Zimmerman, B. J., & Cleary, T. J. (2006). Adolescents' development of personal agency. In F. Pajares & T. Urdan (Eds.), *Adolescence and education: Vol. 5. Self-efficacy beliefs of adolescents* (pp. 45–69). Greenwich, CT: Information Age.

Zimmerman, B. J., & Kitsantas, A. (1999). Acquiring writing revision skill: Shifting from process to outcome self-regulatory goals. *Journal of Educational Psychology, 91*, 241–250.

Zimmerman, B. J., & Kitsantas, A. (2005). The hidden dimension of personal competence: Self-regulated learning and practice. In A. J. Elliot & C. Dweck (Eds.), *Handbook of competence and motivation* (pp. 509–526). New York: Guilford Press.

Zimmerman, B. J., & Schunk, A. (2008). Motivation: An essential dimension of self-regulated learning. In D. H. Schunk & B. J. Zimmerman (Eds.), *Motivation and self-regulated learning: Theory, research, and applications* (pp. 1–30). New York: Erlbaum.

Manuscript received December 20, 2007
Revision received July 27, 2008
Accepted August 3, 2008